KEYWORDS FOR RADICALS

THE CONTESTED VOCABULARY OF
LATE-CAPITALIST STRUGGLE

KELLY FRITSCH
CLARE O'CONNOR
AK THOMPSON

AK PRESS
EDINBURGH · OAKLAND · BALTIMORE

Advance praise for *Keywords for Radicals*

"Not since Raymond Williams's groundbreaking classic *Keywords* has there been such a valuable guide to the world within our words. From its thought-provoking Introduction through its energizing accounts of the tensions underlying our most prized concepts, *Keywords for Radicals* will be indispensable to any scholar or activist who is serious about critique and change. Finally, a worthy successor to Williams!"
—**Stephen Duncombe**, editor of *Cultural Resistance Reader*

"Crafted by scholars and activists whose work has both influenced and inspired me, the succinct essays in *Keywords for Radicals* will be invaluable for political education workshops, reading groups, and classrooms. Drawing on first-hand experience in a wide range of movements, the genealogies that inform these investigations are sure to provoke insight and further the development of contemporary resistance struggles."
—**Dean Spade**, author of *Normal Life: Administrative Violence, Critical Trans Politics, and the Limits of Law*

"*Keywords for Radicals* extends the work of Raymond Williams in directions he could not have anticipated. Marshaling an impressive range of radical voices, this multi-authored collection tackles the new vocabularies of neoliberal capitalism while providing fresh new takes on classic concepts. No mere word list, this book is a crucial window onto radical politics today."
—**Lisa Duggan**, author of *The Twilight of Equality: Neoliberalism, Cultural Politics, and the Attack on Democracy*

"In the tradition of Raymond Williams, *Keywords For Radicals* offers a primer for a new era of political protest. As the editors remind us, language changes, and debates over word usage become more or less intense depending upon the era. Paying careful attention to keywords matters more now than ever, and *Keywords for Radicals* is everything you need to enter into this vital arena of struggle."
—**Jack Halberstam**, author of *Gaga Feminism: Pregnant Men, Heteroflexible Women and The End of Normal*

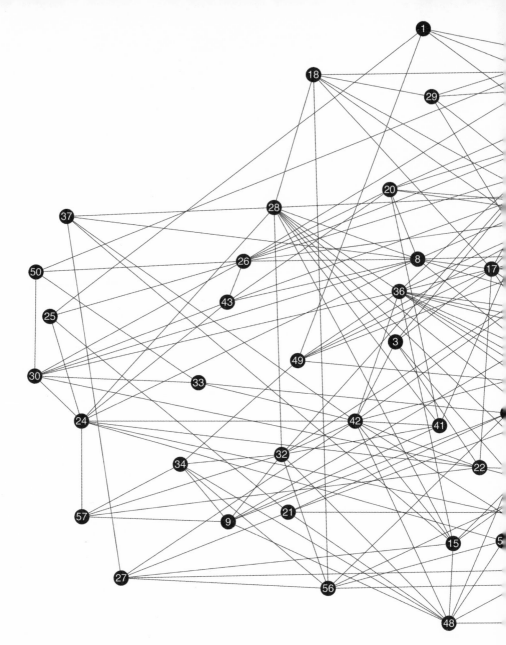

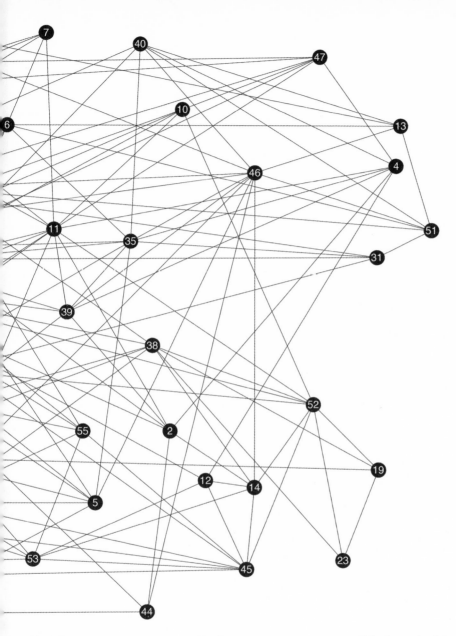

Keywords for Radicals: The Contested Vocabulary of Late-Capitalist Struggle

© 2016 Rests with each contributor, as noted
This edition © 2016 AK Press (Chico, Oakland, Edinburgh, Baltimore)

ISBN: 978-1-84935-242-0 | E-ISBN: 978-1-84935-243-7
Library of Congress Control Number: 2015959321

AK Press   AK Press
370 Ryan Ave. #100   PO Box 12766
Chico, CA 95973   Edinburgh EH8 9YE
USA   Scotland
www.akpress.org   www.akuk.com
akpress@akpress.org   ak@akedin.demon.co.uk

The above addresses would be delighted to provide you with the latest AK Press distribution catalog, which features books, pamphlets, zines, and stylish apparel published and/or distributed by AK Press. Alternatively, visit our websites for the complete catalog, latest news, and secure ordering.

Cover art by Seth Tobocman | sethtobocman.com
Interior design by Margaret Killjoy | birdsbeforethestorm.net
The Editors donate all royalties from the sale of *Keywords for Radicals* to AK Press in the interest of furthering the forms of movement-based education advocated by *Keywords for Radicals*

Printed in the USA on acid-free, recycled paper

CONTENTS

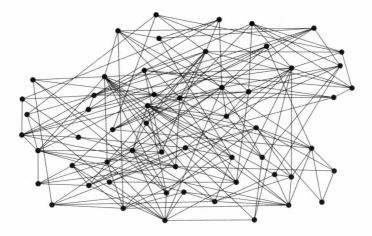

INTRODUCTION

Kelly Fritsch, Clare O'Connor, and AK Thompson

In 1837, Hans Christian Andersen recounted the story of "The Emperor's New Clothes." Working in the fantastical register of fairy tales, he spun a tale in which two swindlers descend upon the town of an emperor enthralled by sartorial decadence. Sensing an opportunity, the swindlers pose as weavers and propose to make the emperor a suit so fine that it will be imperceptible to people who were stupid or undeserving of their post. Seeing the benefit of owning such an outfit, the emperor agrees to their offer. As the swindlers begin their fictive weaving, a novel problem arises. Fearful that their credibility was about to be undermined, the emperor's men repeat the received lie and extol the beauty of the mystery garment. The ruse becomes contagious. Finally, faced with under-lings capable of "seeing" the invisible suit, the emperor succumbs as well. The scene leads inexorably to a procession through the town. Invested in the preservation of the lie, the cheering crowd gives no indication that anything is amiss—that is, until a young boy, lacking in social graces and too naïve to play along, shouts out what the others could not: "But he has nothing on!" (Andersen 1983, 63).

In most riffs on Andersen's story, the lesson is drawn out at this point: by speaking truth to power, we can break the spell that keeps us ensnared. Calling things like we see them forces convenient fictions to give way to more vital truths. Perverse beliefs that fester in shadows get disinfected in reason's light. Things become clear when properly named. For those with radical inclinations, such an account is exceptionally appealing. From the Quaker commitment to "speak truth to power" in the face of the Cold War to Malcolm X's phil-ological injunction to "make it plain," our political struggles have been indelibly marked by the desire for transparency. It's therefore not surprising that radicals have instinctively recognized the impor-tance of Andersen's tale. Indeed, as with Malcolm (and the Quakers before him), *The Emperor's New Clothes* is historically inseparable from revolutionary aspirations. Critical of the mystical claims un-derlying the power of his own era's aristocracy, Andersen became a child of the Enlightenment, which valued the implicitly democratic evidence of sense perception above all.[1] Today, confronted by public

---

1. According to Immanuel Kant (1784), the Enlightenment project was inseparable from the courage to marshal one's own understanding in spite of (and often in opposition to) the positions maintained by the guardians of old. "Laziness and cowardice are the reasons why such a large part of man-kind gladly remain minors all their lives, long after nature has freed them from external guidance. They are the reasons why it is so easy for others to set themselves up as guardians. It is so comfortable to be a minor. If I have a book that thinks for me, a pastor who acts as my conscience, a physician who prescribes my diet, and so on—then I have no need to exert myself. I have no need to think, if only I can pay; others will take care of that disagreeable business for me. Those guardians who have kindly taken supervision upon themselves see to it that the overwhelming majority of mankind—among them the entire fair sex—should consider the step to maturity, not only as hard, but as extremely dangerous." It is worth noting, however, that while the Enlightenment emphasized the commonality of reason as the basis for a new

relations machines still more murderous in their deceit, we strive in our turn to model ourselves after Andersen's child. On guard against the sleights of hand that would keep us in line, we do what we can to tell it like it is. It is therefore not surprising that our campaigns have often taken root at the very point where, beneath the ruse, things and their names begin to coincide. Iraq is a *war for oil*; Israel is an *apartheid state*. The payoff is clear: once proper names have been assigned and mystifications dissolve, the revelation will compel our fellow townsfolk to challenge the emperor's vain conceits.

But if there's one thing such campaigns have made clear, it's that purely nominal shifts are never enough to resolve our political problems once and for all. On the contrary, when radicals become seduced by—and habituated to—the belief that we can assign "true names," we have often ended by hampering our efforts. How, then, should we orient to struggles over word usage and meaning? What other approach might guide our efforts? Covering a wide range of the keywords that currently shape radical discourse and subjecting them to historical, etymological, and political scrutiny, the entries in this volume suggest one compelling path.

■

Leaving aside its literary virtuosity, "The Emperor's New Clothes" owes its popularity to the seductive promise of naming. A major problem, however, is that the fable's lesson tends to get extracted before the story has come to a close. Admittedly, Andersen's tale is brief—not more than a few pages long—and the young boy's mouths-of-babes moment comes in the very last paragraph. Nevertheless, the story does not end with the child's outburst or with the townsfolk shaken from slumber. Instead, it ends with the emperor, and his chamberlains who commit all the more resolutely to keep up appearances: "'But he has nothing at all on!' at last cried out all the people. The Emperor was vexed, for he knew that the people were right; but he thought the procession must go on now!

---

universality, its adherents did not immediately include "the entire fair sex" and others thought to be deprived of such reason within their fold.

And the lords of the bedchamber took greater pains than ever, to appear holding up a train, although, in reality, there was no train to hold" (Andersen 1983, 63).

When approached from the standpoint of its closing lines, Andersen's fable seems to support conclusions that are entirely at odds with those normally derived from it. Significantly, the final scene makes clear that *proper naming* is not enough to bring the royal procession to a halt. Moreover, since the parade does not end (since, indeed, the emperor and his chamberlains redouble their efforts to persevere), it's unclear whether the townsfolk will turn on their sovereign or strive instead to avoid conflict by somehow reconciling the tension between their ruler's charade and their own sense perception.

Of these two outcomes (and despite the Enlightenment), the latter has proven historically to be more likely. Incensed Americans who owe their very hubris to imperialist aggression ask, "Why do they hate us?" Discount shoppers rush to Walmart on Black Friday to revel in the fruits of the global sweatshop without ever curbing their xenophobic injunction to "buy American." Heavily medicated suburban kids insist "it's all good." Through incantations such as these, people symptomatically acknowledge what they stand to lose if the façade crumbles. Faced with the irreconcilability of the given and the evident, those whose lives are beholden to constituted power are more likely to entrench themselves in fictive certainties than they are to renounce them once and for all.

On this point, Andersen's story proves prescient. Populated by townsfolk, servants, high-ranking officials, and entrepreneurial swindlers, the inhabitants of the emperor's kingdom are marked by clear class divisions. But while this taxonomy might imply conflict, Andersen's characters seem for the most part to be enthralled by their sovereign's excess. Indeed, they are *invested* in it. Had they not lined the streets to bask in the glow of his power, the realization that his "new clothes" left him naked would not have been bewildering. Indeed, had it not been for their investment, they might have freed themselves from resplendent misery long before the weaving swindlers made their descent. And who, in the story, is prepared to speak about *that*? Certainly not the swindlers, since they flee the scene before the procession begins. Consequently, even if the people's shock turned to rage (even if their realization foretold a scene of wild defrocking), the profiteering culprits are beyond their grasp. The crowd's indictment cannot touch them. The same holds true today: like Andersen's townsfolk might have done before us, we gradually turned our anger toward the kleptocratic Goldman Sachs. We became smug in our shouting, and for a while we took back the streets. But while we may have "changed the conversation," our hoarse voices ultimately underscored our powerlessness.

Revisiting Andersen's fable in this way is illuminating. By turning our attention toward those aspects of the story that normally escape consideration, it becomes clear that "speaking truth to power" and "making it plain" are no longer enough—and not solely because, today, power has displayed a remarkable capacity to operate under conditions of extreme contradiction.

Apart from ignoring the limits of demand-based politics when trying to achieve revolutionary aims, the idea that we can change things by assigning true names presupposes that those names that are ours to give are somehow outside of and antithetical to power; they are not. We must therefore contend with the fact that the scope of what we can say is delimited not solely by the willingness of others to hear, but also by the concepts at our disposal. These concepts—these *words*—are neither static nor extrinsic to power. Words attain meaning through the history of their usage, and these histories contain traces of the struggle not only to name but also to *create* the world. Read in this way, a concept's historical development (the refinement of its meaning, the management of its contradictory implications) can provide an index of the struggle to shape reality according to particular interests.

To put it another way, because the attribution of names takes the undifferentiated whole and parses it into discrete and manipulable units, the evolution of word usage tends to correspond with developments in what Marx called "the productive forces."

As Raymond Williams noted, "ordinary, everyday language" is "directly subject to historical development" (1980, 50). Consequently, when approached with care, it can be read as an expression or index of that development. Little wonder, then, that naming has historically been a war zone. "Our word is our weapon," declared Subcomandante Marcos. "Names will never hurt me," cried the bullied child, knowing full well it was a lie.

■

At the end of the Second World War, around the time that George Orwell published his "Politics and the English Language," Raymond Williams began to carve a path through this trip-wired land. Noting the significant transformations taking place in English language usage among postwar university students in Britain, he set out to uncover the deeper political developments these shifts expressed. Intuiting—along with J. L. Austin, who tackled the problem in a different but complementary fashion[2]—that words did not merely *describe* a given reality but also played a key role in helping to *produce* it, Williams proposed that transformations in the assigned or implied meaning of words could be read as signals denoting broader transformations taking place in the social sphere. This was analytically significant since—although "society," in its enormity, remained impervious to capture—the words through which it found expression were easier (though not easy) to grasp. By focusing on changes in word usage and meaning, and by constellating the terms that made up the "vocabulary" of the moment, it was possible to begin unfolding something like a sociohistorical map—a map complete with familiar passages, curious footpaths, and advantageous lines of attack.

In the introduction to his *Keywords: A Vocabulary of Culture and Society*, Williams recounted how, since communication ordinarily

---

2. According to J. L. Austin, "a performative" is a particular type of speech act through which the speaking does not amount to a *statement* concerning the act but is rather identical to its doing: "it indicates that the issuing of the utterance is the performing of an action" (1975, 6). Examples of such speech acts in Austin's text include formulations such as "I name this ship" and "I bet you sixpence."

works on account of language's presumed consensual transparency, moments in which this consensus falls apart help to reveal important political, economic, and cultural shifts. In Williams' estimation, language tended to become "brittle" in "periods of change" when the taken-for-granted associations between words and things began to break down (1983, 16).

Such dissolutions are not arbitrary; they arise from the very process by which the thing a word once denoted is itself transformed. The predominantly legal conception of "the sacred" that prevailed in Ancient Rome, for instance, underwent a massive transformation with the advent of Christianity, which endeavored to contest sovereign earthly power by enshrining the outcast savior as king.[3] In our own era, because capitalism owes its being to the unending reorganization of both matter and perception, the development of the productive forces has demanded a corresponding development in our conceptual arsenal. And, indeed, the categories of "development" and "production" must themselves be subjected to scrutiny—the former for its historical association with capitalist notions of "progress" and the latter for its ideological function in certain cookie-cutter Marxisms. Consequently, Williams criticized usages of "production" that narrowed investigation to "the production of commodities, or more general 'market' production, in which all that is ever produced takes the form of isolable and disposable objects." Instead, he advocated usages that would themselves foster *investigation*. "The main result," he declared in a related text, "should be a sustained historical inquiry" (1978, 54). It is toward this project that our attention must now turn.

■

Because they indicate that the aspects of the social world to which they are bound are in flux, developments in word usage and meaning can help us to become aware of political opportunities that might otherwise go unnoticed. But even when changes in usage

---

3. For more on the legal conception of the sacred, see Agamben 1995. For more on the Christian conception of the sacred, see Girard 1977.

or meaning seem to be superficially favorable, there's no guarantee that the developments they express are inherently positive. Within the context of late capitalism, shifts in common word usage have tended to reflect and reiterate the dynamics of post-Fordist development rather than to yield transparency. According to Italian economist Christian Marazzi (2008), recent changes in language use tend to correspond to the modifications that financial markets have brought about in the field of work. In our increasingly service- and consumer-oriented economy, which demands the constant transfer of data and information, work has become communicative-relational in character. As a result, communication of all kinds has been further subordinated to the logic of the market. Meanwhile, employers go out of their way to encourage linguistic cooperation among workers. Previously conceived as a distraction from the production process, horizontal communication—e.g., chatter—has increasingly (and especially at the points of greatest capital accumulation) become its very substance.

In this transition, social media and its attendant linguistic forms have become indispensable for business. At the same time, the prevalence of crowdsourcing, Twitter, and similar tools has transformed the substantive meaning of many words while vastly expanding the field of interaction (laughing out loud, we might say, is not what it used to be). The whole dynamic was enough to lead Paolo Virno (2004) to conclude that, more than in any other era, contemporary wage labor *is* communicative interaction. Moreover, since the new forms of communication have become so well integrated into everyday labor and life, it can be difficult to distinguish between working and non-working hours. Workplace requirements and personal habits entangle while nouns become verbs through the same process by which—through reification—agency is attributed to objects. Let me Google that for you.

But while such word-usage developments are not inevitably "progressive" in the normative sense (and while the prospect of assigning true names remains as elusive as ever), the fights that sometimes arise around contested terms remain *analytically* significant. By highlighting moments in which the taken-for-granted associations between concepts and things become untenable, such skirmishes serve as lighthouses marking hazards—but also opportunities—on the horizon.

When Associated Press editors updated their stylebook in 2013, they recommended that journalists refrain from using the term "illegal immigrant" to refer to undocumented workers in the United States (Colford 2013). On face value, this change constituted a victory for migrant justice advocates who have struggled for more than a decade to popularize the idea that "no one is illegal." At the same time, however, the AP style update reflects broader changes in American labor-market regulation under Obama. Indeed, Obama advanced immigration reform as a strategy for economic growth while simultaneously deporting more people than any other US president, earning himself the grassroots moniker "deporter-in-chief." Viewed from this angle, the new nomenclature speaks less to the cultivation of a humanist ideal than it does to a refinement of the mechanisms of capture and control.

A similar political ambiguity marks other word debates. Sometimes this ambiguity results in contests over the meaning of individual words. At other times it finds expression in struggles to determine which word will be used to designate (and hence, in part, to produce) a given reality. Israel's deceptive references to the apartheid barrier as a fence, for instance, has prompted Palestinians and international solidarity activists to clarify that the obstruction in question is, in fact, a wall. The logic of the skirmish is clear: "fences" are ordinary infrastructure, and good fences (we are told) make good neighbors. In contrast (and especially in the political context), "walls" are burdened by their association with prisons and despised concrete monuments like the one that bisected Berlin for a good chunk of the twentieth century. But while the distinction between "fences" and "walls" is material, the debate's parameters seem to imply that a "fence" used to expropriate land and demarcate colonial borders is somehow less obscene. Instead of clamoring for a change in nomenclature, activists might do just as well to point out that even a fence is a legitimate target if its purpose is to enable mass dispossession. Legislation against sexual violence in Canada has produced similar confusion as the phrase "sexual assault"—intended by feminists as a more encompassing and therefore better alternative to the loaded word "rape"—has itself gradually been stripped of political poignancy for seeming too vague (Makin 2013). In each of these cases, it is difficult to know which tendency will win out.

Regardless of their outcome, contests like these make clear that the points at which language becomes "brittle" constitute important analytic opportunities. When taken seriously, they can foster the development of coherent strategic lines and increase the impact of our political interventions. By honing in on these points of conflict, it becomes possible to uncover the social contradictions that find expression, as Williams observed, "*within* language" (1983, 22). Indeed, because "earlier and later senses" of words often "coexist" within a single moment of enunciation, words themselves can often come to signal "actual alternatives" through which "problems of . . . belief and affiliation are contested" (1983, 22). On this point, Williams comes close to the position advanced by feminist poet Adrienne Rich, who, in her 1971 poem "The Burning of Paper Instead of Children," recounted how "a language is a map of our failures."[4] Such a map is hard to look at and difficult to read. Nevertheless, it remains indispensable when charting our course to freedom.

■

Forty years after it was penned, Williams' text remains an important resource for contemporary radicals. But while *Keywords* has lost none of its intellectual force, many of its specific entries have been overtaken by social transformations. Such an outcome cannot be attributed to shortsightedness; after all, any survey that takes capitalist mutations as its object must necessarily be transitory in

---

4.   Rich's poem was inspired in part by Father Daniel Berrigan's involvement in the destruction of draft files at a military office in Catonsville, Maryland, during an antiwar protest on May 17, 1968. The poem begins with the following epigraph, which is attributed to a statement Berrigan made during his subsequent trial: "I was in danger of verbalizing my moral impulses out of existence."

nature.[5] Through the course of neoliberal market expansion, economic crisis, and the renewed rounds of global austerity that have taken place since Williams' death, words have continued to be important and evolving sites of struggle.

Aware that he was standing on shifting ground, Williams updated *Keywords* in 1983. Since his death in 1988, others have sought to emulate his method. In 2005, editors Tony Bennett, Lawrence Grossberg, and Meaghan Morris published *New Keywords: A Revised Vocabulary of Culture and Society*, a multi-author volume devoted to the continuation of Williams' project. In this spirit, the editors ambitiously added and removed words from Williams' list and updated existing entries to account for "crucial shifts" that had taken place.

Each of the volume's entries reflects great care. However, while Bennett, Grossberg, and Morris strove to honor Williams' intention to "provide a useful, intellectually and historically grounded guide to *public* questions," the *New Keywords* editors—like Williams himself—found it difficult to prevent their work from succumbing to an "overly academic reception" (Bennett, Grossberg, and Morris 2005, 2). Indeed, as one *Guardian* reviewer noted, *Keywords* "powerfully influenced a generation of students, many of whom were fortunate enough to find . . . employment in the looming cultural studies boom" (2005, 2). Thus sequestered, many activists have remained unaware of Williams' legacy—an alarming situation, given the importance attributed to words within radical spheres. Indeed, word-based struggles seem only to have gained prominence since Williams' time, and the "insider language" of activist subculture has

5. To get a sense of the degree to which Williams was not shortsighted, it is useful to recall how, in his "Means of Communication as Means of Production" (1978), he neatly anticipated the development of the Internet: "The creation of democratic, autonomous, and self-managing systems of communal radio are already within our reach," he noted. And such developments suggested "not only 'broadcasting,' in its traditional forms, but very flexible and complex multi-way interactive modes, which can take us beyond 'representative' and selective transmission into direct person-to-person and persons-to-persons communication" (61). What's missing from this prescient account, of course, is an analysis of how the development of such a means of communication would alter the communicated substance itself. It is to this problem that we turn our attention here.

been recognized as a problem to be dealt with in its own right. But while radicals have expressed considerable interest in the question of word usage and meaning, emphasis tends to be placed on the *impact* of words rather than on the dynamic, generative, and contradictory *attributes* of words themselves. It is important to consider why this is so.

■

For radicals, language is—or should be—important because it helps us to describe and "materialize" the world we want to transform. To be sure, language doesn't *produce* the world as various strands of idealist philosophy have maintained;[6] however, it does organize and delimit its objects. In other words, while the configuration of the world's preexisting matter constrains the concepts we can use to make our objects intelligible, the parsing of "matter" into "objects" remains a social accomplishment of the first order. Indeed, by partitioning and organizing matter, our concepts both produce "objects" and determine our orientation to them. Here we need only to think of the distinction between "man" and "animal" (a partition that continues to maintain a whole cosmology despite the material findings of evolutionary biology) or of Iris Marion Young's (2005) observation that the conceptual formation of gender leads many women to "throw like a girl" despite the fact that no matter-based factor demands this particular form of throwing. Given their obvious consequences for struggles in areas like ecology, animal liberation, and feminism, such examples underscore the political importance of the processes by which matter succumbs to meaningful objectification through the application of concepts. Little wonder, then, that words have become such important sites of struggle. "This is the oppressor's language," said Rich, "yet I need it to talk to you."

---

6. Consider, for instance, Kant's proposal from *The Critique of Pure Reason* that, "if I remove the thinking subject, the whole material world must at once vanish because it is nothing but a phenomenal appearance in the sensibility of ourselves as a subject, and a manner or species of representation" (1781, A 383).

Since the "linguistic turn" in social theory that took place during the 1990s, such struggles have been indelibly marked by the insights of Judith Butler. Drawing on Austin's work on performativity, Butler's *Gender Trouble* (1990) highlighted how the act of naming could also be the act of *producing the thing being named* (in Austin's sense, naming would thus be neither a true nor false statement but rather a performative). Emphasizing the constraints inherent in all identifications, Butler proposed that the objective of feminist practice should therefore not be the valorization of marginal identities but rather the "subversion of identity" itself. Here, the project ceases to be one of advancing alternative significations considered to be more true but rather—and as Stuart Hall (1997) proposed in a different but parallel context—to make the sign itself "uninhabitable."

To the extent that Butler's treatment of performativity emphasized the productive dimension of language, her project can be read as an important extension of (and supplement to) Williams' own insights. And to the degree that her work has gained traction among radicals engaged in feminist, queer, and other struggles, this contribution should not be overlooked. But while Butler and Williams share a certain common orientation to language problems, it's important to acknowledge key differences. As Austin makes clear, the performative primarily arises in instances where a proclamation and a production coincide. As a result, performatives tend to be inseparable from verbs like "declare," "authorize," and "pronounce." Such formulations undoubtedly have an effect on the world's matter and, in this way, undoubtedly help to produce the world. However, the production achieved by one's capacity to "authorize" says nothing about the means by which the concept of authorizing was itself constituted. In Williams, this historical question is of paramount importance.

We inhabit a world whose conceptual parsing predates us. Because we are immersed in this world and beholden to its inherited conceptual parsing, we must acknowledge that even our *perceptions* are shaped by this history. Indeed, our perceptions are themselves social products. Revisiting Frantz Fanon's struggle to overcome recognition as the basis for self-worth in *Black Skin,*

White Masks, Sara Ahmed (2007) recounts how the supposed naturalness of certain orientations to the object world is conditioned by a conceptual alignment between the constitution of that world and our own particular perceptions. For this reason, "racism 'stops' black bodies inhabiting space by extending through objects and others; the familiarity of 'the white world,' as a world we know implicitly, 'disorients' black bodies such that they cease to know where to find things—reduced as they are to things among things." Following Fanon, Ahmed concludes by reminding us of how "the disorientation affected by racism diminishes capacities for action" (111).

In light of this fact, it's not surprising that many of us have embarked on projects of re-signification or of attempting to change the valuations assigned to particular terms. But while different conceptual schemas materialize the world differently, changing the words we use or the meaning assigned to given words is not enough to transform the reality that gave these words force in the first place. As Fanon's disavowal of recognition in *Black Skin, White Masks* (1967) makes clear, it is psychologically damaging to fight for better standing within the constituted sphere of objectifications. Consequently, the solution to racism cannot be found in struggling to ensure that blackness gain affirmative recognition. "We shall see that another solution is possible," he said. "It implies a restructuring of the world" (82).

Since the conceptual parsing of matter arises from and corresponds to the organization of a society's social relations, concepts themselves only achieve meaningfulness through the productive sequences they enact. For those of us condemned to participate in—but not to determine the dynamics of—established social relations, conceptual innovation remains at best a signal of our *intent* to change the world in a particular way. Such wish fulfillment recalls the longing for mastery that finds expression in creation myths like the one recounted in Genesis 2:19, where "out of the ground the Lord God formed every beast of the field and every bird of the sky, and brought them to the man to see what he would call them; and whatever the man called a living creature, that was its name."

Although we currently lack the divine power of nomination, committing to the ascription of desirable names can nevertheless guide the imagination toward the realization of particular outcomes. Nevertheless, because a linguistic object's inherited socialization delimits the scope of its possible reconfigurations, radicals are left in the difficult position of having to *complete* or *resolve* the words inherited from injustice rather than simply disavowing them in favor of emancipatory neologisms.

To get a sense of this tension, one could do no better than to consider the exchange that followed the marginal defeat of the proposal to rename the "Occupy Oakland" encampment "Decolonize/Liberate Oakland." In an open letter circulated over the Internet in December 2011, activist Darshan Campos criticized fellow Oakland organizer and hip-hop icon Boots Riley for voting against the motion, arguing that "the name Occupy Oakland replicates the violence of colonialism." In response, Riley cited the American Indian Movement's use of "occupation" to describe some of their own actions and suggested that "problems of race and racism" could not be "solved with a name change." Apart from the fact that the community members he had spoken with did not associate the word "occupy" with colonization, Riley found that "people are excited by OO, if a little confused on the ultimate goal." Moreover, he explained, "the name is the identifier, and they feel that it is connected to the larger movement and that it actually has the ability to change things through direct action. One of the reasons people feel it's connected to the larger movement is the name."

Given its gravity, it's not surprising that variations on this debate quickly spread to other cities. It's also not surprising that, for the most part, these debates remained inconclusive. Nevertheless, if there was a dominant trend in the radical response, it was that disavowals of the movement's putative replication of colonial violence became commonplace. In one diplomatic *post festum* analysis, Baltimore-based authors Lester Spence and Mike McGuire conceded that "to the extent [that] the fight against financial capital *is* a war," the term "occupation" helped to emphasize "the fundamental nature of the struggle" (2012, 56–57). Nevertheless, since "occupation" also "denotes . . . white settler colonialism" and "has a deeply regressive meaning," they concluded by exhorting "future iterations" of the movement to "use symbols that reflect the realities of settler colonialism and refrain from using language that denotes 'occupation'" (63).

■

Why have arguments such as these become so persuasive? If, in the seventeenth century, it was evident that "a rose by any other name would smell as sweet" (that what something was *named* mattered less than what it *was*), the same cannot easily be said today. In a context where radicals have often succumbed to what Butler has called the "utopics of radical resignification" (1993, 224) and the capacity to name has been ascribed with a self-evident liberatory power, how do we find our way back to an awareness of the practical limitations that matter and the dynamics of its historical objectification place on the development of meaningful concepts?

One response has been to stabilize meaning through a renewed emphasis on the definitions of the words we use. In 2012, the Institute for Anarchist Studies (IAS) launched the Lexicon Pamphlet Series, which "aims to convert words into politically useful tools . . . by offering definitional understandings of commonly used keywords." Intended for distribution through existing activist networks, the initial series included pamphlets exploring concepts like colonialism, gender, power, and white supremacy. Similarly, the online archive of the Colours of Resistance network (2000–2006) contains a series of brief entries called *Definitions for the Revolution*, which the group described as "unfinished works in progress, but useful starting-points nonetheless." In his 2007 book *Political Keywords: A Guide for Students, Activists and Everyone Else*, Andrew Levine follows suit by including entries on dozens of words written "to explain what they now mean" (2).

In light of the tremendous challenges posed by the fragmentation of transparent speech communities in the era of late capitalism, such projects should be viewed as important political contributions. However, because they aim to ascribe *definitions*, they fall short of accounting for how meaning is itself the subject of ongoing historical elaboration. Indeed, Levine's direct reference to Williams is primarily a disavowal: "Williams' topic was 'culture and society,' not politics. . . . [M]y aim is not to account for how political keywords came to have the meanings they do" (2007, 2). The problem of accounting for a term's ongoing elaboration is similarly obscured by the fact that, in the IAS pamphlets, in-crowd concepts and formulas seem to be taken for granted.

Tackling the problem in a slightly different way, the CrimethInc. Ex-Workers' Collective has also recognized the importance of intervening in debates about language. From their *Contra-dictionary*, which first began to take shape in the pages of *Days of War, Nights of Love*, to the glossary segment included in each issue of *Rolling Thunder*, the collective has consistently sought to provide a new spin on terms that frequently come up in radical discussions. In stark contrast to projects like the IAS *Lexicon* pamphlets, however, CrimethInc's interventions aim less at producing definitive accounts than they do at undermining common sense in the interest of stimulating novel—and potentially revelatory—habits of thought.

In keeping with their more general orientation, CrimethInc.'s entries foreground wit and push the reader toward action. Their *Rolling Thunder* glossary entry on "Prudence," for instance, reminds readers that it is "better [to] feel once than think twice" (2006, 5). Similarly, their Contra-dictionary entry on "gender" in *Days of War, Nights of Love* ends with the following declaration: "There is no male. There is no female. Get free. Get off the map" (2001, 105). Eschewing definitions, the objective of these passages is clearly not to establish a lexicon. Instead, it is to cultivate new habits of disruptive thinking. Summarizing this position in a recent exchange with Kristian Williams, CrimethInc. (2013a) writes: "If we stay within the bounds of language that is widely used in this society, we will only be able to reproduce consensus reality, not challenge it." Consequently, the task is to "invent new words, styles, and discourses that enable us to say new things while seducing others into the conversation."[7] Such an outlook is undoubtedly important; however, as Raymond Williams' project makes clear, it does little to reveal how our "consensus reality" emerged in the first place. Without this knowledge, it is difficult to imagine how such a reality might be undone.

■

Rather than offering definitions or showing up common sense, our goal throughout this book is to submit the vocabulary of contemporary radicals to historical and analytic scrutiny so that its contradictions might be productively explored. In this way, we hope to devise an analysis of the social world that coincides with the conflicts we uncover in our most intimate utterances. Rather than facilitating communication by proposing an agreed-upon lexicon, our goal is to hasten its "brittle" degeneration so that a new reality and a new understanding might emerge. Practically speaking, this means objectifying language, unearthing its contradictions, and using these contradictions to map the social world they reflect.

Keywords for Radicals draws upon Raymond Williams' legacy while extending it in a few important ways.[8] First, while Williams was interested in capitalist dynamics during the postwar period, our aim has been to come to terms with the significant transformations that have marked the era of late capitalism. The second major difference between the two projects is that, whereas Williams conceived of his vocabulary in fairly broad terms, we have chosen to focus on

---

7. Significantly, this position reiterates one advanced by Butler in defense of her own approach to language problems. Responding to her critics in a 1999 *New York Times* op-ed, she states: "No doubt, scholars in the humanities should be able to clarify how their work informs and illuminates everyday life. Equally, however, such scholars are obliged to question common sense, interrogate its tacit presumptions and provoke new ways of looking at a familiar world."

8. It should be acknowledged that the titular echo of Saul Alinsky's 1971 *Rules for Radicals* is also deliberate. To be sure, radicals have not always favored Alinsky's organizing model. Nevertheless, his emphasis on the importance of "symbol construction" suggests an alignment between his project and the themes that guide our investigation across the following pages.

the contests over word usage and meaning that regularly erupt on the radical left. Finally, whereas Williams authored every entry in *Keywords*, we chose to assemble a multiauthor collection. To understand why, it's useful to recall that the birth of this project coincided with our resignation from the editorial committee of *Upping the Anti: A Journal of Theory and Action* at the beginning of 2012. We had worked together on that project for years and were strongly committed to its mandate, which was to create a nonsectarian space outside of—but in dialogue with—the movements in which we participated. This work was important to us because we found that immersion in struggle sometimes constrained our collective capacity to critically assess our ideas and actions. With our writers and in our pages, we sought to constitute a political "we"—not by asserting a party line but instead through a careful analysis of our collective shortcomings. As editors of *Upping the Anti*, we regularly found ourselves reading drafts in which word usage and meaning seemed very slippery; as a result, editorial meetings often involved discussions in which we noted the contradictory and conflicting transformations that were taking place right before us.

When we began working on *Keywords for Radicals*, we quickly became aware of how many other radicals were working on word-based projects. Although different in their purpose and orientation, these projects helped to make clear how important language had become as a field of struggle. Under such conditions, determining what our keywords would be became extremely challenging. Following Williams, we began by cataloging words that were polysemic and had become "brittle" in radical discussions—words in which taken-for-granted associations had begun to break down. To these, we added words that had clearly established commonsense usages but that were regularly deployed as glosses. When we began to tell people about our project, we also received a large number of recommendations for other words to include. Some of these made it into the table of contents, though we have tried to retain analytic focus by limiting sprawl.

To expect consistency in a volume comprising entries by more than fifty contributors might seem absurd. Nevertheless, the formal constraints with which we proceeded have yielded remarkably consistent results. First and foremost, this owes to the fact that each entry is written as a presentation of what a word does and has done rather than as an argument in support of a particular static definition. Additionally, because each keyword constitutes part of what Williams called a "vocabulary" (a bundled set of historical, etymological, and associational relations that contextualize a term's usage and stabilize its meaning), contributors working autonomously on the analysis of one concept often spontaneously generated the web of associations suggested by another contributor's entry. In order to represent this dense network of associations, we have included "see also" lists at the end of each entry. These lists form the basis of the visual constellation included as a frontispiece to this volume and at the beginning of each entry.[9] By highlighting the networked relations emanating from each individual keyword, these visual representations show how synonymy, homology, and other associations yield a conceptual scaffolding that helps to stabilize the vocabulary despite conditions of brittle linguistic stress.

The confusion that prevails around language today makes clear that we are living through a historical moment in which our speech situation is anything but transparent. In response to this challenging environment, radicals have alternated between trying to "fix" meaning by insisting on particular definitions and trying to subvert it through deconstruction, neologism, or other means. In opposition to both of these approaches, we hope this book will serve as a reminder that contests over word usage and meaning are themselves meaningful. When analyzed closely, words reveal themselves to be symptoms of underlying and overarching social contradictions. By critically illuminating these tensions, it becomes possible to gain additional insight into broader social dynamics. In turn,

---

9.   For more information about these constellations, the means by which they were created, and their political significance, please see Derek Laventure's "Constellations, Cognitive Maps, and the Politics of Data Visualization" included as an Appendix to this volume (Appendix).

these social dynamics constitute the field of struggle upon which we must devise our strategies and play out our tactics. The more we understand this field, the better equipped we will be to win.

Struggles around word usage and meaning are now in a critical state. The cultural logic of late capitalism erodes transparent speech communities while severing tangible relations to the past. Under these conditions, tracing linguistic developments becomes paramount, and for radicals the task is especially urgent. For those of us committed not just to interpreting the world but to changing it as well, becoming aware of language's historical and productive elaboration is an important precondition to meaningful struggle. Means of communication are means of production, noted Williams. And seizing control of such means requires first that we understand them, since only then can we envision how they might be brought into accord with our interests. Without this understanding, all such efforts remain chatter.

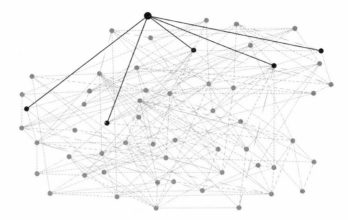

ACCESSIBLE

Kelly Fritsch

ACCORDING TO THE *OXFORD ENGLISH DICTIONARY*, USE OF "accessible" as an adjective dates as far back as the fourteenth century, when it denoted being "capable of being entered or approached" and "readily reached." It was only in 1961 that "accessible" began to be used to denote the ability to be "readily understood." As a noun, "access" derives from the fourteenth-century Old French "*acces*" (denoting both the "coming on" or "attack" of an illness or emotion) and from the Latin "*accessus*" ("a coming to, an approach"). Describing "the power, opportunity, permission, or right to come near or into contact with someone or something," the noun use of "access" derives directly from the Latin. "Access" as a verb emerged in relation to computing in 1962. Within these etymological origins, then, one can detect tensions between "access" as a kind of attack and "access" as an opportunity enabling contact. This tension is important for radicals. Indeed, the concept's dual inflection as both attack and contact highlights the centrality of boundary work to all forms of political struggle.

Within the history of social movements, use of "access" as a noun began to occur frequently throughout the eighteenth and nineteenth centuries, when it was associated with the emergence of liberal politics and calls for "equal access." Drafted during the Reconstruction Era, the US Civil Rights (or "Enforcement") Act of 1875, for example, guaranteed "equal access" to public accommodations regardless of race or color. The use of "access" and "accessible" dramatically increased from the 1950s onward as a result of developments in civil rights, the rise of disability rights struggles, and new forms of technology like the personal computer and the sidewalk curb cut designed to improve urban-landscape navigability.

Following the precedent set during Reconstruction, fighting for "equal access" became a defining feature of the US Civil Rights Movement between 1956 and 1965. On June 11, 1963, John F. Kennedy announced that major civil rights legislation would be submitted to Congress to guarantee equal access to public facilities, to end segregation in education, and to provide federal protection ensuring the right to vote. In this usage, "access" denoted opportunity. According to Bess Williamson, it conveyed "the importance of recognizing external barriers that prevent disenfranchised persons from gaining access to resources" (2015, 15). This meaning is perhaps expressed most obviously through the International Symbol of Access (1969), the ubiquitous white graphic depicting a wheelchair user, faced to the right, presented on a blue background (Fritsch 2013).

Gaining access to resources is the primary meaning "access" takes in activist culture today, where people clamor for "access to jobs," "access to healthcare," and "access to housing" (Williamson 2015, 15). Through "accessibility," people are thought to gain the means of participating in or accessing something that would otherwise exclude them on the basis of mental or physical impairment, educational or class status, or gender identity. In this formulation, "accessibility" is primarily achieved through a checklist approach—accessibility obtains when a space is barrier-free for people using wheelchairs and has non-fluorescent lighting, has gender-neutral washrooms and American Sign Language interpretation available, is free or has sliding-scale fees, has integrated a range of ways for people to participate, offers childcare, is scent-free, et cetera. As a checklist to inclusion, "accessibility" conforms to an understanding in which difference is an individual problem to accommodate. By accommodating and including individuals in this way, the fight for accessibility draws upon and reiterates the liberal rights-based approach to social change. Consequently, it is valorized and celebrated as a self-evident good that solves (or might eventually solve) the problem of exclusion.

In this formulation, "access" is generally conceived as an individual state of affairs in which the problem to be resolved arises from the particular body incapable of gaining access. By taking accessibility into account, and by providing "equal access," this problem is ostensibly solved. Behind this conception resides the assumption that some bodies naturally fit whereas others need "access." As such, the socially just thing to do is to extend access to those who do not easily fit. In this way, demanding access to a space or event can inadvertently reinforce the naturalization of "able" bodies while reinforcing the individualization of impairment, class or educational status, and gender identity. As disability scholar Tanya Titchkosky has pointed out in *The Question of Access: Disability, Space, Meaning*, this is because "access" is not solely about a lack of inclusion; instead, it is a way of "perceiving, talking, and acting" (2011, 13) that is concerned with some aspects of everyday-life access while others remain unnoted. Although every instance of life could conceivably be regarded from the standpoint of access (since establishing access is the precondition to doing anything), current conceptions tend only to implicate those considered abnormal or who do not easily fit into activist spaces as normally constituted. "The fight for the rights to access may get people in," Titchkosky notes, "but that is only half the issue." In her view, "developing critical relations to access that are committed to recognizing how it already interprets embodied difference is the other half" (2011, 28). "Access" can rectify exclusion; however, such efforts remain incomplete without a critical assessment of how those exclusions first came to be and how they continue to function.

Despite attempts by disabled activists to emphasize that it is not the problem of any individual body but rather social relations that set up barriers to access, contemporary mobilizations of "access" tend to reinscribe the idea that access is about some bodies and not others. In this way, and despite the "social model" advanced by many disability activists, the problem is once again individualized. In its dominant figuration of disability access (a wheelchair user who requires a ramp, elevator, or automatic door opener), the International Symbol of Access makes this tension emblematic.

For radical disability activists, the tension in "accessibility" also arises from use of the term to denote inclusion in an unjust system—or, as activist organizer AJ Withers (2015) terms it, "accessing privilege." In this view, a truly radical approach to accessibility requires considering the tensions between "accessibility" as a solution or checklist versus "accessibility" as an ongoing negotiation. For radical disability activists, the potential of "accessibility" is precisely to mark "access" as an ongoing and shifting process rather than as a mode of solving individualized problems. As disability justice activist Mia Mingus (2014) remarks, "we need to go beyond just inclusion and beyond just trying to make spaces accessible" in order to ask what liberatory access would look like, not only for disabled people but for "all of our communities." One strategy for achieving this reformulation can be observed in what Mingus (2011) has termed "access intimacy." Here people are encouraged to "get," "understand," or anticipate someone's access needs and, in so doing, produce or practice "crip-made access" and "crip solidarity."

But even as radicals begin reimagining "accessibility" as a shifting process rather than as a mode of solving individualized problems, and even as we present "accessibility" as a self-evident good, it remains common practice to deliberately limit access in all sorts of ways. And so, while "accessibility" is regularly presented as a way of extending social inclusion to those who have historically been marginalized by ableism or other forms of oppression, this conception of "access" regularly (though rarely explicitly) comes into conflict with "security culture," "safe space," or forms of intellectual engagement such as dense theoretical writing or complicated word usage not deemed to be "readily accessible." Like "accessibility," these forms of exclusion are also commonly presented as a self-evident good, in which access is deliberately restricted for some in order to create a different kind of access, or community, for others. Importantly, the access barriers created by "security culture," "safe spaces," or through particular kinds of intellectual engagement like "inaccessible" writing, are usually taken to be necessary. Indeed, these practices are often necessary in order to create boundaries so as to thwart different kinds of attacks by the state and other enemies. The result is that the assumed good of creating access is pitted against the assumed good of maintaining security, creating community, or deepening our understanding of our ourselves and our world. Here, far from being a self-evident good, "access" functions as a kind of attack upon boundaries that have been constructed for a particular purpose. Thus, while frequently proclaiming the good of access, radicals contradict this proclamation through everyday exclusionary practices that are deemed necessary and important. Historically, this problem has surfaced in fights, for example, over whether or not a revolutionary party should be open or closed (Lenin 1961). This contradiction is also evident in the CrimethInc. Ex-Workers' Collective essay on "Security Culture," in which they ask the reader to "Balance the need to escape detection by your enemies against the need to be accessible to potential friends. In the long run, secrecy alone cannot protect us—sooner or later they are going to find all of us, and if no one else understands what we're doing and what we want, they'll be able to liquidate us with impunity. Only the power of an informed and sympathetic (and hopefully similarly equipped) public can help us then."

Balancing the fight against enemies with the need to be accessible to friends requires that we are able not only to recognize the difference but also to enact that difference through the opening and closing of those boundaries we control.

The question remains: how might we address the divide in radical practices between celebrating access and acknowledging the need for particular exclusionary spaces within radical milieus to defend ourselves from attack? If, despite its violence, exclusion is a category we want to embrace in certain moments (for example, in calls for sovereignty or in contests over occupation), then it may be through "access" as a boundary practice denoting both "contact" and "attack" that we might find the means of navigating this fraught terrain.

SEE ALSO: Bodies; Crip; Intellectual; Rights; Space

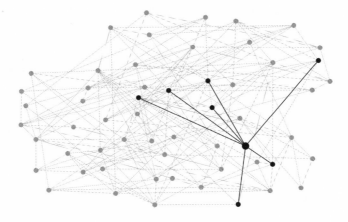

ACCOUNTABILITY

Clare O'Connor

"ACCOUNT" FIRST APPEARED IN THE TWELFTH CENTURY. Its root, "count," derives from the French "*compter*," originally from the Latin "*computāre*" ("reckon"). The prefix "*ac*" ("toward") produced the verb "account," which means "toward reckoning." Usage of "account" as a noun emerged soon after, and both forms referred to the act of considering objects and events in the world with the intent of reckoning (to think, clear, settle) and of relating one's reckoning. In this original usage, the act of "account" was bound to religious or metaphysical contemplation, the movement toward an absolute reckoning with God and his creations. While absolute knowledge was unattainable, "account"— the pursuit itself—heralded passage to the divine.

This metaphysical emphasis continued into the fourteenth century, when "account" first appeared with the suffix "able" (derived from the Latin "*bilis*," meaning "capable or worthy of being"). Poet William Langland (c1325–c1390) wrote, "Men þat ben ryche Aren a-countable to crist": Men that become rich are accountable to Christ (*OED*). Someone was "accountable" as a result of their capability and worthiness of metaphysical reckoning. However, the addition of the suffix "able" also coincided with increasing uses of "count" that emphasized the work of "counting up" for the purposes of financial transaction and providing reckonings of goods held in trust. In the sixteenth century, this usage was extended so that "accountable" meant to "provide an evaluative account of; (also) to answer for (conduct, performance of duty, etc.)." Around this time, "value"— previously a noun denoting "reputation, (personal) merit"—first appeared as a verb and referred to evaluation not of world but "worth" (of goods, property, etc.). Indeed, as scientific observation, realist depiction, and consistent systems of measurement gained traction, "account" became synonymous with the "estimation" of worth. It is in this context that Shakespeare's Lady Macbeth manipulatively reproached her husband for his reluctance to kill their king: "From this time / Such I account thy love" (1963, 76).

By the end of the eighteenth century, bourgeois revolution had rendered this meaning culturally dominant. For someone to be "accountable" meant they were capable of providing an evaluative "report" on their holdings, duties, or actions (notably, the word "bureaucracy" enters English around this time). The prior emphasis on religious metaphysical contemplation was thus supplanted by a model in which positivist accounts could be presented in a form that would enable them to be shared and evaluated.

But while such positivism became culturally dominant, bourgeois revolution didn't extinguish metaphysics entirely; in fact, it relied upon it.[1] "Positivism and metaphysics," notes Stanley

---

1. The division between positivism and metaphysics is commonly acknowledged in analyses of bourgeois epistemology. Stanley Aronowitz explains the problem in his Introduction to Max Horkheimer's *Critical Theory*: "On the one hand, positivist thought denies the relevance, if not the existence, of universals. It asserts the rationality of the given surface reality and documents its permutations.

Aronowitz, "are the unified world view of the bourgeoisie, split according to the prevailing division of labor between science, which serves industry, and religions and secular spiritual ideologies, which serve social domination" (2002, xv). Indeed, the drive to account for things empirically has always come up against the necessary admission that much of what we encounter escapes positivist summary. Consider, for instance, how the phrase "you can count me in" differs from "you can count on me." Both refer to calculation; however, the latter also directs us to the character of the speaker, a residual trace of the original metaphysical meaning. Capitalism draws on this tension to reanimate the disenchanted world: "There are some things money can't buy; for everything else, there's Mastercard."

In commonsense radical usage, "accountability" denotes the measure of someone's willingness to report on their actions. In this usage, someone is "accountable" when they voluntarily engage in processes intended to determine whether or how a situation in which they are involved might be remedied. However, in these processes, the empirical bases for determining accountability often seem inadequate; what we desire tends to exceed what we're able to produce.

In August 2015, activists from Black Lives Matter (what Amy Goodman has called "the accountability movement") confronted Hillary Clinton at a presidential campaign event (Democracy Now 2015a). Citing Clinton's support of the incarceration-inducing Violent Crime Control and Law Enforcement Act of

---

On the other hand, metaphysics abolishes the positivist enslavement to the concrete and searches for a teleology to give meaning to human existence. Science offers no transcendent meaning to men; it simply asserts facts. Its immanent viewpoint is the unity of thought with outer reality. Metaphysics is the other side of positivist nominalism. Its universals are abstract. If not God, then the absolute idea informs its search for purpose so resolutely denied by empirical science" (2002, xv). In his "Theses on Feuerbach" Karl Marx discusses the problem in a similar fashion: "The chief defect of all hitherto existing materialism—that of Feuerbach included—is that the thing, reality, sensuousness, is conceived only in the form of the *object of contemplation*, but not as *sensuous human activity, practice*, not subjectively. Hence, in contradistinction to materialism, the *active* side was developed abstractly by idealism—which, of course, does not know real, sensuous activity as such" (2004, 121).

1994, activist Julius Jones asked her what had changed in her heart: "How can your mistakes be a lesson for all Americans, for a moment of reflection on how we treat Black people in this country?" Clinton accepted Jones' premise, going so far as to call herself a "sinner." "I think there has to be a reckoning," she said; however, she concluded, "I also think there has to be some positive vision and plan . . . . You are not going to change everyone's heart" (Democracy Now 2015b).[2]

Confusion arose when Jones told Clinton that, if she wanted to help, the onus was on her. "If you don't tell Black people what to do, then we won't tell you all what to do. . . . There's not much that we can do to stop the violence against us."[3] Some activists were frustrated with this message. "For a series of protests that hand-waves about 'accountability,'" wrote Douglas Williams, "it would have been beneficial to make concrete demands with which you could actually hold this person, you know, accountable" (2015). MSNBC's Melissa Harris Perry conveyed similar confusion, asking Jones and fellow activist Daunasia Yancey to describe "an encounter that *is* accountable." Yancey explained: "What we're looking for is a reflection on her personal responsibility for being part of the cause of this problem" ("Exclusive" 2015). In an effort to reconcile metaphysical and empirical desires, "accountability" in Jones and Yancey's usage entailed not just the alignment of word and deed but also an account that satisfied their moral standards.

Similarly, although demands for "police accountability" emphasize the need to eradicate impunity, the rare occasions on which officers are indicted tend not to be viewed as evidence of accountability. Indeed, immorality is established through the demand for

---

2. Clinton's argument echoed Martin Luther King's observation that "the law cannot make a man love me, but it can keep him from lynching me. . . . Religion and education must change one's internal feelings, but it is scarcely a moral act to encourage others to patiently accept injustice until a man's heart gets right" (1997, 284). Similarly, Nina Simone insisted, "You don't have to live next to me / Just give me my equality" ("Mississippi Goddamn" 1964).

3. This line of reasoning resembles "yes means yes" (Friedman and Valenti 2008) feminist politics, premised on the notion that resources should be directed toward teaching men not to rape and enshrining in law the requirement of "affirmative consent," now law in California (SB 967 2014).

accountability itself. People thus want to appear accountable *in the moral sense*. Perhaps this is why the US Government Accounting Office (founded in 1921) changed its name to the Governmental Accountability Office in 2004. Or why the word increasingly appears in the business world (Miller 1998; 2004). Claiming that "accountability is an attitude," the "women-owned" Fierce Accountability Training Program, for instance, aims to "create a culture where people choose to hold themselves accountable for delivering results no matter what" (Fierce Accountability Training 2015). However desirable, it becomes evident that moral accountability is here secondary to the ruling forces of market and law.

In radical movements, and especially in the context of anti-racist feminist organizing against gender-based violence and the politics of "community accountability," the term is not beholden in this way. The popular 2011 book *The Revolution Starts at Home: Confronting Violence in Activist Communities* provides a genealogy of community accountability politics. Here the book's editors foreground the founding conference of Critical Resistance in 1999, which "provided a framework for many of us who were involved in the anti-violence movement and were skeptical of its reliance on the criminal legal system." In 2000, this framework inspired the formation of INCITE! Women of Color Against Violence—now the largest North American organization advocating the community accountability model. According to Andrea Smith, INCITE! posed a simple question: "If the criminal legal system is not the solution, what is?" The answer involved adopting preexisting practices of restorative justice while rejecting the state: community accountability.

In theory, this strategy operates through casework. A community supports a survivor by coordinating an "accountability process" by which a perpetrator is held accountable for violence. Varying in form and duration, accountability processes are "collective efforts to address harm" by "challenging the underlying social patterns and power structures that support abusive behavior." These processes allow the virtuous commitment to "accounting for oneself" to be tested. Consequently, "accountability" is typically invoked in reference to its absence, as a response to an "unaccountable" person or group.

In practice, accountability processes have produced confusion and conflict. In 2011, after a decade of community accountability advocacy and organizing, activist Angustia Celeste wrote a controversial article entitled "Safety Is an Illusion: Reflections on Accountability." "Our current models of accountability suffer from an over-abundance of hope," the piece proclaimed. "Safety comes from trust, and trust is personal. It can't be mediated or rubber-stamped at a community level. My 'safe' lover might be your secret abuser. . . . There is no such thing as accountability within radical communities because there is no such thing as community. . . . Community in this context is a mythical, frequently invoked and much misused term."

Similarly, an anonymous online article declared that sometimes "accountability processes . . . just teach men how to appear unabusive" ("Is the Anarchist Man Our Comrade?"). Meanwhile, feminists in New York and Santa Cruz circulated communiqués defending retributive violence against abusive men within their networks. In their view, "alternative accountability processes . . . often force the survivor to relive the trauma of the assault." Moreover, "They end up being an ineffective re-creation of the judicial process that leaves the perpetrator off the hook, while the survivor has to live through the memory of the assault for the rest of her life. The US legal system and the alternative community-based accountability processes are simply not good enough for survivors, and certainly not revolutionary" (Radical Women's Kitchen).

For their part, the CrimethInc. Ex-Workers' Collective weighed in with a zine (2013c) in which they outlined "ten pitfalls of community accountability processes." Despite these efforts, their proposed resolution ultimately reiterated the model's premises: "Without acknowledging and challenging our collective responsibility," they write, "holding individuals accountable won't be enough. . . . So long as our practices around accountability for sexual assault and abuse don't successfully meet folks' needs, vigilantism will continue." Predictably, this intervention didn't solve things. After his friend was "shouted down" at a 2014 activist event for asking why "the forms of accountability processes that we've seen in radical subcultures" have "so regularly failed," activist Kristian Williams contended that "accountability" had generated a framework that fostered a "politics of denunciation" (2014). Since no account can be good enough, the impasse persists.

It is often difficult to determine the specific moment when a new word enters the radical repertoire. Of course, "accountability" appears in political discourse throughout the nineteenth and twentieth centuries. However, it begins to appear more regularly in leftist theoretical and movement-based sources during the 1970s. The publication of Paulo Freire's *Pedagogy of the Oppressed* proved to be decisive. "Sooner or later," he wrote, "a true revolution must initiate a courageous dialogue with the people. . . . It must be accountable to them, must speak frankly to them of its achievements, its mistakes, its miscalculations, and its difficulties" (2005, 128). Over one million copies of the book have been sold since the release of the English translation in 1970.

By 1979, Adrienne Rich could cite the concept as a central category of analysis and struggle: "As I thrust my hand deeper into the swirl of this stream—history, nightmare, accountability—I feel the current angrier and more multiform than the surface shows: There is fury here, and terror, but there is also power, power not to be had without the terror and the fury" (310). In 1982, bell hooks released her influential essay "Race and Gender: The Issue of Accountability" in which she described how white women's racist socialization found expression within the feminist movement in practices that excluded, ignored, and otherwise undermined Black women. As feminists grappled with this observation (elaborated by many women of color), hooks eventually had to issue a clarification: "White people want to deflect attention away from their accountability for anti-racist change by making it seem that everyone has been socialized to be racist against their will" (1992, 14).

Around the same time, the word began to appear alongside "community" in various places. As Patricia Hill Collins explained in *Black Feminist Thought*, "The market model sees community as arbitrary and fragile, structured fundamentally by competition and domination. In contrast, Afrocentric models of community stress connections, caring, and personal accountability" (1990, 222). By the 1990s, the term had become an important point of debate. Reflecting on the undesirability of political fame, Andrea Dworkin insisted that "you can't be accountable to millions of people.... You can only be accountable to people that you really know.... I have to draw a line of accountability and at the same time, increasingly, my behavior does have an impact on other women that I don't know. Then there is some kind of accountability that I owe them, but what is it?" (1996).

This question continues to resonate twenty years later. What account can someone offer that might convince critics that one has redeemed oneself after wrongdoing? In *Giving an Account of Oneself*, Judith Butler suggests that giving an account "takes a narrative form, which not only depends upon the ability to relay a set of sequential events with plausible transitions but also draws upon narrative voice and authority" (2003, 12). However, "the account of myself that I give in discourse never fully expresses or carries this living self ... If I try to give an account of myself, if I try to make myself recognizable and understandable, then I might begin with a narrative account of my life. But this narrative will be disoriented by what is not mine, or not mine alone ... [T]he story of my origin I tell is not one for which I am accountable, and it cannot establish my accountability. At least, let's hope not, since, over wine usually, I tell it in various ways, and the accounts are not always consistent with one another" (36–38).

Insofar as our aim—as Marx proposed in his "Theses on Feuerbach"—is to reconcile the positivist and the metaphysical (the material and the "beyond") and to uphold the latter as a necessary terrain of struggle, we must concede the impossibility of total accountability. In the end, nothing that Hillary Clinton might say or do can truly redeem her. Rather than relying on concepts that obscure these conditions, we might instead speak concretely of the political contradictions that shape our lives, embracing useful—albeit inadequate—reforms while never confusing this with the work of changing hearts.

SEE ALSO: Allies; Community; Demand; Experience; Politics; Privilege; Responsibility

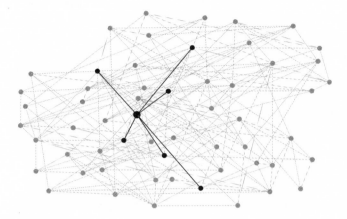

AGENCY

AK Thompson

As noted in the *Oxford English Dictionary*, the first uses of "agency" and "agent" in the English language date from the late sixteenth century and slightly predate the radical Protestant sects that sought to enact God's will without relying on the Church as intermediary and the Enlightenment-era deliberations about human freedom that continue to underscore the concept's modern meaning. Initially designating action pursued beyond or in opposition to determining frames or—in the case of "agent"—the force that actually carried out (rather than merely instigated) a given action, the meaning of "agency" gradually expanded to denote a fundamental but intangible attribute of Being itself. Words associated with this latter meaning include "choice," "freedom," "purposiveness," "volition," and "will."

In North American social movements, popular usage dates from the period following the sex wars of the 1980s, during which sex-positive feminists charged radical feminists with ignoring the capacity for "sex workers" (a term that only came to prominence following the publication of the 1987 anthology *Sex Work*) to engage in purposeful action despite the industry's constraints. Consequently, radical feminists were thought to have *produced* or *exacerbated* (rather than merely to have described) women's victim status. By the first decade of the twenty-first century, this characterization had become so ubiquitous that a sociologist writing in the journal *Critical Sociology* could assert—without citation—that agency "can be defined as the capacity to evaluate and make choices for oneself regarding self definitions as a sexual being and personal sexual performances regardless of the external dominant social forces and social consequences" (Corsianos 2007, 865).

Commonsense contemporary usage of the term by radicals thus emphasized the innate capacity for action possessed by an individual regardless of the particular circumstance in which they found themselves. Consequently, "agency" is perceived to be an intrinsic quality, always in operation, needing only to be recognized. It therefore followed that a major focus for radical action was to further the recognition (and valorize the representation) of existing capacities for agency. On occasion, this emphasis has shown signs of supplanting attempts to modify or extend the field of action itself. Drawn from an article published in a blog maintained by a Harvard law student committed to international human rights and gender justice, the following formulation is characteristic: "One problem with writing about women's rights and poverty . . . is that most such writing ends up denying its very subjects . . . agency. . . . Women and girls are portrayed as victims of abuse, domestic violence, and forced marriage. But even the most 'victimized' of women have a strong voice, and stand up for themselves daily in ways we do not think about. . . . Unfortunately, this strength and beauty is all too often ignored and forgotten" (Kolisetty 2011).

Prior to the term's conceptual mobilization by contemporary social movements in the period following the sex wars, radical interest in the *question* of "agency" arose in part from dissatisfaction with the dominance of various forms of structural analysis in both the social sciences and in socialist organizing during the mid-twentieth century. Figures associated with these trends included Claude Lévi-Strauss, Louis Althusser, and Talcott Parsons. This dissatisfaction, which found practical expression in the New Left's occasional turn toward a subjective politics of self-actualization, coincided with the emergence of similarly inflected intellectual movements. Among others, these included the "people's history" associated with Howard Zinn (1980) and the "history from below" associated with E. P. Thompson (1963).

The point of connection between these various attacks on structural accounts was their common emphasis on people's capacity to make history through individual and everyday actions, and to be present—as Thompson proposed—at the moment of their own emergence. Recalling those figures he took to be precursors to a communist tradition indigenous to Britain, Thompson underscored the importance not only of evaluating but also of *valuing* their experiences—even if they did ultimately prove to be "casualties of history" (1963, 12). "Their communitarian ideals may have been fantasies," he wrote, "but they lived through these acute times of social disturbance and we did not. Their aspirations were valid in terms of their own experience" (1963, 13).

But though these intellectual critiques and the sensibilities of the new social movements combined to ensure that calls to recognize people's agency would become ubiquitous by the beginning of the twenty-first century, the meaning of the term itself remained unclear. As a result, even though the concept is widely used in social movement settings today, it is generally deployed as a gloss. This ambiguity corresponds to (and no doubt arose in part from) disputes taking place contemporaneously in philosophy and the social sciences. Writing at the turn of the century and a decade after the sex wars, two prominent American sociologists recount how "the concept of agency has become a source of increasing strain and confusion in social thought." Indeed, "variants of action theory, normative theory, and political-institutional analysis have defended, attacked, buried, and resuscitated the concept in often contradictory and overlapping ways. At the center of the debate, the term *agency* itself has maintained an elusive, albeit resonant, vagueness" (Emirbayer and Miche 1998, 962).

In light of this ambiguity, the prevailing radical concept of "agency" has been made meaningful primarily through its juxtaposition to "structure," its putative antonym. For its part, "structure" continues to be used (although with decreasing frequency) to denote institutions or relations that give shape and coherence to the social world. The structure-agency dyad gained prominence in the 1980s when it was foregrounded in the work of prominent British sociologist Anthony Giddens.

One of the principal intellectual forces behind the elaboration of a "Third Way" politics and influential during the British Labour Party's rebranding as "New Labour" during the 1990s, Giddens' work had a disproportionate effect on social democratic and labor movement forces. Along with his canonization in the field of sociology (a status that has since begun to wane), this traction facilitated the broad diffusion of his concepts into radical scenes. And though these scenes tended not to endorse Giddens' (1984) sociological solution—"structuration"—to the posited irreconcilability between structure and agency, they proved less reluctant to adopt the antithetical terms themselves.

In contrast to Giddens' structuration, contemporary radicals have tended overwhelmingly to line up on the side of agency in an effort to undermine structural accounts and even structures themselves. Coextensive with this development has been the increasing importance attributed to recognition and representation within the political field. If, as this position maintains, agency is always operative, and if it is the means by which people make history, it follows that radicals must cultivate the capacity to recognize agency in action. It is in this context that other terminological shifts that took place around the same time can be understood. These include the "empowering" new emphasis on "survivors" rather than "victims" of various forms of violence, and on "clients" or "consumers" rather than "patients" in various health industry settings. Significantly, the *Oxford English Dictionary* (*OED*) lists "patient" as one among several antonyms to "agent." Meanwhile, "empowerment" itself has become a contested term under neoliberalism, where it is frequently invoked to justify forms of deregulation purportedly aimed at broadening the realm of choice.

But while the characterization of agency as an ever-present force undermining the determining power of social structure has achieved a commonsense ubiquity within radical scenes, it's important to recall that, from the seventeenth century onward, "agency" has in fact denoted two separate and nearly antithetical ideas. In the first, and as already described, it coincides with the desire expressed by moral philosophers and political liberals to pinpoint the force that generates action among free subjects. In the second iteration, however, the term is associated with organizational coordination, instrumentality, and even the division of labor.

According to the *OED*, "agency" in this second sense denotes "one who acts for another." Significantly, the *OED* also highlights how, in the seventeenth century, the "agitator" (a figure who stands as an obvious precursor to today's radical) was regularly conceived as "a person who acts on behalf of others, an agent." Although less widely acknowledged by radicals today, this second usage continues to enjoy widespread traction in both popular culture and institutional settings.

In the social sciences, the concept of "agency" as instrumental action carried out at the behest of an instigating force gained traction again in 1974, when Stanley Milgram published his now-famous study *Obedience to Authority*. Theorizing his findings, Milgram advanced the position that "agency" described the tendency for autonomous individuals to subordinate themselves—and thus to become agents—when doing so produced less direct conflict with authority than would defiance. In Milgram's words, "a person is in a state of agency when he defines himself in a social situation in a manner that renders him open to regulation by a person of higher status. In this condition the individual no longer views himself as responsible for his own actions but defines himself as an instrument for carrying out the wishes of another" (1974, 134).

Although this characterization is a near-perfect antithesis to the current dominant conceptualization among radicals, it aligns more clearly with commonsense usage, for example, "an agent of the state" or "the Central Intelligence Agency." In a similar but distinct move away from conceptions of "agency" that posit it as a unique and intrinsic quality of the free individual, social scientists following the Actor Network Theory (ANT) of Bruno Latour have recently begun contemplating the agency of *objects*. According to Latour (2005), "ANT is not the empty claim that objects do things 'instead' of human actors." Instead, "it simply says that no science of the social can even begin if the question of who and what participates in the action is not first of all thoroughly explored, even though it might mean letting elements in which, for lack of a better term, we would call non-humans" (2005, 72).

In a similar way, feminist philosopher Karen Barad has also sought to decouple agency from the autonomous liberal subject. For Barad, "agency is not an attribute of a subject or an object." Instead, it is "an enactment . . . of iterative changes to particular practices" (2007, 178). Following this observation to its logical conclusion, Barad maintains that agency can therefore and in no way be limited to humans.

Elaborated in movement-related scholarly works, these shifts have also been echoed in contemporary radical discourse, where "people" have come regularly to be designated in their object status—for example, as "bodies." This nominal-conceptual change—noted by both David McNally (2001) and John Sanbonmatsu (2004) in their respective accounts of the explosion of scholarly works that, since the 1990s, have prominently featured "the body" in their titles—may itself be read as an indication that the philosophical concern with the body, which can be traced from Spinoza through to Deleuze and Guattari, has now become an inexact but hegemonic preoccupation suturing together currents as various and contradictory as neoliberal biopolitics and radical posthumanism.

Practically speaking, all of these developments have meant that the tension between radical evocations of "agency" and common-sense ones has been exacerbated. If agency is not an innate individual and subjective capacity that can be cast as antithesis to both structure and object, and if—by extension—recognizing a subject's agency can no longer be considered a sufficient means of overcoming objective structural constraints (and, indeed, if objective constraints and objects themselves are now viewed as constitutive aspects of agency), then the formulation that holds agency (once recognized) to be the source of historical transformation begins to reveal its limit.

SEE ALSO: Bodies; Experience; History; Liberal; Representation; Vanguard

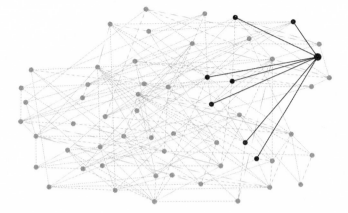

ALLIES

Mab Segrest

FOR CONTEMPORARY ACTIVISTS, THE TERM "ALLY" IS used to refer to people in historically dominant groups who align themselves politically with historically oppressed groups with the goal of dismantling oppressive systems. Feminist intersectional theory and praxis during the 1970s and 1980s led the way in making the multiple valences of power clear so that such alliances are—at best—complex negotiations of positionality and privilege. Historically, the term "ally" referred most often to relationships of marriage and kinship, as well as to those state and military alliances that often preceded or followed them. In contrast, most recent radical usages designate relationships not so much *within* but *across* systems of power and biological kinship, working against the grain of deeply embedded historical misapprehensions of Others.

A survey of book titles and activist blogs illustrates how contemporary radicals use the term today. For example, *Some Men: Feminist Allies and the Movement to End Violence against Women* (Messner, Greenberg and Peretz 2015) gives voice, in Gloria Steinem's words, to "a diverse activist community of men who understand that feminism is their movement, too—not only because they support daughters, wives, mothers and coworkers, but because they see violence against females as a normalization of all violence, and a powerful way of limiting men's full humanity too." Karen Dace's *Unlikely Allies in the Academy: Women of Color and White Women in Conversation* (2012) collects essays by four white women and five women of color in an attempt to create alliances toward more inclusive structures on campuses and beyond. J Love Calderón's *Occupying Privilege: Conversations on Love, Race & Liberation* (2012) defines allies as "members of the advantaged group who act against the oppressions from which they derive power, privilege and acceptance." Cynthia Stokes Brown's *Refusing Racism: White Allies and the Struggle for Civil Rights* (2002) takes its definition from Beverly Tatum: "An antiracist activist, a white man or woman who is clearly identifiable as an ally to people of color in the struggle against racism." Such people identify themselves by "taking a public stand against racist assumptions that surround one, against the prevailing system of white supremacy, when one is the beneficiary of the system" (Tatum 1994, 474).

Paul Kivel's early and influential *Uprooting Racism: How White People Can Work for Racial Justice* (1996) devotes its third chapter to "Being An Ally," which explains topics such as what an ally does, getting involved, making a commitment, working with white people, and including family and friends. Generating such lists became a staple for authors struggling to define the term. Usage often arises in conjunction with group identities: white allies to people of color, heterosexual allies to queers or LGBT people, middle- or upper-class allies to poor and working-class people, and male allies to women. For example, Calderón refers to herself as "a heterosexual ally for queer liberation" (2012, 100). Meanwhile, current contests over the concept's meaning detach "allies" from individual identities ("I am") to refocus on collective actions and movements ("We do"). Contestants within these debates have also discredited the "ally industrial complex," which they associate with the professionalization of political work carried out by nonprofits.

Derived from the Latin "*alligare*" ("to bind to"), "ally" passed into English through the Old French "*alier*" and the Anglo-French "*aillaier*" between AD 1250 and 1300. Its antonyms include "enemy," "foe," and "adversary." According to the *Oxford English Dictionary*, the earliest uses of the noun denoted a "relative, relation" (usually from marriage) among "kinsman, kinswoman" from elite families. This usage can be seen in Chaucer's Second Nun's Tale (circa 1405): "This day I take thee for myn allye Seyde this blissful faire mayde." The relation expands quickly from personal heterosexual binding to a "state, military force, etc., united or associated with another league by formal treaty, esp. for political or military purposes," as in Grenewey's 1598 translation of Tacitus' *Annales*: "The like number of citizens and allies should be under Corbuloes charge." Standing apart from state and familial relations, one strand of meaning denotes "a person who helps or cooperates with another; a supporter, an associate, a friend." A third strand indicates "something similar to another thing in nature of characteristics, or placed near it in classification; esp (Biol) an organism which is related to another by common evolutionary origin." World Wars I and II elevated state military alliances to new heights. In this context, "the Allies" became a proper noun denoting the military forces, as the *OED* explains, "who fought in alliance against Germany and her allies in the First World War (1914–18) or the Second World War (1939–45)." The *OED* also acknowledges the verb form: "to ally."

During the Cold War, radicals began reimagining the concept of "ally" so that its emphasis fell less on close political affinities within existing regimes of power. Instead, they sought to emphasize calls for accountability across systems historically justified by biology (for example, by way of social Darwinism) and across psyches defined as non-normative or Other.

This alternate use of "allies" emerged during the liberation movements of the 1960s and 1970s as people of color began insisting that white people take on white supremacy in their own communities. In 1966, the Student Nonviolent Coordinating Committee (SNCC) urged the white people who had been working with them to stop trying to "escape the horrible reality of America by going into the black community . . . while neglecting the organization of their own people's racist communities." Although their position paper on "The Basis of Black Power" (Carmichael 1966) does not use "ally," it does refer to "white people who desire change in this country" who are "just as disgusted by this system as we are." Acknowledging the valuable role that whites played in helping to "give blacks the right to organize," the Committee declares: "that role is now over." Talk of coalitions was meaningless, they argued, because—at present—"there is no one to align ourselves with, because of the lack of organization in the white communities." Organizing in white communities meant, in part, working to change white individual and collective psyches: "Whites are the ones who must try to raise themselves to our humanistic level." If carried out effectively, such work might result in "talks about exchange of personnel, coalition, and other meaningful alliances."

This new orientation established the role to be played by the "ally" on a terrain that was rapidly being transformed by a resurgent right-wing politics. By the 1970s, even as the US government worked to violently suppress radical movements, the Civil Rights Act (1964), the Voting Rights Act (1965), and initiatives launched during Lyndon Johnson's War on Poverty (1964) opened up new government jobs (such as those in Head Start, founded in 1965) as well as positions in a growing nonprofit sector of "501-c-3s" overseen by the Internal Revenue Service. These opportunities provided a base for some 1960s radicals. Some sectors of the emerging second-wave feminist and gay and lesbian rights movements also organized within nonprofits. Meanwhile, multinational corporations created a highly feminized global assembly line, undercutting labor organizing in the United States. Reagan-era neoliberal structural adjustment policies encouraged the accumulation of profits from information and service industries and resulted in massive new inequalities. In 1976, China turned toward "state capitalism." The collapse of the Soviet Union in 1989 brought the "era of the three worlds" to a close, thus unleashing a triumphant new wave of capitalist globalization. Under such circumstances, what is an ally to do?

Raising the collective white psyche up to a "humanistic level" would prove to be difficult in the newly emerging "non-profit industrial complex" (Incite! Women of Color Collective 2009) as various sectors of the well-funded right deployed an array of identity-based scapegoats for a 99 percent losing footing in the new global capitalist economies.

The movement of "ally" (against etymology's grain) from a relation between kin to one between Others explains some of the difficulties associated with "training allies" in the twenty-first century. In his *Uprooting Racism*, Paul Kivel (1996) provides a translation of people of color's requests to whites: respect us, listen to us, find out about us, stand by my issue, provide information, don't assume you know what's best for me, take risks, make mistakes. Such lists are useful, but they have been replicated to the point of becoming formulaic. Consequently, disclaimers have emerged, such as that found in the CrimethInc. Ex-Workers' Collective essay on "Undermining Oppression": "To gain an understanding of the workings of white supremacy, one need not attend endless workshops or become involved in an obscure subculture."

A more full-blown cri de coeur from the Colours of Resistance Archive gives voice to the emerging disquiet. In "Whose ally? Thinking Critically about Anti-Oppression Ally Organizing, Part 1," an anonymous author laments the 2003 global demonstrations against the US invasion of Iraq. According to the author, although white people have sometimes "become a part of these efforts in ways that resist white supremacy and substantively support the struggles of people of color," they run the risk of becoming "part of a growing culture of self-identified white, antiracist allies" who participate in a "highly specific modality of political practice" with "mostly white people" who "impose a new culture onto the work . . .

of what constituted anti-racist white allies." The author concludes: "Almost none of the groups I'd worked with had ever successfully worked on a cross-racial campaign without inviting major disasters and irreversible fuck-ups. Looking around, I saw many other white activists who had been raised through years of a very similar culture of talking about white privilege equally unable to make any concrete changes in their lives and work."

Indigenous Action Media (2014) put forward one of the most frontal assaults on "allies" to date when they referred to them as "non-profit capitalists." In their view, "the ally-industrial complex has been established by activists whose careers depend on the 'issues' they work to address. . . . Commodification and exploitation of allyship is a growing trend in activism today." In response, they suggest that people adopt the role of "accomplices, not allies," since "accomplice" denotes "a person who helps another commit a crime." In the ongoing struggle against settler colonialism, such a person would be among those "who has our backs, or more appropriately: who is with us, at our sides."

Without trashing the concept of "allies" altogether, Black Lives Matter recently accomplished another strategic shift from alliances based on single fixed identities to ones based on an intersectional approach. The movement grew out of social media and social movement responses to the murder of Trayvon Martin and the police killing of Michael Brown. Both events pointed to the lethal police and paramilitary violence in Black communities. Fifty years after SNCC, Black Lives Matter emerged to defend Black people from heinous state violence. The movement speaks to any and all who will hear. As movement cofounder Alicia Garza put it, "We call on black people and our allies to take up the call that . . . Black lives, which are seen as without value within White supremacy, are important to your liberation." At the same time, the movement's Black queer creators drew upon an intersectional approach by focusing on "those who have been marginalized within Black liberations movements" in order to affirm "the lives of Black queer and trans folks, disabled folks, Black-undocumented folks, folks with records, women and all Black lives along the gender spectrum"

(Garza 2014). "Black lives" are not a monolith; instead, and as a collective, they are constituted by other systems of oppression and resistance. As movement activists make clear, such an intersectional understanding has been expected of white allies as well.

These contests over the meaning of "ally" are at the core of radical efforts to define our relationships-in-action when we are moved into alliances by the desire for justice. No amount of flip charts or weekend workshops can teach courage and fortitude, the desire to earn trust, or the imagination to envision a different world (although those flip chart meetings can refine strategies and sharpen understandings of our active commitments). Instead, courage, fortitude, and trustworthiness are acquired when collective struggles forged in political crises stimulate the imagination, show possibilities in action, and provide occasions for us to hold our breath and leap.

SEE ALSO: Accountability; Community; Conspiracy; Oppression; Privilege; Queer; Solidarity

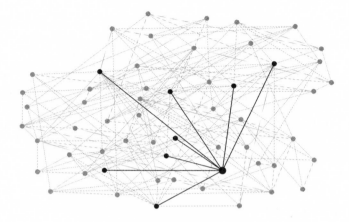

AUTHORITY

Maia Ramnath

ALMOST BY DEFINITION, RADICALS ARE IN CONFLICT with "authority" and "the authorities." Our instinct is not to obey but to question—and, if necessary, to refuse and rebel. Coming from an authority figure, "because I said so" carries no weight; in fact, it's an invitation to defiance. Nevertheless, the term itself is filled with ambiguity.

According to most dictionaries, "authority" is defined as the right or the power to judge, adjudicate, control, command, enforce, or direct the actions of others. By extension, it can be used to denote the person or group who holds that right or power, or the rank, office, or position that confers the right or power on the person or group. The word encompasses both the aura of rectitude bestowed upon certain actions and the agents responsible for that bestowal.

There are several things to notice about this definition. First, it says nothing about the *content* of the enforced norms but instead refers only to the enforcement capacity itself. Second, it seems to encapsulate each of the different modalities that Max Weber noted in his analysis of charismatic, traditional, and rational-legal or bureaucratic modes of rule. Weber (1978) used the concept of *"Herrschaft"* (which lacks a direct English translation but is often rendered as "authority," though the word *"Autorität"* also exists in German) to offer a typology of *legitimate* forms of power—power that must be recognized as justifiable by both ruler and ruled. In this view, "authority" requires consent and is closer to hegemony than to domination.

Finally, one notes a gaping crack at the very heart of the definition, since having "power" and having the "right" are two very different things. This is the crack that radicals wedge open when they challenge authority. It's also the source of the term's conceptual ambiguity. Without separating these two streams of meaning, coercion and legitimacy begin to appear co-constitutive. To regain the distinction, it's useful to return to the Latin *"auctoritas."*

In addition to its specific legal and political implications in Ancient Rome, this concept variously entailed a decree, order, or "suggestion" that could not be refused, legal title or ownership, the capacity to sanction or validate, and the transcendent quality that bestowed stature, prestige, and reputation—which in turn could manifest as influence or command. As bearer of *auctoritas*, the *auctor* was filled with (and could transmit) a powerful aura of gravitas, which then became the vector of authority. Depending on the context, the *auctor* was the one responsible for founding, originating, generating, proposing, initiating, guiding, sponsoring, advising, augmenting, enlarging, increasing, or cultivating.[1]

---

1. In *Lectures on the History of Political Thought*, Michael Oakeshott (2006) expands upon the technical and legal meanings of *"auctoritas"* as a category central to Roman theories of power and social organization. Fundamentally, both *"auctor"* and *"auctoritas"* are related to the verb *"augeo,"* meaning "to increase or augment."

Etymologically, "authority" developed through its passage from Classical to Medieval Latin and onward through the Latinate vernaculars. It advanced from Rome along with churches, kings, and emperors.[2] Derived from the Old French "*auctorité*" ("prestige, right, permission, dignity, gravity; the Scriptures"), the thirteenth-century French word "*autorité*" meant a "book or quotation that settles an argument." In this way, it bore the layered sense of its Latin root: a source of definitive knowledge or expertise, the power and legitimacy to use it, and the offices, institutions, or qualities that conveyed that legitimacy.

In English (where the word was spelled the Latin way—with a "c"—until the sixteenth century), the meaning "power to enforce obedience" dates from the late fourteenth century, and "people in authority" from the early seventeenth century. "Authoritative," meaning "possessing authority," followed in the mid-seventeenth century. In the early nineteenth century, "authorities" emerged, denoting "those in charge, those with police powers." These meanings remain current in common usage, where they usually refer to law enforcement but also include the civic functionaries of public health and safety, social services, environmental standards, and licensing (whether of dogs or drivers). If "the authorities" are those who maintain rules and norms, then whether they induce feelings of security or threat depends upon one's relationship to the system they represent.

To take one recent example, the Catalyst Project circulated an announcement concerning egregious police violence against African Americans that declared, "There is no going back. . . . People know there are no significant attempts at justice being made by the 'authorities'" (2015). The scare quotes could imply that this particular claim to authority is illegitimate, and that someone else might have a better claim. Alternately, they could imply that the very concept of authority is—by definition—oppressive. This is where the tradition of anti-authoritarianism comes in. If "authoritarianism" assumes

---

2. In Christian angelologies like the one produced in the thirteenth century by Thomas Aquinas, "Authorities" (or "Powers") were one of the ranks in a complex celestial hierarchy. It is worth noting that, in the various contemporary English translations of New Testament verses concerning the concept of authority, some use "authority" while others use "power."

that power and right coincide, "anti-authoritarianism" assumes that unleashing power means forfeiting right. The question becomes whether the problem is intrinsic to "authority" itself or if it lies in its abuse by particular claimants. This distinction underlies the spectrum running from more socialist or rationalist iterations of anti-authoritarianism to more individualist or romantic ones.

Anti-authoritarianism developed in tandem with the Enlightenment Era's libertarian tradition, broadly defined. In this political context, attitudes toward authority were inextricable from attitudes toward those who had held it in the ancient regime. The new political philosophies of the eighteenth century challenged traditional social formations by claiming that authority derived not from god and king but from empiricism and individual reason, which was to be institutionalized in secular democratic republics based on contractual agreement, civil rights, and equality before the law.

Genealogically, this philosophy branches into both classical liberalism and anarchism. Classic examples of the former include Voltaire's 1751 remark that "it is dangerous to be right in matters on which the established authorities are wrong" and Thomas Jefferson's 1816 injunction to "leave no authority existing not responsible to the people." Sharing this wariness, anarchists applied the critique of power not only to traditional authorities but also to emergent ones. The notion of an explicit anti-authoritarianism subsequently crystallized through debates between authoritarian and libertarian socialists in the First International. When that body eventually broke apart over the issue, members of the dissident Jura Federation wrote: "If there is one incontrovertible fact ... it is that authority has a corrupting effect on those in whose hands it is placed." "How can we expect an egalitarian and free society to emerge from an authoritarian organization? Impossible. The International, as the embryo of the human society of the future, is required in the here and now to faithfully mirror our principles of freedom and federation and shun any principle leaning towards authority and dictatorship" (quoted in Robert Graham 2005, 96, 98).

After the depredations of twentieth-century fascism, totalitarianism, and war, anti-authoritarianism enjoyed another surge in popularity and has remained a significant tendency within radical movements ever since.[3] Although some view "anti-authoritarianism" as interchangeable with anarchism, others believe it to have a wider scope and, as a result, observe anti-authoritarian tendencies in many feminist, pacifist, radical queer, anti-oppression, indigenous, and radical anticolonial movements that do not self-identify as anarchist.

Whereas anti-authoritarian movements favor participatory democracy, nonhierarchical decision-making, decentralized organization, egalitarian social relations, and horizontal grassroots initiatives, authoritarian regimes represent the opposite: top-down centralized power, harsh disciplinary and penal systems, coercive conformity, and fetishized virile dictatorship. Such "authority" is rigid, not flexible; homogenizing, not diversifying; craving stasis, not change. Around 1950, the term "authoritarian personality" appears in the work of critical theorists like Theodore Adorno and Erich Fromm, who were struggling to understand the social psychology of fascism.

In addition to these usages, "authority" also has more neutral connotations. "Moral authority" denotes strength of character, integrity, courage, and a commitment to justice. It adds force to the words and actions of those in whom we recognize it. However, classical formal logic and legal discourses use "argument from authority" to describe the logical fallacy underlying appeals to tradition rather than to reason. Mid-twentieth-century philosopher A. J. Ayer had this meaning in mind when he announced that "no moral system can rest solely on authority" (1968, 4). In the realm of knowledge, someone is "an authority" on a given topic when one is thought to know the most about it. In relation to this usage, no less an anti-authoritarian than Mikhail Bakunin (1871) wrote: "Does it follow that I reject all authority? Far from me such a thought. In the matter of boots, I refer to the authority of the bootmaker; concerning houses, canals, or railroads, I consult that of the architect or the engineer. . . . But I allow neither the bootmaker nor the

---

3. Chris Dixon's *Another Politics* (2014) traces the genealogy of a prominent "anti-authoritarian current" in North American social movements.

architect nor savant to impose his authority upon me. I listen to them freely and with all the respect merited by their intelligence, their character, their knowledge, reserving always my incontestable right of criticism." Bakunin concluded that "there is no fixed and constant authority, but a continual exchange of mutual, temporary, and, above all, voluntary authority and subordination." Nevertheless, contemporary anti-authoritarians often aim to foster self-sufficiency by reducing their dependence on those who would monopolize knowledge and skills.

Is there, within the existing etymology of "authority," some concept that could open a space not only between power and right, but between power and knowledge as well?

Besides "authority," the Latin *auctoritas* also gives us "author" (as both verb and noun). The "author" is the writer of a text; however, "to author" something is also to be responsible for its conception and form. The author of events influences their unfolding. Is there some connection between the controller of text and the controller of action? Since the linguistic turn in the social sciences and humanities, it has become commonplace to equate writing with doing, text with matter, and inscription with action. Meanwhile, outside of the academy, everyone from politicians and pundits to organizers and entrepreneurs speak of "controlling the narrative" and "crafting the message." Whether for political power, military victory, commercial success, or social change, battles today are fought as much on the level of language and perception as on the level of physical force. To be sure, text and action are not equivalent; nevertheless their relationship is crucial.

In societies predating mass literacy, written texts required specialized, trained interpreters to convey religious or legal decisions. The text's "authority" came in part from restricted access. Today literacy is commonplace (though far from universal), and the Internet (where still uncensored and unlocked) allows the sharing of information from an array of sources. Consequently, the relationship to texts and their authorship has been decentralized and democratized. While not all writings are equally valid, it is now up to all readers to critically evaluate and judge. What's "authorized" today may rest as much on what's verifiable and sourceable as on what's orthodox and official.

Some activists and intellectuals express skepticism about any authorial claim, whether from distrust of authority or as a result of the idea that writing itself constitutes an act of logocentric dominance over orality. By this logic, "author" equals "authority" equals "authoritarian." However, this conclusion is no more necessary than is the idea that the dispersal of authorship (and subsequently authority) lies in hive-mind crowdsourcing. If authorship is multiplied, then every author exists (at least theoretically) in conversation with interlocutors who may in turn author further installments in an expanding dialogue. And if we reject the sources of official authorization, then we must choose which ideas to empower—to realize—by virtue of our actions. Just as actors interpret, shape, and sometimes transform the possibilities inherent in a script, we endow ideas with retroactive authority by putting them consciously into practice.

SEE ALSO: Domination; Experience; Hegemony; History; Liberal; Oppression; Rights; Sovereignty

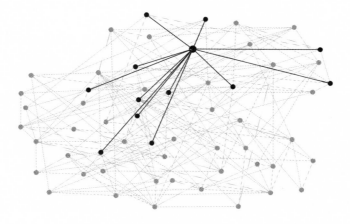

BODIES

Anna Agathangelou[1]

ACCORDING TO THE *OXFORD ENGLISH DICTIONARY*, A "body" is the "physical form of a person, animal, or plant" and also "the main portion; the trunk." The latter meaning stems from the Old English "*bodig*" and Old High German "*botah*," meaning the trunk or chest of a human or animal. "Body" was extended to mean "person" (e.g., "somebody") during the late thirteenth century after a series of famines, plagues, and wars generated fears about how to protect life. In German, for example, "life" is replaced by "lived body" ("leib"). "Body" has been contrasted with "soul" since the mid-thirteenth century, and since the

---

1.   I would like to acknowledge the considerable assistance I received from Kelly Fritsch and AK Thompson in crafting this entry.

late thirteenth century it has been associated with "corpse." Using "body" to refer to matter ("heavenly body") occurred in the late fourteenth century. By the sixteenth century, "body" also began referring to those emerging political forms that would become the nation-state ("body politic").

Given this history, it is not surprising that tensions exist between various meanings of "body," which is cast variously as a soulless phenomenon capable of "mechanistic explanation and manipulation" (Kirmayer 1988, 59), as the medium of self expression, language, feelings, and connection, as a fleshy corpse, and as a site of political struggle. These tensions make the body—in both word and matter—a pivotal site of radical engagement today. In radical movements and the social sciences, and especially in studies concerning race, gender and sexuality, class, and disability, references to "the body" and "bodies" have proliferated since the 1990s (Sanbonmatsu 2004; McNally 2001). Following from the nineteenth-century Romantic insights of Walt Whitman, who could not help but to "sing the body electric" (1855), these contributions have often worked to unsettle mind-body and soul-body dualisms. By Whitman's account, "was it doubted that those who corrupt their own bodies conceal themselves?"

> And if the body does not do fully as much as the soul?
> And if the body were not the soul, what is the soul? . . .
>
> The thin red jellies within you or within me, the bones
>   and the marrow in the bones,
> The exquisite realization of health;
> O I say these are not the parts and poems of the body
>   only, but of the soul,
> O I say now these are the soul!

Tackling the conceptual partition between body and soul from another angle a century later, Malcolm X highlighted the philological connection between "Negro" and the Greek words "*necro*" (death) and "*nekros*" (corpse). In this way, he helped to underscore how white supremacy entangled Black bodies—and following W.E.B. DuBois, the very "souls of Black folk" (1903a)—with death. Between the publication of Du Bois' groundbreaking work and Malcolm X's pivotal "Ballot or the Bullet" speech of 1964, this entanglement found vivid expression in Abel Meeropol's "Strange Fruit" (1939). A protest against lynching, the song conjures "black bodies swinging in the southern breeze" while conjoining the smell of magnolias to that of burning flesh. In a 1969 interview, Nina Simone (who had recorded a famous rendition) recounted that "Strange Fruit" was probably the ugliest song she had ever heard: "It is violent and tears at the guts of what white people have done to my people in this country. I mean it really really opens the wound completely raw when you think of the man hanging from a tree and to call him strange fruit" (Combe 2012).

Around the time that Simone was revisiting the rawness of the wounds endured by Black folks reduced to "bodies," Black Panther Party cofounder Huey Newton began to confront the contest surrounding the Black body as well. For Newton, however, the body was not solely a target for racist violence. It was also a "number of persons regarded as a group" (i.e., the body politic). Pressing against the limits of the mind-body dualism, he outlined his program as follows: "We give white people the privilege of having a mind and we want them to get a body." Concretely, this meant: "arm yourselves and support the colonies around the world in their struggle against imperialism" (1968, 8).

Such a struggle was necessary since, according to Frantz Fanon, "there are times when the black man is locked into his body" and subjected to a "crushing objecthood" as a result of colonialism (1967, 110). Influential for Newton and the Black Panthers, Fanon's account of the colonial encounter stood at odds with theories of democracy presaged by the 1679 Habeas Corpus Act, which associated the body with political representation. According to Giorgio Agamben, the modern democratic states that emerged in the wake of this legislation could distinguish themselves from ancient and medieval regimes because, at their inception, it was "not the free man and his statutes and prerogatives . . . but rather *corpus* that [was] the new subject of politics" (1998, 124). Still (and along with other contradictions arising from the modern democratic framework), the histories of racism, slavery, and colonial rule ensured that some bodies were not the *subject* of politics but rather its dead matter.

But even as embodiment became the foundation for legal and political representation for Europeans, the new situation did not apply to all. Indeed, workers were still often viewed as the objects and not the subjects of politics. According to the 1714 British Vagrancy Act, "All Persons able in Body, who run away, and leave their wives or Children to the Parish, and not having wherewith otherwise to maintain themselves . . . and refuse to work for the usual and common Wages . . . shall be deemed Rogues and Vagabonds." For Marx, the vagrant body amounted to a "specter outside its domain" (1964, 121) since capitalism acknowledged the body only inasmuch as it labored and reproduced. Today, this struggle continues through slogans such as "the body must be ours. It is not the state's or the market's" (Agathangelou forthcoming).

The fight for bodily self-possession builds on feminist movements that have also oriented toward the body as a site of protest, highlighting how control of women's bodies through domination has been a central dynamic of modern societies (Federici 2004). "In our culture," said Andrea Dworkin, "not one part of a woman's body is left untouched, unaltered. No feature or extremity is spared the art, or pain, of improvement." According to Dworkin, this constant requirement was not cosmetic but disciplinary; ultimately, it prescribed "the relationship that an individual will have to . . . her motility, spontaneity, posture, gait, the uses to which she can put her body" (1974, 113–14). Around the same time, Audre Lorde began to describe the Black body as an anachronism. With this insight, she challenged the feminist movement to take account of the particular experience of feminized Black embodiment. "We have been sad long enough to make this earth either weep or grow fertile," she stated. "I am an anachronism, a sport like the bee that was never meant to fly. Science said so. I am not supposed to exist. I carry death in my body like a condemnation. But I do live. The bee flies. There must be some way to integrate death into living, neither ignoring it nor giving in to it" (1980, 13).

According to Cherríe Moraga, feminists like Audre Lorde and June Jordan helped to give lesbians "a body, a queer body in the original dangerous, unambivalent sense of the word" (quoted in Gumbs 2010, 14). Similarly, 1970s health movement activists brought abortion "out of the closet where it had been hidden in secrecy and shame" (Sullivan 2006, 158). With slogans like "my body, my choice," feminist movements made bodily autonomy and sovereignty the very site of politics. In 1973, the Boston Women's Health Collective published the first edition of *Our Bodies, Ourselves*, a book whose title effectively erased the formal conceptual distinction between embodiment and subjectivity. By 1989, however, the degree to which women's bodily sovereignty was under attack became clear when feminist artist Barbara Kruger designed her famous "Your Body Is a Battleground" image to support the March on Washington in defense of reproductive choice. Since then, ecological justice movements have stretched the feminist "my body, my choice" paradigm to protest the broader social conditions that force women to confront "the results of toxic dumping on their own bodies (sites of reproduction of the species), in their homes (sites of reproduction of daily life), and in their communities and schools (sites of social reproduction)" (Merchant 1995, 161; Shirley Thompson 2003).

Toward the end of the 1980s, activists in ACT UP challenged the widely held belief promoted by arch-conservatives like Senator Jesse Helms (R-NC) that being HIV-positive meant being a contagion in need of quarantine within the national body politic. For Helms, quarantine was justified to prevent AIDS-infected inmates from taking "revenge on society" upon release from prison (United Press International 1987). ACT UP members responded in a variety of creative ways, including updating their iconic "Silence = Death" poster to read "Helms = Death." Jon Greenberg, an ACT UP activist who died of AIDS, used to say to his friends, "I don't want an angry political funeral. I just want you to burn me in the street and eat my flesh." At a 1988 demonstration against the Food and Drug

Administration, AIDS activist and artist David Wojnarowicz wore a black leather jacket emblazoned with the words "If I Die Forget Burial Just Drop My Body on the Steps of the F.D.A." The Marys, another AIDS activist group during this period staged open-casket funerals to politicize AIDS deaths as well as the dead body itself (Debra Levine 2009). Under the slogan "LEAVE YOUR BODY TO POLITICS," they placed an advertisement in the August 1992 *PWA Coalition Newsline* that recounted how, "throughout the AIDS crisis, furious activists with advanced HIV disease have been saying they want their deaths to help further the fight against this country's neglect and incompetence in the face of AIDS" (Debra Levine 2012).

Whether motivated by xenophobia or purported altruism, public health movements have tended to emphasize "well-being" over individual liberties; however, the conceptual distinction between these two concerns is not always clear. In response to the question "Why is cancer a feminist issue?," biologist, activist, and cancer survivor Sandra Steingraber highlights how "the parts of women's bodies that have been affected—our ovaries, our uterus, our breasts—are the parts of the body that have been despised, objectified, fetishized" (quoted in Tarter 2002, 200). More recently, health and reproductive rights activists grappling with the medical industrial complex have drawn inspiration from theorists like Latour, for whom "the body is . . . a dynamic trajectory by which we learn to register and become sensitive to what the world is made of" (2004, 205–6). Rather than "theorizing the body directly," Latour has instead advocated what he calls "body talk." He asks, "Under what conditions can we mobilize the body in our speech [without reiterating] the usual discussions about dualism and holism?"

Similarly, feminist materialists have begun to push understandings of embodiment beyond discursive construction (Barad 2007) to explore the means by which bodies both resist and conform to normative gendered and sexual scripts. According to Anne Fausto-Sterling, "labeling someone a man or a woman is a social decision. We may use scientific knowledge to help us make the decision, but only our beliefs about gender—not science—can define our sex. Furthermore, our beliefs about gender affect what kinds of knowledge scientists produce about sex in the first place" (2000, 3). Proclaiming that "genitalia isn't destiny," actress and activist Laverne Cox has similarly underscored how "lots of lived experience defies that trapped-in-the-wrong-body narrative" (2014).

On December 14, 2012, Canada voted Bill C-45 into law, thus amending the Fisheries Act, the Canadian Environmental Protection Act, and the Navigable Waters Protection Act. In this way, they removed thousands of lakes and streams from federal protection and made it easier for economic development projects—including tar sands mining and oil pipelines—to be approved. In response, Idle No More leader Chief Spence challenged Bill C-45 with a hunger strike. Under the slogan "Bodies of Water, Not Bodies of Women," Chief Spence aimed to redirect media attention, which "began to conflate the Idle No More movement with Indigenous women's bodies, focusing on objectification, discrimination, and violence" while neglecting to consider the struggle around water that initially prompted the mobilization (Rutherdale, Dolmage, and Podruchny 2014). Nevertheless, as Anishinaabe grandmother and "water walker" Josephine Mandamin reminds us, "We are all water. We are born of water. We are all water people. We are all water carriers. We carry water within us. . . . We have a duty to care for the water" (King 2014). Such observations force us to reconsider Chief Spence's distinction between water and women's bodies. From the struggle to secure autonomous integrity to the challenge of recognizing fluid co-implication, the "body" remains a battleground.

SEE ALSO: Accessible; Agency; Care; Crip; Experience; Gender; Labor; Nation; Oppression; Politics; Race; Trans*/-

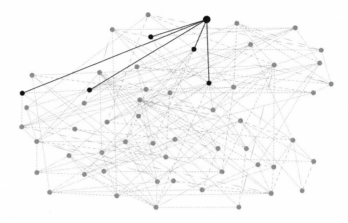

CARE

Christine Kelly

THE ORIGINS OF "CARE" ARE AS CONTESTED AS THE contemporary policies and practices that surround it. Michael Fine (2007) has argued that efforts to link the concept to the Ancient Greek "*charis*" (grace or favor) or to the Latin "*caritas*" (charity) reflect later interpretations by the Roman Church. The *Oxford English Dictionary* defines "care" as "mental suffering, sorrow, grief, trouble" and traces its etymological roots to the Old English "*caru*" or "*cearu*." Notably, both the affective intonations of love and the embodied sense of physical help evolved out of the word's roots in sorrow and grief. According to Fine (2007, 28), "Conflicting sets of meanings—care as a 'worry', 'concern' or 'responsibility' and care as 'love' and 'charity' seem to adhere to the word 'care' in the English language today." This troubled double sense finds expression in modern activist usage. For many disability and feminist activists, current iterations of "care" are burdened with historic injustices, which have contributed to systematic exclusion. Consequently, it seems that "care" must today be conceptualized as a tension between competing definitions—including those with oppressive potentials and histories—in order to be fully understood.

Many basic human dignities have been denied through the mobilization of "care" as either "taking care of" or "caring for" disabled people. As Willig Levy notes in *A People's History of the Independent Living Movement* (1988), disabled people "are neither patients to be cured, children to be taken care of, nor brave souls to be admired." In many disability activist contexts, "care" is understood as a form of oppression that controls, segregates, and dehumanizes disabled people through practices like sterilization. However, at the same time physical support can be a necessity for participation in an able-bodied world. As a result, much of the disability rights movement in the global North formed around a critique of "caring" approaches, instead emphasizing the rights of disabled people to live in the community with home-based support as opposed to segregated settings controlled by health professionals. As Ed Roberts, a disability activist in Berkley, California, remarked, "[It was only when the nurses left that] I realized that I could have a life, despite what everyone was saying. I could make choices, and that is freedom" (2015).

To acknowledge this history, some disability activists continue to avoid the term "care" and instead use terms like "personal assistance," "attendant services," and "support." For example, the Centre for Independent Living in Toronto (2015) specifies that "Attendant Services do NOT include . . . 'care' or taking responsibility for the person with a disability." Similarly, the American grassroots nonviolent direct action group ADAPT stages dramatic protests outside of nursing homes, demanding "Free our people!" The group's national actions also push for individual choice concerning living arrangements and challenge aspects of US Medicaid policy, which gives preferences to institutions and nursing homes. Meanwhile, radical disability activists have challenged the move from "care" to "choice" and "independence," alleging that the latter concepts bolster neoliberal policies and rationales. As disability justice artist and activist Patty Berne has observed, "even the idea of independent living is a little difficult. I mean, I support it, obviously. It's incredibly important. But it's a capitalist framework; there's nothing about collective interdependency" (Berne, quoted in Lamm, 2015).

The ADAPT slogan "Free our people" is tied to ongoing deinstitutionalization efforts, which also highlight how "care" can become a form of oppression. In 2013, survivors who lived in large-scale residential regional centers in Ontario, Canada, between 1945 and 2009 reached a $35 million settlement in acknowledgment of the abuses that took place in these institutions. The settlement included a public apology from the Ontario premier, who acknowledged that residents "were failed by a model of institutional care" (Wynne 2013). In the United Kingdom, the "Justice for LB" group was established in 2014 to contest the death of Connor Sparrowhawk ("LB"), an eighteen-year-old man with autism and epilepsy who drowned in July 2013 while under the care of an assessment unit in a public hospital. The campaign resulted in a number of social media actions and a shadow report outlining new forms of support.

As with many demands arising from radical disability perspectives, the left has not uniformly endorsed closing large-scale care institutions. For example, labor movements have occasionally opposed efforts to close institutions and establish independent living–style attendant services (Cranford 2005; Parker et al. 2000). For some labor activists, the closure of institutions signals the loss of unionized jobs and makes work more precarious for women and people of color. The Alberta Union of Provincial Employees applauded the provincial government for reversing its decision to close the Michener Centre in 2014 despite the well-documented abuse that took place there (Malacrida 2015).

In some discussions, disability activists have invoked "care" to refer to the daily help a person might require. On February 6,

2015, the Supreme Court of Canada moved to reverse its decision on physician-assisted suicide, thereby making it legal. Leading up to the case, the Council of Canadians with Disabilities (2015) argued that "for those who receive care . . . the risk is palpable. Dependence upon others will come to be seen as a suffering too great to bear." Although critiques of care arise most frequently around attendant services and deinstitutionalization, in contexts like physician-assisted suicide, questions of service provision and quality become secondary since activists feel that reliance on others will be interpreted as evidence of a meaningless life. In these literal life-or-death debates, complexities around the notion of "care" are temporarily displaced to emphasize survival.

Social justice activist Mia Mingus has challenged the disability rights approach to "choice" and "independence" by endorsing "interdependency." By her account, "interdependency is not just me 'dependent on you.' It is not you, the benevolent oppressor, deciding to 'help' me. It is not just me who should be grateful for whatever I can get" (2010b). Disability justice activists' use of "interdependence" is grounded in the experiences of those who need support as well as in an awareness of the structural conditions that shape gendered, racialized, and globalized care work.

Critiques of gendered and racialized care work are rooted in feminist organizing and scholarship that emphasizes the physical and reproductive labor involved in caring for children, partners, and older people, and highlights how women (particularly women of color) are often coerced into caring servitude (Glenn 2010). Women continue to carry out the majority of formal and informal care work globally, often affecting our ability to participate in political activities. While women's care work is essential for maintaining and reproducing capitalism, this work is often made invisible by the public-private distinction (Kittay 1999). Feminist approaches to care have sought to make this reproductive work visible; however, they run the risk of objectifying people with disabilities and casting them as "burdens" rather than as active members of feminist communities. As a result, this perspective has led to ongoing tensions, especially in the form of scholarly and policy debates. For example, some UK feminists in the 1980s infamously opposed the shift to community care policies, arguing that this framework relies on women's informal and unpaid labor (Thomas 2007).

Outside the academy, feminist organizing has achieved piecemeal success around issues like child care, working conditions for formal care workers, and hierarchical transnational care chains. Although promoting affordable day care has been a feminist issue since the second wave, little headway has been made in Canada, the United States, or the United Kingdom. In March 2013, two hundred protesters gathered at the premier's office in Vancouver, Canada, to call for a "$10-a-day plan" for affordable day care. The demand was denied. Earlier, the US-based National Organization for Women had advanced radical demands for "free 24-hour child care for all," and feminists lobbied for the 1971 Child Development Act (CDA), "which would have established federally funded community centers with a sliding fee scale based on income" (Berlatsky 2013). President Nixon vetoed the Act. Considering why feminists in Britain did not mobilize around day care as extensively as they did elsewhere, Randall (1996) has suggested that the second-wave feminist movement's ambivalence toward motherhood contributed to its lack of political headway.

Areas in which feminists have had greater success, including birth control, choice in labor and delivery, and other pro-choice measures, have also worked to expand conventional understandings of health care to encompass reproductive justice. However, unlike in disability organizing, the concept of care is here used in neutral or even positive ways. For example, Gaye Demanuele (2013), an Australian reproductive rights activist, birth-worker, and member of Radical Women, implores: "Who could care more about her baby than the woman herself?" Academic investigations that frame "care" as coercive and limiting are not always intelligible within the context of feminist-informed services.

Interestingly, the idea of "self-care" has become a point at which disability-informed perspectives on embodiment come into tension with disability perspectives concerning the coercive aspects of care.

In radical scenes, the concept of "self-care" has been invoked with the aim of preventing activist burnout. Audre Lorde (1988, 131), for example, notes: "Caring for myself is not self-indulgence, it is self-preservation, and that is an act of political warfare." Self-care confronts the reality that organizing against large systems of oppression can be physically and emotionally draining (a problem more severe for activists who are survivors of abuse, harassment, and online trolling). From 2010 onward, there has been a notable proliferation of resources devoted to self-care on activist blogs and within nonprofit organizations. The Self-Care Project (2015) advances slogans like "Because there's much to do and never enough time" and "Because we want a movement that builds us up, instead of burning us out."

Meanwhile, in "An End to Self-Care," National Day Laborer Organizing Network activist B. Loewe (2012) critiqued the individualizing undertones of self-care while arguing that those who most benefit from it are "middle-class people with leisure time." In contrast, Loewe promotes "community care" while pointing out that "movement work *is* healing work." Objecting to this characterization, Hande suggests that Loewe's account reflects the reluctance of able-bodied activists to engage with disability politics (Hande and Kelly 2015). Similarly, activist Dori Midnight (2012) has noted that what is required is not the end of self-care but rather an end to "the privatization of healing, the illusion that our struggles are also private and separate, the marginalization of disabled and chronically ill people and people who struggle with mental illness, disassociation from our bodies, and the pervasive disconnection from *all* of our indigenous healing traditions and ancestral wisdom."

For their part, the CrimethInc. Ex-Workers' Collective (2013a) has also questioned whether "self" and "care" should be "universally acknowledged values in this society," highlighting the ways that self-care individualizes embodied experiences of pain and fatigue, creates simple dichotomies between health and illness, and discounts the radically transformative history of some self-destructive behaviors. This position seems to confirm Van Meter's observation

(2012) that care is continually seen as irrelevant to activist movements. Today activists are beginning to question the notion of self-care and make linkages to broader questions of care related to disability, gender, and labor.

The tensions currently playing out on the terrain of "self-care" suggest that social movements have become better at incorporating a broad range of issues beyond parceled identity politics. This trend is perhaps best reflected in the work of disability justice organizers who have ongoing relationships with pain and suffering, embodiment, and the shifting dynamics of identity, while connecting to broader social justice issues. Disability justice activist Mingus's public speaking engagements begin not only with an acknowledgment of the organizing work required for such events to take place, but of all the local and global work that maintains the physical building, the legacies of colonization and genocide that shape our realities, and the activist work that came before as well. In such moments, the responsibilities, burdens, love, and charity of "care" collide, challenging us to see both the potential and the limitations of "caring" approaches to social justice.

SEE ALSO: Bodies; Community; Labor; Love; Sustainable

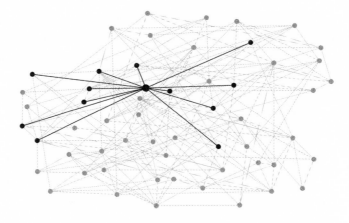

CLASS

Johanna Brenner

REFERRING TO A *SOCIAL* DIVISION, "CLASS" FIRST APPEARED in English in the early eighteenth century; however, until the early nineteenth century, it competed with other notions of social stratification such as "rank" and "order." According to Raymond Williams (1976), "middle classes" and "working classes" had become common terms by the 1840s, although—as today—they had confusing referents. "Middle" implied insertion between higher and lower, whereas, at its origin, "working classes" referred to those engaged in productive or useful activity. By the late nineteenth century, however, "working-class" had come to refer more clearly to the economic relationship between wage earners and their capitalist employers.

When Occupy activists defined themselves as the 99 percent, they evoked a populist language in which "the people" are arrayed against "the trusts." Yet, rather than reflecting the largely agrarian movement that fueled nineteenth-century American populism, the movement's efforts to recast the ruling class as "the 1 percent" reflected an almost complete exclusion of Marxist notions of class. Indeed, the idea of a "ruling class"—or of capitalist class relations constituting a revolutionary subject (e.g., the proletariat with a common interest in overthrowing capitalism)—seems completely foreign to contemporary political discourses. It is therefore not surprising that Occupy found a different concept to convey the idea of common interest against the ruling few.

Although the concept of class has not dropped from use, its contemporary meaning has become restricted to describing social stratification. Even in this sense, in which "class" denotes a hierarchy of "differences" (e.g., of income, education, culture), there is no agreed-upon meaning of class categories. In dominant usages, the class system comprises a "middle class" defined by its difference from the poor or lower class on the one hand and the rich or upper class on the other. When surveyed about their place in the class system, most Americans choose to place themselves somewhere in the middle class, though the proportion naming themselves "lower middle class" is growing due to ongoing assaults on working people's lives (Morin and Motel 2012). This "middle class" has long dominated the rhetoric of the labor movement. A 2015 AFL-CIO report on "10 Ways to Rebuild the Middle Class for Hard Working Americans," for instance, argues that "the middle class . . . exists because people worked hard to win at the legislative level and in the workplace." Mainstream political discourse is similar; through 2015 Obama used the term "middle class" twenty-eight times in his State of the Union addresses and the term "working class" only once (Cherlin 2015).

Another spin on "class" emerged in the 1970s from social movement and academic invocations of "classism." In 1976, Dykes for an American Revolution declared their "full power to levy war against sexism, racism, classism, and all other oppressions." The decline of radical movements led "class"—originally linked to critiques of imperialism and capitalism—to be understood as a social category homologous to race, gender, sexuality, disability, and other forms of identity shaped by power and privilege. Class Action, a Massachusetts nonprofit founded in 2004 and dedicated to "building bridges across the class divide," defines "class" as "relative social rank in terms of income, wealth, education, status and/or power" and hosts popular education workshops to "create safe spaces for people across the class spectrum to explore class and begin to dismantle classism" (2015). The dividing line of class privilege is typically drawn between the poor and working class on the one hand, and the middle and owning class on the other. No matter how boundaries are drawn, however, the concept of "classism" aligns class with other dimensions of power and privilege that have been the focus of many contemporary social movements.

"Classism" would be unthinkable without the recognition that white supremacy, patriarchy, and heteronormativity are foundational aspects of US society. In a 1977 statement, the Combahee River Collective asserted: "We are actively committed to struggling against racial, sexual, heterosexual, and class oppression, and see as our particular task the development of integrated analysis and practice based upon the fact that the major systems of oppression are interlocking." Feminists subsequently incorporated these challenges through the concept of "intersectionality," which gained prominence in the 1980s and is commonly attributed to Black legal scholar Kimberlé Crenshaw. Most intersectional analysis focuses on social, cultural, economic, and political relations of relative power and privilege. Consequently, the meaning of "class" is restricted to defining a place within capitalist social relations rather than describing—as it did for Marx—the foundational premise of the social whole.

Yet, even with Marx, the term had a double meaning. On the one hand, "class" refers to the social relations of production through which an owning class appropriates the social surplus. Not all societies are class societies, however, and Marx envisioned communism as a classless society. In his view, class relations did more than create social categories (classes), they also transformed every feature of society. Indeed, "in all forms of society there is one specific kind of production which predominates over the rest, whose relations thus assign rank and influence to the others. It is a general illumination which bathes all the other colours and modifies their particularity. It is a particular ether which determines the specific gravity of every being which has materialized within it" (1857, 106–7).

Under capitalism, labor is carried out by a class of wage laborers who are "free" to enter into contracts with employers and "free" from ownership of the means of production. Since they cannot produce for themselves, they are compelled to sell their labor power to survive. This "freedom" distinguishes the proletariat from the capitalist class. In this sense, "class" denotes a group of individuals sharing a similar position within the social relations of production. However, Marx additionally argued that the proletariat was not simply a social category but a historical subject, that it was the agent of revolutionary transformation. In the *Communist Manifesto* (1976b), he argued that—by creating the proletariat—"what the bourgeoisie . . . produces, above all, are its own grave-diggers."

Another important dimension of class is therefore the shared experience of a common situation. As E.P. Thompson (1963) recounts:

> class happens when some men, as a result of common experiences (inherited or shared), feel and articulate the identity of their interests as between themselves, and as against other men whose interests are different from (and usually opposed to) theirs. The class experience is largely determined by the productive relations into which men are born—or enter involuntarily. Class-consciousness is the way in which these experiences are handled in cultural terms: embodied in traditions, value-systems, ideas, and institutional forms. . . . Consciousness of class arises in the same way in different times and places, but never in just the same way. (9)

With respect to the distinction between "class in itself" and "class for itself," Marx understood that there was nothing automatic about class-consciousness. Indeed, "separate individuals form a class only insofar as they . . . carry on a common battle against another class," he wrote. "Otherwise they are on hostile terms with each other as competitors" (Marx and Engels 1978, 82).

During the twentieth century, the conditions of work and life for the working class became less homogeneous due to factors like de-skilling, the destruction of old industries and the rise of new occupations, and the expansion of the managerial strata. If, in the nineteenth century, it was possible to speak of "class consciousness" as an expression of workers recognizing their common interests, the rise of white-collar workers (administrators, managers, and new salaried professionals) in the early twentieth century already complicated the picture. Not only did the proletariat become more diverse, it also became riven by serious divisions in working conditions, life chances, experiences, and culture. In response to these changes, the idea of a "new middle class" emerged ("new" because it included employees in contrast to the older middle class, which was composed of small business owners). Increasingly, "the working class" became defined by manual work. As a result, social democratic theorists and politicians began to argue that, rather than overcoming divisions within the proletariat, socialist politics demanded a cross-class alliance between the middle and working classes (Speier 1939).

By mid-century, Marxist ideas about class had been further marginalized by the Cold War and the Fordist regime of accumulation, which offered economic security and expanded consumption to male blue- and white-collar workers. In a society where so many could access previously unavailable lifestyles through consumer power, "proletariat" and "working class" became anachronistic terms. Published in 1962, Michael Harrington's *The Other America* shocked readers because it described conditions that many thought had been left behind. Harrington focused on the 25 percent of Americans mired in isolated rural communities and slums—the "poor" whose lives were culturally, socially, and economically distinct from those of the affluent society around them.

Rank-and-file rebellions during the 1960s and early 1970s opened new terrain for thinking about class (Brick and Phelps 2015). But while radicals during this period argued about how to draw the boundary between the middle and working classes, few expressed concern with differences in social status, income levels, nature of payment (salary versus wage), and cultural distinction—all of which were then at the center of mainstream social science debates about class (Meiksins 1986). Instead, New Left theorists focused on corporate capitalism's power relations and on the role of professionals and managers in surplus value extraction. In this context, Barbara and John Ehrenreich developed the concept of the "professional/managerial class" (PMC), a class "between labor and capital" defined by its functions in controlling labor within the production process and exercising social control over the working class in society as a whole. Critics of the idea that professionals and managers constituted a distinct class argued that the Ehrenreichs had reified a temporary situation. And, as the Ehrenreichs (2013) have acknowledged, de-skilling, offshoring, defunding, and other developments are rapidly changing this group's levels of autonomy and security.

For their part, contemporary Marxists tend not to view the middle class and the owning class as equal bearers of "class privilege." Based on the degrees of power and authority they exercise at work, Zweig argues, professionals are in the working class or the middle class (2012, 23). Similarly, labor relations scholar Bob Carter (2014) attributes the contradictory class position of managers to their functions in the production process. Professionals and managers find themselves between a working class defined by its lack of control over working conditions and a capitalist class that directs production and investment decisions. And since workplace power relations change over time, so too can an occupation's class position. For example, public school teachers now share conditions that are more similar to those of skilled manual or service workers than to those of research scientists or tenured university professors.

Concurrently, upper managers have become owners through stock holdings while some professionals (e.g., corporate lawyers and accountants) enjoy close relationships with the capitalist class (Zweig 2012).

Almost from the moment that Occupy proclaimed itself to be "the 99 percent," the idea of a common condition was vigorously contested. While acknowledging that "we" have a common enemy, women and activists of color protested that such a "we" can't simply be proclaimed. As a result, the #OWS POC Working Group (2011) organized to "unite the diverse voices of all communities . . . and to demand that a movement to end economic injustice must have at its core an honest struggle to end racism." Similarly, the authors of a feminist flyer asked: "What do Equal Pay, Reproductive Rights and Sexual Assault Have to do with the Occupy Movement?" In response, they answered: "EVERYTHING! We cannot successfully Occupy Wall St unless we also OCCUPY PATRIARCHY" (Occupy Patriarchy 2011). These statements reflect the theoretical and political gains won through four decades of struggle. However, the strategy they reflect risks being enveloped in a liberal discourse that focuses on individual transformation (e.g., "recognizing one's privilege") while advancing moral imperatives (e.g., achieving more equal relations among people). Meanwhile, the connection between capitalism's particular class features and the reproduction of oppressive relations is at risk of being lost.

Developing an alternative to liberal identity politics is a burning issue for the radical left. This requires reintroducing a conception of class as "class relations of production" to encourage people to discover their common interest in overturning capitalism. Starting from the dynamics of the capitalist system, this strategy fosters demands that directly address existing divisions within the proletariat. Today's new social justice unionism represents one important expression of these politics (Peterson 2014/2015). When Chicago school teachers join Latino mothers and children in civil disobedience to stop a school closing, when they demand an end to "stop and frisk" policing of students, and when they fight for a contract that demands $15 an hour for all school employees, they fuse identity struggles with class politics.

SEE ALSO: Commons; Experience; Gender; Ideology; Labor; Liberal; Materialism; Oppression; Populism; Privilege; Reproduction; Violence

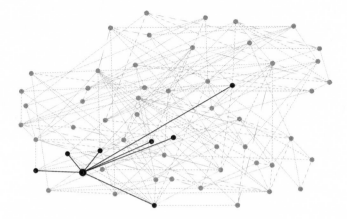

COLONIALISM

Lorenzo Veracini

THE TERM "COLONIALISM" DERIVES FROM THE LATIN *"colere"* ("to cultivate"). A *"colonus"* was a tenant farmer inhabiting a settlement removed from the motherland (a *"colonia"*). Today "colonialism" designates one of the unequal relations. After the inception of colonial studies during the "age of decolonization" in the 1950s and 1960s (Memmi 2003; Fanon 1967), the study of colonialism fragmented into a variety of discourses, approaches, and terminologies. "Neocolonialism" emerged almost immediately to denounce relations that ostensibly acknowledged the equality of former colonizer and colonized but did not actually affect structuring inequalities (Nkrumah 1965; Sartre 2001). "Internal colonialism" emerged in the

1970s to focus on the resilience of colonial relationships *within* a specific polity (Casanova 1965; Hechter 1975). This designation was eventually applied to a remarkable variety of polities and realities, including Apartheid South Africa, Appalachia, the position of African Americans, and the Celtic "fringe." "Postcolonialism" (or "post-colonialism") emerged in the 1980s to emphasize the ways that colonial regimes continue to inform relations after the end of formal colonial subjection.

All of these approaches foreground what historian Partha Chatterjee has defined as "the colonial rule of difference" (1993, 19, 33). A relative latecomer, "settler colonialism" consolidated in the 1990s and 2000s to designate the "settler societies" and the relations they still entertained with colonized indigenous minorities. Settler Colonial Studies emphasized circumstances primarily characterized by a determination to erase colonized subjectivities rather than reproduce their subordination (Veracini 2010). Unlike the other colonial formations, "settler colonialism" supersedes rather than reproduces the colonial rule of difference; settlers win by discontinuing unequal relationships rather than maintaining them. Patrick Wolfe's seminal theorization was often referred to during the consolidation of this new scholarly field. "What if the colonizers are not dependent on native labour," he asked. Indeed, "what if the natives themselves have been reduced to a small minority whose survival can hardly be seen to furnish the colonizing society with more than remission from ideological embarrassment? . . . In contrast to the kind of colonial formation that Cabral or Fanon confronted [i.e., 'franchise' or 'dependent'], settler colonies were not primarily established to extract surplus value from indigenous labour" (1999, 1).

Like scholars of "internal colonialism," scholars contributing to Settler Colonial Studies have emphasized the *continuing* operation of an unchanged set of unequal relations. The former, however, assumed the state as given and already formed, whereas the latter have focused on locales that would once have been referred to as "frontiers"—sites where, by definition, the state is absent and in the process of being formed. Settler colonialism as a mode of domination, it was often noted, has typically resisted formal decolonization.

Today, "colonialism" is often referred to outside of academia. In Europe, for example, *Les indigènes de la République* (a French political movement inspired by a political manifesto denouncing the ongoing "indigenisation" of significant segments of the population) recently mobilized against the infiltration of typically colonial forms of rule.[1] However, the term is adaptable and can be used in a variety of contexts. European right-wing movements opposing immigration, for instance, recurrently refer to the "risks" associated with "reverse colonisation" (Sasha Williams and Law 2012). More recently, draconian austerity measures imposed by international creditors on the Greek government have prompted one Greek MP to refer to "neo-colonial servitude" (Evans-Pritchard 2015).[2]

Outside of Europe, widespread "land grabbing" in Africa and elsewhere is often interpreted as a "new" colonialism (Liberti 2011). The Zapatistas (whose 1994 insurgency coincided with the five hundredth anniversary of the colonial encounter) have revived the term's common use throughout Latin America, where colonialism has long been a significant structure of reference (Galeano 1997). Indeed, attempts to undo ongoing colonial orders in the context of variously defined Indigenous "resurgencies" even prompted the pope to decry economic austerity as "colonialism" during a trip to Bolivia (Arvinth 2015).

"Settler colonialism" is also often invoked in the diverse struggles of Indigenous peoples and their allies in contemporary settler societies like Australia, Canada, Israel, Aotearoa/New Zealand, and the United States. Indigenous activists in these contexts have been particularly wary of "postcolonial" approaches, since ongoing uninterrupted domination does not fit with that paradigm's implicit temporalities. Australian Aboriginal militant and poet Bobby Sykes' ironic quip epitomizes this approach: "What?

1.   On the 2006 Paris riots and the *banlieus* as sites of colonial warehousing where noncitizen inhabitants are managed like "colonised natives" located beyond the borders of an exclusionary democracy, see Castel 2007.
2.   This is a recurrent reference in analyses of Greece's current predicament vis-à-vis international creditors (see, e.g., Terki-Mignot 2015).

Postcolonialism? Have They Left?" (quoted in Linda Tuhiwai Smith 1999, 24).

As specific modes of domination, colonialism and settler colonialism are not new. In the ancient world, the alternatives of creating dependent polities out of existing populations or displacing existing populations with settlers were already apparent. Phoenicians, Greeks, and Romans all practiced both modes of domination at different times, in different locales, and in relation to the vast diversity of peoples they encountered during their respective expansions (Graham 2016).

Europe's colonial expansion only began in earnest during the fifteenth century. While its meteoric rise to global hegemony enabled a number of western European polities to accumulate vast colonial dependencies and to contend with each other for domination over international trade networks, the term initially indicated a variety of practices. Gerrard Winstanley and the Diggers, for example, used "colony" to refer to their settlements (Bradstock 2013). Their usage, however, was probably more due to the original Latin meaning of the term (i.e., to "cultivate") than an indication that the Diggers were thinking of the "colonies" that were being planted in Ireland and America at the time. After all, they always involved local people in their efforts and were determined not to displace—clearly an anticolonial stance. Indeed, Winstanley was probably keen on *returning* to an original uncorrupted order (in this case, an original uncorrupted meaning).

Europeans practiced settler colonialism as a mode of domination in sixteenth-century Ireland, the Cape of Good Hope, and in North America. However, the practice only went global as a result of what historian James Belich (2009) has called the "settler revolution." The ideology that accompanied this "revolution" during the nineteenth century reformed the generalized perception of settlers and their societies. In places where "rebarbarised" demi-savage Europeans lived at the margins of civilization, the "frontiers" of settlement eventually became sites of political experimentation and manly regeneration—a conservative escape from both debilitating social contradictions and growing revolutionary tensions.

But revolutionary analyses were linked to the dynamics of settler colonial expansion as well. Indeed, the concept of primitive accumulation developed through reflection on what Marx defined as the only "real colonies, virgin soils colonised by free labour" and what Engels defined as the "colonies proper" (which he contrasted to those "countries inhabited by a native population, which are simply subjugated—India, Algeria, the Dutch, the Portuguese, and Spanish possessions") (Marx 1976, 931; Engels 1882; see Piterberg and Veracini 2015). Marx was responding to the theory of "systematic colonisation" advanced by Edward Gibbon Wakefield, who had originally "discovered" primitive accumulation upon noting how the presence of "free lands" in settler-colonial peripheries enabled servants to abscond and rely on a subsistence economy that undid their previous subjugation (Wakefield 1968).

As a specific term, "settler colonialism" was first used in the 1920s to indicate a particular type of British colonialism in the Australian context, where it was distinguished from convict colonialism and used to differentiate between South Australia and New South Wales (Veracini 2013). As a compound term, however, it originally developed in relation to "bona fide" or "actual" settlers. In the United States and in the British Empire during the nineteenth century, these widely used expressions identified "migrants" or "colonists" who had displaced with the intention of remaining in a particular locality or colony. The difference between colonialism and settler colonialism was clear to most observers (Foley 2011), and British historian J. R. Seeley aptly encapsulated the socio-political distinction: "The [settler] colonies and India are in opposite extremes. Whatever political maxims are most applicable to one, are most inapplicable to the other" (quoted in Bell 2009, 8). The distinction was also abundantly clear in the United States and was epitomized by the different ways in which conquered areas were treated during the Mexican War of 1846–48 ("occupation" south of the Rio Grande, organic incorporation north of it). One could approve of one mode of domination and *precisely for that reason* dislike the other. John A. Hobson, for example, approved of "settlement" although he disliked "imperialism."

Lenin's theory of imperialism overturned the perception that these modes of domination were separate. For him, the rise of globalized "monopoly capitalism" made their differences irrelevant (1952). Lenin emphasized imperialism's ability to structure *all* "peripheries." During the twentieth century (and especially during the period of decolonization, when many settlers "repatriated" to their respective motherlands), the analytical difference between colonialism and settler colonialism became blurred.

During the 1970s, and in the context of bitter anticolonial insurgencies in Africa, "settler colonialism" was used again to identify a type of ultra-colonialism through which settlers held power without a demographic majority (Emmanuel 1972). However, beginning with Donald Denoon's seminal work (1983) on the settler economies of the Southern Hemisphere, "settler colonialism" once again became associated with polities in which settlers and their descendants were in power *and* a normalized majority. While the United States and Israel were for some time not included within the bounds of Settler Colonial Studies, they eventually became important case studies (Hixson 2013; Piterberg 2008). Today the concept is applied to locales including postcolonial African nations, Latin America, Taiwan, and even Pakistan (Devji 2014). As scholarly field and analytic paradigm, Settler Colonial Studies have gone global in recent years (Veracini 2015).

While radicals routinely engage with "colonialism," engagement with "settler colonialism" is more rare. Nevertheless, radicals used the latter concept before academics did. Japanese-American Maoist activist J. Sakai, for example, noted how he originally wrote *Settlers* after realizing in the 1970s that white people were actually the "problem," and because the revolutionaries he met from Zimbabwe, South Africa, and Palestine "kept using the term 'settlers'" and "kept talking about 'settler colonialism'" (2014, 421–22). For the indigenous peoples of the settler societies, talking about settler colonialism reminds settler majorities of the need to decolonize relationships and reform the constitutional bases of the settler polities. Reference to settler colonialism is also essential for indigenous communities striving to avoid being lumped together with "diverse" groups in multicultural contexts. Indigenous activists routinely contest attempts to extinguish their sovereign claims through multicultural "recognition" (Byrd 2011).

Palestinians and their supporters have also found reference to Israeli settler colonialism to be a powerful mobilizing device (see, for example, Salamanca, Qato, Rabie, Samour 2012). The paradigm has been especially useful to those opposing the Palestinian Authority's two-state solution (a classic decolonizing approach that does not recognize a settler colonial reality). Similarly, indigenous protesters in Canada have recently prompted an indigenous "renaissance" through Idle No More (Coulthard 2014) and other struggles against neoliberal exploitation. For these movements, colonialism and settler colonialism never ended. Although "colonialism" is typically used to refer to unequal relationships linking the Global North to its southern counterpart, reflections on settler colonialism highlight the foundational illegitimacy of ongoing settler colonial regimes.

Settler colonialism constitutes a privileged point for thinking about capitalist accumulation. Primitive accumulation separates future laborers from their means of subsistence so that they might subsequently be exploited through the wage relation. But while at times there is indigenous labor under settler colonialism, there is never an indigenous proletariat. Under settler colonialism, Indigenous peoples become disposable. Similarly, other sectors of the population increasingly face accumulations that demand everything we have but do not particularly need us as labor. In contrast to the "old" enclosures, these "new" enclosures resemble the dispossessions that indigenous peoples confronted under settler colonialism (Veracini 2015). By highlighting this similarity, it becomes possible to devise a collective response.

SEE ALSO: Domination; Nation; Occupation; Oppression; Race; Sovereignty; Zionism

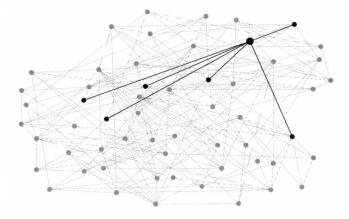

COMMONS

George Caffentzis

AFTER CENTURIES OF MARGINALIZATION, THE TERM "commons" is now at the center of a wide-ranging political dialogue among radical scholars and activists, including urban gardeners, hackers, ecologists, anarchists, feminists, and Marxists. This discussion ranges from a shack dwellers' organization in South Africa (Abahlali baseMjondolo, whose stated aim is to "recreate the commons") to the protesters in Istanbul's Gezi Park (who carried signs bearing the slogan "Reclaim the commons!" when the government threatened to convert the park into a shopping mall) and to the activists of the Great Lakes Commons in the United States, who call on those who dwell near the Great Lakes to regulate the use of this watery wealth according to commons principles. In fact, the discussion is so wide-ranging that some—like David Bollier (2014)—argue that we are now witnessing the emergence of a "commons movement" that is bringing together the defense of "natural resource commons" with "digital commons" like free software.

When it first appeared in medieval-era English property law, the term "commons" referred to a set of legally recognized "assets"—including meadows, fisheries, forests, and peat bogs—that a community used but *did not own*. Most of the land the commoners used was royal territory or belonged to a manor's owner or to the Church. Although commoners did not "own" these resources, they had customary and collectively managed usage of them. This "usufruct" was generally the result of prolonged struggles between commoners and landlords. When landlords had the upper hand, they abrogated the "customs" by violence or through parliamentary legislation. These were the usual means of "enclosure," which had both legal and physical dimensions; they consisted both of acts of Parliament and the encirclement of formerly common resources with bushes or fences to prevent access to them. As Marx observed through his analysis of primitive accumulation (1976), such separation of the peasantry from its "means of production" was one of the main conditions for the rise of capitalism.

While enclosure in the sixteenth century was carried out by "ex-lege" (extrajudicial) force, in the eighteenth and nineteenth centuries a legislative strategy was more often employed. In both cases, however, enclosure caused a dramatic drop in the percentage of land held in common in England. According to conservative estimates, up to 26 percent of the land in sixteenth-century England was held in common, whereas barely 3 percent can be considered communal today—and even this modest stretch is threatened by privatization.

In the twentieth century, as communal land became privatized worldwide, commons became conceptually invisible as well. They were either romanticized (with the trappings of "merrie old England") or demonized, as in ecologist and population theorist Garrett Hardin's 1968 article "The Tragedy of the Commons." According to Hardin, since human nature is driven by self-interest, commons were a path to self-destruction. In this model, a rational herder would maximize advantage by placing as many of his cattle on the common land as possible. However, since every other rational herder would do likewise, the pasture would quickly be "tragically" overgrazed and thus become useless to all herders.

Hardin's thought experiment had a profound effect on a scholarly world seeking easy retorts to the call for more communal forms of social reproduction that arose with the anticapitalist movements of 1960s. By the late-1970s, however, the argument's power began to fade as anthropologists, political scientists, and social researchers pointed out that the "open-access" situation Hardin assumed had rarely occurred in reality. The empirical work of political economist Elinor Ostrom and her colleagues at the US-based International Association for the Study of the Commons was crucial in amassing evidence to counter Hardin's thesis. Looking at property as "a bundle of rights," Ostrom showed that, in both common-property and common-pool resource systems, commoners have always set rules limiting access to the resources they shared due to their awareness that their long-term livelihood depended on self-imposed limitations. Since the Middle Ages, for instance, herders in Switzerland have brought their cows to graze on communally held Alpine meadows. They have also collectively determined rules and created surveillance networks to sanction those who violate them.

Ostrom's 1990 critique of Hardin was a crucial counterpoint to neoliberalism's sweeping privatization of public and communal property. These "New Enclosures" (as *Midnight Notes* labeled them in 1990) were especially devastating in the formerly colonized world where, in the name of a highly engineered "debt crisis," the World Bank and International Monetary Fund went to war against the remaining communal regimes. Since the 1980s, whether through "structural adjustment programs," free trade agreements, or intellectual property rights and patenting regulations, customary regulations have been declared extinct. In the "developed" world, privatization has extended to include not solely land, public spaces, and services, but life forms as well.

In the context of widespread struggles to defend against neo-liberal assault, radical interest in "the commons" revived. On New Year's Eve 1993, the Zapatistas sparked an international solidarity movement when they re-appropriated and communized thousands of acres of land in Chiapas, Mexico. Their call for land and freedom and a world beyond state and market resonated far beyond the region, heightening consciousness of the commons and providing new principles for anticapitalist organizing.

However, the concept of the commons that has taken shape in radical discourse since the 1990s is quite different from the concept that appeared under English property law. The older notion was *geographically* tied to England's territory, was *ontologically* rooted in the use of lands, forests, waters, and the subsoil, and originated *historically* and *politically* in the class struggle on the medieval manor. In contrast, the present notion has a wider geographical and historical application. Radicals now realize that commons exist on every continent and have been the dominant form of economic production and reproduction for most of humanity's existence, including most pre-Columbian indigenous societies on the American continent. Ontologically, our present concept includes seeds, genes, urban spaces, electromagnetic waves and software programs, languages and cultural works, and many other social realities. Commons are conceived as a product both of struggle and of new forms of co-operation. In this way, they are brought into existence every day. Politically, commons are the way in which anticapitalist and anti-state movements increasingly express their demands and identity.

Reflecting upon the 1999 anti-WTO protests in Seattle, Naomi Klein identified a "radical reclaiming of the commons" as the spirit linking different campaigns and movements (2001). Indeed, as worldwide privatizations, expropriations, and economic crises have become permanent features of everyday life, interest in the commons as a principle of self-government and of "non-commodified . . . social cooperation and production" (De Angelis 2009) has sharpened.

Nevertheless, the concept can be co-opted. According to Massimo de Angelis, "increasingly the idea of the commons seems to function less as an *alternative* to capitalist social relations and more like their *saviour*" (2009, 32). Citing discourse on climate change, he explains that neo-Keynesian economists use the phrase "global commons" to couple the contradictory goals of environmental sustainability and economic growth. The same concept has also been used by the World Bank to justify—in the name of protecting our natural wealth—the expulsion of various indigenous groups from their habitat in forested areas (Isla 2009). A further contribution to this distorted use of "the commons" has come from the United Nations' classification of particular cities as part of the "heritage of humanity" and thus subject to specific international regulations. This policy has undermined residents' control over the urban environment and opened the "heritage" cities to commercial exploitation (Lixinski 2011). The danger of co-optation is also evident in the proliferating use of "commons" in real estate jargon and in the labeling of public buildings (e.g., as when libraries become "information commons"). Even shopping malls are now frequently branded as "commons."

Different interpretations of the concept have also emerged in leftist discourse. Followers of the Ostrom School (best exemplified by the work of David Bollier and Silke Helfrich, inspired also by the Hungarian economist Karl Polanyi) do not view the commons as a road to an anticapitalist society. Instead, they argue that it constitutes a "third" social and legal space beyond state and market that can serve as a buffer against neoliberalism's extremes. Through various conferences and publications—including Bollier's *Think Like a Commoner* (2014) and Bollier and Helfrich's *The Wealth of the Commons* (2012)—they have helped to make "the commons" a household phrase. Nevertheless, their assumption that commons are compatible with capitalist relations has led many radicals to reject this conception.

Consequently, many contemporary radicals tend to view commons as embryos of a developing non-capitalist society. In the 1990s, *Midnight Notes* described the creation of commons as the precondition for refusing exploitation (2001). For his part, historian Peter Linebaugh has described the struggle for the commons as the red thread joining centuries of class struggles (2008; 2014a; 2014b). For Massimo de Angelis (2009), commons are capitalism's *outside*, which the class struggle constantly creates. Drawing from a political tradition shaped by the experience of indigenous peoples and especially the Zapatistas, Gustavo Esteva (2012) has argued that commons are not a utopia but—for populations marginalized by development plans—the organizational form of everyday reproduction.

Marxist autonomists Antonio Negri and Michael Hardt (2009) proposed another radical conception by counterpoising the singular "common" to the "commons." In this way they differentiate between cooperative forms of production (which they see as necessary and already underway) and "nature's commons." Convinced that the new phase of capitalist production requires more autonomous and cooperative forms of work, Negri and Hardt seek the production of the common in the interactive space of the Internet and the densely articulated world of the city.

This perspective stands in contrast to the one advanced by eco-feminist activists and writers like Maria Mies and Vandana Shiva, who have described the commons as a relation to the land, the basis of livelihood, and the expression of our "responsibility for the continuation of life" (Mies 1999, 153). According to Mies, the reclamation or reinvention of the commons begins with taking responsibility (a central concept in ecofeminist analysis) for waste, which she defines as a "negative common" (1999, 153; 155). Similarly, Vandana Shiva has argued that land, forest, water, and the systems of knowledge produced through their care have been rural India's "survival basis," as well as the "domain of the productivity of women" and the condition of communal self-reliance (1989, 83). Feminists are also increasingly interested in applying the principle of the commons to everyday life in an effort to break with the isolating conditions of reproductive work under capitalism (Federici 2012).

Despite the differences in conceptualization and emphasis described above, it is possible to deduce several areas of agreement concerning the commons as a political project. The first is that commons are not given but have to be produced. Secondly, commons are not things or "resources" (a term suggesting commercial use) but relations of cooperation and solidarity. Peter Linebaugh (2008) has suggested using the term "commoning" (a verb) instead of "commons" (a noun) to make this point. Finally, there can be no commons without "community."

There is also some agreement that the politics of the commons pose problems when conceptualized as the basis for mass movements. Through their actions, the Zapatistas have demonstrated that tens of thousands of people, spread over more than a hundred miles in southern Mexico, can carry on a commons-based subsistence project together. Nevertheless, it remains analytically and strategically difficult to reconcile the scale of commons in the past (when communal forms of property had continental dimensions) with the smaller commons of today. In a more practical vein, how can we construct a world based on the commons when the very means that enable our cooperation—predominantly the Internet, which relies extensively on mineral extraction and water consumption—require their destruction?

We do not have complete answers to these questions. But if we view the commons not as a distant goal but as the movement that negates the present order of things (not as a given reality but as something evolving through our struggle), then the outline of a path emerges.

SEE ALSO: Class; Community; Reproduction; Solidarity; Space; Utopia

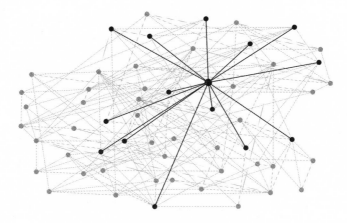

COMMUNITY

Sarah Lamble

OF ALL THE KEYWORDS CURRENTLY CIRCULATING AMONG activists, "community" is perhaps the most frequently used, least explicitly defined, and most elastic in its meaning. Whether referring to a physical location (a neighborhood or social center), a group of identities or interests ("the queer community"), a network of relationships (an online activist community), or a set of shared values or practices ("living in community" or engaging in "community organizing"), the term is used in myriad ways. Everyone seems to know what the concept refers to when it's invoked, yet its precise meaning remains elusive. As a result, attempts to delineate its boundaries invariably result in contentious debate.

According to the *Oxford English Dictionary*, the word first emerged in the fourteenth century, deriving from the Old French "*comuneté*" and the Latin "*commūnitāt*," which both broadly referred to joint possession, ownership, or use, as well as to shared social relations, fellowship, or association. When translated from Latin, the term's root ("*common*") literally means "together under obligation" (Raymond Williams 1983, 70). Today "community" still invokes senses of mutual obligation or collective social responsibility. Between the fourteenth and the twentieth century, "community" came to denote a range of more specific meanings, including "the people of a district," "the quality of holding something in common, as in community of interests, community of goods," and "a sense of common identity and characteristics" (Williams 1983, 75). Indeed, the *OED* provides no less than thirteen specific definitions for "community," which are grouped under two broad categories: (1) "a body of common" and (2) a "shared or common quality or state."

Among the meanings that have since become obsolete, several are noteworthy. Between the fourteenth and seventeenth century, the term referred both to "the generality of people" or "the people as a group" and to "common people," as in "the body of people having common or equal rights or rank, as distinguished from the privileged classes" (*OED*; Williams 1983, 75). The term also referred to "the commons," describing the right to shared access to land or water. Along these lines, one passage from 1630 recounts how "Every Neighbour claimeth communitie to feed his Cattell." While these particular definitions have fallen into disuse, they linger in contemporary activist usage, where "community" is bound to the idea of "the people" as distinguished from governments, states, or social elites. Likewise, "community" still often denotes a sense of shared ownership; "the community" belongs to everyone who is part of it rather than being the domain or property of one individual. In this sense, "community" is part of the "commons." Organizers of guerrilla gardening projects like those that emerged in New York City during the 1970s, for example, called their efforts "community gardens" to emphasize collective ownership and use by neighbors working in opposition to private urban developers.

Alongside these meanings, the word "community" also previously referred to a commonwealth, nation, or state. However, in the context of changing social relations under industrialization and urbanization from the nineteenth century onward, it tended toward denoting local, direct, and immediate social relationships rather than the more abstract, formal, and impersonal ones suggested by "society" and "state" (Williams 1983, 75–76). Today activists still conceive of "community" as both the basis and the forum for connections that are "stronger and deeper than rational or contractual associations of individuals such as the market or the state" (Yúdice 2005, 51). Likewise, although the concept is still sometimes linked to discourses of nationhood (particularly in diasporic or immigrant contexts where non-majoritarian identities are marshaled in opposition to nationalist hegemony), such invocations tend to refer more to cultural and ethnic affiliations than to "the nation" per se.

Often "community" is uttered to express fear about its perceived disappearance. Activists describe a waning sense of collective belonging as a "loss of community" and invoke the rhetoric of "community-building" both as a vehicle of social change and as an antidote to the alienation of modern life. According to Eric Hobsbawm, "Never was the word 'community' used more indiscriminately and emptily than in the decades when communities in the sociological sense became hard to find in real life" (1995, 428). Indeed, anti-globalization activists at the turn of the century invoked "community organizing" as a strategy for challenging state and corporate power while advancing visions of "community" that cast it as a reprieve from the bleakness of contemporary capitalism—as a place where the disenfranchised, isolated, and oppressed could forge bonds of solidarity with people of similar identities, interests, or values and build alternative social relations.

Here the ideological underpinnings of the term come into view, as "community" gets invoked not solely as description but also as a normative conception indexed to aspirational values. As sociologist Zygmunt Bauman has noted, "Whatever the word community may mean, it is good 'to have community', 'to be in a community' . . . community is a 'warm' place, a cozy and comfortable place" (2001, 1). Likewise, for Raymond Williams, "community" is "the warmly persuasive word to describe an existing set of relationships, or the warmly persuasive word to describe an alternative set of relationships. . . . [U]nlike all other terms of social organization (state, nation, society, etc.) it seems never to be used unfavorably, and never to be given any positive opposing or distinguishing term" (1983, 76).

Today many radicals view "community" as the proper location from which activism should arise. Consequently, organizing efforts perceived to lack a strong basis "in community" are considered suspect. This lack is typically attributed to a disconnection from the people most directly affected by the issue at hand. During the rise of the Black Power movement in the 1960s, Black organizers called for "community control" of schools, workplaces, and social services to ensure that these institutions were run by community members rather than by elites (Goldberg and Griffey 2010; Peniel Joseph 2009). Similarly, appeals to community-based culture, values, and organizing often figure prominently in struggles for economic and political self-determination, and especially around claims for indigenous sovereignty. In this way, the concept has become infused with a set of normative and affective qualities that reinforce its status as an inherent social good.

In response, movement intellectuals have cautioned against overly romanticized views of community, arguing that communities can just as easily become sites of oppression, discipline, and control (Bannerji 2000; Miranda Joseph 2002; Pavlich 2001). Internal conflicts, unequal power dynamics, and fraught social relations can generate feelings of alienation, loss, and exclusion for those who fail to conform to the norms, customs, and expectations of a given community. Likewise, although they may appear to share a basis of alliance, the needs and values of different communities can often exist in tension with one another. The 1968 teachers' strike in New York City, for example, provoked fierce conflicts as the struggle to establish "community control" over predominantly Black schools came into conflict with the rights of unionized workers (Goldstein 2014). In this way, communities may mirror or replicate the structural inequalities they ostensibly seek to challenge.

These problems arise in part because the ideal of community tends to privilege unity over difference (Iris Young 1986, 13). Invocations of "community" can thereby homogenize groups and risk suppressing the needs and identities of individuals in favor of the imposed will of the collective. Subjected to white-centric definitions of feminist community and male-centric definitions of Black community, Black feminists have often been chastised, silenced, or ignored for raising concerns that are perceived to threaten the "unity" of either group (Sudbury 1998, 177–223; Bannerji 2000, 151–74). In Britain, where "Black" has historically been mobilized to refer both to a range of racialized identities as well as to people of African or Caribbean descent more exclusively, organizers have responded to debates about who constitutes "the Black community" by shifting to the plural "communities." In this way, they signal their intention to recognize and affirm rather than deny or suppress difference (Sudbury 1998, 93–142). Symptomatic of broader changes in the social understanding of identity, these shifts reflect long-standing debates about the politics of representation and belonging. Nevertheless, questions about who belongs and the conditions under which someone may legitimately be excluded from a community remain highly contentious. The protracted debates about the inclusion of transgender women in "women-only" spaces, for example, underscore the high stakes involved in contests over belonging.

Tensions between inclusion and exclusion, sameness and difference, persist in part because the very notion of "community" is predicated on the establishment of an inside/outside boundary. Establishing the "we" of community inevitably generates a corresponding "they" or "other." For this reason, many activists remain wary of appeals to community and highlight how seemingly benign efforts to forge collective identities can simultaneously reinforce marginalization and exclusion. Indeed, as Iris Marion Young has pointed out, "the desire for community relies on the same desire for social wholeness and identification that underlies racism and ethnic chauvinism, on the one hand, and political sectarianism on the other" (Young 1986, 1–2).

Meanwhile, there is no "pure" community that can be set apart from social formations like the state, capitalism, and the individual. As Himani Bannerji has pointed out, communities are invariably entangled in broader social relations (2000). As such, Miranda Joseph (2002) has cautioned against the "romance of community" and argued that "community" is itself constituted through capitalist relations of production and consumption. Indeed, Joseph has shown how "communities of difference" are appropriated to generate new niche markets to serve capitalist interests. Meanwhile, the state increasingly invokes the language of "community" for policing and development purposes, as well as to lend legitimacy to new forms of power, control, and colonization. Ultimately these efforts are designed to channel local concerns into state objectives. For instance, criminal courts deliver "community sentences" to put a progressive spin on punitive measures that amount to forced, unpaid labor (e.g., picking up garbage or cleaning graffiti from public spaces) with little meaningful connection to the neighborhoods in which the sentence is to be carried out. In light of the strong identification that radicals have expressed toward the concept, Clare O'Connor has cautioned that "community" is in fact "politically ambivalent. Our enemies draw upon its promise as often as we do" (2011, 266).

Aware of the word's limits, some left thinkers have begun proposing alternatives. These include "the un-oppressive city" (Iris Young 1986), "the inoperative community" (Nancy 1991), and the "unavowable community" (Blanchot 1988). To date, however, these formulations have remained largely contained within academic circles. "Community," it turns out, is not easily replaced. In part, this is because it is conceived as the place (literal or metaphoric) where political aspirations emerge and get channeled. As Miranda Joseph notes, "attachments to particular communities of belonging and activism run deep: they are our sites of hope in a difficult world" (2002, ix). The word also retains currency because it is symbolically and pragmatically linked to other key concepts, including solidarity, self-determination, collective action, and empowerment. As Anthony Cohen has argued, "people construct community symbolically, making it a resource and repository of meaning, and a referent of their identity" (1985, 118).

As a result, some have argued that community is best understood as something created though the very process of organizing—that it is less a concrete entity than a set of practices and relationships that are made, cultivated, and reiterated on an ongoing basis. As Brian Alleyne has suggested, "community is so fundamental a concept . . . that it quite unsurprisingly is a term which is impossible to define with any precision. Indeed, there are good reasons why such definition should be avoided . . . it is a term best understood in action" (Alleyne 2002, 608). Conceived in this way, communities are never clearly bounded and are always changing; they have multiple, fluid, and porous boundaries; they are constantly in a state of flow and flux. Moreover, the tensions, conflicts, and challenges that arise within these practices are a central part of community rather than a threat to it. These tensions are what enable people to ask strategic questions, build relationships, make decisions, and grapple with key problems. This redefinition is appealing. However, it remains to be seen whether it will be enough to resolve the analytic and strategic dilemmas the word so frequently yields.

SEE ALSO: Accountability; Allies; Care; Commons; Experience; Friend; Love; Nation; Privilege; Representation; Solidarity; Sovereignty; Space; Utopia

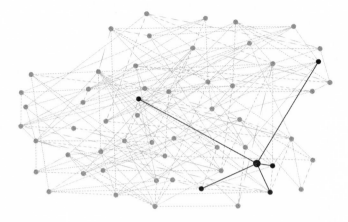

CONSPIRACY

Mandy Hiscocks

DERIVED FROM THE LATIN "*CONSPIRATIONEM*" ("TO breathe together"), the word "conspiracy" denoted "agreement, union, unanimity" when it first appeared in 1386. The immoral connotation we're familiar with to-day—"combination of persons for an evil or unlawful purpose"—emerged much later, in 1863, with the creation of the criminal offense of conspiracy: the agreement of two or more persons to do an illegal act, or to do a lawful act by unlawful means. Although the *Oxford English Dictionary* acknowledges neutral and positive definitions (e.g., "union or combination . . . for one end or purpose; harmonious action or effort"), in contemporary usage people are pre-sumed to conspire to do "bad" things rather than "good."

Many aspects of revolutionary organizing are necessarily conspiratorial, but we rarely name them as such. For example, "conspiracy" doesn't appear in the Colours of Resistance Network's *Definitions for the Revolution*, Gene Sharp's 2012 *Dictionary of Power and Struggle*, or even the "Definition of Terms" section of the CrimethInc. Ex-Workers' Collective's website. Indeed, although radicals sometimes attempt to reclaim the word, social movements tend to conceive of "conspiracy" primarily as a criminal charge to avoid, a description of what opponents are doing, or a "fringe" belief ("conspiracy theory").[1] Each of these usages presents a specific challenge for radicals.

In law, conspiracy is a crime of planning, not of doing. A charge can be laid at or after the moment a plan is set, even if it is never executed. In its earliest legal usage, "conspiracy" was associated with crimes like treason and murder and often referred to revolutionary activity; to overthrow a king you needed to kill him. As conditions of governance changed, the purview of conspiracy law was expanded to preserve its use as a tool of political repression. Leaders of the 1919 Winnipeg General Strike, for instance, were convicted of seditious conspiracy as a result of their purported efforts to "bring into hatred and contempt and to excite disaffection against the government and . . . promote feelings of ill-will and hostility between different classes" (*Rex v. Russell* 1919). Today activists charged with conspiracy have typically been arrested for "conspiring" to commit mischief or to obstruct police—the two minor offenses most associated with demonstrations and direct actions. As Wes Wilson explains, "The substantive and procedural features of the law in this area offer the State a singularly convenient weapon with which to suppress political dissent or augment the criminality of essentially political trials" (1984, 60). Indeed, although maximum conviction sentences for conspiracy can't exceed those imposed when criminal plans are actually carried out, the word "conspiracy" makes the charge sound worse; it often prompts a gut reaction similar to ones produced by words like "terrorism" and "extremism."

---

1.   The radical circles I'm in, and those I read about, predominantly comprise young to middle-aged white people based in Canada, the United States, and parts of Europe. I am by no means attempting to speak for or about any other groups or communities.

Well-known political conspiracy cases typically involve the arrests of activists who engaged in specific collective actions, such as the Chicago 7 (arrested after massive protests against the 1968 Democratic National Convention) and the Vancouver Five (charged after the 1982 bombing of Litton Industries in Toronto). In "The Age of Conspiracy Charges," CrimethInc. chronicles many of the major movement conspiracy cases since 1999, including SHAC 7, Operation Backfire, San Francisco 8, RNC 8, AETA 4, and Asheville 11. These cases involved various accusations (e.g., planned bombings and arson, conspiracy to riot, and even "conspiracy to violate the Animal Enterprise Terrorism Act for protest activity relating to home demonstrations in which they wrote on a sidewalk with chalk"), but many of the charges were dropped. Indeed, for activists, conspiracy charges are serious mainly because of the way evidence of conspiring is gathered and used against the accused and their comrades; conspiracy convictions are rarely the state's main goal. As Tom Hayden, one of the Chicago 7, notes in *Conspiracy to Riot in Furtherance of Terrorism*:

> In virtually every "Seattle" occasion, the FBI declared that an anarchist threat was descending on local citizenry. . . . Wiretapping, informants and provocateurs were liberally employed. The alleged ringleaders were rounded up before their menacing actions could take place. . . . The round ups were accompanied by press conferences where dangerous anarchist tools were placed on display. . . . After the crisis passed, in virtually every instance the conspiracy, felony and misdemeanor charges were dismissed, plea-bargained out, or rejected by local juries. . . . No one seemed to notice that the numerous conspirators across America were released without jail time. (2011, 2)

In the legal context, the word "conspiracy" is meant to refer to a self-evidently bad act. It makes sense then that radicals readily adopt it to describe what our opponents are doing. Consider the suburbanization of America, which Noam Chomsky (2013) traces back to "a literal conspiracy of General Motors, Standard Oil of California, and Firestone Rubber to buy up and destroy the fairly efficient electric transport system in Los Angeles and other cities." The courts convicted and fined the participating parties. However, due to limited access to information and to the spaces of official decision-making, it is not always possible to substantiate our suspicions of conspiracy— let alone to build legal cases in response. Under these conditions, investigative journalists do much of the heavy lifting.

The 2014 documentary *Cowspiracy* (Anderson and Kuhn), for example, uncovers how large environmental NGOs intentionally refuse to discuss industrial meat and dairy production's contributions to climate change—despite a United Nations report (2006) that found it to be the largest contributor—in order to placate corporate funders with investments in the industry and individual donors who don't want to change their lifestyles. Lacking resources for investigation, radicals often operate under the assumption that secret deals can and will be struck between corporations and government, police and state prosecutors, union officials and management, and so on. This reinforces our normative views of conspiracy, which entail not just deception, secrecy, and exclusion, but also harmful intent.

When people conceive of conspiracy as the enemy's primary strategy, they are more likely to generate "conspiracy theories." During a 2011 talk at Occupy Wellington in New Zealand, one speaker defined a conspiracy theory as one that "flies in the face of evidence or science" while insisting that "its correctness can be shown by the paucity of evidence in favour of it. . . . Conspiracy theories often encourage an 'us few enlightened folk versus everyone else' world view. This creates an atmosphere where conspiracy theorists look down on people (or sheeple as they are often called) and ignores the fact that people, by and large, are actually pretty intelligent" ("Against Conspiracy Theories" 2011).

Many radicals openly disparage conspiracy theories (e.g., the idea that 9/11 was an inside job, that the world is ruled by the

Illuminati, or that vaccinations are a ruse to give children autism) as distractions from the real work of revolutionary struggle. We are additionally suspicious of such theories because their proponents often include people on both the far left and the far right.

These negative orientations toward the word—a crime, an enemy strategy, a fringe distraction—tend to occlude the historical use of "conspiracy" as a tool of progressive political change. Prior to democracy and mass movements, conspiracies were one of the only ways to unsettle monarchs and affect change. Those in power lived in constant fear of conspiracy—and justifiably so, since such plots were numerous and often successful (Coward and Swan 2004). Although it is difficult to know whether "conspiracy" was used as a point of pride in the aftermath of the Gunpowder Plot of 1605 or by French courtiers in the eighteenth century, the term's etymology encourages us to consider meanings beyond the normative negative one.

Contemporary positive usage typically arises in the form of defiant reactions to state repression. After the 2010 protests against the G20 summit in Toronto, for example, the group of activists charged with conspiracy called their website *Conspire to Resist*. For their part, Canadian hip-hop artists Test Their Logik wrote a song called "Conspiracy Rap" (2011). And, to raise legal funds for the defendants, local activists created and sold "co-conspirator" T-shirts. Perhaps not surprisingly, insurrectionary anarchists have been most likely to use the word in a positive way. CrimethInc. demonstrates this tendency, as do many black bloc participants. In some cases, the word is used playfully, as by the New Left–era socialist-feminist formation WITCH, the "Women's International Terrorist Conspiracy from Hell!" ("Bring Back"). In others, its positive inflection derives from association with other words, as with Amnesty International's 1986 Conspiracy of Hope tour, which strove to raise awareness about the prisoners of conscience supported by the group.

Hesitation among radicals to invoke the word in these ways may stem from discomfort arising from the term's proximity to vanguardism. These days, many radicals differentiate themselves from mainstream social movements by adopting consensus-based approaches, and these models are difficult to reconcile with small clandestine groups carrying out anonymous actions. Affinity group actions and late-night sabotage (perhaps the most conspiratorial tactics in today's repertoire) are often disparaged for being small-scale and ineffective. Examples that disprove this position include the arson attack on a horse-killing facility recounted in the documentary film *If a Tree Falls*. This action immediately closed the facility down, thus ending a ten-year campaign of unsuccessful protest and lobbying (Curry 2011).

Reluctance to use the word "conspiracy" may also simply reflect unwillingness to part with our comforts. Although arrest and incarceration have different consequences for each of us (and some radicals have good reasons to avoid these outcomes), conspiracy will inevitably divide the left on the basis of risk aversion so long as it remains tied to imprisonment. At the same time, however, the *imagery* of conspiracy can be powerfully mobilizing. The Gunpowder Plot may have been a religiously motivated aristocratic attempt to change one leader for another (by people who fled to their summer estates after the failure) (Sharpe 2005). However, with the help of the popular film *V for Vendetta* (2005) and the activity of the hacker group Anonymous, the Guy Fawkes mask has come to symbolize the power and possibility of large-scale solidarity and risk-taking. Indeed, although it's difficult to measure their resonance, positive utterances of "conspiracy" have recently begun to appear in movements against anti-Black violence and the prison industrial complex. In this context, the term has been juxtaposed with the concept of "allies." In June 2015, the *Guardian* ran an article entitled "'We Need Co-conspirators, Not Allies': How White Americans Can Fight Racism," featuring a quote by social worker and activist Feminista Jones: "I am not interested in white allies. What we need are co-conspirators" (Hackman 2015). Similarly, special Projects Coordinator of the National Domestic Workers Alliance and #Blacklivesmatter cofounder Alica Garza says she is looking for more "white co-conspirators . . . who are interested in dismantling systems of oppression" (Walker 2015).

In this usage, the co-conspirator is someone willing to take greater personal risk than the risks perceived to be associated with "allyship."

Engaging with the historical development and political use of the word "conspiracy" could help today's radicals to think more broadly about the stakes of serious organizing and the kind of commitment it requires. It forces us to consider whether there are ways to conspire without succumbing to vanguardism. Is it possible, for instance, to divorce conspiracy from the practice of exclusion? Is this what the Animal Liberation Front and Earth Liberation Front have accomplished or are trying to do with their membership-free, principle-based actions? Is this what H. G. Wells was getting at with the 1928 publication of *The Open Conspiracy: Blueprints for a World Revolution* or what Anonymous intends with the use of the Guy Fawkes mask and the idea that anyone can take part?

Most importantly, reorienting to the word's history and etymology can help us better understand the positive role that conspiracy has played in the past. Not all covert organizing is sinister, shady, and nefarious. We conspire because we know that, at its root, conspiracy means "breathe together."

SEE ALSO: Allies; Demand; Politics; Revolution; Vanguard

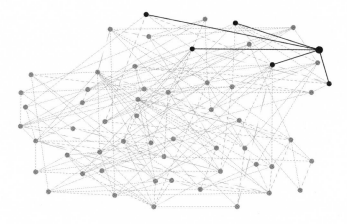

CRIP

Robert McRuer

LIKE THE WORD "QUEER," "CRIP" HAS HAD A LONG AND variegated history. For almost two decades, it has been a recognizable term within the academic field of Disability Studies, generally marking (as "queer" did in relation to LGBT) a more radical alternative to an assimilationist or reformist disability politics. Long before it was an acknowledged word in the academy, however, disabled activists and artists used it to mark a flamboyant sense of collective identity characterized by both defiance against able-bodied norms and often by what Carrie Sandahl identifies as "wicked humor, including camp" (2003, 37). In the United States, "crip" has also had a parallel, racialized history, signifying inclusion in a prominent African American gang.

The degree of overlap between these two uses depends in part upon how the history or mythology of the gang name is narrated.

"Crip" is derived from the English word "cripple," which has more than a thousand-year history as both a noun and verb. According to the *Oxford English Dictionary*, the noun—meaning "one who is disabled (either from birth, or by accident or injury) from the use of his limbs; a lame person"—dates from 950; the verb—meaning "to deprive (wholly or partly) of the use of one's limbs; to lame, disable, make a cripple of"—dates from 1307. The *OED* cites Shakespeare's *Timon of Athens* (1607), where Timon himself uses the word as a curse: "Thou cold sciatica, Cripple our senators, that their limbs may halt as lamely as their manners!" For much of the word's history, the noun "cripple" has been deployed as a harsher, more demeaning, or pitiful version of words perceived to be more neutral (like "impaired," "handicapped," or "disabled"). The *OED* includes, for example, an 1865 usage from Anthony Trollope describing "a poor cripple, unable to walk beyond the limits of her own garden." In our own moment, "cripple" (especially as a verb) continues to circulate freely as a negative metaphor to describe virtually any natural catastrophe. Following a devastating earthquake on April 26, 2015, for example, MSN and other news outlets quickly reported that "Nepal's Earthquake Could Cripple Its Vital Tourism Economy."

"Crip" will always carry traces of this painful history of stigma and derision. In the face of this pain, however, "crip" has been reclaimed. Collective reclamations of words are never simplistic reversals. They do not offer a one-to-one replacement (a singular positive meaning for a singular negative one). Instead, as collective revaluations, they simultaneously allow for the germination of multiple, unexpected meanings that can be "worldmaking" (Muñoz 1999, 195).

As a term, "disability" itself has been reclaimed. If, in the past, it automatically connoted loss, lack, or exclusion, it can now mark an identity or inclusion in disability culture. Even more than "disability," however, "crip" has become the marker of an out-and-proud cultural model of disability (Snyder and Mitchell 2006, 5). This model stands in opposition both to medical models (which reduce disability to pathology, diagnosis, and treatment/elimination) and to the well-known social model (which suggests that "disability" is located not in bodies but rather in inaccessible environments requiring adaptation). The flamboyant defiance of "crip" ties it to models of disability that are more culturally generative (and politically radical) than a merely reformist social model.

Since disability haunts many stories of the gang name's origins, the LA Crips are not absolutely autonomous from this history. There are many origin stories for the LA Crips, and several are likely apocryphal. In a 1988 report, the *Los Angeles Times* captured the role of rumor in this history: "Some said they wore earrings. Some said they carried canes. Some said they walked with a limp, like cripples. The nickname spread: Crips" ("Modern Gangs"). In 1992, the *Guardian* more directly tied the gang's name to a person, suggesting that Raymond Washington, who founded the Crips in 1969, was himself disabled: "Crip is an abbreviation for cripple, nickname of the gang's founder, who walked with a limp" (Martin Walker 1992, 21). Over the past four decades, numerous other accounts have confirmed, contradicted, proliferated, and (perhaps most importantly) disseminated these stories.

Some stories of the gang name's origin suggest that it was an acronym for either "Continuous Revolution in Progress" or "Community Resources for Independent People"; others suggest that these acronyms emerged only later to explain the name. Nevertheless, media accounts of the gang often point either to a way of walking *as though* impaired or as *definitely* impaired. In these accounts, "crip" marks either a stylized way of walking or a way of walking necessitated by mobility impairments. The fact that canes are sometimes part of these stories substantiates the spectral disability histories connected to the gang's origins. It is in no way apocryphal, however, that—at some moments (as when a truce was signed with the rival LA Bloods following the 1992 riots)—the Crips have explicitly focused on issues directly linked to disability, such as community health care clinics or HIV/AIDS services. As part of the 1992 truce, the Crips promised to match funds for an HIV/AIDS awareness center that would be operated by minority researchers and physicians (Browning 1998, 108).

Although the historical connections of "crip" to "cripple" seem to tie the term to mobility impairment, it has proven to be far more flexible. A set of two special issues of the *Journal of Literary and Cultural Disability Studies* (2014) focusing on "Cripistemologies" (a term coined by Merri-Lisa Johnson), position "crip" as describing non-normative or non-representative disabilities. The essays focus on borderline personality, anxiety, hysteria, chronic pain, HIV/AIDS, trans identity, and a range of other impairments or states of being not comprehended by the signifier "disability." Likewise, throughout her important *Feminist, Queer, Crip*, Alison Kafer (2013) uses the term to think about issues, mental states, behaviors, or forms of embodiment that might not, on the surface, appear to be about disability at all. For Kafer, "crip" has the capacity to encompass forms of embodiment or states of mind that are arguably in excess of the able-minded or able-bodied/disabled binary. Like "queer" at its most radical, "crip" has the potential to be simultaneously flamboyantly identitarian (as in, "We are crip and you will acknowledge that!") and flamboyantly anti-identitarian (as in, "We reject the capacity of your ableist categories to describe us!") (cf. Duggan 1995, 171). In *Crip Theory: Cultural Signs of Queerness and Disability*, I wrote that "crip" should be "permanently and desirably contingent: in other queer, crip, and queercrip contexts, squint-eyed, half dead, not dead yet, gimp, freak, crazy, mad, or diseased pariah have served, or might serve, similar generative functions" (2006, 40, 41). Both *Crip Theory* and *Feminist, Queer, Crip* trace the term's emergence from activist and artistic locations.

Artist and activist Eli Clare has also written thoughtfully about "crip." In *Exile and Pride: Disability, Queerness, and Liberation*, Clare explicitly uses the first-person plural to explain how "we in the disability rights movement create crip culture, tell crip jokes, identify a sensibility we call crip humor" (1999, 68). For Clare, creative deployments of "crip" differentiate it from the more individualistic "supercrip." Supercrips have often been critiqued for participating in ableist "overcoming" narratives, as though disability represented an adversity over which one must "triumph" (through athletic competition or daring adventures, for example).

Both Clare and Sandahl appeared with numerous other artists in David Mitchell and Sharon Snyder's groundbreaking 1995 documentary *Vital Signs: Crip Culture Talks Back*, with the very title suggesting that "crip" is connected to community, solidarity, outspokenness, and defiance. "Crip," in all of these senses, has not been contained to the United States. In the United Kingdom, the cartoonist Crippen has generated biting critiques of ableist ideas and performer Liz Carr has created "crip radio" through a podcast called "Ouch!" available on the BBC's disability website (O'Hara 2006). In Australia, comedian and disability activist Stella Young produced a comedy performance called "Tales from the Crip" aimed at affirming disabled people's sexuality while mocking ableist notions that disabled people should be "inspirational" (she even wore a T-shirt that read "Inspiration Boner Killer"). "I identify with the crip community," Young said in an interview. "I didn't invent the word—it's a political ideology I came to in my late teens and early 20s. People often say to me 'You can't say that!' and I say, 'Well, my people have been saying it for decades so I reckon I probably can'" (Northover 2014).

Back in the United States, Mike Ervin has blogged as "Smart Ass Cripple" since 2010 on the "official site for bitter cripples (and those who love them)." For his part, Leroy Moore has invented an African American, disabled, and genderqueer cultural form called Krip-Hop—with the K marking a distance from the C of the LA Crips. Aiming to bring hip-hop artists and poets with disabilities to a wider audience, Krip-Hop has been integrated into some of the performances of Sins Invalid, a troupe celebrating the beauty, desirability, and diversity of queer and disabled people of color.

Usage of the term as an adjective in cases such as these underscores its generative character: when combined with a noun, "crip" as adjective is not simply additive. Describing something like culture as "crip" remakes the substance in question: "crip culture" is not simply crip + culture (as if we all agreed in advance what the latter term might mean). In the same ways that "crip" as noun does not simplistically mark a form of existence that can be known in advance, "crip" as adjective cannot be reduced to a mere descriptor.

The term's power when used as a verb emanates from its uses as a noun or adjective. Queer disability theorist Mel Chen has written about "animacy," which describes the degree of "liveness" associated with an entity or term. For Chen, "a queer-crip approach to disability" is marked by a "disentangling of the discourses . . . that contain and fix dis/abled bodies" (2012, 215). Whether as noun, adjective, or verb, such animacy is evident in "crip."

We are still collectively discovering what it might mean "to crip." As a verb, the term is still perhaps best defined by what it might become. Two important conferences in Prague—Cripping Neoliberalism in 2010 and Cripping Development in 2013—implied in their titles that "cripping" entails radically revisioning, from committed anti-ableist positions, the taken-for-granted systems in which we are located. Both conferences interrogated fetishized notions of capitalist growth and highlighted how bodies and minds are unevenly caught up in global processes. Similarly, the location of these conferences outside of the United States or western Europe indicated a desire to find new languages for thinking about disability in the Global South or in post-socialist countries.

"Crip" has, at this point, moved in and out of various languages. One of the first special issues of an academic journal on crip theory was a bilingual (English and Swedish) publication out of Sweden, *lambda nordica* ("Cripteori"). The anticapitalist *Crip Magazine* out of Vienna, Austria, was also bilingual (English and German). "Crip" resonates strongly with some radical queer and disability activists in Spanish-speaking and German-speaking locations as well (in German, the contemporary history of "crip" partially intersects with the longer history of the *Krüppel* movement, although the ways the term currently travels seem to be semi-autonomous). In Spain, Melania Moscoso has begun to talk about "cripwashing" as a complicated process of domesticating radical disabled energy by using the very language of disability activism (2013, 170). Theorizing similar appropriations in a Czech context, Kateřina Kolářová uses the idea of "the inarticulate post-socialist crip" to describe impaired or disabled modes of being silenced by neoliberal appropriations of disability (2014, 257).

"To crip," like "to queer," gets at processes that unsettle and make strange or twisted (Kuppers 2011). "Cripping" also exposes the ways that able-bodiedness and able-mindedness get naturalized, and the ways that bodies, minds, and impairments that should be at the center of a space, issue, or discussion get purged. Such purging has tended to be in the service of a globalized neoliberal capitalism, which is one reason that "crip" has had such resonance for radicals.

When AIDS activists protested outside New York's Trump Tower in 1989, they sought to expose the ways that dominant meanings of development, housing, luxury, or the good life actually *depended upon* eviction, homelessness, and literal death. Trump received massive tax abatements to construct his towers, while activists calling for housing to keep people with HIV/AIDS from dying in the streets saw their applications for hospice care languish in the mayor's office (Crimp 1990, 122). We might retrospectively term this action "cripping" and identify its affinity with later cultural work—not simply for its linguistic, deconstructive maneuver, but also for its insistent focus on the materiality of impaired bodies and minds caught up in, or purged from, unjust systems.

"Cripping," then, always attends to the materiality of embodiment at the same time that it attends to how spaces, issues, or discussions get "straightened"—though it does so in a more expansive sense than we might think of "straightening" in queer studies, activism, or art. This is in part because the radical power of "queer" has been diluted by global commodification processes that have not yet domesticated "crip." For radicals, "crip" is a keyword that currently connects to what many have begun to call "disability justice" (Mingus 2010a). Disability justice moves beyond mere rights-based and nation-state–based strategies (represented most prominently by the Americans with Disabilities Act). It also forges anti-neoliberal coalitions in the interests of a global crip imagination, which can invent new ways of countering oppression and generate new forms of being-in-common.

SEE ALSO: Accessible; Bodies; Queer; Rights; Trans*/-

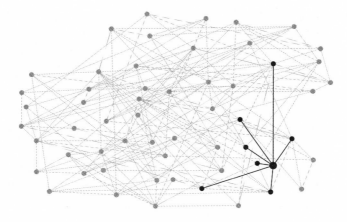

DEMAND

Nina Power

To DEMAND SOMETHING FROM SOMEBODY (WHETHER it be from an individual or a state) is often to accept, as many thinkers have pointed out, at least the broad outlines of the existing situation. To demand something—better working conditions, political representation, compensation—is at the same time often to recognize the framework and the institutions that could (but most often will not) acquiesce to that demand: employers, the government, the state. But does that mean that all demands are inherently reformist and therefore anti-revolutionary? It is clear that, as a political tactic, advancing demands has historically benefited workers and civil rights groups in many situations, especially when these demands have been backed up by strikes, mass protest, or other forms of collective action. The politics of demand need not always be realistic: sometimes demanding the impossible—as in the popular May '68 slogan, "Be Realistic, Demand the Impossible!"—changes the way in which a particular political debate is framed and how people act within that framework. Nuanced takes on the idea of demand (e.g., "transitional demands," "directional demands") seek to fuse a desire for immediate change with a long-term desire for the abolition of the status quo. Only the most puritanical thinkers and actors would deny the necessity of improving things on the way to a revolutionary overhaul of the entire system.

"Demand" can be both a noun and a verb ("a demand"; "to demand something") and stems from the Latin "*demandare*" (meaning "to entrust," "commit to one's charge," or "to hand over"). So, while radicals are accustomed to thinking of "demand" simply as a request (or "mandate," also from "*mandare*," meaning "to order") conveyed to someone else or to a larger institution, the word also etymologically implies trust. We might thus ask what it is that we trust about any person or institution we demand something from; what it is in their constitution that causes us to "commit" our demand to their charge? Moreover, if to demand is to place something in someone's hand, it stands to reason that the hand must at some point be extended. This etymological relationship between demanding and being offered has important political implications. Even as we repeat abolitionist Frederick Douglass' famous claim that "power concedes nothing without a demand" (1857), we must consider how the act of demand implies our trust in the very relations of power we seek to undermine.

"To ask for as a right"—the dominant contemporary conception of political demands—stems from early-fifteenth-century Anglo-French legal language. The noun form of "demand," as in a request or claim, dates from the fourteenth century. Hovering in the background behind these usages is the economic sense of demand, as in the laws of "supply and demand" considered by Adam Smith in *The Wealth of Nations* from 1776. The legal and economic senses of the word remain present to some extent in contemporary activist and political uses, in which "demand" often stands in for (or is linked to) an insistence on the recognition of existing "rights" or appeals for new ones. "Demands" in this sense can be put forward by specific groups (trans rights, rights for indigenous peoples, and so on) or they can appeal to ostensible universalities, as was the case with the demands first advanced during the French revolution (e.g., the "rights of man"—now human rights—or "citizens' rights," including recent demands for a basic guaranteed minimum income). Specific demands need not be in tension with universal demands and may even complement them. The demand for fairer treatment by and for particular groups, for instance, will arguably benefit the majority insofar as a more equal society benefits everyone.

There have been several historical attempts to radicalize the concept of "demand." In 1938, Trotsky marked the relationship between what he described as the minimum and the maximum program. These programs respectively correspond to reformist social democratic demands, on the one hand, and the replacement of capitalism by socialism on the other. Due to the "contradiction between the maturity of the objective revolutionary conditions and the immaturity of the proletariat and its vanguard," Trotsky in his "Transitional Programme" (1938) proposed a series of "transitional demands" that would ultimately lead to the "conquest of power by the proletariat." He argued that transitional demands, demands made from the "revolutionary perspective," should replace the reformist minimum program. This sense presents "demand" in a processual rather than static light, as an ongoing series of mobilizations designed to undermine the basis for bourgeois and capitalist rule. Through this process, Trotsky envisioned that the proletariat would start to see itself as part of a growing revolutionary movement committed to the overthrow of capitalism. In this way, he aimed to overturn the formal distinction between revolutionary and reformist demands while ensuring that demands made to the bourgeoisie would no longer need to be articulated in piecemeal fashion.

Although many radicals choose to distance themselves from the legacies of Trotsky and Trotskyism, a great deal of the contemporary discussion concerning the nature of "demands" similarly views them less as fixed ends in themselves than as part of an ongoing process. The historical opposition between reformism and revolution is perhaps less rigid than it used to be. Today one can operate on multiple political fronts at once using a variety of different tactics. To see the demand for reductions in work hours as being in opposition to the abolition of the wage-labor system, for example, is to set up a false sense of scarcity ("if this change is made, this larger change can't happen"). Many activists and theorists do not view demands made to states or employers as being in opposition to the greater desire to create a situation in which the original lesser demand would become redundant. In *The Problem with Work* (2011), Kathi Weeks advances a similarly important distinction between "utopian" and "nonutopian" demands. A utopian demand, she writes, "should point toward the possibility of a break, however partial, with the present." In contrast, a non-utopian demand fails to "animate the possibility of living differently." In her discussion of the Wages for Housework campaign, where feminists demanded that unpaid reproductive labor (e.g., childcare and cleaning) be economically remunerated, Weeks acknowledged, "None of its supporters presumed that wages for housework would signal the end of either capitalism or patriarchy. But they did hope the reform would bring about a gendered system characterized by a substantially different division of labor and economy of power, one that might give women further resources for their struggles, make possible a different range of choices, and provide discursive tools for new ways of thinking and imagining" (220).

Seemingly impossible or improbable demands can open up a significant political and conceptual space for thinking about the world differently. What would it mean, for example, to understand that "work" includes everything that keeps humanity going, is highly gendered, and is not merely restricted to wage labor? Even if there was no hope of achieving any form of economic recognition for housework, utopian demands of this kind force us to think differently.[1] For example, what if—rather than profit—we took "care" to be the most fundamental value in society? What would it mean to adopt the standpoint of prison abolitionists who begin from a vision of the world in which incarceration didn't exist at all and then work backward from there?

In a similarly "utopian" vein, philosopher Simon Critchley has written about the idea of the "infinite demand." Following the work of Knud Ejler Løgstrup and Emmanuel Levinas, Critchley argues that ethical subjectivity is constituted through our commitment to the unfulfillable ethical demands that befall us upon recognizing the other. Arguing that we live in an age in which the proletariat is no longer the revolutionary subject, Critchley suggests that contemporary anarchism—as the "continual questioning from below of any attempt to impose order from above" (2007, 13)—is where hope for democracy lies. Here "demand" is understood as an ethical imperative "whose scope is universal and whose evidence is faced in a concrete situation" (132).

In recent years, activists have begun to strongly criticize the traditional logic of demand, particularly when it comes to strategy. In "Preoccupied: The Logic of Occupation," a text about the New School occupation of December 2008 written by the Inoperative Committee, the authors attack what they describe as "radical liberals" who operate within the logic of "[n]ames, demands and identities." Like Critchley, they oppose "infinite demands" (which are held to be "compelling, but ultimately an alibi for reform, a series of binding delays which blunts the force of any potential upheaval") and advance the call to become "infinitely demanding." With this reversal of the logic of "demand," the authors make clear that it is no longer a question of asking someone in power for something. Instead, what is required is the recognition that something is ethically and politically demanded of *them* (or, indeed, *us*): "Those who occupy, strike, or sabotage

---

1. It should be noted that the Wages for Housework campaign has recently achieved some material gains: a 2013 Venezuelan law pays full-time mothers a wage and a pension, recognizing their contribution to social reproduction and altering the traditional conception of work.

are not the ones who infinitely demand, rather it is occupation, striking, and sabotage themselves which are infinitely demanding in their fulfillment. We do not demand something infinite by means of occupation; we are demanded by occupation to infinitely extend it. This is why there is no excuse for conceding in an occupation. Every demand is already a defeat, and the only genuine failure is one that occurs in the attempt to expand it" (Inoperative Committee 2001, 10).

But even as the Inoperative Committee engaged in their polemical reversal and overhaul of "demand," other movement thinkers were in the process of salvaging the concept and giving nuance to its meaning. In the 2007 article "Walking in the Right Direction?" Ben Trott recounts discussions—in particular, those taking place in Germany—around the idea of "directional demands" (*Richtungsforderungen*). While Trott acknowledges that there is currently "no single unified position" determining what constitutes such a demand, he presents their deployment as an expression of "the desire to constitute a social actor, movement or counter-power capable of intervening in, and influencing, social and political developments" in the hope of bringing about a class recomposition capable of disrupting capitalism. In his account, Trott explicitly opposes such directional demands to Trotsky's "transitional demands," arguing that the latter might be "realisable in bourgeois society" while the former look for "a way out." In this view, directional demands are global (i.e., not dependent on nationality or citizenship status recognition) and they don't give primacy to the industrial proletariat as political vanguard. Instead, and in conjunction with the insights of post-Fordist thinkers like Antonio Negri, Michael Hardt, and Paulo Virno, directional demands favor "the Multitude." No single actor can claim a monopoly on the right to advance directional demands. Moreover, such demands cannot be said to have "necessary stages." Like Weeks' notion of utopian demands, directional demands in Trott's account "open up the potential for possible future worlds."

Historically, "demand" has shifted between reformist and revolutionary conceptions, as well as between utopian and non-utopian ones. Severed from an understanding of "demand" in a strictly legal rights--based sense, activists and theorists have sought to re-formulate the concept to emphasize processual, infinite relations and an open-ended series of tactics. The old image of "demand" as asking for something concrete from someone in power within a particular national context has mutated into something much more global, infinite, and universal.

SEE ALSO: Accountability; Conspiracy; Prefiguration; Revolution; Rights; Utopia; Vanguard

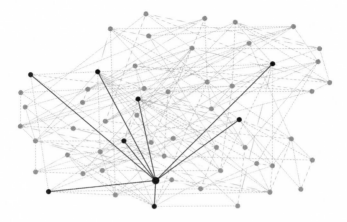

DEMOCRACY

Donatella della Porta

BUILT FROM THE GREEK ROOTS *"DEMOS"* (PEOPLE) AND *"kratia"* ("power or rule"), the concept of "democracy" is inextricably bound to the idea of people power. Today radicals often cite *The Port Huron Statement* (1962) as a manifesto of "participatory democracy." Emphasizing free speech and the right to collective self-governance, the historic document reads, "We seek the establishment of a democracy of individual participation, governed by two central aims; that the individual share in those social decisions determining the quality and direction of his life; that society be organized to encourage independence in men and provide the media for their common participation."

Participation is often a central theme in activist debates about democracy. Indeed, the very concept of "politics" (with its etymological root in the Greek *"polis"*) suggests democratic participation. However, modern "representative democracy" has little in common with the so-called "ancient democracy" of the Greek *polis.*

Where "liberal democracy" foresees the constitution of bodies of specialized representatives, "participatory democracy" posits strong constraints on delegation, which is seen as an instrument of oligarchic power. If liberal democracy is based on formal equality—one head, one vote—participatory democracy underscores the need to create conditions of real equality. While liberal democracy is often bureaucratized, with decision-making concentrated at the apex, direct democracy insists on bringing decisions to the people. The very idea of popular sovereignty presupposes participation.

Theorists of participatory democracy criticize liberal conceptions by pointing to the asymmetries that a purely political equality fails to neutralize. For Carole Pateman, *full* participation is a "process where each individual member of a decision-making body has equal power to determine the outcome of decisions" (1970, 70–71). In a similar vein, "strong democracy" has been defined as a government in which citizens participate at least some of the time in the decisions that affect their lives (Barber 1984). To contest inequality, radicals call for greater transparency and the democratization of institutions. The democratization of parties and associations is considered particularly important, since these mediate between society and the state. In this conception, participation is oriented toward rebalancing power.

In the history of the labor movement, attention to the social dimension of democracy often finds expression through attempts to develop a democracy of the workplace through workers' councils. As Anton Pannekoek noted in the 1940s,

> In the present and coming times, now that Europe is devastated and mankind is impoverished by world war, it impends upon the workers of the world to organize industry, in order to free themselves from

want and exploitation. It will be their task to take into their own hands the management of the production of goods. To accomplish this great and difficult work, it will be necessary to fully recognize the present character of labor. The better their knowledge of society and of the position of labor in it, the less difficulties, disappointments and setbacks they will encounter in this striving. (Dawson 1950)

To a certain extent, participation has survived in representative regimes. As Pierre Rosanvallon noted, modern democracy grew alongside institutions of electoral accountability. For Rosanvallon, these institutions are not "the opposite of democracy, but rather a form of democracy that reinforces the usual electoral democracy, a democracy of indirect powers disseminated through society—in other words, a durable democracy of distrust which complements the episodic democracy of the usual electoral representative system" (2006, 8).

Supporters of participatory democracy criticize ritualistic forms of participation, calling instead for real empowerment to allow for more informed decisions. Participation is seen to have a positive effect on citizens, and spaces of participation like social movements become "schools of democracy." Indeed, participation in civic activity educates individuals with respect to how to think in public, given that citizenship permeates civic activity with the necessary sense of publicity and justice (Pateman 1970).

In European history, participatory democracy developed with the labor movement. The initial phases of the democracy were characterized by widespread activism in the public sphere. Movements applied pressure through public demonstrations to influence representatives. Democracy signaled what sociologist Bendix called "the entrance of the masses into history." Indeed, "the 18th century represents a rupture on a grand scale in the history of western Europe. Before that moment, the masses were barred from exercising their public rights. From that moment, they became citizens and in this sense members of the political community" (1964, 72). In Europe, between the end of the eighteenth century and beginning of the nineteenth, the importance of demonstrations and strikes grew. Workers formed associations for the defense of wages and working conditions but also to call for democratic reforms.

A central element of this conception of democracy was the collective dimension attributed to rights. The social and political demands of the workers' movement intertwined with claims addressing the very conception and practice of democracy. The battle for the freedom of the press was a founding experience. The emerging social movements operating in the public sphere not only discussed specific political reforms but also constituted arenas in which different conceptions of democracy could meet and raise an explicit challenge to the minimalist, individualistic, and liberal vision favored by the developing democratic state. A central demand of the worker movement concerned the right "to combine," which began with the right to associate but differentiated itself over time. In this way, liberal democracy unintentionally provided the resources for its own transformation.

Other models of democracy were introduced through the protest campaigns to expand citizenship rights. These included conceptions of direct, horizontal, and self-managed democracy. Under pressure from social movements, the system of representation soon evolved to recognize emerging collective actors through the extension of civic, political, and social rights. Notwithstanding its individualizing rhetoric, the democratic state developed traits of organized or associative democracy.

Social movements during the 1970s and 1980s also insisted on the legitimacy of participatory democracy. Indeed, "the struggle of the left libertarian movements thus recalls an ancient element of democratic theory, which promotes the organization of the collective decision-making process variously defined as classical, populist, communitarian, strong, grassroots or direct democracy, against a democratic practice defined in contemporary democracies as realist, liberal, elitist, republican or representative democracy" (Kitschelt 1993, 15). Through their participatory conception of democracy, the new social movements of the 1970s criticized mass-party mediation and aimed to make policy-making more visible and controllable.

The protests against austerity that arose during the 1990s were pathbreaking from an organizational point of view. While neo-liberal reformers criticized unions for jeopardizing the free market, new organizational forms developed to promote alternative models of democracy. These ideas emerged from the Zapatistas in Mexico, the Sem Terra in Brazil, the Piqueteros in Argentina, and elsewhere to challenge representative and majoritarian models. As Subcomandante Marcos put it in his greeting to activists participating in the first intercontinental encounter in the Lacandon rain forest, "no major strategic or policy decision is made until it has been considered and approved by consensus in every community's assembly" (quoted in della Porta 2015, 168). This approach influenced the global justice movement, which combined participatory and deliberative qualities—a communicative process based on reason that could transform individual preferences and prioritize the public good (della Porta 2009a; 2009b). For example, the World Social Forum defined itself as an "open meeting place" in its charter, exempting only political parties and those advocating racist ideas or using terrorist means. Its functioning testifies to the importance given to the production and exchange of knowledge. What seems to make cognitive exchanges especially relevant for the global justice movement in general, and for the Social Forums in particular, is the positive value assigned to openness toward "the others," considered by some activists to be a most relevant attitude for building "nets from the local, to the national and the supranational" (quoted in della Porta 2015, 176). The development of inclusive arenas for the creation of knowledge emerged as a main aspiration in the Social Forum process.

Inspired by the deliberative and participatory model of democracy of the global justice movement, recent anti-austerity protests introduced some new radical twists. In Tahrir Square, Kasbah Square, the Plaza del Sol, Syntagma Square, and Zuccotti Park, the *acampada* represented a major democratic experiment. Conceptions of participation from below were combined with efforts to create egalitarian, inclusive public spheres. As activist and sociologist John Postill (2011a) noted about the protest in Madrid,

> the encampments rapidly evolved into "cities within cities" governed through popular assemblies and committees. The committees were created around practical needs such as cooking, cleaning, communicating and carrying out actions. Decisions were made through both majority rules vote and consensus. The structure was horizontal, with rotating spokespersons in lieu of leaders. Tens of thousands of citizens were thus experimenting with participatory, direct and inclusive forms of democracy at odds with the dominant logic of political representation. Displaying a thorough admixture of utopianism and pragmatism, the new movement drew up a list of concrete demands, including the removal of corrupt politicians from electoral lists, while pursuing revolutionary goals such as giving "All power to the People."

The camps were set up in the open air to enforce the public, transparent, and inclusive nature of the process. Similarly, the refusal to appoint delegates represented a further emphasis on equality.

In Spain, the 15M introduced a political logic into these spaces that allowed people to learn new skills. The assemblies were described as "a massive, transparent exercise in direct democracy" (quoted in Postill 2011b). As the main institutions of the *acampada*, the general assemblies testified to a broadly inclusive effort. The more-or-less permanent occupations of squares were thus seen as creating a new agora in publicly owned spaces. "Because the squares belong to us," one activist noted, "they are locations of a new communitarian and participatory democracy" (Italian Revolution Milano 2011). Assemblies aimed to mobilize not just activists but communities of people.

Another key democratic tool that was further developed during the anti-austerity protests was the consensual method. In some cases, this method was aimed at reaching agreement while in others their purpose was to create community (della Porta 2009b). Democracy in the square was defined as inclusive and respectful of people's experiences. As activist and anthropologist David Graeber noted regarding the use of the consensual method at Occupy Wall Street, "Anyone who feels they have something relevant to say about a proposal ought to have their perspectives carefully considered." Moreover, "Everyone who has strong concerns or objections should have those concerns or objections taken into account and, if possible, addressed in the final form of the proposal. Anyone who feels a proposal violates a fundamental principle shared by the group should have the opportunity to veto ('block') the proposal" (2012, 214–15).

Like the social forum, the *acampadas* were sites of contention—but also of information exchange, reciprocal learning, individual socialization, and knowledge building. In their discontent with mainstream politics, participants saw the occupations as occasions for experimenting with participatory and deliberative forms of democracy. As one activist wrote, "Democracy starts with people caring about one another and acting responsibly on that sense of care, taking responsibility both for oneself and for one's family, community, country, people in general and the planet" (quoted in Langman 2013). According to a speaker of a commission in Puerta del Sol, Madrid, "What unites us is a general dissatisfaction. We want a new model of society, based on the participation of all persons, an effective participatory democracy, where people can take part in decisions on the social, economic and political plans" (Nez 2012, 80).

For radicals, democracy is therefore a work in progress. While our practices often fall short of our ambitious aims, self-reflection allows us to learn from the mistakes of the past and experiment with innovative ideas.

SEE ALSO: Leadership; Liberal; Politics; Populism; Prefiguration; Representation; Rights; Sovereignty

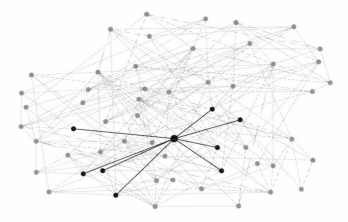

DOMINATION

Ruth Kinna

WHILE THERE IS DISAGREEMENT ABOUT ITS PRECISE definition, the prevailing view is that "domination" describes a form of power institutionalized in social and economic hierarchies and experienced through cultural bias. By this account, non-domination demands the equalization of power. An alternative view, common in historical anarchisms, is that domination is a type of unfreedom. These different conceptions support different strategies for change, with the first focused on processes that confront privilege and the second on activism against enslavement.

The Colours of Resistance Network's (CRN) "Definitions for the Revolution" has no entry for "domination"; however, they list it as a synonym for "oppression."

Accordingly, they define an oppressor as "one who uses her/his power to dominate another, or who refuses to use her/his power to challenge that domination." For CRN, "domination" is also linked to privilege, defined as "unearned social power accorded by the formal and informal institutions of society to ALL members of a dominant group (e.g., white privilege, male privilege, etc.)" The CrimethInc. Ex-Workers' Collective, in contrast, distinguishes domination from oppression. In "Undermining Oppression," they suggest that domination occurs "when an individual or group coerces, controls, or intimidates others" and that oppression describes "the systematic privileging of one group over another." While it is possible to imagine members of oppressed groups dominating the privileged, it is impossible "for a more privileged group to be oppressed by a less privileged group." Meanwhile, it is likely that the oppressed will also be dominated, though this is not spelled out in CrimethInc.'s account. In all these cases, "domination" is linked to privilege and defined as power. In "No Masters," CrimethInc. argues that the control of "domineering authorities"—landlords, employers, magistrates—is a power that supports hierarchy. This is also the way that Sam Clark defines the concept in *Living without Domination*. Here "domination" denotes a capacity to exercise power. Through the state, such power is distributed unevenly to centralize, monopolize, and create hierarchical systems (2007, 38, 76, 143).

Such usages of "domination" distinguish the critical politics of contemporary activism from historical movement struggles. Examining shifts in the postwar period, Cindy Milstein argues that "anarchists agree on the necessity of a world without capital and states" (2010, 35) but adds that the "generalized critique of hierarchy and domination" serves as "the prism" through which contemporary activist politics find expression (39). As anarchist author Uri Gordon puts it, "domination" designates "the paradigm which governs both micro- and macro-political relations" (2008, 32). As such, it is a generic concept for the "systematic features of society whereby groups and persons are controlled, coerced, exploited, humiliated, discriminated against, etc." (2008, 32).

Gordon explains the pervasiveness of "domination" in contemporary discourses of resistance as a result of the "convergences of radical feminist, ecological, anti-racist and queer struggles" in the late 1960s that fused during subsequent waves of global protest. He also points to the concept's generic application to describe multiple forms of "oppression, exclusion and control." In this view, the contemporary rejection of domination challenges and corrects anti-statist critiques, now deemed outmoded and associated with faulty conceptions of power. Domination does not reduce to class division, nor is it derived exclusively from law or realized through police, schools, and religious institutions. Instead, "domination" today refers to broader sociological and cultural processes. "Regimes of domination," Gordon notes, "are the overarching context that anarchists see as conditioning people's socialisation and background assumptions about norms, explaining why people fall into certain patterns of behaviour and have expectations that contribute to the perpetuation of dominatory relations." By identifying particular instances of domination, activists can work to "transcend specific antagonisms towards the generalised resistance that they promote" (2008, 31–33).

The term "domination," Mark Antaki notes, "comes from the Latin *dominus*, the master or lord of the household who rules over his household with absolute power." The related term *dominium* "designates ownership as well as rule over others. Accordingly, slavery appears as an instance, perhaps a key instance, of domination" (2010, 400). In ordinary language, "domination" has long been defined in the first sense, with reference to power. Conventional dictionary definitions describe it narrowly, typically with reference to church and state. Webster's 1828 *American Dictionary of the English Language* defines domination as the "exercise of power in ruling; dominion; government" or to "one highly exalted in power." Here it refers to the Christian hierarchy to describe "the fourth order of angelic beings." Various editions of the *Dictionnaire de L'Académie française* give comparable definitions. Also referring to the Christian hierarchy, the 1762 entry defines domination as "power, empire, sovereign authority." The 1913 *Webster's New*

International Dictionary of the English Language includes some modernizing inflections; although the references to the fourth order of angelic beings and to "the act of dominating; exercise of power in ruling; dominion; supremacy; authority" remain, "domination" now refers to a "ruling party; a party in power" as well. Moreover, the word is linked to the particular power of the tyrant or the absolute ruler. "Arbitrary authority" and "arbitrary or insolent sway" are included in the new definition. The 1762 and 1798 editions of the *Dictionnaire de L'Académie française* refer to the "domination of the Turk," playing to a cultural bias about the democratic predisposition of European peoples in order to underline the dangers of domination. Although the Orientalist prejudice was removed from the 1832 and 1932 editions, the concept's association with ideas of injustice, absolutism, and usurpation remains.

In this sense, "domination" describes the power of a master to deny liberty to others by instituting relations of dependence and reiterating the principle of ownership found in "*dominium.*" When Edmund Burke (1775) observed that the "haughtiness of domination combines with the spirit of freedom," he established "domination" as an antonym to slavery. For Burke, "domination" was the denial of liberty, epitomized in slavery, and the eagerness of masters to enslave others was by the same token a measure of freedom's value. Intervening in the independence debates of the 1770s, Burke judged the spirit of freedom to be higher in Virginia and the Carolinas than in the northern American states because people in the former regions owned a "vast multitude of slaves." His general observation was that "where this is the case in any part of the world, those who are free, are by far the most proud and jealous of their freedom."

Discourses of slavery and freedom such as these were prominent during the radical movements of the nineteenth century. "If there is a state," Michael Bakunin argued in *Statism and Anarchy*, "then necessarily there is domination, and consequently slavery. A state without slavery, open or camouflaged, is inconceivable—that is why we are enemies of the state" (1990, 178). This association of "domination" with slavery and the denial of freedom highlighted the continuity between absolutist and representative regimes, which conventional dictionary definitions keep apart. Peter Kropotkin made the same point—though he added that the institutions in which power was vested reinforced domination through culture and socialization. "During and after the revolutions, when the lawyers rose to power, they did their best to strengthen the principle upon which their ascendancy depended," he wrote. Correspondingly, because "the people received it as an improvement upon the arbitrary authority and violence of the past," they "bowed their neck beneath the yoke of law to save themselves from the arbitrary power of their lords."

> The middle class has ever since continued to make the most of this maxim. . . . It has preached this doctrine in its schools, it has propagated it in its writings, it has moulded its art and science to the same purpose, it has thrust its beliefs into every hole and corner—like a pious Englishwoman who slips tracts under the door—and it has done all this so successfully that today we behold the issue in the detestable fact that men who long for freedom begin the attempt to obtain it by entreating their masters to be kind enough to protect them by modifying the laws which these masters themselves have created! (1970, 199–200)

The historical transformation from chattel slavery to wage slavery, which also featured as a theme in Marx's work from the mid-nineteenth century, was a key to this particular understanding of "domination." Kropotkin condemned attempts by economists to represent "the enforced contract (under threat of hunger) between master and workingman as a state of freedom" since they obscured "the surviving influence of past centuries of serfdom and religious oppression." Political citizenship similarly meant being "a serf and a taxpayer of the State" (2014, 638). Although Kropotkin spoke primarily of "workingmen," it seems evident that the unfreedoms entailed by domination and slavery also encompass forms of oppression like racism, sexism, classism, heterosexism, anti-semitism, ableism, and ageism, which the CRN "Definitions for the Revolution" treat as power relations. For Selma James (2012), enslavement means being dependent on the will of another and being forced to do things contrary to one's own will. Although work is fundamental to slavery, James focuses her analysis on women's domestic enslavement to show how it colonizes life in particular ways. Here the struggle against enslavement is not solely a struggle for financial independence; instead, it is about factors including "abortion, sterilization, housework, rape, divorce, child custody and care, lesbianism, dress, personality, orgasms" (144–45).

Overcoming domination involves organizing. For Milstein (2010), the commitment to non-domination underpins an ethical, prefigurative politics designed to promote autonomy, community, and local control. It captures the fluid, practice-based dimensions of horizontal activism and underscores the commitment to enact changes in everyday life. For Kropotkin (1970), the struggle against domination involved the construction of alternative systems of production, distribution, and exchange in revolutionary union and community networks based on mutual aid and free agreement. Similarly, James' (2012) activism emphasized the importance of mobilizing against capitalism in community networks and work-place organizations. But despite the similarities in the objectives and approaches of these strategies, however, different conceptions of "domination" as either power or unfreedom give rise to distinctive practices. Where domination is linked to privilege, contemporary activists call for the adoption of practices that confront and address undeserved power advantages. In Gordon's terms, non-domination is about exercising "power with" rather than "power over" (2008, 49–55). It demands the adoption of forms of nonhierarchical, de-centralized, and consensus-based organization that can "uncover, challenge and erode" the dynamics of domination (2008, 32). From this perspective, and as the CRN makes clear, an important measure of non-domination is the willingness to organize "against our privilege" and not simply "against our oppression" (Colours of Resistance Network n.d.). For their part, CrimethInc. collective members note in "Undermining Oppression" that resisting domination means developing "the self-awareness to resist dominating social situations" while working simultaneously to "prevent others from dominating them." In their view, such a process is bound to be "emotionally intense and challenging" and likely to involve anger and guilt.

In contrast, where "domination" is defined as a condition of unfreedom or slavery, non-domination expresses itself as a strategy of resistance through which the enslaved take direct action against institutions and practices that deny freedom. This might be understood as a demand for autonomy, as has been argued by Daniel Colson (2001). Alternatively, it may be linked to the recognition of interdependence, a position favored by Martha Acklesberg (2010). In either case, however, overcoming domination depends on the willingness or ability of the dominated to defy the master. While this approach is compatible with the repertoires of action designed to address power advantages rooted in social privilege, it downplays the political significance of the advantages that accrue to individuals by virtue of their membership in particular social groups and focuses instead on the structural forces that undermine resistance.

SEE ALSO: Authority; Colonialism; Hegemony; Nature; Prefiguration; Privilege; Violence; War

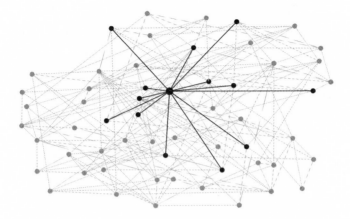

EXPERIENCE

Kate Kaul

"Experience" is built of two compounded prepositional prefixes. Its "ex" has a range of uses, applying to space ("out of," "from"), time ("immediately after," "since"), cause ("by reason of"), transition ("from being"), and means ("by means of"); it also distinguishes a part from a whole ("out of," "from among," "made of") (Traupman 1979). "Per" is "through," in the multiple senses of space ("through," "along"), time ("through," "during"), agency ("through," "by means of"), means ("through," "by") and—anticipating the claims-making function, the legal uses of "experience"—in oath ("by") (Traupman 1979).

More specifically, "experience" comes from Latin's *"experire"* ("to try," "to put to the test") and overlaps in early usages with "experiment," which shares the same origin. In this overlapping usage, "experience" was a testing-out, in the sense of "proof by actual trial." The *Oxford English Dictionary* tells us that this sense has passed into "the observation of facts or events, considered as a source of knowledge," but this learning by observation is difficult to separate from "experience" in another sense, describing "an event by which one is affected." Finally, "experience" is also the "knowledge resulting from actual observation or from what one has undergone." This etymology points to an interesting shift in the relationship between the subject and the world; in "experience" as experiment, the subject tests out a possibility and learns from observation—out of, and through, a trial, a testing, an observed event. Later (and still now), it is the subject and not the world outside that undergoes events, who goes through and emerges out of them, who is tested, changed. The subject observes not only the outside world, but also herself.

"Experience" thus simultaneously presents a claim to knowledge and a refusal of knowledge; its radical possibility lies in our ability to take this simultaneity seriously. In the March 25, 1978 entry of her *Cancer Journals*, Audre Lorde writes: "The idea of knowing, rather than believing, trusting, or even understanding, has always been considered heretical. But I would willingly pay whatever price in pain was needed, to savor the weight of completion; to be utterly filled, not with conviction nor with faith, but with experience—knowledge, direct and different from all other certainties" (1980, 24).

To claim "experience" is to claim knowledge and authority based on imminence and immersion, on identity and life lessons, rather than on expertise; however, it is also—as Lorde demands— to claim knowledge that moves from these immediacies, these events, into an awareness based on reflection and return, a knowledge that can only be collective. The "belief," "trusting," and "understanding" that Lorde opposes to "knowing" have often been considered heretical in an epistemology that opposes feelings to truth. It is "experience" as knowledge, at the end of Lorde's statement, which brings them together. Lorde's title, "Breast Cancer:

A Black Feminist Lesbian Experience," asserts that experience can be both individual ("A") and collective ("Black," "Feminist," "Lesbian"). Lorde's claim to experience as knowing brings an experience of breast cancer into Black, feminist, lesbian knowing; at the same time, it sets Black, feminist, lesbian knowing into a long, troubled, tradition of knowing and experience. The heresy lies not so much in Lorde's knowing through experience as in her bringing knowing, believing, trusting, and "even understanding" together.

In his *Keywords* entry on "experience," Raymond Williams presents the word's dual structure, its insistence on both immediacy and reflection. Williams distinguishes between "experience past" (lessons) and "experience present" (full and active awareness); the two are, he suggests, "radically different, yet there is nevertheless a link between them, in some of the kinds of action and consciousness which they both oppose" (1976, 127). At its most serious, "experience past" includes those processes of consideration, reflection, and analysis that the most extreme uses of "experience present" as unquestionable authenticity and immediacy exclude (128). "Experience past" (lessons) suggests that "experience present" (immediacy) constantly offers to the present the possibility of knowledge that has traditionally been understood as available through "experience past." As Williams suggests, there is a dialectic relationship between these two senses of experience. The etymology he offers demonstrates not a replacement of one sense by the other but, instead, a historical ambivalence in which the careful consideration of what has happened and a physical immediacy that defies consideration are set against each other.

Lorde is not alone in pointing out that writing, or expression, is the work that turns the things we live through into the knowledge we share with others—a knowledge she identifies with experience. Michel Foucault's (1991) notion of the "experience-book" recognizes that the production of knowledge from experience involves many more of us, and asks more of us, than any writer, reader, or actor, can anticipate. The experience-work that moves us from surviving events to thinking through them, from individual encounters to collective response, is discursive. As discourse, what has been said and what can be said about (and through) "experience" depends on relations of power and knowledge (Foucault 1972). Bringing knowledge, language, and power together, "experience" moves different kinds of subjects in and out of recognition and intelligibility.

At the first Disability Studies conference I ever attended, there was heated debate over whether able-bodied people should be working in Disability Studies. "I don't care who does this work, as long as they have the disability experience," a woman behind me said as the conference hallway around us filled with blind people, Deaf people, people with invisible disabilities, and (presumably) people without any. Standing in a crowd of unfamiliar bodies, I was thrown off balance by this statement. What was "the disability experience"? What was it in that moment? According to Mikhail Bakhtin, "there is no experience outside its embodiment in signs. It is not experience that organizes expression, but, to the contrary, expression that organizes experience, that, for the first time, gives it its form and determines its direction... Outside material expression, no experience. More, expression precedes experience; it is its cradle" (quoted in Todorov 1981, 43).

The "disability experience" to which the speaker referred was a claim to authenticity, to life lessons, to the immediacy of living with, or near, disabled bodies. But it was not only this; in offering me a term—a sign—for something I had not thought about, it asked me to pay attention to two questions: what was "the" disability experience? And what was this work that "we" needed to do?

Historian Joan Scott suggests approaching—rather than appealing to—experience and, instead of embracing it uncritically, "focusing on processes of identity production, insisting on the discursive nature of 'experience' and on the politics of its construction. Experience is at once always already an interpretation and something that needs to be interpreted" (1992, 797). This focus, this critical attention, is part of experience itself. And, in the discourse of "experience," no appeal to experience can be entirely reduced to "experience present" or "experience past"; each extends into the other.

Slogans like "the personal is political" and "nothing about us without us" present the urgency of appeals to "experience" and reveal the extent to which we need one another to understand and assert ourselves as individual subjects. In the context of disability rights activism, "nothing about us without us" makes the crucial claim that there is an "us," that "we" exist and have a collective opinion—or, at least, that we are a collective that includes opinions. "Nothing about us without us" points to the dual function of experience: living-through and making knowledge from. It also reminds us that the relationship between the personal and the political is corporeal—we live it, think it, experience it, through and in our bodies—and we experience not only as individuals but always in a social context (Kruks 2001, 149). Activists use "experience" as a way of understanding identity—sameness, collectivity— but the claims to experience that ground identity politics have taken many different forms. "What counts as experience is neither self-evident nor straightforward," Scott argues; "it is always contested, and always therefore political" (1992, 797). Whose experience counts (and, as a result, who counts) is also always contested, always political.

In Lorde's frame, the work of experience is collective, epistemological action; it produces knowledge. Violence can be felt individually, but oppression—like epistemology—is collective. Experience emphasizes perspective; the sense-making of "experience past" relies on the testimony (the account) of someone to whom things are happening, or have happened, in some "experience present." This extension from the collective to the individual, and from the individual to the collective, is the only way "experience past" can work and the only way "experience present" can mean. Who is that collective? Whether it is the Black feminist lesbians to whom Lorde extends her identification, the women she addresses in her memoir, or the reader she cannot anticipate, the collective is not defined in advance of or in anticipation of meaning-making; instead, it arises through it. For Bakhtin, the "utterance" is only recognizable when it ends with a response. In listening, recognizing, responding, we declare ourselves a "we" capable of experience.

For Giorgio Agamben (1993), along with language, "experience" marks the move from infancy to history; similarly, for

William Blake, "experience" is the end of innocence (Jay 2004, 1). As in Williams' formulation, these frameworks remind us that nothing yells "time" quite like experience. As imminence, "experience" is a being-in-the-present moment; however, experience is also the move from infancy and innocence into language and knowledge. Experience represents the impossibility we live: only ever in one moment, always aware of others, in a knowing that embodies this tension and is only possible through our awareness of time. Experience joins the urgency of the immediate to the lessons of the past, enabling our imagination of the future—and it is only this imagination that makes action possible in the present.

Like "experience," "radical" has a dramatic, dual, relationship to time. In its 21-page entry, the *OED* connects "radical" securely to "root": "relating to a root," "fundamental," "inherent." A radical medical treatment, then, is not necessarily a drastic one but one that is directed at the root cause of a disease. In connection to change or action, "radical" means: "going to the root or origin; touching upon or affecting what is essential and fundamental; thorough, far-reaching." Like "experience," then, "radical" reaches both backward and forward; radical action and radical knowing identifies what is fundamental to determine what must be changed. Like "radical," "experience" calls for a close attention to change, to authenticity, and to knowledge. It summarizes the work involved in bringing belief, understanding, and knowing together. Each present moment is a crystallization of this complicated path.

Claims to experience are claims to identity, knowledge, and community, but the notions of identity they appeal to are necessarily provisional, imperfect, and contested. Experience makes subjects but it also makes collectives—even if these are better described in terms of "allegiance" (Joyce 1987, 382) than of sameness or familiarity. Arguments that a transgender woman's experience is not and does not represent women's experience, and that a celebrity transgender transition is not and does not represent transgender experience, reenact the old drama of experience in which individual and collective can never neatly align. Despite fierce debates over whose experience counts (and who is counting), "experience" presents a way to value difference rather than to insist on sameness. If, as Sonia Kruks suggests, feminists orient toward the vast social differences between women rather than foregrounding "minimal commonalities," then focusing on experience may be a way toward "solidarity" rather than similarity (2001, 152).

An appeal to "experience" is always an attempt to connect individual experience to something collective—and it involves collision and failure as much as it does connection. Claims to experience may be imperfect; however, they are part of how we make sense of ourselves and one another, of how we make ourselves—and are made—in the world. We no longer think of "experience" as the experiment that a subject carries out on the world, learning from the results; in the twenty-first century, "experience" is something in which we are all entangled together.

SEE ALSO: Accountability; Agency; Authority; Bodies; Class; Community; Friend; History; Misogyny; Oppression; Politics; Queer; Space

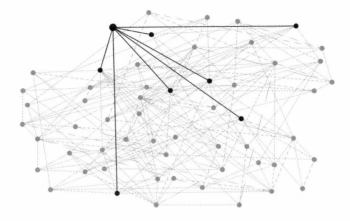

FRIEND

Simon Wallace

FRIENDS WERE LOVERS AND LOVERS WERE FREE. OLD
English knew no distinction between these words.
According to the *Oxford English Dictionary*, the verb
"*frī*" (or sometimes "*frīg*," which meant "to free from
bondage" and "to love") became a noun when the suffix
"*end*" was appended to it. Inspired by the Germanic
goddess of love Frigg (the namesake for Friday), a friend
was someone with whom one chose to develop a love relationship outside of and beyond networks of kin. Few
people, however, could have friends. Friendship depended on a measure of mobility and freedom that was only
available to those with legal entitlements; "*frī*" is also a
root of "freeborn," which denoted having rights of full

citizenship at birth (something that could not be claimed by slaves and those in servitude). Friends were exceptional and were markers of privilege, of a life beyond family.

The extraordinary character of the friend is apparent in early English literature. In ancient epics dating from the eighth to the eleventh centuries, friends were absent or played only minor roles when compared to those played by kings, fates, and gods. Narratives did not turn on friends, though heroes sometimes sought solace from their supra-kin relationships. According to literary historian Albrecht Classen, the friend relationship was important but primarily sentimental: "true friendship reaches the surface after all, especially in face of imminent death" (2011, 123). The friend was a rare, revered figure whose company was premised on the freedom to choose, with whom one developed great feelings of love, but who existed outside the sustaining dynamics of people's small communities.

The medieval period turned the friend into a disruptive figure. The first self-conscious political deployment of "friend" is found in the frith-guilds. Frith, a now obsolete relation to the word friend (also from "*frī*"), connoted peace and security. Frith-guilds were mutual-aid societies that sought to replicate family networks amongst friends during the economically and socially unstable period of the Norman Conquest, the eleventh-century invasion of England led by Norman the Conqueror. Frith-guilds produced and relied upon the friend to restructure life amongst previously disconnected people and, in so doing, bound people together along new lines (Kropotkin 1902, 145; Green 1881, 216).

During the fourteenth and fifteenth centuries, the English language was supplemented with several French words that parsed out aspects of "friend," narrowing its meaning. The word "love" was introduced, along with "amicable," "fidelity," and "filial." Linguistically, "friend" began to denote a more specific relationship, separate from romance and family.

The process of urbanization that coincided with capitalism's emergence heralded new spaces of social interaction. Forced into cities by enclosure and new economic imperatives, individuals found new horrors but new pleasures as well. Whereas the feudal lord controlled much of one's life, the proto-capitalist boss laid claim only to one's work. The pub, coffee house, and music hall emerged as people began to exercise more control over their own time and movements. And, unlike the Church or the Court, these new spaces functioned as "levellers." As urban sociologist Ray Oldenberg notes, "within these places, conversation is the primary activity and the major vehicle for the display and appreciation of human personality and individuality" (1999, 42).

Under such conditions, those with the freedom and compulsion to engage in the new public life began to orient more to the stranger than to the family member. New labor dynamics could bring two people into the same craftsman shop, or oblige another person to travel to a new, larger market. Meanwhile, the upper classes' increased idleness—financed by the wealth appropriated from others—prompted regular travel (for education, recreation, and business) across previously unimaginable distances; courts expanded, universities and garden parties proliferated.

By the time of Shakespeare, the friend held an important social position: Hamlet had Horatio and Rosencratz had Gildenstern. Whereas ancient heroes would call out to friends as they died, Mercutio's death drives *Romeo and Juliet* to its tragic conclusion. Indeed, as much as young free love, it is Romeo's cabal of chosen friends that tears at the power and proscriptions of ancient families. Shakespeare's work of historical fiction portended what was to come: close, non-familial networks challenging established networks of kin and power. The play ultimately resolves with the reconciliation of two great houses, illustrating a theme familiar to Shakespeare's audience: to survive the coming change in relations, power would have to consolidate and leave its old prejudices behind.

The emergence of friendly societies—large associations modeled on frith-guilds—induced a final major shift in meaning: "friend" came to denote not only close, amicable relationships between specific individuals, but also important connections between people who never had, and never would, meet. In reaction to the "charity" of the Poor Laws that first emerged in medieval times, friendly societies self-consciously invoked the idea of mutual aid, encouraged the pooling of resources, and united people who were vulnerable to similar emergent class-based calamities—the penniless death, the doctor's collections agent, the workplace injury. For their part, Quakers (founders of the Society of Friends) posited that, since all persons were friends with Christ, all persons could be friends. Radically egalitarian, Quaker doctrine contended that a pre-existing relationship with God could unite everyone (Moore 2013, 12).

The word's primary contemporary tension thus arose: "friend" denotes someone with whom you choose to cultivate a relationship of amity *and* someone with whom you are presumed to have amity by virtue of one or more similarities, which were not chosen. Importantly, these competing definitions both assume that the friend is a real person, and not an unrealizable theoretical figure. Whether friends are united by Christ, by working-class experience, or because they like interacting with each other, the friend is an actual person in a specific moment. The friend is someone with whom we relate because of who they are. This is in contrast to a comrade or a mentor: someone to whom we relate for what she—or we—might become.

In the twentieth century, Nazi jurist Carl Schmitt imbued the newer conception of the word with concrete political significance. For Schmitt (whom some leftists embraced as a leading critic of liberalism after World War II), all politics were reducible to the relationship arising from the distinction between friend and enemy. And, since politics presupposed struggle as its defining extreme case, he argued (as the friendly societies had before him) that friends would carry out the struggle. According to Schmitt, such friends were united by their national "form of existence" (1996, 27); although they were alike, they did not need to like—or even to know—each other personally.

The long ascendance of the friend—flipside to the erosion of the family as the basic economic relationship—reaches its apex with neoliberalism. Equipped with the ultimate power to choose, the liberal subject is encouraged to select their "social networks"; friendship is the modern relationship *par excellence*. Parents want their kids to treat them as friends. Friend dates are as common as romantic dates. Romantic partners are boyfriends and girlfriends. This dynamic is captured best by Facebook, which binds people with a few clicks. Just as "community" today is constituted not only on the basis of what is common but also through chosen identification, the neoliberal friend is a conscious and intentional creation—not to mention a verb, "friend me." In contrast to familial relationships based on obligations of "unconditional" love (or hate), contemporary friendships affirm people's individual agency.

Simultaneously, inferences that we are friends with strangers or, indeed, friends with everyone, have proliferated. Invitations to become a friend of the environment (or of the public broadcaster, health research, or symphony) are ubiquitous. In place of the desire to interact with like-minded people, we discover the desire to advertise the "profile" choices we make about the company (even the fictional company) we keep. "Friend" increasingly denotes illusory or distant acquaintances between people who never meet. Neoliberal friendship unites the concept's two strands (the stranger and the amiable relationship) but hollows out both; all relationships are now friend relationships.

Radicals recognize the danger of an economy that presents limitless opportunities to befriend while diminishing the quality of friendship itself. Often, the response is to double down on *meaningful* friendship—to acknowledge that capital would have us make friend after friend but none with real emotional or political significance. The radical friend thus harkens back to the original friend (the heroic figure existing beyond the dominant patterns and relationships that order contemporary life) while defining the basis of friendship as a shared political commitment to a different world. However, radicals have not escaped the word's legacy, and we deploy the word in two opposite but now-familiar ways.

Some aspire to have friendships that prefigure the world to be built. Along with family, the friend becomes a symbol of perseverance and an example of a basic human truth in need of cultivation. The contributors to the anthology *Don't Leave Your Friends Behind: Concrete Ways to Support Families in Social Justice Movements and*

Communities specifically link friend and family together as components of an ideal revolutionary strategy. Because activists can be caustic toward friend and family, the authors argue that it is necessary to "create new, nonhierarchical structures of support and mutual aid, and include all ages in the struggle for social justice…" (Law, 3). Indeed, to push back against neoliberalism, the friend is asked to reassume some of the concept's more traditional trappings, in which it exists as a supplement to family. Partly a riposte to the large, centralized movements of the nineteenth and twentieth century that tended to turn people into "masses," friend and family are appreciated in this formulation for their smallness, localness, and personal authenticity. Real feelings of human connectedness are seen as intrinsically valuable in a world that seems to foster their dissolution.

In this alternate activist use, the friend is a pre-made revolutionary subject. As the Crimethinc. Ex-Workers' Collective figures it, "if your idea of healthy human relations is a dinner with friends, where everyone enjoys everyone else's company, responsibilities are divided up voluntarily and informally, and no one gives orders or sells anything, then you are an anarchist, plain and simple" (2002, 4). More emblematic, however, is the Invisible Committee's *To Our Friends*. Throughout its pages, the authors consider the global revolts that arose in response to the 2008 economic crisis and ask why the insurrections had come but the revolution had not. Travelling the world, members of the Committee find conspiracy everywhere ("in building hallways, at the coffee machine, in the back of kebab houses, at parties, in love affairs, in prisons") that they interpret as the basis of "friendships [that] are forming a historical party in operation…" Of absolute significance is the fact that "the party to be built is the one that is already there." However, factionalism has prevented that party from producing revolution. The Invisible Committee's admonition is therefore clear: "our strategic intelligence comes from the heart and not the brain" (2015, 46) To wit: we must grasp our shared experience, and operate as friends. Echoing the sensibilities of the earlier friendly societies and of Schmitt's friend-enemy distinction, strangers can count as friends when they convey a shared understanding of how it is to be done.

Despite their differences, contemporary radical conceptions of the friend place the accent on emotional connection. This privileging of emotional connection is the most unique aspect of the contemporary radical friend. Although such a friend speaks to an optimistic politics (we are surrounded by revolutionary raw material!), perhaps a darker truth lurks in the innovation: we do not command a movement, we do not belong to mass parties, the ruling classes do not tremble at our utterances, we are without an institutional base—still, we will always have our friends.

SEE ALSO: Community; Experience; Liberal; Love; Prefiguration; Solidarity; War

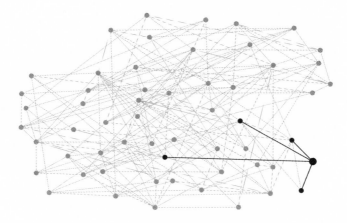

FUTURE

Rasheedah Phillips

THE WORD "FUTURE" DESIGNATES A TIME PERIOD OR temporal space that is not now, but that is situated ahead of us and is distinctive from times that precede the one in which we are currently situated. According to the *Oxford English Dictionary*, it developed out of Old French ("*futur*") during the late fourteenth century, when it denoted "a time after the present… yet to be." It derives from the Latin "*futurus*" via the stem "*fu-*" ("to grow" or "become"), which is the future participle of the word "*esse*" ("to be").[1]

---

1. Both "*esse*" and "*futur*" share "be" at their root," which may explain why the word "be-fore" can both denote an event that has already passed and is now in the past, or an event that has not yet happened.

Notions of the future—that which lies ahead—vary greatly. In traditional indigenous African spatiotemporal consciousness, time is experienced as a matter of "pacing" (akin to walking). Time begins when you arrive at your destination. African time also has a backwards linearity: when events occur, they immediately move backward to what John Mbiti (1990) calls "Zamani time" or "macrotime." All future events exist in "potential time" until experienced or actualized. These events do not depend on some specific clock time or calendar date; instead, time itself depends on the quality of the event and the person experiencing it. Once the future event is experienced, it instantaneously moves backward into the present and past dimensions. Those two dimensions bear the most ontological significance: "a person experiences time partly in his own individual life, and partly through the society which goes back many generations before his own birth" (Mbiti 1990, 17).

In contrast, traditional European spatiotemporal consciousness conceives of time as flow and inevitability. Abstract conceptions of time as a continuous duration first emerged during the fourteenth century, within the European Judeo-Christian order (Postone 2003, 203). In this context, Biblical apocalyptic visions of the end being near inspired strict regulation of work and prayer times.[2] As Jeremy Rifkin notes in *Time Wars*, "western culture has institutionalized its images of the future by way of religion and politics," making sure that "the future can be made predictable and controlled" (1989, 146–147). It is through religion and politics that a linear temporal orientation first came to be discerned, concurrent with the development of Western culture. The structure of time eventually came to be organized discretely and causally into a past, present, and future, with fixed events set against a forward moving timeline—one that would eventually come to a climactic, chaotic end. Born in northern Africa but buried in Italy, prominent religious philosopher Saint Augustine was among the first

---

2.   According to the *OED*, the word "time" uncertainly derives from the word "tide" or "tidiz", derived from the Sanskrit word for "division," "to cut up" or "to flood" (as in "the time of high water").

western thinkers to view Christianity-inspired, irreversible linear time as an important feature of his philosophy. In his *Confessions,* written in Latin around AD 400, Augustine asks, "How can... the past and future, *be,* when the past no longer is, and the future is not yet? As for the present, if it were always present and never moved on to become the past, it would not be time, but eternity" (1961, 264).

This progressive unidirectional future was subsequently consolidated through significant events in science and technology. As Gerhard Dohrn-Van Rossum notes, "Only since the scientific revolution in the middle of the seventeenth century can one speak of experimentally qualifying scientific procedures and conceptions of time as a scaled continuum of discrete moments" (1996, 287). The increased use of public clocks (and eventually of personal watches and timepieces) further inscribed a mechanical order of time, impacting all aspects of Western life.

Developed around 1854, the second law of thermodynamics reinforced the linear notion that time was speeding into the future toward a chaotic end. Meanwhile, significant temporo-historical events like the invention of the telegram and the construction of the first long distance railroads allowed people to conceive of the future in terms of conquest. Considering the relationship between "the future" and imperialism and colonialism, Stephen Kern notes how the "annexation of the space of others" and the "outward movement of people and goods" amounted to "spatial expressions of the active appropriation of the future" (2003, 92). In 1839, British Foreign Minister Lord Roseberry noted that the motivations for colonizing Africa were not about the present, "not what we want now, but what we shall want in the future" (Kern 2003, 92). Roseberry viewed the future as something to be mined; he and his fellow imperialists were engaged in the business of "pegging out claims for the future" as trustees "to the future of the race" (92).

In the US context, both during and after slavery, "the future" offered a potential source of hope in the struggle against racial oppression. On July 4, 1852, abolitionist and former slave

Frederick Douglass attacked the hypocrisy of Independence Day, observing that "America is false to the past, false to the present, and solemnly binds herself to be false to the future." Consequently, it was liable to commit the same atrocities it had inflicted against those it had enslaved against humanity more broadly. Decades later, in 1892, he told a group of Black students at Atlanta University: "Be not discouraged. There is a future for you and a future for me" (Hamilton 2002, 117). Marcus Garvey, founder of the Universal Negro Improvement Association, ensured his followers that "we have a beautiful history, and we shall create another in the future that will astonish the world" (Garvey 2012, 6).

At the turn of the century, the avant-garde Italian social movement known as "Futurism" attempted to revolutionize notions of the future in art, architecture, literature and culture. Believing that the reverential cult of tradition should die, they created manifestos, artwork, music, and critical theory to capture a future that was rapidly speeding toward them. Much like Einstein's relativistic future, the Futurists' future had run into *now*. Or, as Filippo Marinetti wrote in his *Manifesto of Futurism*, "Time and Space died yesterday" (1909). In the "Manifesto of Futurist Painters," Boccioni et al. (1910) declared that "the triumphant progress of science makes profound changes in humanity inevitable." In their view, such changes were "hacking an abyss between those docile slaves of past tradition and us free moderns, who are confident in the radiant splendor of our future." They embraced a violent, clashing, chaotic, technological future—one that was constantly changing and perpetually at war with its own ideas. Because the future was transient, there could be no permanent buildings, monuments, or empires.

Notions of the future have virtually defined the modern day genre of science fiction. Following the Victorian era of wonder, space travel, and high technology, these future visions began to take on a dystopian tone. H. G. Wells spent much of his career time traveling into dystopian futures through fiction, essays, and speeches. Meanwhile, George Orwell's novel *Nineteen-Eighty Four* famously warned that "who controls the past controls the future; who controls the present controls the past" (1950, 37). The imaginations of science fiction writers have both been stimulated by and contributed to developments in science and technology. Indeed, many sci-fi writers are scientists, or are consulted by scientists when their work predicts the future or thinks up new possibilities and uses for technology.

One inevitable consequence of the rapidly changing future envisioned by the Italian Futurists and illustrated by science fiction is what Alvin Toffler called "Future Shock": the "shattering stress and disorientation that we induce in individuals by subjecting them to too much change in too short a time" (1970, 11). According to Toffler, the greatly accelerated rate of social and technological change in our society produced mostly negative personal and psychological consequences, which arose from "the superimposition of a new culture on an old one" and produced a form of culture shock from which the victim cannot recover (11). This was what Marinetti and the Italian Futurists wished for: a "future now," permanently split from the past, and brought about by a violent expansion of the scope of change. For Toffler, we were racing too far into the future, too quickly.

The term "future shock" itself spread through popular culture, theory, and media after the release of Toffler's book. In 1973, Curtis Mayfield released his song "Future Shock," which Herbie Hancock covered as a title track in 1983—a jazz-funk-electronic fusion that was considered futuristic for its time. For Mayfield, future shock entailed a world of poverty, drug addiction, hunger, and desperation:

> When won't we understand
> This is our last and only chance
> Everybody, it's a future shock

His words evoke a "presentism time orientation,"—the darker side of "the future is now." This represents how oppressed people today, particularly the descendants of enslaved Africans, embody temporal tensions, a disunity between cultural notions of time.[3]

Today this temporal orientation is connected to class, poverty, oppression, racism, and the legacy of slavery. Maintaining presentism over futurism has been both a defense against Black communal trauma under conditions of class warfare and racial oppression deriving from slavery as well as a harkening back to a more natural, ancestral temporal-spatial consciousness. Michelle M. Wright cautions that, "if we use the linear progress narrative to connect the African continent to Middle Passage Blacks today, we run into a logical problem, because our timeline moves through geography chronologically, with enslavement taking place at the beginning, or the past, and the march toward freedom moving through the ages toward the far right end of the line or arrow, which also represents the present" (2015, 57).

In a similar vein, Jeremy Rifkin explains that use of the linear progress narrative among oppressed peoples keeps them "confined in a narrow temporal band, unable to anticipate and plan for their own future . . . powerless to affect their political fate." For those deprived of access to the future, they become stuck planning for the present while the society around them speeds forward in illusory, linear progress. The future thus becomes "untrustworthy [and] unpredictable" (1989, 192). This narrow temporal band is used to penalize people; being ten minutes late to court, for example, can mean losing your job, kids, home, and freedom. Hierarchies of time and lack of access to the future inform intergenerational poverty in the same way that wealth passes between generations in

---

3. Usage of the "presentism time orientation" is class and race-based. It has been recently appropriated by New Age philosophy (being "present" in meditation); however, when presentism is applied to Black people, it is often cited negatively. In this view, Black people are seen as lacking a sense of future and thus concerned solely with present pleasures and immediate concerns. In studies on increased presence of heart disease in African Americans, for example, "presentism time orientation" is often cited as one of the causal factors. African Americans with a present-time orientation "may not see the need to take preventative medication or to finish antibiotics when symptoms disappear," or "may delay seeing a physician until symptoms are severe, and begin interfering with their work or life" (Cunneen n.d.).

traditionally privileged families. In a famous speech given at the Founding Rally of the Organization of Afro-American Unity in 1964, Malcolm X attempted to address this imbalance by under-scoring how "education is the passport to the future, for tomorrow belongs to those who prepare for it today."

For his part, Toffler identified change as "the process by which the future invades our lives" (1970, 3). Relying on a similar concep-tion, Barack Obama structured his entire 2008 presidential cam-paign around "change," using it as a slogan to appropriate a specific vision of America's future. In 2009, he boldly told a joint session of Congress that, "we did not come to fear the future. We came here to shape it." In a 2011 interview, Obama was asked, "If hope and change defined the 2008 campaign, what words are going to define 2012?" In response, he said "what'll define 2012 is our vision for the future." His 2012 campaign slogan, "Forward," appropriates the same visionary, future temporality.

How do we begin to map our return to our own futures? One way that contemporary radicals can more affirmatively claim or create the future is by actively engaging temporalities and adopt-ing alternative temporal orientations and frameworks. This, in turn, helps to shift the meaning or placement of the future and shifts the means of accessing it. As Rifkin notes, "the new time rebels advo-cate a radically different approach to temporality" (1989, 12). In this spirit, the concept and community of "Afrofuturism" has emerged over the last twenty years as a tool, medium, and lens with which marginalized Black communities across the diaspora might evaluate and shape our futures. According to Ingrid LaFleur, Afrofuturism is "a way of imagining possible futures through a black cultur-al lens" (quoted in Womack 2013, 9). For D. Denenge Akpem, it is "an exploration and methodology of liberation, simultaneously both a location and a journey" (2011). Along with Afrofuturism, a number of other alternative movements have emerged over the past few years (e.g., Chicano futurism, Queer futurism, and Crip futurity) to appropriate or redefine notions of "future" while actively exploring what the future might look like for marginalized people. For its part, Afrofuturism lends itself well to exploring pathways to liberation, unearthing our true histories, mapping our futures, and understanding our present conditions in the flow of time. Because it provides a perpetual bridge between the past, present, and future, Afrofuturism and the Black speculative imagination can be used as liberation technologies to build future worlds.

SEE ALSO: History; Hope; Prefiguration; Utopia

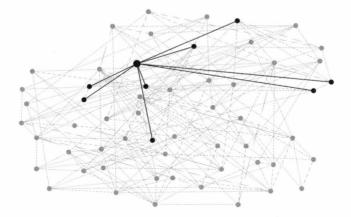

GENDER

Tammy Kovich

DESIGNED BY THE FEMINIST ARTIST BARBARA KRUGER, the poster used to promote the massive pro-choice rally that descended on Washington DC on April 8, 1989, read: "Your Body Is a Battleground." Indeed, our bodies are both the vehicles through which we engage the world and the medium through which the world affects us. At times functioning as a site of discipline and regulation, at others acting as a site of resistance and liberation, the body marks a fundamental plane of political struggle. Within the context of contemporary radicalism, "gender" is key to understanding this battleground. As defined by Heckert, gender is "a system of categorizing ourselves and each other (including bodies, desires, and behaviours) running through every aspect of culture and society, and intertwining with other categories and hierarchies (race, class, sexuality, age, ability, and so much more)" (2012, 1). Conceptualized broadly as pertaining to how bodies are experienced, categorized, and inscribed with meaning, "gender" exists as a system of social organization with far-reaching implications.

Predominantly associated with women at the height of the feminist movements of the 1960s and 1970s, the term "gender" has since "come to collate much of what the category of women is said to exclude: from men, masculinity, and queer sexualities to trans and intersex identities and analysis" (Wiegman 2012, 38). Including—but not limited to—considerations of women's subordination, "gender" is now deployed in more inclusive ways to reflect the complex and constitutive interactions between identity, sex, sexuality, and power relations. The term is invoked both to examine and to challenge the various ways in which interpretations of particular bodies correspond to systemic oppression. Under the broad umbrella of "gender activism," radicals work on issues as diverse as ensuring reproductive self-determination, fighting violence against women, supporting trans* prisoners, challenging heterosexist social conventions, and advocating for the rights of sex workers (Pan 2013).

According to the *Oxford English Dictionary*, the word "gender" has been in use since the fourteenth century as a grammatical term denoting nouns variously classed as masculine, feminine, or neuter. In "Gender: A Useful Category of Historical Analysis," feminist author Joan Scott (1986) notes that the term's "connection to grammar is both explicit and full of unexamined possibilities." She explains: "explicit because the grammatical usage involves formal rules that follow from the masculine or feminine designation; full of unexamined possibilities because in many Indo-European languages there is a third category—unsexed and neuter" (1053). With its root in the Old French "*gendre*" (modern "*genre*"), the term also suggests a system of classification and the refinement of particular styles. Expanding beyond the consideration of grammatical and literary-aesthetic categories, "gender" took on broader usage in the mid-twentieth century to encompass questions pertaining to sex and sexual difference.

Ever since the publication of Simone de Beauvoir's *Second Sex* in 1949, feminists have argued that one is not born but made a woman. From this perspective, "woman" is an ideological construction reproduced through political and economic institutions, disciplinary mechanisms, and micro-level interactions. This observation set the stage for the subsequent adoption and broad use of the term "gender." During this period, the term was also introduced into the lexicon of medical and psychoanalytic researchers studying sexual pathologies (Mann 2012, 69). Initially used to describe people's subjective understanding of their sex as it related to their biological anatomy, "gender" rapidly developed as a concept used to "contest the naturalization of sexual difference in multiple arenas." As feminist author Donna Haraway has noted, it served both to "explain and change historical systems of sexual difference, whereby 'men' and 'women' are socially constituted and positioned in relations of hierarchy and antagonism" (1991, 131). Marked by contestation, "gender" became an analytic tool to counter claims that presupposed natural or biological bases for either sex differences or the hierarchies they yielded.

The publication of Ann Oakley's *Sex, Gender, and Society* in 1972 provided a critical account of research done on the differential psychology of the sexes. One of the first works to deploy "gender" in a systematic way, Oakley offered the following definition: "'Sex' is a word that refers to the biological differences between male and female: the visible difference in genitalia, the related difference in procreative function. 'Gender' however is a matter of culture: it refers to the social classification into 'masculine' and 'feminine'" (Oakley 1985, 16). Critiquing positions maintaining that women's differences from men were biologically determined, Oakley argued that psychological differences between sexes were the result of social conditioning. Commenting on this work in "Rethinking Sex and Gender," Delphy noted that, while Oakley found that a division of labor based on sex was universal, "the content of the tasks considered to be feminine or masculine varies considerably according to the society" (1993, 3). In this view, "gender" is socially determined and based on the exaggeration of what would otherwise amount to minimal biological sex differences.

Published three years after *Sex, Gender, and Society*, Gayle Rubin's "The Traffic in Women: Notes on the Political Economy of Sex" continued examining the production of gender. In this influential essay, Rubin introduced the concept of a "sex/gender system," which she described as "the set of arrangements by which a society transforms biological sexuality into products of human activity, and in which these transformed sexual needs are satisfied" (1975, 287). As Haraway noted, Rubin viewed the sexual division of labor and the psychological construction of desire to be the foundations of a system that turned females into "the raw materials for the social production of women" (1991, 137). Updating this perspective, McCann and Kim have argued that the sex/gender system "takes the raw material of human babies/bodies and produces gender-differentiated beings with complementary skills and personalities" (2013, 15).

Following a similar logic to Rubin's in her essay "One Is Not Born a Woman," Monique Wittig (2012) theorized the relationship between *the myth of woman* and compulsory heterosexuality. Presenting sexuality as the foundation of gender, Wittig argued that "woman" emerged through a relationship of categorical dependence upon man. As Haraway explains, "what makes a woman is a specific relation of appropriation by a man. Like race, sex is an 'imaginary' formation of the kind that produces reality. . . . 'Woman' only exists as this kind of imaginary being, while women are the product of a social relation of appropriation, naturalized as sex" (1991, 138). Within this framework, Wittig argued that the task of materialist feminists was to destroy "the class of women within which men appropriate women." For Wittig, this project was to be accomplished through "the destruction of heterosexuality as a social system which is based on the oppression of women by men and which produces the doctrine of difference between sexes to justify this oppression" (2012, 250). The idea of women as a natural group is destroyed through the creation of a lesbian society operating outside of heterosexuality's political economy.

Interrogating the limitations of dominant scientific thought in *The Science Question in Feminism*, Sandra Harding (1986) set out to challenge the androcentrism of science. In the process, she contributed to the further conceptual development of "gender." Asserting that "our social and natural worlds" themselves arose in relation to "gender meanings" (17), Harding outlined the means by which gender has been produced and maintained through several interrelated processes: ascribing meaning via the assignment of dualistic metaphors to perceived dichotomies (gender symbolism); appealing to gender dualisms to divide and organize social activities (gender structure); and, finally, as a form that constructs individual identity (individual gender). By highlighting these various elements, Harding emphasized the symbolic, institutional, and personal implications of gender.

The concept of gender continued to develop during the 1990s. Contributions such as Judith Butler's (1990) *Gender Trouble* presented "gender" variously as a matter either of performance or of performativity. For Butler, "gender" is realized "through a stylized repetition of acts" (179). At the same time, however, "there need not be a 'doer' behind the deed," since "the 'doer' is variably constructed in and through the deed" itself (181). Unstable and contradictory, "gender" in this account becomes a cultural ideal created and perpetuated through the repeated performance of specific signs and norms that simultaneously constitute the actor who enacts them. Although feminists had been asserting for decades that gender was a social construct, it was widely held that biological sex constituted a fixed foundation upon which gender roles were subsequently elaborated. This presumption was challenged, however, as activists and scholars began arguing that "even the body and its sexed components (such as genitals, gonads, chromosomes, secondary sex characteristics, hormones, and so forth) are given shape and meaning by pre-existing beliefs about gender" (Mann 2012, 249). Writing at *She Is Revolutionarily Suicidal*, Shanice McBean noted: "The realization of biological potentials is shaped by social environment. . . . our biological features and capacities have a fundamentally social interpretation, meaning and value. Hence not even sex—with its basis in biology—is a fixed or immutable part of nature." Unsettling the assumption that biological sex is pre-social, queer and transgender theorists began to challenge the idea of a gender binary in which humans exist in one of two essential forms—male or female. For example, in the zine *Politicizing Gender: Moving toward Revolutionary Gender Politics*, Carolyn (1993) points out that "people who do not fit into the gender binaries of female and male have always been with us."

In "Transgender Liberation: A Movement Whose Time Has Come" (2006), Leslie Feinberg presented the case of those who transgress the gender binary. Exploring the histories of those whose self-expression "is 'at odds' with their sex" (150), Feinberg argued that, although those who present non-normative gender configurations have been subject to intense repression, transgender individuals have always existed. Refuting the assumed connection between the biological body and gender, Feinberg defined "gender" as a matter of "self-expression, not anatomy" (148). Proceeding along similar lines, Emi Koyama argued in "The Transfeminist Manifesto" that "we construct our own gender identities based on what feels genuine, comfortable and sincere to us as we live and relate to others within a given social and cultural constraint" (2003, 251). Having disentangled gender from both social constructs and biology, J. Rogue found that "gender can only be defined by individuals for themselves—or perhaps we need as many genders as there are people, or even further, that gender should be abolished" (2012, 29). This may entail living as a member of a sex different from the one assigned at birth (transsexual), identifying outside of the male/female binary altogether (genderqueer), moving freely between genders (gender-fluid), or any other manifestation of gender variance that deviates from prescribed norms.

The evolution of "gender" has unearthed important considerations for political struggle. By expanding and problematizing our understanding of sexual difference and its repercussions, current usage speaks to the seemingly endless possibilities of doing gender. Liberating us from binary constraints, "gender" is now presented in many radical circles as a site of playful experimentation in which people might create gender in line with their specific desires and inclinations. While previous iterations emphasized the interplay between gender, structural relations, and social organization, current iterations largely gloss over these connections. This is a problem. In "She Came to Riot," Jennifer Pan (2013) notes that contemporary approaches to gender struggles run "the risk of diluting feminism to bumper-sticker banalities, rather than constituting a serious political force, let alone revolution." Detached from considerations of material groundings and social relations, current usage reflects a conceptualization of gender as something rooted primarily in individual choices and actions. However, there is nothing about gender transgression or deviance that is in itself revolutionary.

Indeed, our political system can assimilate any number of supposedly subversive identities, while capitalism easily commodifies them. As noted by an anonymous author in *Baeden 1: Journal of Queer Nihilism*, "There is nothing about the production of new genders and sexualities that resists capitalism; to the contrary, this production is fertile terrain for new economic growth" ("Identity in Crisis" 2012, 137). Drawing on the work of *Theorie Communiste*, they argue that "through struggle, one must reach the point at which it becomes impossible to both continue to struggle and to maintain one's self" (139). Along with race and class, "gender" is thus presented as that which must be abolished. This cannot be accomplished through the individual expression of what feels "genuine, comfortable and sincere" alone. As a system of classification that organizes the world's matter in accordance with particular productive principles, "gender" cannot be liberated without broader collective struggle. Understanding "gender" as a relation rooted in social and symbolic organization implies that gender is altered and potentially destroyed only by attacking the material processes and institutions that generate gendered subjects.

SEE ALSO: Bodies; Class; Labor; Misogyny; Queer; Race; Reproduction; Trans*/–

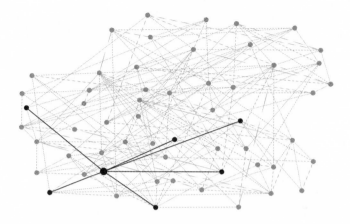

HEGEMONY

Richard Day

Like so much in the Western tradition, the concept of "hegemony" originated in Ancient Greece, where the term "*hegemonia*" was used in a variety of contexts and with various shades of meaning. In one of its common deployments, a "hegemon" denoted a leader or commander, as in the "Catalogue of Ships" recounted in Book II of Homer's *Iliad*, which listed the leaders of the formidable Archaean army that sailed on Troy. Featured in this list are many of the great heroes we continue to know today, including Odysseus, Ajax, Achilles, and Menelaus. This historical connection between "hegemony" and "leadership" subsequently becomes codified in the *Oxford English Dictionary*, which marks "hegemony" as originating during the sixteenth century from the Greek "*hegemon*" ("leader") and from "*hegeisthai*" ("to lead").

In this usage, hegemony implies consent—or at least acceptance—of the primacy of one individual over others within a community. In such contexts, the concept might best be translated as "leadership." However, by drawing on Liddell and Scott's canonical *Greek-English Lexicon* (1968), which has provided a comprehensive lexicographical overview of Ancient Greek since the nineteenth century, political scientist David Wilkinson has suggested that "*hegemonia*" often "carried a weightier meaning" (2008, 122). Indeed, "power, leadership, command, supremacy, dominance, dominion, lordship, sovereignty, empire: classical *hegemonia* sits somewhere in their company" (2008, 124). Consequently, "the entry for *hegemonia* in the 'middle Liddell' [the second condensed version of the lexicon, first published in 1889]" read as follows:

> hêgemonia . . . [II.2] the hegemony or sovereignty of one state over a number of subordinates, as of Athens in Attica, Thebes in Boeotia—*the hegemony of Greece was wrested from Sparta by Athens; and the Peloponn[esian] war was a struggle for this hegemony.* (quoted in Wilkinson 2008, 122)

This is why the Athenians lamented "the Spartan Hegemony" as an exceptional time during which they were governed by someone other than themselves.[1] Not another class, or even another nation—Spartans, Thebans, and Macedonians were all Greeks, after all—but a political formation that deprived the governed of meaningful participation in their government. As a mode of political relationship between city-states in Ancient Greece, "hegemony" was very clearly seen as an imposition of rule from outside, achieved and maintained through violence.

---

1. Of course, when it was the Athenians who had the upper hand, they assumed this was because of their excellent leadership qualities. For example, Aristotle saw armed force as being justified in securing hegemony in foreign affairs if one was not acting despotically, but "for the benefit of those who are ruled" (quoted in Keyt 1993, 144).

According to intellectual historian Perry Anderson, it was the Russian Marxists Georgi Plekhanov and Pavel Axelrod (Anderson 1976a, 16) who introduced discussions of "hegemony" into modern social and political theory near the beginning of the twentieth century.[2] The concept was subsequently picked up by Lenin, who argued in 1911 that the proletariat "must be the leader in the struggle of the whole people for a fully democratic revolution. . . . The proletariat is revolutionary only in so far as it is conscious of and gives effect to this idea of the hegemony [*gegemoniya*] of the proletariat" (1963, 232–33). In the hands of Lenin and his predecessors, "hegemony" shifts away from referring either to individual leaders or to inter–city-state domination. Instead it comes to refer to the leadership of "the whole people" by one group within a national state formation. Moreover, rather than being an external imposition upon an otherwise democratic process within a given political formation, the struggle for hegemony came to be viewed as a normal, internal part of the revolutionary-democratic process itself.[3]

While the inflexion given to the concept by the Russian Marxists had a lasting impact, Antonio Gramsci's subsequent elaboration came to dominate the meaning of "hegemony" during the second half of the twentieth century. According to Lenin, revolutions required both violence and hegemony (as leadership) by one class over "the whole people." This formulation implied that establishing hegemony was not itself a violent process—the violence was in the revolution. In contrast, Gramsci argued that—in the context of struggles within a national-state formation—establishing hegemony necessarily required both democratic consent *and* violent coercion. By his account, a group seeking "supremacy" must "lead" kindred and allied groups who recognize and accept

---

2. David Wilkinson (2008, 120), however, presents quite convincing evidence that scholars such as J. C. F. Manso (writing on the Spartan *Hegemonie* in German) and Groen van Prinsterer (on the Athenian *hegemonia*) were using the term in a similar way to the Russians, in the early nineteenth century.

3. This is not to say that Lenin denied the necessity of a violent component in what he called the Social Democratic revolution. In his discussion of the notion of the "withering away" of the state, he argues very clearly that, for Marx and Engels, "[t]he supersession of the bourgeois state by the proletarian state is impossible without a violent revolution" (1964a, 405).

its moral, intellectual, and political superiority (1971, 57–58). For those who do not display this recognition, however, the hegemonic group must deploy "the apparatus of state coercive power which 'legally' enforces discipline on those who do not consent either actively or passively" (1971, 12). In times of "crisis," Gramsci argued, a group seeking hegemony might even strive to "liquidate" antagonistic groups using armed force (1971, 57). Here the disparate elements, meanings, and contexts of "hegemony" discussed thus far become fused into a self-conscious whole.

At the same time, Gramsci's theory also brought an important new inflection to the concept. In his view, every human community always already contained a hegemonic force. By this account, even before the Spartans managed to put the Athenians under their thumb, the latter were already being dominated—by *themselves*. For Gramsci, since hegemony amounted to a pluralized play of antagonistic forces within the boundaries of a nation-state, the natural and inevitable result was that "only one" of the contending forces would "tend to prevail" and "propagate itself throughout society" through control of the state apparatus (1971, 181).

This is the meaning of hegemony that is most common today. It is ascribed to that which is dominant and maintains a relative sway over the thoughts, actions, and habits of everyday people within a given geographic-administrative space. But while it establishes an enveloping narrative with very little in the way of "choice" at any point along the way, "hegemony" itself is not static. Totalizable in the abstract, it always remains partial and relative under concrete circumstances.

Gramsci's theory of hegemony became the bedrock of Western Marxism—an eclectic grouping of ideas that Anderson (1976b) contended turned away from revolutionary politics to embrace what Lenin would surely have called reformism. In a coterminous move toward reformism, rather than seeking state power in the name of a proletariat-led revolution, twentieth-century social-democratic parties aimed instead to mute capitalism's worst effects by rewarding workers with decent wages and working conditions. As Anton Pannekoek put it, "the conquest of political power by the proletariat became," for social-democratic bureaucrats, "the conquest of a parliamentary majority by their Party, that is, the replacement of the ruling politicians and State bureaucracy by themselves" (1927, 4).

The shift away from revolutionary politics during the inter-war period was accompanied by a shift in the understanding of hegemony, which came increasingly to be viewed as "cultural" and "consensual" in nature. This is not to suggest, however, that the theorists of the time entirely forgot the coercive aspect of hegemony as analyzed by Gramsci (the best among them most definitely gave a nod in this direction). It is, rather, a matter of nuance. Beginning with Stuart Hall's Gramscian reading of hegemonic culture, the following series of moves drawn from media theorist Dick Hebdige's influential late-twentieth-century analysis of youth subcultures might be taken as exemplary: "The term hegemony refers to a situation in which a provisional alliance of certain social groups can exert 'total social authority' over other subordinate groups, *not simply by* coercion or by the direct imposition of ruling ideas, but by 'winning and shaping consent so that the power of the dominant classes appears both legitimate and natural'" (Hall 1977, quoted in Hebdige 1993, 366, emphasis added).[4]

Here the "coercive" moment of hegemony as understood by Gramsci is acknowledged; however, this acknowledgement is simultaneously displaced through Hebdige's reference to the work of Marx and Engels, in which he writes: "The ruling ideas are *nothing more than* the ideal expression of the dominant material relationships grasped as ideas; hence of the relationships which make the one class the ruling class, therefore the ideas of its dominance" (1993, 365, emphasis added). Finally, the displacement of the coercive moment of hegemony is installed directly into Gramsci's analysis: "This is the basis of Antonio Gramsci's theory of *hegemony*

---

4. Hebdige here cites Stuart Hall, who was to a great extent responsible for the resurgence of interest in the concept of hegemony in the 1980s. It is important to acknowledge that Hall was always aware of the dual nature of Gramsci's concept, which involved both coercion and consent. It is also important to acknowledge that the move made by most practitioners of Cultural Studies (the move toward a "merely cultural" understanding of hegemony), was often made, as I have shown with the example from the work of Dick Hebdige, through a reliance on Hall's work.

which provides the most adequate account of how dominance is sustained in advanced capitalist societies" (Hebdige 1993, 365).

This is the reading of Gramscian theory that came to permeate Cultural Studies, where it intermingled with the burgeoning politics of identity associated with the "new social movement" struggles of the 1960s and 1970s. With the publication of Ernesto Laclau and Chantal Mouffe's *Hegemony and Socialist Strategy* in 1985, the field of action was extended beyond the working class to encompass anyone with a grievance against the existing order. Meanwhile, the physically coercive aspect of the struggle for hegemony disappeared entirely. Instead of seeking to "liquidate" staunch adversaries as Gramsci had proposed, political actors were said to strive for the "articulation" of interests that—though they were conceived into being (i.e., rather than being discovered as preexisting)—could nevertheless serve as points of common identification. In this view, "hegemonic transitions" are "fully dependent on political articulations and not on entities constituted outside the political field—such as 'class interests'. Indeed, politico-hegemonic articulations retroactively create the interests they claim to represent" (Laclau and Mouffe 1985, xi).

In plainer language, hegemonic articulation refers to a process by which a particular demand can connect with and come to encompass a whole network of related demands, thus universalizing (and hegemonizing) them. The practical ramifications of Laclau and Mouffe's analysis could be seen in the "movement of movements" that converged to fight corporate globalization at the beginning of the twenty-first century. The more recent Occupy and *indignado* movements operated according to similar premises.

Laclau and Mouffe's "hegemony" bears the marks of the Western Marxism and Cultural Studies traditions in that, rather than trying to *take* state power, the agents of hegemonic articulation are said merely to want to *influence* its flows. Consequently, many Marxists (e.g., Geras 1987, Bertram 1995) argued that Laclau and Mouffe's theory abandoned the revolution and wandered sadly into the territory of liberal reformism. This apparent "retreat from class" (Wood 1999) would soon be taken even further. With the concept of "post-hegemony" developed by Scott Lash (2007) and Jon Beasley-Murray (2010), the Western Marxist tradition had been fully deconstructed, with representation and even discourse being supplanted by affective, biopolitical, unconscious actors.

Since the beginning of the twenty-first century, the theory and practice of non-hegemonic (Day 2005) or prefigurative (Graeber 2004) modes of struggling for social change have gained traction in the radical scene, especially among anarchists and autonomous Marxists. Unlike their counter- or anti-hegemonic counterparts, these struggles focus on the creation of alternative spaces and on living, here and now, the life that one wishes to lead without mediation by the state or other apparatuses of power. With their "one no and many yeses," the Zapatistas are the iconic movement-image of this approach. Examples of this politics in action also include the land occupations of the Landless Rural Workers' Movement (MST) in Brazil and the recovered enterprises of Argentina. More broadly, they find symptomatic expression in the negative slogan *"Que Se Vayan Todos!"* ("They all must go!"), which was advanced in Argentina during the struggles of December 19 and 20, 2001. These struggles culminated in then-president Fernando de la Rúa fleeing the Casa Rosada by helicopter.

Proponents of non-hegemonic modes of social change do not deny the existence of currently hegemonic structures and systems; indeed, they know these exist and are quite wary of their interventions. But rather than trying to take over the structures of power, prefigurative actors seek to render them redundant and ward off their reemergence. It could be argued that these new currents are simply in denial of the fact that they themselves are involved in a struggle for hegemony with the very logic of hegemony itself, and that they are therefore validating the very process they wish to overcome. Similarly, it could be said that those who want to work hegemonically are displaying an autonomous orientation toward those with whom they must articulate to achieve their aims. Considering these possibilities, it becomes clear that hegemony and autonomy are locked in an intimate embrace and that each cannot do without the other. Still, there are rumblings of a new meta-logic, one that treats hegemony and autonomy not as ideological deadweights but as tools to be deployed where they can be most efficacious. "Instead of erecting a wall between horizontalism and hegemonic processes," writes Yannis Stavrakakis, "wouldn't it be more productive to study their irreducible interpenetration, the opportunities and the challenges it creates?" (2014, 121). To this I can only respond: yes, indeed, I think it would.

SEE ALSO: Authority; Domination; Intellectual; Leadership; Prefiguration; Sovereignty

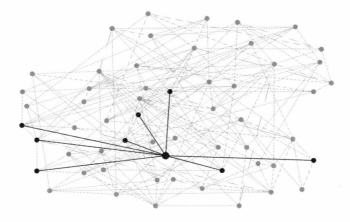

HISTORY

Bryan D. Palmer

At its most basic, "history" designates what happened in the past. However, the past is not a simple uncontested truth. Although radicals can all allude to how "history shows that *x*," the "lessons" drawn from history would, of course, be very different depending on what any particular radical wanted to emphasize.

Feminists, for instance, can point to how *his*-story has too often been a record of male presence. According to feminist historian Sheila Rowbotham (1973), this left half of humanity is "hidden from history." In response, American radical feminist Robin Morgan (1970) coined the counter-term "*her-story*" in *Sisterhood Is Powerful*, a pioneering anthology of 1960s feminism. As a corrective to the neglect of women's experiences and contributions to history, *her-stories* aimed to reinsert women into the frameworks used to understand the past and to transform everyday gender practices in the present.

For his part, Henry Ford exemplified the reactionary tendency to repudiate history when he declared that, as far as he was concerned, "history is bunk" (*New York Times* 1921). The narcissism of the present-minded (and radicals can sometimes themselves be guilty of this) follows this course by declaring that only what currently exists is of importance. Yesterday's news is outmoded and inconsequential, apparently of no importance: "That's history."

In the CrimethInc. Ex-Workers' Collective's *Days of War, Nights of Love*, this repudiation is taken to new heights. Here CrimethInc. excoriates "the dead hand of the past" while insisting that "those who cannot forget" what is over and done with are condemned to repeat it. In contrast, "if we dare to throw ourselves into the unknown and unpredictable, to continually seek out situations that force us to *be* in the present moment, we can break free of feelings of inevitability and inertia that constrain our lives—and, in those instances, step *outside* of history." To accomplish this aim, CrimethInc. confidently calls for a revolutionary embrace of myth and its ostensibly democratic storytelling impulse. Such raconteur radicalism, moreover, claims to sidestep the twin traps that CrimethInc. rejects: false impartiality and objective truth (109–14).

Obviously extreme, this approach flies in the face of centuries of radical thought. Radical thinkers have long posited history not as some all-encompassing straitjacket but as a field within which agency and determination wrestle. Between structured imposition and human activity mobilized to critique, challenge, and change social inequalities lay histories that we jettison, as radicals, at our peril. Myth may seem like an attractive alternative (and indeed at times myth grows out of this confrontational past); however, myth has also sustained a range of far more dubious possibilities. Every nationalist project, for instance, is sustained by myth; so too are all racist and xenophobic endeavors.

In the reciprocities of past and present, there is no getting around the fundamental realities of social struggle. This is the stuff of both history and myth. The fact that the form in which this past has been related to the present has privileged conventional histories that justify power (on the one hand) and myth-type storytelling that seemingly leaves more room for alternative outcomes (on the other) is no reason to refuse the radical potential of "history." Rather, the task is to remake historical understanding so that, in the words of E.P. Thompson, "the enormous condescension of posterity" does not silence dissent or reduce history to prepackaged inevitability (1966, 12). Radicals therefore tend to have a more consistent regard for history (both as precedent and as illustration of possibility) than do either those on the left who reject history or those on the right committed to preserving the status quo. This radical appreciation of history itself has a long history.

Karl Marx and Friedrich Engels (1978), for instance, drew upon Hegel's world-historic spirit of human development—albeit in ways that turned it on its head. What resulted was a materialized appreciation of the past that revised understandings of causality and shifted the analysis of society so that interpretation could aid in charting socio-economic transformations. In this way, they replaced metaphysics (God) and the primacy of thought ("In the beginning was the word") with concrete considerations of physical environments, modes of production, class formations, and the ways that changes in these realms ordered human history. Known as historical materialism, this orientation reconfigured how "history" was understood. Subsequently, no serious radical project could ever jettison historical consideration. For Frederic Jameson, the maxim became: "Always historicize!" (1981, 9).

Social justice is by no means assured by or confirmed within history. Nevertheless, addressing the past with a sophisticated appreciation of its struggles over a terrain marked by difference and contradictory demands can strengthen the hand of those committed to ending oppression. For this reason, "history" is never far from the radical imagination. In contemporary radical circles, however, such imagination is increasingly informed by questions of identity. As a result, current interpretations of history have tended toward the particularistic, and "history" is rarely invoked as a totality encompassing all peoples.

Postmodernism's influence, moreover, has left many radicals increasingly suspicious of "master narratives" and categories. As Perry Anderson succinctly noted, "the defining trait of the postmodern condition is the loss of credibility of these meta-narratives" (1998, 25). Ostensibly composed of discrete constituencies, history within such postmodern paradigms is often reduced to the recounting of experiences of marginality. However important, such a focus tends to fragment realities that are in fact consolidations of power and authority. As the operations of the multicultural state suggest, particularized identities can be de-radicalized through celebration. The mainstreaming of Black History Month, for instance, has had the ironic effect of cleansing a history of racist oppression through representations of advancement. In this way, it both dulls the radical edge of past struggles for equality *and* suggests that ongoing struggle has become unnecessary (see Palmer 1990, 2000; Jacoby 1994).

History, of course, is not new. Its record is physically etched wherever men and women first gathered. Later it would take form within oral traditions. In the Hellenic world, "history" emerged as a word alongside other linguistic designations associated with "civilization," including "academy," "school," and "logic." The Greek word "*historia*" first meant merely "knowledge gained by inquiry" (Barfield 1967, 37, 105). Between the fifteenth and the eighteenth century, "history" came to be understood as a narrative of human developments linked to and shaping the present. "History" was thus separated from earlier writings, including the fifteenth-century Shakespearian dramas that had been "histories" (as opposed to "comedies" or "tragedies") at the time of their writing. As a genealogy of power (concerned with war and the human face of governance), history struggled to be less didactic and to rely on more than the privileged oral tradition of select interlocutors.

Philosophically, this move was captured in the eighteenth century by Giambattista Vico's meditations on history. A professor of rhetoric, Vico's *The New Science* (1968) suggested ways of appreciating how the complex weave of determination set a stage upon which humans struggled and produced outcomes that were both paradoxical and progressive. According to E. P. Thompson, Vico's work stood as an important "precursor of historical materialism" (1978, 86). Combined with the Enlightenment, political upheavals like the French Revolution, and the emergence of socialism and historical materialism in the nineteenth century, this expansive sense of "history" established the foundation upon which the radical appreciation of history would consolidate during the twentieth century.

Revolutions, rebellious social movements, and popular insurgencies prompted radical understandings of both the past and its potential contributions to struggles in the present—a dynamic reflected in Leon Trotsky's canonical *History of the Russian Revolution* (1932). Concurrently, "history" was also being constructed in more mainstream and academic ways. Ordered by a compilation of empirical facts, the so-called "scientific history" of Leopold von Ranke adopted an approach that coincided with capitalism's Industrial Revolution and, in its fixation on ostensibly empirically verifiable fact, channeled historical investigation in decidedly conservative directions (Iggers and Powell 1990; Grafton 1997). This approach came to dominate the study of history in universities, where consensus (not conflict) tended to be the interpretive paradigm.

Historicism resulted. A reigning ideology of the mid-twentieth century, it fit well with Cold War orthodoxies, in which championing capitalism meant demonizing collectivist projects like the Soviet Union. As an approach, it repudiated radical understandings of "history" by insisting that all inquiry into the past rely on the seeming transparency of known evidence while eschewing abstract thought. Theorizing was increasingly suspect; overarching analytic frameworks were rejected. By the mid-twentieth century, consensus within history, structural functionalism within sociology, and a generalized agreement about what Daniel Bell (1960) called "the end of ideology" congealed to produce complacency within the university. One of the attractions of Thompson's (1966) influential study of class formation in England's Industrial Revolution was that it took direct aim at this consolidated paradigm by attacking structural functionalist views of class, pillorying notions that history was governed by consensus, and rejecting claims that ideas had ceased animating struggles for human betterment. Through the challenge to conventional thought that erupted in the 1960s, and especially through the protests of 1968, the radical approach to "history" blossomed (see Bernstein 1968; Lemisch 1975).

Over the course of the past half-century, conventional understandings of history have been shattered. This process was well underway when, during the 1970s, Raymond Williams concluded that history, "in different hands, *teaches* or *shows* us most kinds of knowable past and almost every kind of imaginable future" (1976, 120). The women's/feminist history that emerged during the late 1960s has spawned gender history (in which both femininities and masculinities are considered), lesbian history, family history, cultural histories of various kinds, and histories of bodies and emotions inspired by the work of Michel Foucault. What counts as a historical subject or historical evidence has changed to the point that what counts as "history" today bears little resemblance to how it was imagined in the past.

Conveying the democratizing, critical, and anticapitalist substance of historical gains to mass audiences has been an enduring radical concern. The notion of a "people's history" opposed to mainstream academic wisdom has been around since at least the 1880s and the Knights of Labor, though it gained momentum in the 1930s with the rise of various national communist parties. Radical movements have developed educational forums in which such histories are routinely discussed as a central component of organizational recruitment and education. Howard Zinn's (1980) *A People's History of the United States* made important contributions to the development of such histories. For their part, more radical historians like Paul Buhle and Nicole Schulman (2005) have promoted comics format presentations of historical social movements, while groups like Canada's Graphic History Collective have produced comic-book style histories of May Day and other mobilizations stretching from the 1880s to the 1990s. Justseeds, a decentralized artists' cooperative, celebrates people's history with a poster series.

In knowing more history, and in knowing history differently, radicals are required to see their present struggles with more sophistication than was demanded of any previous generation. Recognition of history's differentiated multitudes runs the risk of particularizing politics. The balance that radicals must achieve today entails a sensitive appreciation of diversity that does not undermine a strategic sense of the ways these specificities form a whole. Similarly, knowing how various groups have experienced lives of both subordination and struggle is indispensable to forging resistance in the present. For radicals, reflection on how resistance can be rallied (history as pedagogy) and on how history can inspire (history as example), suggests that "history" can inform the present in important ways. Significantly, it can help make our period one of activism rather than accommodation. If this is to happen, however, an appreciation not only of difference but also of the totality of social forces is necessary.

If, as the radical historian E. J. Hobsbawm (1971) once wrote, the task is to move from a fully grasped social history to a history of society, the radical informed by history will be cognizant of the complexities of identity while grasping the importance of waging struggles that address the totalizing means by which exploitation and oppression are deepened. Such universalism will also inform the project of creating alternatives to our current destructive reality.

SEE ALSO: Agency; Authority; Experience; Future; Ideology; Materialism; Representation; Zionism

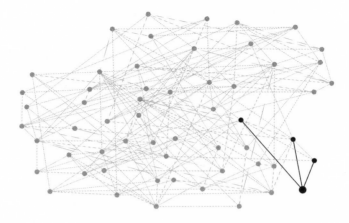

HOPE

Ana Cecilia Dinerstein

THE TERM "HOPE" DESIGNATES A DESIRE FOR CHANGE and the belief in a situation that is better than the existing one. The *Oxford English Dictionary* defines hope as "a feeling of expectation and desire for a particular thing to happen." In Hesiod's *Works and Days*, the most famous myth of hope in Greek mythology, hope (Elpis) is depicted as Zeus' punishment to humanity. Zeus sends Pandora—the first mortal woman—to Earth to become the spouse of Epimetheus. With her she brings a jar full of gifts or vices. Despite Prometheus advising his brother against it, Epimetheus accepts the offering. Pandora opens the jar and all the contents escape except hope. To Nietzsche, hope was Zeus' revenge: "Zeus intended that man, notwithstanding the evils oppressing him, should continue to live and not rid himself of life, but keep on making himself miserable. For this purpose he bestowed hope upon man: it is, in truth, the greatest of evils for it lengthens the ordeal of man" (1908, 102). In this account, "hope" misleads humans into believing that happiness is attainable. This reading contrasts with those that recall that hope was a gift. Pandora's contested myth thus compelled new philosophical understandings of "hope" as a value, a psychological state, and as an "anthropological" feature of humanity (Geoghegan 2008). The Latin word for "hope" is "*esperanza*" (a word that has the same root as "*esperar*," from Latin "*esperare*" ("to wait"). The Latin root "spe" is usually related to the Indo-European root "spe" ("to expand"). In the etymology of the Latin verb "*prosperare*," "*pro*" means "for" and "*spe*" means "hope" (i.e., anticipation, expectation; object, embodiment of hope). *Prosperare* means to flourish, to succeed, to thrive, to prosper. In this sense, to bring hope is also to bring prosperity.

Hope is also a theological category. To Thomas Aquinas, "hope" was "a movement of appetite aroused by the perception of what is agreeable, future, arduous, and possible of attainment" (quoted in Nicholas Smith 2008, 8). For Christians, "hope" refers to a reality witnessed but not yet realized, which—although already inaugurated by Christ—will not be fulfilled in this world (Dinerstein and Deneulin 2012). For example, the Epistle of Paul the Apostle to the Romans (in Romans 8:24) recounts how "we were saved in this hope, but hope that is seen is not hope: for why does one still hope for what he sees?" (Holy Bible, 785). Saint Augustine highlights: "As we do not yet possess a present but look for a future salvation, so it is with our happiness. . . . Salvation such as it shall be in the world to come, shall itself be our final happiness" (1962, 133).

In the late 1930s and during the 1940s, the German philosopher Ernst Bloch articulated a new meaning for "hope" outside of the religious framework in a context marked by profound political disappointment and the horrors of war and the Holocaust. As a "religious atheist," Bloch regarded religion as "one of the most significant forms of utopian consciousness, one of the richest expressions of the Hope Principle" (Löwy 1988, 8). He distinguished the "theocratic religion of the official churches, opium of the people, a mystifying apparatus at the service of the powerful" from "the underground, subversive and heretical religion" in a way that refuses to see religion "uniquely as a 'cloak' of class interests" (Löwy 1988, 8). Bloch (2009) engaged with Marx's view that religion is "an *expression* of man's real misery and a protest against it." Indeed, for Marx, "Religion is the sigh of the oppressed creature, the heart of a heartless world, and the soul of soulless conditions . . . the opium of the people." Consequently, "The abolition of religion as the illusory happiness of the people is the demand for their real happiness" (1982, 131). For Bloch, "The critique of religion in the spirit and context of Marx's thought liberates from undiscriminating taboos far more than Marxism does. One cannot of course expect miracles from a consideration of the opium-quotation in its entirety . . . but it might at least open the way, as they say, to conversations between believers purged of ideology and unbelievers purged by taboo" (2009, 51).

Bloch's three-volume treatise *The Principle of Hope* portrays hope as the most genuine feature of what makes us human. Hope is not fantasy, faith, optimism, or wish, but rather the strongest of all human emotions. "Hope, this expectant counter-emotion against anxiety and fear *is therefore the most human of all mental feelings and only accessible to men, and it also refers to the furthest and brightest horizons.* It suits that appetite in the mind which the subject not only has, but if which, as unfulfilled subject, it still essentially consists" (Bloch 1995, 75). In this view, hope possesses a utopian function, which enables us to engage with the "not-yet" dimension of reality that inhabits the present and can be anticipated here and now. Hope in this sense is willful rather than wishful (Levitas 1997): it informs people's concrete endeavors to forge a better life.

During the 1950s, Martin Luther King Jr. revitalized the idea that hope amounted to the possibility of a new reality. As one of the twentieth century's best-known advocates for nonviolent social change, King inspired a generation of activists. In his famous "I have a dream" speech of 1963, he envisioned a world in which people were no longer divided by race. This dream became institutionalized in 1964 when Congress enacted the Civil Rights Act and King received the Nobel Peace Prize. Many of his statements—compiled in James Washington's book *A Testament of Hope: The Essential Writings and Speeches* (1986)—seem inspired by Bloch's ideas. For example, in Bloch's 1961 lecture "Can Hope Be Disappointed?" he claimed: "Hope must be unconditionally disappointable." This was because "hope is not confidence. If it could not be disappointable, it would not be hope. However, hope still nails a flag on the mast, even in decline, in that the decline is not accepted, even when this decline is still very strong (Bloch 1998, 340; 16–17). Speaking in a similar fashion to an audience in Washington, King insisted that "we must accept finite disappointment, but never lose infinite hope."

During the 1960s, "hope" became essential to various revolutionary theologies. In his *Theology of Liberation: History, Politics, Salvation* (1971), Peruvian priest Gustavo Gutiérrez conceived of theology as a hope-inspired praxis. Drawing on Bloch's insights, he suggested that "the hoped-for salvation of humanity comes about not in the historical incarnation of hope represented in the activities of Jesus and a community of believers but, rather, in a transcendent future which makes the promise available to a receptive humanity" (Moylan 1997, 101). This characterization, in which hope appears as a guide to revolutionary action, developed alongside revolutionary politics in Latin America. It also coincided with the concurrent discussion among bishops at the 1968 Latin American Episcopal Conference about how to adapt the Christian message to the world. As conceived by Father Gustavo Gutiérrez, liberation theology called on the church to relate to popular movements and their struggles.

Similarly, new radical pedagogies put hope at the center of liberation struggles during the 1970s. Brazilian radical educator Paolo Freire (2004) connected hope with dialogical learning experiences. In *Pedagogy of the Oppressed* (1970), he contended that pedagogical dialogue cannot exist without hope: "Hope is rooted in men's incompletion, from which they move out in constant search—a search which can be carried out only in communion with others. . . . Hope, however, does not consist in crossing one's arms and waiting. As long as I fight, I am moved by hope; and if I fight with hope, then I can wait." (Freire 2000, 91–92).

After the "no future" politics of the 1980s, the 1994 Zapatista uprising explicitly reinserted "hope" into contemporary social movement discourse. For Subcomandante Marcos, indigenous struggle amounted to an "experience of hope" pursued by an "army of dreamers" (Lorenzano 1998, 157). Throughout their declarations and communiqués, the Zapatistas make clear that "hope" is neoliberal globalization's antithesis. Echoing Bloch's formulation, their First Declaration recounts how "a new lie is sold to us as history." Specifically, this is "the lie about the defeat of hope, the lie about the defeat of dignity, the lie about the defeat of humanity." At a time when global capitalism asserts itself as "dreamlessness in regard to the future . . . [where] there is fear, not hope" (Bloch 1971, 32), the Zapatistas propose: "Against the international terror representing neoliberalism, we must raise the international of hope. Hope above borders, languages, colors, cultures, sexes, strategies and thoughts, of all who prefer humanity alive. The international of hope" (SIM 1996a).

Today many social movements define themselves as mobilizers of hope, with prefiguration as their main strategy (Dinerstein 2015). Hope was the implicit motif in the global justice movement's declaration: "Another World Is Possible." Here hope is indexed to the real *possibility* of transforming the world. At its best, then, the global justice movement marshaled hope as a tool to counteract transnational capitalism.

Other political and religious forces have tried to leverage hope from positions of power in order to articulate new senses of possibility. On July 9, 2015, Pope Francis called for the "globalization of hope" in a speech to the Encounter of Popular Movements in Santa Cruz de la Sierra, Bolivia: "The globalization of hope, which emanates from the peoples and grows among the poor must replace this globalization of exclusion and indifference." Upon winning his second presidency, Barack Obama declared that his supporters had "reaffirmed the spirit that has triumphed over war and depression, the spirit that has lifted this country from the depths of despair to the great heights of hope." He went on:

> I've never been more hopeful about our future. I have never been more hopeful about America. And I ask you to sustain that hope. I'm not talking about blind optimism, the kind of hope that just ignores the enormity of the tasks ahead . . . [and] I'm not talking about the wishful idealism. . . . I have always believed that hope is that stubborn thing inside us that insists, despite all the evidence to the contrary, that something better awaits us so long as we have the courage to keep reaching, to keep working, to keep fighting. (2012)

Syriza leader Alex Tsipras' 2014 election as prime minister of Greece prompted similar utterances. "Today we are opening the road to hope," he declared. "Today we open the road to a better tomorrow with our people united, dignified and proud" (Euronews 2015). With both Obama and Tsipras, "hope" is articulated to invoke a new social imaginary to challenge catastrophic reality (Letts 2009). As Marcus Letts recounts, by describing hope vaguely (e.g., as "that thing inside us" or "what led me here today"), Obama was able to reach a multitude.

New theorizations of radical change associate "hope" with "utopia," "prefiguration," and an immediate temporal conception of the "future" (i.e., not as something that will occur later but something that is unfolding now) partly to escape the concept's appropriation by institutionalized politics and policy. Here radical change is no longer conceived as a revolution that involves taking state power, but instead as a process of learning and teaching hope. According to critical scholar Sarah Amsler, "In conditions of intellectual, political and cultural foreclosure such as exist now in extreme neoliberal societies, the learning of hope is both a critical element of radical democratization and a practical politico-educative activity that can be cultivated anew at each new conjuncture" (2015, 6).

The utopia that emerges from the process of learning hope is not an "abstract utopia" that follows the plan of the party for a future-oriented revolution. Instead, it is a "concrete utopia," a praxis-oriented category (Levitas 1997, 70). In these praxis-oriented concrete utopias, "knowing-concrete hope subjectively breaks most powerfully into fear [and] objectively leads most efficiently towards the radical termination of the contents of fear" (Bloch 1995, 5). Concrete utopia ventures into the *not yet*, the seeds of which already exist in latent form within the present reality. As Bloch highlights, the idea of concrete utopia is "only seemingly paradoxical." This is because it is "anticipatory" in nature and, for this reason, "by no means coincides with abstract utopia dreaminess, [or] is directed by the immaturity of merely abstract utopian socialism" (1995, 146). The distinction between these two modes found concrete expression through the tension between the neighbors' assemblies and the traditional left party activists during the radical mobilizations in Buenos Aires in late 2001 and early 2002. The party activists regarded the neighbors' mobilization as a tool for the attainment of a future abstract revolution led by the party. For the neighbors, however, this attitude undermined the development of alternative political practices here and now. For them, the future did not lie ahead in a linear sequence but could be anticipated by movements through collective action.

Gift or vice? Today conflict persists between those radical scholars and activists who perceive hope to be a guiding praxis that must be cultivated and protected against opportunistic appropriation, and those who argue that hope undermines movements' capacities to change the world. Derrick Jensen is in the latter camp: "The more I understand hope, the more I realize that all along it deserved to be in the box with the plagues, sorrow, and mischief; that it serves the needs of those in power as surely as belief in a distant heaven; that hope is really nothing more than a secular way of keeping us in line" (n.d.). For Bloch, however, hope "is not content just to accept the bad which exists" and "does not accept renunciation." Instead, educated hope (*docta spes*) guides praxis: "It is a question of learning hope" (1995, 3).

SEE ALSO: Future; Prefiguration; Utopia

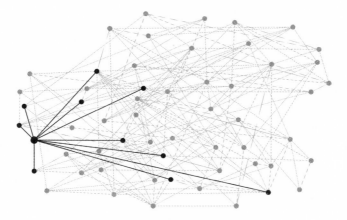

IDEOLOGY

Himani Bannerji[1]

THE ROOT OF "IDEOLOGY" IS THE GREEK *"IDEIN,"* WHICH refers to patterns or forms that can be seen. The "idea" that is "seen" thus implicates the "seer" and designates the object that is brought into view. Here "visibility" highlights the tension between perception and representation, between those conceptions that hold ideas to be inward constructions and those forms of scientific observation that locate ideas in the perceived objects themselves.

In his *Keywords*, Raymond Williams reviews the emergence of "ideology" during the French Enlightenment.

---

1. I would like to acknowledge the considerable assistance I received from AK Thompson, without whom this piece would not have been possible.

During this period, the mind and ideas became uprooted from their putatively divine origin and entered the profane world. Correspondingly, the origin of ideas became a central topic of exploration; do they originate "within" or "outside" the knower? These inquiries gave rise to two schools of thought, through which associationists or empiricists became set against intuitionists or idealists. For Locke, Hume, and their colleagues, the faculties of perception etched impressions onto the mind. In contrast, the English and German Romantics viewed ideas as subjective creations emanating from the mind itself. Epistemological inquiry thus became divided between those who viewed the "science of mind" as an empiricist matter and those, like the idealists, who situated ideas within the metaphysical realm.

Both the *Oxford English Dictionary* and Williams' *Keywords* (153–57) agree that "ideology" denotes a special kind of knowledge in which the author imaginatively invests objects (whether mental or physical) with certain properties. As such, "ideology" is associated with and held to be a product of idealism. This emphasis on idealization (and hence on imagination and creativity) connects ideology with art; however, it does so in a negative light—suggesting fiction, lies, or false representation. At the same time, however, ideology's "idealism" also suggests identification with (an aspiration toward) the not-yet-realized and the universal. Williams (153) points out that the tension between these meanings still finds expression in current coexisting uses of the term.

For radicals throughout much of the twentieth century, the views Lenin expressed during the Second International became key reference points for discussions concerning ideology. In conventional communist usage during this period, "ideology" evoked three distinct but related ways of thinking about the relationship between world and idea, base and superstructure. In this paradigm, "ideology" could indicate a) the neutral organization of ideas and beliefs, b) false consciousness, and/or c) political ideas. Lenin deployed the neutral use when, in his 1902 "Letter to the Northern League," he referred to socialism as "the ideology of the class struggle of the proletariat" (1977, 161). However, a tinge of the political can be detected even in this neutral usage, since Lenin's objectives put him in close alliance with this struggle.

For its part, the idea of false consciousness—a formulation coined by Engels in his 1893 correspondence with historian Franz Mehring—also contains both political and content-based connotations. According to Engels, "ideology is a process accomplished by the so-called thinker consciously, indeed, but with a false consciousness." This was because, syllogistically, "the real motives impelling him remain unknown to him, otherwise it would not be an ideological process at all" (1968).

Today, the overlapping usages of "ideology" to denote false consciousness, political allegiances, or organized ideas arising from or pertaining to the superstructure can be seen especially clearly in reportage by periodicals like *Foreign Policy*, which run stories recounting how, for instance, "after 13 years of conflict in Afghanistan, money has replaced ideology and vengeance" as the motivating factor for many Taliban fighters (Weir and Azamy 2014). Indeed, according to authors James Weir and Hekmatullah Azamy, although "ideology and retribution still remain," they "grow less relevant to the movement." In this formulation, "ideology" is deployed as an antithesis to money, which stands in for the material world. A similar deployment can be observed in *Toronto Star* Provincial Affairs columnist Martin Regg Cohn's finding that "the arguments against unions" marshaled by the Progressive Conservative Party of Ontario "are entirely ideological, not empirical," since the thesis that jobs are created by lowering union density remains "unprovable" (2013).

Given this usage, some radical, left, and labor movement forces have come to perceive "ideology" as an obstruction to the realization of concrete aims. About a decade before Britain's Liberal Democrats adopted the slogan "Neither Left nor Right but Forward," socialist folk singer Billy Bragg released "Ideology" (1986), a song in which "the voices of the people" could not be heard "above the sounds of ideologies clashing" in a parliament comprised of "old men grinding axes." More recently, CrimethInc. has proposed that "resisting ideology" means asking questions rather than presupposing answers and "ceasing to regard our ideas as possessing meaning apart from the ways we are able to put them into practice" (2010).

Although Marx and Engels drafted the *The German Ideology* prior to the formation of the Second International in 1889, it was not published until the middle of the twentieth century. Consequently, it did not have an immediate effect on the conceptualization of ideology within radical milieus. Nevertheless, since its publication it has exerted a powerful influence on contemporary understandings. By tracing the relationship between the developing modes of production and conscious human existence, Marx revealed how ideas and objects of observation informed each other to produce reality through "human sensuous activity." In this way, Marx's historical materialism dispensed with abstract, objectivist materialism (empiricism) as well as with an equally abstract and empty idealism.

According to a famous passage from *The German Ideology*, "the ruling ideas" of any age are "nothing more than the ideal expression of the dominant material relationships . . . grasped as ideas." Since its publication, this statement has taken on a slogan-like quality and has tended to favor interpretations that associate ideology mainly with content (e.g., with the manifestation of "ruling ideas" in concrete propositions). For Williams, therefore, Marx and Engels equate all reliance on ideas with illusion and false consciousness (1977, 57–59).

However, this assessment is not exactly accurate, since Marx and Engels judged ideology to be an epistemological *procedure* rather than merely an amalgamated content. Through this procedure, the relation between ideas and natural or social reality became inverted; in the end, ideas themselves appear to take precedence over reality. "If in all ideology men and their circumstances appear upside-down as in a camera obscura," they note, "this phenomenon arises just as much from their historical life-process as the inversion of objects on the retina does from their physical life-process." Ideology, then, is indeed a mystification; however, it is a mystification that arises from—and thus corresponds to—a particular moment in the historical development of human social and productive relations.

By the middle of the twentieth century, Herbert Marcuse began to note how the formal distinction between ideology and reality, base

and superstructure, had begun to dissolve—a dynamic he attributed directly to the historical development of productive relations. In
his view, this situation did not amount to "the end of ideology" as
some commentators had proclaimed. Instead, he found that "advanced industrial culture is more ideological than its predecessor,
inasmuch as today the ideology is in the process of production itself."
Indeed, the organizational forms associated with mass transportation, communication, entertainment, and information "carry with
them prescribed attitudes and habits, certain intellectual and emotional reactions which bind the consumers more or less pleasantly to
the producers and, through the latter, to the whole" (1964, 11–12).

The most in-depth contemporary application of Marx's critique
of ideology as epistemological procedure can be found in the work of
the feminist sociologist Dorothy Smith, for whom "much conceptual
work is a secondary ideological efflorescence" (1990, 54–55). In her
analysis of the "Ideological Practices of Sociology," Smith mobilizes
the conceptual tools developed in *The German Ideology* to reveal how,
in sociology, "the actualities of living people become a resource to
be made over in the image of the concept." Here "the work becomes
that of transposing the paramount reality into the conceptual currency in which it is governed." Finally, once this work is complete,
"sociological procedures legislate a reality rather than discover one"
(1990, 53). From this perspective, ideology is not solely a body of
ideas with political connotations; it is a process of knowledge production arising from the division between mental and manual labor.

Inquiring into ideology's social organization as an aspect of
ruling regimes, Smith's institutional ethnography in some ways
echoes Louis Althusser's mid-twentieth-century analysis of the
"ideological state apparatus." In that analysis, Althusser claimed
that the work of ideology was to ensure the reproduction of labor
power, not only through "a reproduction of its skills, but also, at the
same time, a reproduction . . . of submission to the ruling ideology for the workers, and a reproduction of the ability to manipulate
the ruling ideology correctly for the agents of exploitation and repression" (1977, 127–28). However, unlike Althusser's perspective,
which granted to ideology an absolute and ahistorical dimension,

Smith's approach emphasizes the means by which all forms of knowledge production—including but not limited to the ideological—arise from people's everyday lives.

Outside of the Marxist intellectual tradition, treatments of ideology show a distinct path of development. Throughout the nineteenth and twentieth centuries, sociological thinkers like Emile Durkheim, Karl Mannheim, and Max Weber followed a content-based trajectory in which distinct values added up to a worldview that both prompted and offered an interpretive schema for understanding socio-economic developments. Although marked by what he considered an "artificial simplicity," Weber nevertheless insisted that his "ideal types" might help to make historical reality sensible. In this view, "because of the impossibility of drawing sharp boundaries in historical reality," the researcher could only "hope to understand" phenomena through a consideration of "their most consistent and logical form" (2003, 98).

Considering the problem from the standpoint of social experience itself, and though he stood in opposition to the limits of the "ideological method" of analysis (1982, 86), Durkheim observed that "the soldier who falls defending his flag certainly does not believe he has sacrificed himself to a piece of cloth." Consequently (and through the process of idealization), he concluded that, in such cases, "the idea creates the reality" (1995, 229). Finally, according to Mannheim, whose *Ideology and Utopia* endeavored to outline the historical development of ideology in the modern era, "We begin to treat our adversary's views as ideologies only when we no longer consider them as calculated lies and when we sense in his total behavior an unreliability which we regard as a function of the social situation in which he finds himself" (1954, 54).

In each of these cases, ideas are presented as prime movers of history. Notions of *zeitgeist*, cultural essences, and the attribution of a single consciousness to whole societies are found widely in such works, which remain influential in contemporary investigations of society, culture, and art. This epistemological practice can also be detected in postmodern theories of discourse, which tend to make it logically impossible to think beyond, prior to, or outside of discourse itself. Indeed, as Frederic Jameson has noted, the "depthlessness" of postmodern analytic patterns ensures that even the past is reduced to little more than a semiotic "referent" (1991, 19). This entanglement is especially evident in the work of Gilles Deleuze and Félix Guattari, who compare discourse to that "molecular assemblage of enunciation that is not given in my conscious mind" but upon which I must "always depend" (1987, 84). Still, they maintain, "there is no ideology and never has been" (1987, 4).

Today fields like Cultural Studies, Postcolonial Studies, Communication Studies, and others have provided new opportunities to consider the cultural roots of capitalism, the state, and its modes of governance. Although "ideology" is not always directly mentioned in this work, analyses of dominant and oppositional modes of thought and culture continue to be elaborated under the banners of "hegemony," "discourse," and "representation." Overwhelmingly issue-oriented in their approach, however, these readings have tended to be directed more toward social reform and gradualist transformation than toward anticapitalist revolution.

Nevertheless, even as the late twentieth century witnessed forms of cultural determinism supplant economic ones, it was still possible for figures like Stuart Hall—whose analysis focused on dynamics including neoliberalism, racialization, and nationalism—to generate invaluable insights into the relationship between ideology, culture, and politics. A product of his time, Hall nevertheless echoed earlier Marxist insights when he conceived of ideology as "the mental frameworks . . . and the systems of representation" that found differential distribution among the social classes and were used by them to "make sense of, figure out and render intelligible the way society works" (1996b, 26). In a moment characterized by pervasive social refraction (a refraction that, from Marcuse to Deleuze, has led some to conclude that there is in fact no ideology), the task of mapping these "systems of representation" is more pressing than ever.

SEE ALSO: Class; History; Intellectual; Liberal; Materialism; Representation; Reproduction; Revolution; Victory; Zionism

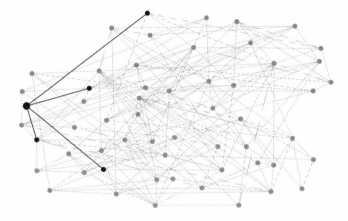

INTELLECTUAL

Sumayya Kassamali

IN THE HILLS OF 1970S LEBANON, ARABIC NOVELIST AND
spokesperson for the Palestinian Front for the Liberation
of Palestine Ghassan Kanafani gathered circles of refugee
children to teach them of freedom and resistance. In the
early mornings of 1920s New York City, working-class
Jews congregated before the start of the workday to
debate the finer points of left-wing ideology as recounted
by Yiddish-language Communist newspapers. In 1960s
California, the leaders of the Black Panther Party for Self
Defense made Mao's *Red Book* (1964) and Frantz Fanon's
The Wretched of the Earth (1967) required reading for all
party members, while—back in the New York City area—
poet Amiri Baraka launched the Black Arts Movement as

the literary branch of the Black Power movement. Decades after his assassination in 1967, the prolific writings of Che Guevara on everything from guerrilla tactics (2006) to the economics of Afro-Asian solidarity continue to be published, translated, and distributed. What is the relationship between radical politics and intellectualism? The question requires an exploration of the term "intellectual" both as the name ascribed to an individual social role and as a particular form of labor associated with the "work of the mind."

"Intellectual" derives from the Latin "*intellectus*" (discernment, understanding) and the root verb "*intelligere*" (to understand). Its earliest use was as an adjective meaning "grasped by the mind" (rather than by the senses) and dates back to the fourteenth century. According to the *Oxford English Dictionary*, "intellectual" as a noun originally referred to the faculty of the intellect itself. This usage has been rendered obsolete. However, the use of "intellectual" to refer to a person of allegedly superior intellect—or to one who pursues higher learning—can be found as far back as the mid-seventeenth century. In his own *Keywords*, Raymond Williams noted that the early usage of "intellectualism" carried distinctly negative connotations. In turn, "it acquired implications of coldness, abstraction and, significantly, ineffectiveness" (1983, 170). By the early twentieth century, one notes the use of the plural "intellectuals" to describe a class of writers prone to emotionally devoid rationalism, further connected to the group noun "intelligentsia." The latter term entered English through the Russian, where it was first used to refer to the educated and patriotic bourgeoisie. It is this social class that Vladimir Lenin famously referred to as being "not the brains of the nation but its feces" (1919). Similarly, Leon Trotsky found the bourgeois intellectuals to have been "irrevocably absorbed by capitalist industry" (1910). Writing a decade after Trotsky, French philosopher Julien Benda (2007) launched a damning critique against what he took to be "the treason of the intellectuals." In his book by the same name he argued that, since European intellectuals had become subservient to the nationalist ideologies of war and racism, they were better off retreating into an ascetic life of the mind.

According to Edward Said, "there has been no major revolution in modern history without intellectuals." However, he was quick to note that "there has been no major counterrevolutionary movement without intellectuals" either (1994, 11). A radical orientation to the problem of the intellectual must therefore begin by attending to a central contradiction. Historically, intellectuals have often served state power, and their distinctive social role is inextricable from histories of elitism and the devaluation of physical labor. At the same time, activism must contend with the danger of romanticizing experience or focusing exclusively on day-to-day organizing to the detriment of developing sustained political analyses. It is in this context that leftists have worked to develop an understanding of "the intellectual" as someone who is both grounded in knowledge production and accountable to social movements, someone positioned against dominant interests while constantly engaged in public conversation.

Today it is common to hear that "public intellectuals" have retreated into the academy and lost their once-prominent social role (see Greif 2015; Kristof 2014; Warren 2015). Within social movements, activism and formal scholarship are often conceived as irreconcilable, with the latter deemed inaccessible and isolated from realities on the ground. Similarly, academics in various disciplines regularly struggle with this tension as they reflect upon how their teaching and training might contribute to radical social transformation (e.g., Fletcher 2001; Murphy 2005). While such debates arise from contemporary conditions, they reiterate questions that have long been posed by thinkers on the left.

References to "the intellectual" in Marxist thought often arise within broader debates about revolutionary consciousness, its relationship to the working masses, and the constant dialectic between theory and practice. Nevertheless, the Marxist tradition has "struggled with the contradiction between a theoretical identity rooted in the vision of proletarian self-emancipation, and the political reality of a movement dominated by intellectuals" (Boggs 1979, 7). Writing from prison in the aftermath of the Italian workers' council movement and the rise of Mussolini's fascism, Antonio

Gramsci famously formulated the distinction between "tradition-al" and "organic" intellectuals. This distinction was predicated on a notion of intellectual work as a general human capacity. "All men are intellectuals, one could therefore say: but not all men have in society the function of intellectuals" (1971, 115).

For Gramsci, every social group included a category of intellec-tuals that traditionally served functions tied to knowledge produc-tion and control. "Traditional intellectuals" of this kind included teachers and priests. At the same time, under capitalism, each class organically generated its own intellectuals in the interest of orga-nizing itself and increasing its power. "Organic intellectuals" of this kind could be identified by their role within broader social relations and not solely by the nature of their work. For Gramsci, bourgeois intellectuals played a key role in the production and maintenance of hegemony: "The intellectuals are the dominant group's 'deputies' exercising the subaltern functions of social hegemony and political government" (118). In contrast, working-class intellectuals would be key to the development of radical consciousness.

Emma Goldman (1914) presciently drew attention to the pro-letarianization of intellectuals at the beginning of the twentieth century. By her account, material constraints limited artists or journalists in ways that were comparable to conditions faced by workers in shops and mines. In fact, she argued, "This terrible de-pendence upon those who can make the price and dictate the terms of intellectual activities, is more degrading than the position of the worker in any trade." In his turn-of-the-century *Representations of the Intellectual*, Edward Said (1994) drew on Gramsci's observa-tions to remark upon the rising number of professions organized around highly specialized areas of expertise. From digital jour-nalism to government bureaucracy, consultancy firms to think tanks, "intellectual work" is now part of the job description for large segments of the North American workforce, particular-ly since the outsourcing of industrial manufacturing. The recent growth of copyright restrictions has also focused on legislating "intellectual property," producing associations between intellectu-alism and the ideologies of private ownership and individualism

(Barron 2006). Meanwhile, between the 2003 U.S.-led invasion of Iraq and today's unceasing media punditry, a new coterie of intellectuals has emerged to loudly serve the combined interests of state, capital, and war (Robin 2014). Said referred to the group of men who championed the first Gulf War—many of the very same voices heard today—as "scholar-combatants" (Harlow 1991). In contrast, he maintained that the designation "public intellectual" presupposed a clear opposition to constituted power.

The Saidian intellectual occupies a uniquely lonely position, unpopular yet resolutely unafraid. The role demands distance from national belonging as well as from the filial loyalties of ethnicity or family. The task of the intellectual is to bring together rational investigation with firm moral judgment while anchoring herself to a political cause based on "justice, principle, truth, conviction" (Harlow 1991). Writing in the decades following decolonization, Said drew upon Frantz Fanon's distrust of the nativism that would dilute its critical gaze when it came to the assessment of indigenous powers (the critical gaze that stopped at the moment of independence rather than continuing to struggle toward liberation). Such an intellectual works at the point where Gramsci's aphorism "pessimism of the intellect, optimism of the will" (1971) and Fanon's proclamation "Oh my body, make of me always a man who questions!" (1986, 181) converge.

Prompted by the 1987 publication of Russell Jacoby's *The Last Intellectuals*, Said's writings are part of a larger debate concerning the decline of intellectual life in America as a direct consequence of the growing dominance of the university. According to Jacoby's controversial claim, members of the last generation of American intellectuals were born in the early twentieth century; after that, disappointment prevailed. Jacoby's text popularized the phrase "public intellectual" in North America. In his estimation, the demise of the American intellectual tradition owed to the growing impossibility of surviving as an independent worker and the need to seek corporate employment, the inaccessibility of affordable urban life in areas like Greenwich Village, and the monopoly of universities over scholarly life after World War II. Although the glaring whiteness of Jacoby's list of prized American intellectuals should give all readers serious pause, his provocative argument continues to ring true as the social transformations he described have continued apace.

A growing contemporary conversation within (but on the margins of) higher education has questioned the increasing corporatization of the North American university. As student debt skyrockets along with administrative salaries, and wealthy universities become key real-estate owners, gentrifiers, and transnational business partners in a globalized economy, their capacity to nurture radical thought appears doubtful. For Said, the intellectual working against the pressures of professionalization must embrace a certain "amateurism," a willingness to intervene even in areas where one is not a declared expert. Such an intellectual is identified not by their "elevated polemic" but by a criticism that works to reinterpret assumed common sense and reshape the parameters of public debate (1994, 72). Said insisted upon broadening the forms in which intellectual intervention might be recognized so that the artist, musician, or journalist could epitomize this work just as readily as any widely published professor.

"The most radical ideas often grow out of a concrete intellectual engagement with the problems of aggrieved populations confronting systems of oppression," writes Robin Kelley (2002, 30). Indeed, intellectual work is regularly conducted from the margins of society. According to scholar Dylan Rodriguez, American prison writings reveal a lineage of "captive intellectuals" uniquely positioned to demonstrate the nature of modern state power and articulate an expansive vision of freedom while writing behind bars (2005). In 1956, British historian E. P. Thompson resigned from the Communist Party over the Soviet invasion of Hungary. Writing the following year in the inaugural issue of the journal *Universities and Left Review*, Thompson cautioned intellectuals against their retreat from humanism and into dogmatic party politics. Beautifully, he implored: "We continue our intellectual work because we believe that, in the last analysis, ideas matter; it is man's business, if he is not to be mere victim of involuntary reflexes or of a predetermined historical flux, to strive to understand himself and his times and to make reasonable and right choices. This gives to all our imaginative work a significance at once terrible and hopeful" (1957, 33).

Today, intellectualism sometimes appears as though it were the dusty purview of those who live solely within books. While groups of activists constantly pursue new models of collective organizing, learning, and leadership, we have yet to see an adequate theorizing of the relationship between the intellectual as individual and the work of solidarity. What of explosive figures like Frantz Fanon (who gave us the language to connect racism, decolonization, and liberation) or June Jordan (whose poetry expanded what the English language could do for a feminist spirit)? We must recall Eqbal Ahmad, who became known both for his generosity and for his association with radical nuns accused of a conspiracy to kidnap Henry Kissinger. Ahmad was a scholar of guerrilla warfare who learned from the FLN in Algeria and advised Yasser Arafat in southern Lebanon. He later became a key figure of the American anti–Vietnam War movement and a staunch defender of secularism and anti-imperialism in his native Pakistan.

We might similarly turn to Grace Lee Boggs, labor and women's rights activist, comrade of C. L. R. James and Malcolm X, translator of Marx, and inspiration to multiple generations of American youth; or to Arundhati Roy, acclaimed Indian novelist, anti-globalization activist, and vocal commentator on environmental and political issues within India and across the world. Such are the intellectuals who offer both hope and guidance for a radical imaginary.

SEE ALSO: Accessible; Hegemony; Ideology; Labor

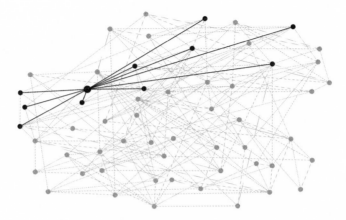

LABOR

Sam Gindin

THE WORD "LABOR" STEMS FROM THE LATIN "*LABOREM*," meaning "toil, exertion, hardship, pain." Early economists and political philosophers of capitalism understood labor in instrumental terms: it was an onerous activity done out of necessity. "Labour for labour's sake is against nature," John Locke asserted at the beginning of the eighteenth century (1828, 549). Near the end of that century, Adam Smith professed in *The Wealth of Nations* that "the sweets of labour consist altogether in the recompense of labour" (1993, 121). Early in the nineteenth century, Jeremy Bentham declared that "love of labour is a contradiction in terms" (1817, 20), and, as the twentieth century approached, the then-dean of economics Alfred Marshall summarized this perspective by defining labor as "any exertion of mind or body undergone partly or wholly with a view to some good other than the pleasure derived from the work" (Reisman 2011, 208).

It fell to Marx (1867) to address labor not just as a necessity but also as a capability: the universal human capacity for purposeful action in transforming nature to address our material needs. The qualification "purposeful" was intended to highlight that "what distinguishes the worst architect from the best of bees" is the ability to imagine that which does not exist, and then to realize that vision. In laboring to meet their needs, humans make and remake the context in which they live, and so also remake themselves. Marx highlighted the disjuncture between labor as necessary drudgery and the potentials of labor as a value in itself and as a liberating force. The realization of that potential, however, was contingent upon addressing the tension between necessity and capacity—a tension organized by relations of power and inequality, as well as by competing conceptions of rights, democracy, and social justice, and by our relationship to nature.

By the mid-twentieth century, "labor" had come to be commonly conceived as a particular subset of work: work that is "hard, difficult, or painful" (Raymond Williams 1976, 337). For its part, "work" now holds the same negative connotations. In the 1999 movie *Office Space*, a worker is called into the manager's office. "Looks like you've been missing a lot of work lately," says the manager. "Well," replies the worker, "I wouldn't say I was *missing* it." In the rebellious sixties, Bob Dylan expressed similar reservations in *Maggie's Farm*. Not for him the *Cinderella* injunction to "whistle while you work." For Dylan, work—like labor—meant toil and alienation: "They say sing while you slave / and I just get bored."

When Dylan defiantly sang "I ain't gonna work on Maggie's farm no more," he wasn't just tapping into student disaffection but also to the frustrations of a generation of militant young industrial workers. Disaffected by the mindless work, angry over incessant speed-ups, and resentful of management's authority, workers expressed their "Blue-Collar Blues" (Gooding 1970) by sabotaging products, slowing down the line, and walking off the job. Today the protests of another generation of workers are in the news: service workers at Walmart, McDonald's, Starbucks, and IKEA. However, unlike those of their 1960s counterparts, their demands are less concerned with ending alienating work/labor than they are with trying to increase meager wages while securing steady hours and full-time status.

Workers today don't feel any better about their labor. However, decades of defeats and a heightened sense of permanent insecurity have lowered expectations, modified attitudes to work/labor, and narrowed the scope of rebelliousness. A telling example of this shift is the prevalence of unpaid positions and internships. Speaking at a 2014 press conference about the desperate condition of unemployed youth, the governor of the Bank of Canada unashamedly counseled taking any job—"even if it's for free"—since this could at least be listed as experience on a resume (Poloz 2014).

It's important not to exaggerate generational differences, however. Workers in the 1960s were not unambiguously revolutionary. For all the bravado in Dylan's song, the actual rebellion he describes is limited to hoping for reprieve: "Well, I wake up in the morning / Fold my hands and pray for rain." Since it doesn't always rain, radicals confront a challenge: how can we overcome what seems like a depressingly inevitable part of the human condition?

Answering this question requires an understanding of how capitalism transformed the essence of labor. In the transition to capitalism, individual consumption became systematically linked to pay earned through the sale of individual labor power. Capitalism stripped a majority of the population down to one asset: the capacity to labor. Peasants, farmers, and families who had lost their land or who could not compete against the machinery and tools of large workplaces faced the necessity of "voluntarily" converting their human capacity for labor into a commodity for sale.

Having to sell their labor power left people dependent on employers. However, like exploitation, dependence itself was not novel. Those who labored had previously been dependent on kings and lords for protection, on merchants and banks for credit, and to some extent on markets to sell or trade their production. The difference was that, in previous circumstances, the tools workers used were their own and they themselves organized their labor. Capitalism created the modern working class, which depends on those who buy labor (and who own capital: machinery, tools, finance) for the organization of their labor. The capitalists not only kept a share of the output but also largely determined how workers' capacity to labor would develop over time.

This dramatic change in the nature of work changed how we think and speak about "labor" (Raymond Williams 1976). The word began to appear alongside adjectives in now-familiar phrases ("paid labor," "wage-laborers," "labor markets") and also came to refer to the overall supply of labor power in the economy. New oppositional political terms and concepts also emerged ("working class," "class consciousness," "unemployment," "strikes," "pickets," "international solidarity"). This discourse is subject to perpetual modification, as ongoing transformations *within* capitalism prompt yet more specific uses of the word: "social wage," "breadwinner," "equal pay," "Big Labor," "guest workers," and so on.

Although the prevalence of paid labor has grown considerably over the past century, it would now seem anachronistic to speak of more "laborers" in the economy. The word "laborer" brings to mind a male worker carrying out, under supervision, the mindless physical or "manual" work (from the Latin "*manus*" meaning "hand") of laying tracks, digging ditches, or carrying bales of hay (Raymond Williams 1976, 146). This link to "heavy work" is generally distinguished from the "lighter work" done by women often deemed "unsuited to engineering work, skilled jobs and any tasks deemed 'physical'" (Wright 2003, 31).

Today half the workforce in the developed world is now female, the largest employment sectors are retail trade and health care, and a good many workers seem to be part of a "cybertariat," enthusiastically doing work that includes a significant degree of autonomy, encourages innovation, and seems to approach play (Huws 2003). But while work has certainly changed over the past century, it would be wrong to suggest that work is no longer "laborious" in the earliest sense of the word. That North Americans can view work today as distant from that of earlier "laborers" is not only an outcome of technological advances and globalization but also reflects a systemic under-appreciation of the fact that "women's work" has always been arduous. Personal, in-home care work and institutional long-term care—both exceptionally difficult jobs predominantly done by women—are the fastest-growing occupations in North America. Meanwhile, the labor union gains of the twentieth century have been eroded and jobs have become increasingly strenuous, stressful, and overloaded. For its part, even the cybertariat has confronted "increasing professionalization, greater specialization, decreasing utopianism, and more commercialism" (Gill 2007, 7).

At the same time, a new category of worker—much more significant numerically, and even referred to as a new class—has risen to prominence in public discussions: the "precariat" (Standing 2011). With precarious work, the commodification of labor power seems to have reached its ultimate form, where no stable employment relationship is offered and employer commitments beyond the wage (such as benefits) are minimized, while flexibility in hiring, firing, and applying labor are maximized. But here too the significance of this change has been misunderstood. The Latin origin of "precarious" is *precarius*," which means "to entreat through prayer" and "held through the favor of another"—expressions emphasizing the condition of having to beg for work. Under capitalism, working-class life has always been more or less precarious, and degrees of precariousness have corresponded less to technical changes than to shifts in the relative strength of workers. Those who sold their labor power were precarious before unions emerged. Similarly, precariousness increased again as unions weakened (Palmer 2013). Though precarious work is currently concentrated in sectors like fast food and hospitality, precariousness has also spread to sectors once identified with the "aristocracy of labor." The proliferation of two-tier union agreements in the automotive industry, for example, sees precarious and not yet precarious workers laboring side-by-side with different standards, prompting one worker to lament how "we are all precarious now" (Shotwell 2014).

The first organized opposition to precarious labor emerged in the late-nineteenth century and corresponded to the concentration of capitalist production in large workplaces. The strategic position of workers in production opened the door to collective action; "labor" became shorthand for the "labor movement." Soon unions fighting for the democratic rights that then applied only to property owners emblazoned the Latin adage *"Labor Omnia Vincit"* ("Labor Overcomes Everything") on their banners. This phrase originated in 29 BC with the poet Virgil, writing in support of Augustus Caesar—who, in response to landowners' concerns that a falling supply of slaves would increase their price, initiated a "back to the land" drive to encourage more Romans to become farmers. The American Federation of Labor subsequently adopted it as its official motto. The slogan spoke to the fundamental contribution made by those who provide the labor for the improvement of life, linked the dignity of work to broader themes of justice, and raised the Marx-inspired possibility of workers as transformative social agents. For the first time in history, an underclass went beyond sporadic rebellions to establish *permanent* organizations (unions and political parties) with the brazen aim of challenging and eventually overthrowing those in power.

It is the defeat of that early promise that defines our times. In this context, "the labor movement" now means "unions," and unions have come to be perceived as bureaucratic institutions detached from any radical potential. Where socialists once related to unions by "boring from within," many jaded activists now find unions to be *boring* from within. This shift is evident in the celebration of May Day, an energetic cultural expression of working-class solidarity that emerged in the last decades of the nineteenth century. Since World War II, May Day has been marginalized and superseded in the United States and Canada by a government-sanctioned Labor Day reduced to formalized marches to nowhere. The shift in labor's zeitgeist is also apparent in the tendency among unions and workers to self-identify as "middle class."

Intended or not, this usage excludes those who are decidedly not middle class: the poor, the part-time and low-waged, and new immigrants. The diminished usage of "working class" also highlights the retreat from the heady notion that the working class is a key agent in social transformation.

Lin Chun (2014) has poignantly addressed this problem in the case of China, which now includes the world's largest and fastest-growing working class—in this case transitioning from a socialist society to capitalism. Where once the language of "the working class" was constantly used, capitalist imperatives turned such language into a problem. The subsequent "refusal of the language of class," Chun asserts, is "a titanic act of violence on the part of the Chinese state" (25), which robs workers of a central tool for understanding their condition and their underlying unity.

In highlighting the current weakness of organized labor, it would be a mistake to romanticize the past. In an 1895 speech entitled "*Labor Omnia Vincit*," US socialist and labor leader Eugene Debs asked: "With all these grand achievements to the credit of labor, how stands labor itself?" His sober answer was that its condition was "humiliating beyond the power of exaggeration." Similarly, in 1828, Henri Saint-Simon asked, since "the worker is exploited materially, intellectually, and morally," can he "develop his intellectual faculties and moral desires?" Most perceptively, he added: "Can they even *desire* to do so?" (Saint-Simon 1972, 73).

For radicals, the question of social transformation is inseparable from the tension between labor's integration into capitalism and its potential to move beyond it. Absent the support of organized labor's resources, coordination, and numbers, no protest movement can be taken *beyond* protest. Even if the spark for rebellion comes from outside organized labor, its involvement is a condition for eventually winning. The Occupy movement, for example, could only have grown if unions had brought their own members into the fray by extending the occupations from symbolic sites to factories, hospitals, schools, and government buildings.

Whether organized labor can participate in such a project depends on reviving the conceptual relationship between "labor power" and capacities. From this perspective, the core critique of capitalism is that some own and control the labor power of others and affect the development of their capacity to create and produce in the widest sense. The alternate vision this suggests is a society structured to support the full and mutual development of everyone's capacities—"mutual" because our respective capacities develop in relation to one another. Realizing this vision requires that we convert the broadly defined "laboring class" into a social force that can figure out how to overcome capitalism's narrowing of working people's capacities and contribute instead to developing the capacities to analyze, understand, evaluate, dream, and build structures capable of realizing the most radical version of *"Labor Omnia Vincit."*

SEE ALSO: Bodies; Care; Class; Gender; Intellectual; Materialism; Reproduction; Rights; Solidarity; Sustainable

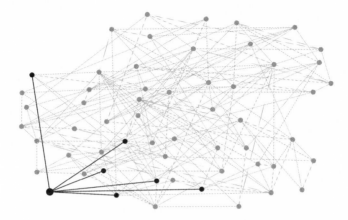

LEADERSHIP

Joy James

THE ROOT WORD "LEAD" COMES FROM THE OLD ENGLISH
"*lædan*" ("to guide") and is derived from the Proto-
Germanic "**laiđâ*" ("road, journey") (*OED*).[1] In the fourteenth century, it came to denote the fact of being "in first
place." Indeed, the word "leader" has always referred to
actions at the fore. Not surprisingly, conceptions of the
conditions ("*-ship*") that define and guide these actions
have varied across time and place. As a result, they form
the basis of political disagreements about what constitutes true leadership. Among radicals, the tension among

---

1. In translation, the word "lead" has always been used to render the
   Latin "*ducere*" ("to lead, consider, regard") and this association has
   influenced English usage.

and between leaders and the people they aspire to lead arises at every political scale.

Much of the imagery and analysis that informs contemporary activist conceptions of "leadership" can be traced to the mid-twentieth century Civil Rights Movement and the influence of radical black leadership on social movements during the sixties and seventies. Ella Baker, who helped to found the Student Non-Violent Coordinating Committee in 1960, argued: "Strong people don't need strong leaders" (Moye 2013; Ransby 2005). Baker's conception influenced the future leadership of feminist, white student anti-war, and gay liberation collectives, who also adopted SNCC's multi-racial organizational practices, consensus-building model, and non-elite assumptions regarding community-based leadership (Holsaert et al. 2010). SNCC's impact continues to find expression today in programs like the Children's Defence Fund (headed by former SNCC activist Marian Wright Edelman), which runs "freedom schools" to produce "young servant leaders."

Meanwhile, prestigious colleges and universities funded in part by nineteenth-century magnates with wealth accumulated from the convict lease system now have campus Community Engagement Centers mandated to teach social justice leadership. Because culture produces context for "leadership," it also diversifies its meanings. In "Reclaiming MLK Day," Black Lives Matter founders Opal Tometi, Alicia Garza, and Patrisse Cullors-Brignac remark on the significance of context in their description of BLM's "new layer of leadership." In their view, "We create much more room for collaboration, for expansion, for building power when we nurture movements that are full of leaders, and allow for all of our identities to inform our work and how we organize. This then allows for leadership to emerge from our intersecting identities, rather than to be organized around one notion of Blackness. Because of this, we resist the urge to consolidate our power and efforts behind one charismatic leader" (Tometi, Garza, and Cullors-Brignac 2015).

Emphasizing "Black love," BLM organizers describe leadership as a collective phenomenon requiring the diminishment of ego: "When we center the leadership of the many who exist at the margins, we learn new things about the ways in which state sanctioned violence impacts us all." Consequently, political prisoners are among those setting the movement's tone. Wearing T-shirts emblazoned with the proclamation "Assata Taught Me," organizers invoke the guidance of former Black Panther and Black Liberation Army leader and political fugitive Assata Shakur. In her memoir, Shakur described the need for "a Black revolutionary party, led by Black revolutionary leaders" (1987, 192) capable of both criticism and self-criticism. "My awareness of class difference within the Black community came at an early age," she wrote. "Although my grandmother had taught me more about being proud and strong than anyone i know, she had a lot of Booker T. Washington, pull yourself up by the bootstraps, 'talented tenth' ideas. . . . She was determined that i would become part of Wilmington's talented tenth—the privileged class—part of the so-called Black bourgeoisie" (1987, 21).

Instead, Shakur's Black radicalism exemplifies a rejection of the "uplift ideology" associated with W. E. B. Du Bois' concept of the "talented tenth." According to Du Bois, "The Negro race, like all races, is going to be saved by its exceptional men. The problem of education, then, among Negroes must first of all deal with the Talented Tenth; it is the problem of developing the Best of this race that they may guide the Mass away from the contamination and death of the Worst, in their own and other races" (Du Bois 1903). Shakur's rejection of this strategic orientation is apparent in BLM calls for collective leadership. However, although Du Bois radicalized and later repudiated the idea that Black elites could effectively lead oppressed Blacks (Robinson 1983), his conception of Black leadership (which differed greatly from that of Booker T. Washington, who by some accounts was Du Bois' "nemesis" [Gates 2013]) endures.

In *Dusk of Dawn* (2007), Du Bois revisited a historic controversy which revolved around education and competing visions of Black leadership. Rejecting Booker T. Washington's emphasis on industrial training and accumulation of wealth, Du Bois advocated for liberal arts education: "I knew that without [higher education] the Negro would have to accept white leadership, and that such leadership could not always be trusted" (35–6). Indeed, Du Bois' "talented tenth" was a direct critique of Washington's strategy but it was not a critique of elitism or sexism.[2]

> There was no question of Booker T. Washington's undisputed leadership of the ten million Negroes in America . . . But there were discrepancies and paradoxes in this leadership. . . . At a time when Negro civil rights called for organized and aggressive defense, he broke down that defense by advising acquiescence or at least no agitation. . . . All this naturally aroused increasing opposition among Negroes. (2007, 36–7)[3]

These debates and differences continued throughout the twentieth century. Issued by the Black Liberation Army's Coordinating Committee in 1976–77, the section of *A Political Statement from the Black Underground* devoted to "Leadership of the Struggle" recounts how "The problem of leadership has always been a vexing one for Black people. We must break with the old style of leadership forced upon us by the prevailing class standards or we will fail in our struggle. Nonetheless, leadership is important, especially to Black people, and without it we will never triumph in our struggle." Rather than disavowing Black intellectuals on the basis of their upward mobility, however, the authors emphasized the need for more direct, critical action from such figures: "It is past time that Black intellectuals, professionals, and so-called Black scholars assumed a more active role in the leadership of the liberation struggle, instead of laying back theorizing and writing essays in a

2. Henry Lyman Morehouse, a white northerner who headed the American Baptist Home Missionary Society coined the phrase "talented tenth" seven years before Du Bois published his influential essay. Du Bois helped to marginalize anti-lynching crusader Ida B. Wells from leadership in the NAACP.
3. Interestingly, Du Bois indicates more than once that he did not view himself as a leader. Reflecting on his public controversy with Washington, he wrote: "I was in my imagination a scientist, and neither a leader nor an agitator" (2007, 35).

vacuum, or in various Black bourgeois publications" (Coordinating Committee Black Liberation Army 1976/1977).

Despite the popularity of democratized conceptions of leadership, the "talented tenth" model still finds symptomatic expression in leadership from academics, nonprofits and government elites. Similarly, the tensions that mark debates over the role of class in leadership are apparent in contemporary social movements. In *The Wretched of the Earth*, Frantz Fanon highlighted how these tensions played out during the period of decolonization. "Before independence," he wrote, "the leader, as a rule, personified the aspirations of the people—independence, political freedom, national dignity. But in the aftermath of independence . . . the leader will unmask his inner purpose: to be the CEO of the company of profiteers composed of a national bourgeoisie intent only on getting the most out of the situation" (1967, 112). Fanon's analysis makes clear that tensions concerning movement leadership tend to unfold within a context of state repression—a third conception of "leadership" that, while denounced, nevertheless influences our understanding of leadership qualities.

Conscious that repression is an inevitable response to effective radical leadership, contemporary social movements have adopted democratized conceptions of leadership partly as a survival strategy. Like Black Lives Matter, Occupy Wall Street described itself as "a leaderless (and leaderful) movement"—though it has largely disappeared under the pressure of police surveillance and arrests (Wedes 2014). Anonymous, which emerged in 2003, also abides by a decentralized and democratized leadership structure (Kushner 2014). In 2010, *The Guardian* cited one of the infamous hacktivists explaining that the group has "no central command structure" (Halliday and Arthur). On another occasion, *Salon* quoted former Anonymous activist Gregg Housh, who explained: "There is no leadership. There can't be. That is the point of it all" (Boon 2013). Taken together, OWS, BLM, and Anonymous illustrate that the prevailing radical usage of "leadership" is less concerned with the capacity of rare, great individuals than it is with the agency of ordinary people. Although the implications of this orientation remain ambiguous, it seems likely that attachment to the promise of "leaderful" movements will shape our political imaginary for years to come.

SEE ALSO: Democracy; Hegemony; Populism; Representation; Vanguard; War

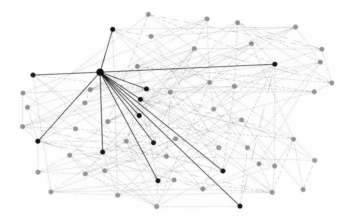

LIBERAL

Robin Marie Averbeck

THE ROOTS OF THE TERM "LIBERAL" REACH AS FAR BACK
as the thirteenth century, when it was first used to denote
a form of freedom specific to individuals with access to
financial and personal independence. Moreover, it also
took on the meaning of "generous" or "unrestrained,"
thereby acquiring connotations that could run in both
positive and negative directions. These connotations
in turn inflected a political meaning, which—by the
eighteenth century—was used to refer to individuals with unorthodox views who sympathized with the
Enlightenment project of questioning traditional hierarchies while placing emphasis on the liberty of individual
subjects (Williams 1976).

Most historians agree that the development of "liberalism" as a political philosophy built around the notion of "liberty" for the individual took place during the eighteenth century. This "liberty" depended on the destruction of traditional social obligations and entailed a restructuring of the economy along capitalist lines. As historians Neil Jumonville and Kevin Mattson write, "This early and still very weak stage of individualism took the name of Protestantism in religion, capitalism in economics, and liberalism in politics" (2007, 2).

In Europe, use the term "liberal" by political actors was commonplace by the mid-nineteenth century. In North America, however, it was not frequently used to refer to a political position until the mid-twentieth century—at precisely the time when the term itself began to take on somewhat altered meanings. These new meanings first began to find expression when a faction of turn-of-the-century liberals—who usually called themselves "Progressives"—sought to address the social dysfunction and suffering caused by capitalism through remedial programs and policies. This "liberalism," however, was never intended to fundamentally alter social relations. Instead, as historian Daniel Rodgers argues, it was rooted in the assumption that "the most promising counterforce to the injustices of industrial capitalism was the enlightened conscience of capitalism itself" (1998, 16–17).

It was not until the Great Depression that "liberal" and "liberalism" came into widespread use as terms identifying a discrete political association rather than a broad political philosophy. In this context, liberalism became the creed of the New Deal and of the coalition the Democratic Party constructed around it. Although this liberalism remained deeply committed to maintaining capitalist relations, the emergency programs of the New Deal enabled the concept to become associated as much with intervention in the market as with the defense of property rights (Rotunda 1968). At the same time, Depression-era popular organizing by socialists, communists, and other leftists—a coalition referred to as the Popular Front—occasionally intersected with New Deal programs (Brinkley 1995). As a result, "liberal" became a common term against which radicals defined themselves at the very moment when, in the United States at least, the two forces collaborated the most.

The historical experience of having at one time worked closely with liberals, and perhaps even of having invested hope in their administrations, helps explain the intensity with which most radicals turned to using "liberal" as a clear derogative during the Cold War years. Of course, long-time leftists had never identified closely with liberalism. Still, many left-leaning baby boomers reared in a political culture that heralded liberalism as the last defense against totalitarianism began identifying with the term. As the social upheavals of the 1960s unfolded, however, many young radicals went through an educational process that eventually led to their rejection of liberalism. Once again the term "liberal" became derogative.

In the early stages of the student movement, for example, many white activists who still identified with liberalism encountered a Black movement that was much more skeptical about liberals' capacity to advance the struggle. Tom Hayden writes of encountering Black organizers in the early 1960s who were "miles ahead of us . . . chuckling knowingly about the sterility of liberals" (2011, 228). By the time Mario Savio spoke to the crowd at UC Berkeley during the Free Speech Movement of 1964, few people missed the scathing critique implied in his reference to "a well-meaning liberal." Shortly thereafter, radical songwriter Phil Ochs distilled this disdain into his satirical masterpiece "Love Me, I'm a Liberal."

The inflection given to "liberalism" by social movements during this time was mirrored in leftist scholarship that sought to disassociate the term from its mid-century progressive overtones. In his 1963 book *The Triumph of Conservatism,* historian Gabriel Kolko argued that the major legislative achievements of Progressivism ought to be understood not as left-leaning policies enacted by those opposed to unregulated, unmediated capitalism but rather as the accomplishments of the representatives of business and capitalism itself. Such legislation, Kolko argued, secured the establishment of what he called "political capitalism," a system of liberal democratic governance that exists to ensure and preserve capitalist social relations (1963). From this critique grew the conjunction "corporate liberalism," a term that became widely popular as a way of referring to liberalism's function in maintaining capitalism.

Originating in 1920s Germany but best known through the mid-century work of Max Horkheimer, Herbert Marcuse, and Theodor Adorno, the Frankfurt School also shaped radicals' understanding of "liberals" and "liberalism." Their critique provided postwar radicals with an analysis of liberal, bourgeois society that criticized its endless capacity for alienation and the sickening effect of its consumerism on the well-being of individuals and society alike. This critique resonated with young New Leftists who had been reared in the cradle of postwar affluence only to find the results of consumer- and market-based society to be spiritually devastating. In this sense, "liberalism" referred not only to a political philosophy but also to a social disease that led individuals to seek meaning in empty places (Jay 1973).

Other radical scholars also made valuable contributions. Since the 1980s, literary critic and Marxist theorist Fredric Jameson has worked to expose the political content in contemporary cultural output that presents itself as apolitical. By Jameson's account, liberalism distinguishes itself from other ideologies by denying that it is, in fact, an ideology. Only liberalism, for instance, seeks to distinguish an artist from his or her art, since "such a separation is possible only for a world-view—liberalism—in which the political and the ideological are mere secondary or 'public' adjuncts to the content of a real 'private' life, which alone is authentic and genuine. It is not possible for any world-view—whether conservative or radical and revolutionary—that takes politics seriously" (1981, 289).

In this view, liberals are seen as advocating a definition of "politics" that is far narrower than the one that radicals embrace. "Politics," in the liberal sense, refers only to those institutions and practices explicitly concerned with the distribution of power, like parties and election campaigns. When Jameson argues that liberalism does not take politics seriously, he highlights the liberal tendency to segregate social and cultural life from political life while depicting "politics" as a contaminant to a true human nature that transcends the political realm.

The significance of this critique arises from contemporaneous developments in the field of politics itself. During the 1980s, the reaction against the global liberation movements that had exploded in the middle of the century began to consolidate. In the United States, the election of Ronald Reagan heralded this triumph—as did the administration of Margaret Thatcher in the United Kingdom. Over the next three decades, social democratic institutions eroded, and the market expanded into previously public arenas throughout the world. The ideology that accompanied these developments was "neoliberalism," with the term intended to highlight the connection between the privatizing agenda and the free-market ideals of the eighteenth century (Harvey 2005).

This new use of "liberalism" thus requires some attention, since "neoliberal" is usually used to distinguish advocates of a theoretically "free market" from the inheritors of Progressive and New Deal–era liberalism, who advocate limited use of the state to ameliorate, but not alter, capitalist relations. However, radicals today often use "neoliberalism" and "liberalism" interchangeably, a practice that suggests a critique of the most commonly received meaning of "liberalism," which continues to be associated with the New Deal. From a radical perspective, the experience of the past sixty years has exposed liberalism's inability—as a philosophy of what Raymond Williams (following C.B. Macpherson) called "possessive individualism,"—to resist capitalist market relations in any significant way (1976, 181). Indeed, the 1960s rejection of liberalism can be understood as a realization that liberalism—in its many valences—ultimately failed to provide any path out of capitalism's social inequality and suffering. Moreover, the failure of liberal parties in the United States and elsewhere to maintain ideological independence from neoliberal policies seems to legitimize the radical tendency to blur the distinction between the two categories. The affinity between liberalism and neoliberalism becomes especially clear when it is understood that neoliberal policy aims less for "the retreat of the state so much as its remaking" according to the interests of capital (Heideman 2014).

Despite this new dynamic, the most common meaning of "liberal" in North America continues to evoke the descendants of the New Deal who argue against socialism and other radicalisms. A liberal, in common radical usage, is someone who ultimately sides with capitalism despite personal commitments to social justice. As a result, radical discussions of liberalism are often punctuated by accusations of naiveté. This is not surprising since, as Jameson pointed out, a crucial component of liberalism is its insistence that it is not an ideology.

In the end, liberal naiveté—or delusion—is both a limit to liberal conceptions of the political and a highly useful ideological defense against radical claims. Contemporary radicals often confront this dynamic when leftist and liberal circles overlap. Under such conditions, the term "liberal" becomes synonymous with ignorant adherence to moderation and mainstream political pieties. Such was the joke, for instance, behind a banner carried by anarchists in Washington DC during the Occupy movement, which read: "Liberals: Can We Riot Now?"

Along with hapless credulity, the moderation of liberals is often experienced as infiltration. With the rise of Black Lives Matter, many organizers became frustrated with what they perceived to be elite liberal encroachment on a radical grassroots movement. Liberals, they argued, shifted the discourse away from challenging institutionalized racism and toward a politics of "practical" reforms. As one commentator put it, "liberalism in the movement encourages working with the police and the government to reform state violence" while "ignoring the fact that the system cannot reform itself" (Black Communist 2014).

Reminiscent of the laments of mid-century Civil Rights activists, the Black Lives Matter movement drew attention to how race shaped political responses. Articles and essays written about the shortcomings of liberalism during this period often described their subjects not merely as liberal, but also as white. These interventions included articles with titles like "It's Not about You, White Liberals" and even a personal blog entitled "STFU, White Liberals!" (Cooper 2014). Similar to the dynamic of social movements in the

1960s, activists today increasingly understand liberalism to refer not solely to a politics of class but also to a politics of race.

Despite these variations, the most common radical usage of "liberal" today remains as a point against which to define ourselves. Liberalism, as a political philosophy committed to capitalism, is what radicalism is not. To speak critically or satirically about liberals (from a vantage other than that of the right) is to identify one's self as a radical. For this reason, liberalism has a deep social meaning and function for radicals. If, as Lewis Coser and Irving Howe once argued, "socialism is the name of our desire," then liberalism today is the name of our enemy. Through our shared opposition to its machinations, we identify our friends and build solidarity (Kazin 2011, 277–78). At a time when liberal control over international politics seems nearly complete, such an alliance is of great importance. It surpasses in value the merely functional negative definitions upon which we've come to rely.

SEE ALSO: Agency; Authority; Class; Democracy; Friend; Ideology; Nation; Politics; Populism; Race; Responsibility; Rights

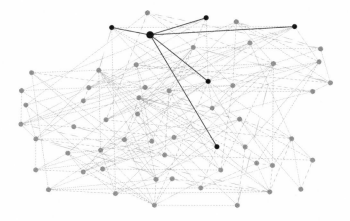

LOVE

Heather Davis

In a town hall meeting in Seattle that took place shortly after the 2014 Ferguson uprisings, Cornell West described Black Lives Matter and its future challenges in the following way: "These folks start channeling all of this rage in a way that is headed towards justice rather than killing each other. . . . But the challenge is going to be can we pass on to the younger generation the expression of that rage . . . through love and justice rather than hatred and revenge?" (West 2014). The pairing of love and justice in West's comments is part of a long tradition with roots in Christian theology. It continues to find expression in social movements today.

The slogan "Black Lives Matter" itself came from a sentiment of love (Kurwa 2014). It started as a conversation on Facebook between Alicia Garza and Patrisse Cullors. Garza thought it was extremely troubling that people were not surprised when George Zimmerman was found innocent after murdering Trayvon Martin, an unarmed Black teenager. Garza wrote, "Black people, I love you, I love us, we got us and our lives matter" (Kurwa 2014). Her friend turned the sentiment into the hash tag #blacklivesmatter and connected it to a burgeoning movement that would grow even stronger after the police killings of Eric Garner and Michael Brown (Kurwa 2014). The insistence on "love" in the movement's first enunciations is fundamental to cultivating both solidarity and self worth, which are consistently undermined by white supremacist culture. Here, "love" operates not solely as an affirmation but also as an indictment of racism. The call to love is thus necessarily a call for self-organizing and racial justice.

As noted in the *Oxford English Dictionary*, "love" has been used in English to describe affection and attachment since at least the eighth century, with etymological roots in Old Frisian, Old Saxon, Old High German, and Gothic. Love itself has certainly been part of human consciousness long before this. Organizing through calls of love also has a long history—especially in movements that adhere to nonviolent direct action, like the Civil Rights Movement. Here, "love" and "justice" are twinned through the imperative to "love thy neighbor as thyself." According to the Book of Mark, "there is none other commandment greater than these" (Mark 12:31). This imperative has influenced contemporary social movements through traditions like nonviolent resistance and liberation theology. The two most prominent examples of nonviolent direct action from the twentieth century are the Quit India movement led by Mahatma Gandhi and the Civil Rights Movement in the United States. Both frequently invoked "love" as a guiding principle and force for change.

Early on, Gandhi was influenced by "A Letter to a Hindu," which Leo Tolstoy published in the *Free Hindustan*. In it he argued that all of the major religions were united through the principle of love, which represented the highest form of morality. For Tolstoy, this did not mean that people should be subservient; on the contrary, the principle of love compelled opposition to all forms of violence and—in the case of colonial India—the overthrow of English rule. "Love is the only way to rescue humanity from all ills," Tolstoy wrote, "and in it you too have the only method of saving your people from enslavement" (Tolstoy n.d.). Gandhi adopted this principle and subsequently developed his understanding of nonviolent direct action through reference to "*satya*" (truth) and "*ahimsa*" ("action based on the refusal to do harm"), which he drew from Hinduism (Bondurant 1971, 23). This principle—that love can overcome oppression—was put to work on a grand scale and contributed to the overthrow of British colonial rule.

Drawing on Baptist theology, Martin Luther King Jr. developed a similar conception of love as resistance. He understood the destructiveness of hate and the transformative potential of loving one's neighbor even while actively working to resist violent actions. According to King, hate distorted the personality of the person who hates. In contrast, love was radical, redemptive, and transformative. In a recently discovered 1964 address, "Speech on Civil Rights, Segregation, and Apartheid South Africa," King insisted that "love can be a powerful force for social change":

> I'm not talking about a weak love, I'm not talking about emotional bosh here. I'm not talking about some sentimental quality. . . . It would be nonsense to urge oppressed people to love their violent oppressors in an affectionate sense and I have never advised that. . . . Love is understanding, creative, redemptive goodwill for all men. Theologians talk about this kind of love with the Greek word *agape*, which is a sort of overflowing love that seeks nothing in return. And when one develops this, you rise to the position of being able to love the person who does the evil deed, while hating the deed that the person does. . . . I believe firmly that it is through this kind of powerful

> nonviolent action, this kind of love that organizes it-
> self into mass action, that we will be able to transform
> the jangling discords of our nation and the world into
> a beautiful symphony of brotherhood. (King 1964b)

King similarly asserted the connection between love and social transformation during his 1964 Nobel Peace Prize address: "Negroes of the United States, following the people of India, have demonstrated that nonviolence is not sterile passivity, but a powerful moral force which makes for social transformation. . . . If [peace] is to be achieved, man must evolve for all human conflict a method which rejects revenge, aggression and retaliation. The foundation of such a method is love" (King 1964a). In this way, "love" became a fundamental principle of the Civil Rights Movement, and the churches became important sites for organizing people on this basis. Identification with love's radical promise continues today and can be seen in social movements like Black Lives Matter. West made this connection explicit while speaking at the Seattle town-hall meeting mentioned above: "Love is subversive; it's revolutionary because when you really love folk, especially when you really love poor and working people, you hate the fact that they are being treated unjustly. You loathe the fact that they are being treated unfairly and if you don't do something then the rocks are going to cry out. That's the fire in the bones that you get in Jeremiah and Hebrew scripture" (West 2014). In this Christian formulation, people are called to action and to achieve social justice through their love for others.

But despite the strong associations of love with nonviolent direct action, other revolutionary leaders have recognized the importance of love as a mobilizing principle while remaining open to violent tactics. In his "Socialism and Man in Cuba," Che Guevara makes this explicit by asserting ("at the risk of seeming ridiculous," no less) that "the true revolutionary is guided by great feelings of love." In fact, he thought, "it is impossible to think of a genuine revolutionary lacking this quality" (Guevara 1968). This sentiment, with its seemingly contradictory impulses, would later be expressed by liberation theologian Oscar Romero in the midst of El Salvador's armed struggle. In opposition to the movement's detractors, Romero insisted that "the violence we preach is . . . the violence of love" (AK Thompson 2014). Here, "love" is understood as political transformation and upheaval—not unlike the personal experience of falling in love, where the boundaries between self and other dissolve in a feeling that compels people to act beyond themselves. In this iteration, violence and love are not antithetical. Instead they work in tandem toward the larger goal of social revolution.

In a similar fashion, the notion of "brotherly love" (as in the Greek "*philia*") has also been a powerful organizing tool. Poland's Committee for Workers' Defense (KOR) illustrated the power of friendship to transcend and transform the political by bringing politics itself into contact with people's most intimate being. As researcher Nina Witoszek writes, politics in Poland from 1976 to 1978 was conducted "via unpolitical means: a bohemian community sharing things, money, food; a 'warm circle' which provided a sense of security and an awareness that 'you can risk everything because there will always be people who love you, who will help you and who will be with you to the end'" (Witoszek 2007, 106). This sense of solidarity between friends is thus presented as being essential to any kind of meaningful change. However, it is not without its risks. Although the idea that we are "in it together" can bond people and create the necessary emotional and physical structures to keep fighting, this same love can become a tool of social coercion capable of shutting down dissent within radical communities. Recalling a conference of NGO workers, Yasmin Nair describes how "it was expected that we would throw our lives out there and reveal our vulnerabilities. To justify all this, the word 'love' was thrown around a lot: we were not only expected to love our work—and what that meant for those whose work was unpaid or underpaid was quite unclear—but to love each other, to believe that we were all in the struggle together" (Nair 2011). Love, as Nair's account makes clear, can be marshaled as a semantic tool to quell dissent or obscure structural problems (especially concerning the organization and division of labor) within activist communities.

Political theorist Michael Hardt has recently considered how love can appear both as an expression of solidarity and as a force of transformation. By his account, love is a useful metaphor for revolution since it provides a framework to think about duration within transformation. Everyday experiences of love, ones that create relations of responsibility and radical change, parallel the need for forms of revolutionary action that are simultaneously transformative and ongoing. Hardt writes, "On the one hand, a political love must be a revolutionary force that radically breaks with the structures of the social life we know, overthrowing its norms and institutions. On the other hand, it must provide mechanisms of lasting association and . . . create enduring institutions" (2012, 6). For this to work, he offers two different concepts. One is the idea of "composition," which denotes a body composed of smaller parts that interact with other bodies. This happens both at the level of the individual and at the level of society, encouraging experimental configurations while not insisting on unity. The second concept is that of "ritual." Through ritual, people continually return to the things or people they love. It is a means of creating stability and repetition, and of bringing habit into our lives. Far from being mere repetition, this understanding of ritual offers a way of thinking about political structures as a source of constant revitalization. As a result, we can commit ourselves again and again while recognizing that each return is new. For Hardt, this model amounts to a form of revolutionary institution-making arising from the need to create stable structures for enduring change. We need places from which we might gain strength without those places becoming fixed or dogmatic.

Love is not just a useful metaphor for thinking through revolutionary transformation. It is also the site at which the personal connects with the political—as can be seen in the "free love" movement, which developed in the mid-nineteenth century. This movement argued that questions regarding love, sex, and partnership should be decided by individuals and not by the church or state. Connected to first-wave feminist politics, free love practitioners advocated women's bodily and reproductive autonomy and showed how these rights were often foreclosed by marriage. Victoria Woodhull, the first woman to run for the US presidency, proclaimed her adherence to free love in 1871 when she wrote: "Yes, I am a Free Lover. I have an inalienable, constitutional and natural right to love whom I may, to love as long or as short a period as I can; to change that love every day if I please, and with that right neither you nor any law you can frame have any right to interfere."

Free love also had close associations with anarchism and found a venue in publications like *Lucifer, the Light Bearer*, which addressed matters concerning birth control, women's suffrage, and other topics. Emma Goldman (1932) also famously championed free love and reproductive rights and assisted with abortions. Like other anarchists, she argued that liberation could not be achieved without addressing issues of sexuality and the questions of women's equality (Goldman 1969, 227–39). Noting a connection between sexual and racial slavery and developing an interracial ethic through jazz and poetry, currents within the free love movement also forged alliances with abolitionists (Buhle 1998, 243). The movement also incorporated the insights and commitments of the early gay rights movement into its analysis through the writings of Edward Carpenter. These included a commitment to sex radicalism in the interest of overthrowing patriarchy and "the authoritarianism of heterosexual domination" as well as alignment with the "widespread movements to decriminalize homosexual activity" (Buhle 1998, 244). These attempts to redefine sexuality outside of the regulative norms of church and state anticipated the subsequent rise of LGBTIQ and polyamorous communities. Among other things, these projects attempt to re-invent sexual and intimate relations by allowing for ambiguity, incommensurability, and openness in order to cultivate a form of politics that refuses patriarchal heteronormativity.

Love is central to contemporary social justice projects as a guiding principle, a metaphor, and a practice. Love of the world and for others compels us to act. Love as attachment has—through the efforts of queer radicals—transformed notions of family, community, and intimacy. Through nonviolent direct action and civil rights, love has also been a means of structuring our resistance. However, despite its power as a tool of resistance, love's invocation has not always been benign. Because it necessarily blurs the distinctions between the personal and political, love can be used for social coercion on intimate and national scales; consider the phrase "for the love of one's country." Indeed, it is often for love of family, friends, children, and others that we find ourselves in conflict with our own principles. Radicals must therefore cultivate love for and through social justice work while resisting its use as a tool of manipulation. For this reason, love's political promise must constantly be rediscovered.

SEE ALSO: Care; Community; Friend; Solidarity; Violence

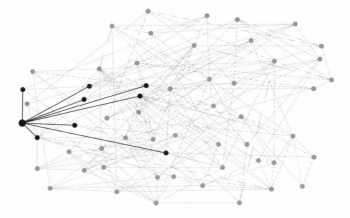

MATERIALISM

Rosemary Hennessy

ACCORDING TO THE *OXFORD ENGLISH DICTIONARY*, "materialism" entered the English lexicon in the mid-eighteenth century to denote the opinion that nothing exists except matter. In its contemporary commonsense usage, "materialism" refers to the tendency to value possessions or consumer products more than spiritual ideals. Pop singer Madonna's 1984 hit song "Material Girl" conveys this connotation by foregrounding her desire for a man with "cold hard cash." The distinction between "the material" and "the spiritual" also finds expression in philosophical discourse, where "materialism" constitutes a line of inquiry into the nature of reality. Generally differentiated from idealism, materialism takes as its premise not spirit or mind but, rather, social conditions and relations or (in some versions) physical matter itself. Two recent versions of materialism—cultural materialism and the new materialism—elaborate the social and ontological features of the concept while departing to some extent from the formulation of historical materialism most commonly associated with Karl Marx.

Philosophical materialism dates back to Heraclitus who, in the sixth century BC, conceived of material life as a dynamic process: "things whole, things not whole, (something) being brought together, (something) being separated; (something) consonant, (something) dissonant" (1987, Fragment 15). This attention to a vibrant and interrelated world reappears in the seventeenth century, where it found expression in the radical early-modern materialism of Baruch Spinoza. In his *Ethics*, Spinoza aimed to restore divine and human life to their proper place in nature, claiming that "it cannot happen that a man is not a part of Nature and can undergo no changes apart from those that can be understood through his nature alone, and of which he is the adequate cause" (2000, 231). His attention to affect and to the body, which challenged the dualistic materialism of his contemporaries, has been rediscovered and embraced by twenty-first century intellectuals.

One of the most theoretically and politically powerful iterations of materialism to emerge from capitalism's industrial phase is historical materialism. Elaborated by Karl Marx and Friedrich Engels in *The German Ideology*, historical materialism begins not with culture or consciousness but with "real individuals, their activity and the material conditions of their life" (1976a, 31). For Marx and Engels, the "material" comprises "the existence of living human individuals." Such existence is made possible by (and reproduced through) interactions in and with the natural world through labor, political organization, and cultural practices—all of which vary historically. Distinct from other materialisms, historical materialism was conceived as enabling forms of action that could make social life more just. As Marx asserted in his *Theses on Feuerbach*, "the philosophers have only interpreted the world in various ways; the point is to change it" (Marx and Engels 1976a).

On this basis, Marx developed his critique of capital as a property relation between those who own only their labor and those who own and control the resources that enable them to accumulate value (profit) in the form of surplus (or unpaid) labor. According to this perspective, the material basis of capital's value relation is the labor time stolen during the working day and the time for regeneration stolen through the plunder of both nonhuman resources and human capacities as they are drawn into exchange markets. As marxist feminist Selma James has noted, capital "takes our time, which happens to be our life" (2012, 149).[1]

Marxist feminists like James strive to make visible what Marx could not see—that the social reproduction of material life presupposes both the labor of care crucial to survival and the time required for living organisms to regenerate and rest. In redefining domestic labor as value-bearing, marxist feminists uncover the material underside of the wage labor market—the unwaged domestic labor of women that remains invisible as labor yet enables and enhances the capacities that workers exchange for a wage. As Silvia Federici explains, "recognition of the importance of reproduction and women's domestic labor for capital accumulation led to a rethinking of Marx's categories" and highlighted how women's oppression was materially bound to capitalist development (2012, 96).

Such an analysis can also help to reveal the value that capital has reaped through the historical process of colonization, in which value accumulation is achieved through the production of what Ariel Salleh has described as "ecological and embodied debts" (2009, 27). These debts represent the value of the raw materials, human bodies, and labor harvested from the Global South as well as the time required to reproduce the resources for sustaining life that was stolen along with them (Mies 2014; Federici 2004). A systemic materialist analytic understands that the oppression of subalterns, women, sexual dissidents, and people of color is an integral feature of capitalism. By calling on scholars to "[put] materialism

---

1.   I use the lowercase "m" for "marxist feminism" to signal its *critical* affiliation with Marxian theory. For additional examples of marxist feminist contributions to materialist thought, see Federici (2004, 2012); Hennessy (2013); Hennessy and Ingraham (1997); Mies and Shiva (2014); Vogel (1987).

back into race theory" (2006), Robert Young has advanced a political economy of race in the interest of emancipatory politics.

Since the beginning of the twentieth century, the most widely recognized materialist approaches to culture were developed by intellectuals associated with German critical theory, British cultural materialism, and French Althusserian Marxism and post-Marxism. The Frankfurt School of critical theory (Walter Benjamin, Theodor Adorno, Max Horkheimer, and Jürgen Habermas) directed their attention toward the impact of alienated rationality in advanced industrial societies. According to Adorno, materialism needed to take account of "the increasing strength of modern mass culture," including the destructive impact of culture as ideology (1992, 71). The cultural materialism of British Marxists Raymond Williams and E. P. Thompson confronted the limits of the concept of ideology and conceived culture as a contested historical and material force. Drawing upon Gramsci's concept of hegemony, Williams conceptualized culture as "a whole body of practices and expectations over the whole of living" in which "forms of domination and subordination correspond much more closely to the normal processes of social organization and control" (1977, 110). For Williams, "the reality of any hegemony . . . is that while by definition it is always dominant, it is never either total or exclusive" since alternative or oppositional politics have effects on the hegemonic culture (1977, 113).

Stuart Hall pursued this materialist conception of culture as hegemonic while devoting particular attention to popular culture. As Hall asserts, "For something to become popular entails a struggle; it is never a simple process, as Gramsci reminded us" (Hall 1996a, 141). Founded by Hall and Richard Hoggart in 1964, the Birmingham Center for Critical Cultural Studies (CCCS) brought materialist analysis to investigations of race, gender, working-class subcultures, and postcolonial subjects. Much of this work drew upon continental (and especially French) Marxist theories. Notable among these reference points was the work of Louis Althusser who, in the wake of the failures of the 1968 general strike in France, sought to forge a more robust materialist account of the state's relation to ideology. In his widely read essay, "Ideology and Ideological State Apparatuses," Althusser proposed that, contrary to prevailing conceptions, "ideology has a material existence" (1971, 165). "This existence is material," he noted, because it "always exists in an apparatus, and its practice, or practices" (1971, 166). As such, it "has the function of constituting concrete individuals as subjects" (171). A student of Althusser's, Michel Foucault broke from the Marxist conception, which emphasized culture's material relation to the reproduction of class structures, in order to consider how the materiality of discourse found expression in genealogies of punishment, discipline, and subject formation. Here power is exercised not through ruling-class control but through "a multiplicity of force relations," which function through norms and forms of governmentality (2009, 92–93).

For its part, materialist feminism draws upon both marxist and post-marxist analytics.* Post-marxist materialists tend to depart from theories that presume causal and structural relations between culture and political economy in order to posit more flexible formulations of power. In such formulations, change is conceived as contingent and propelled by gaps in signification that offer opportunities for novel iterations. Famously articulated in Judith Butler's reading of performativity, this attention to the material character of cultural indeterminacy punctuates queer and postcolonial theory and has been taken up in multiple struggles for recognition. Butler's (1990) widely adopted performative theory of gender and sexual identity brings several materialist problematics into critical conversation. These include Monique Wittig's (1992) materialist critique of heterosexuality and Foucault's (1978) concept of the discursively constructed subject. In attending to the "materiality of the body," Butler calls for "a return to the notion of matter, not as site or surface, but as a *process of materialization that stabilizes over time to produce the effect of boundary, fixity, and surface we call matter*" (1993, 9)—in short, a cultural materialism in which "matter is fully sedimented with discourses" (1993, 29).

For cultural materialists, the material constitutes "what matters" in the double sense of culture having a material existence that is given priority. Although this work has sought to bring formerly unrecognized subjects and bodies into view, the materiality of these subjects often remains subsumed within the discourses that make them meaningful. As various critics have argued, cultural materialism's exclusive attention to culture runs the risk of obscuring other features of material life while foreclosing sustained analysis of culture's relation to capital. As Joan Sangster and Meg Luxton point out, "class was often named but remained a theoretical ghost, an absent presence" in much feminist materialist work carried out in this vein (2013, 300).

Toward the end of the twentieth century, capital's pursuit of new sources of value through the exploitation of human capacities, living organisms, and scientific advances in genetics, subatomic particle physics, and biochemical technologies encouraged renewed theoretical attention to the ontological dimensions of materialism—that is, to material as (non-discursive) matter. This so-called "new materialism" aims to draw attention to the life processes occluded by the historical separation of reason from nature. It also probes the institutionalized division between nature and culture while striving to reconsider the boundaries between the organic and inorganic as well as the human and nonhuman (Alaimo and Hekman 2009). According to Diana Coole and Samantha Frost, what makes the new materialism "new" is its contention that matter itself possesses agency (2010, 6–7).

Some new materialists build on Foucault's concept of bio-power (the "power over life" enacted by a host of technologies and practices) while others emphasize the intimate interactions within and among species. Still others expand "the material" to include the active participation of nonhuman and inorganic forces in the creation of material reality. The "vital materialism" of Jane Bennett, for example, attends to the "lively materialism" or "thing power" of objects that cannot be reduced to the meanings those objects have for humans (2010). For her part, Karen Barad (2007) has aimed through her "onto-epistemological materialism" to account for the "entanglement" and indeterminacies of matter and meaning, the apparatuses and relations that structure them, and the openings that arise and play out at all scales (subatomic, social, cosmic).

The material entanglements of human and natural forces is fundamental to many indigenous concepts like "*buen vivir*" or "*suma qamaña*" that connote collective striving for a good life (Gudynas 2011; Artaraz and Calestani 2014). Although indigenous critiques of modernity tend to depart from the Eurocentric archive of materialist perspectives, their post-capitalist and post-socialist politics share historical materialism's systemic attention to the structural inequalities of capitalism while emphasizing a bio-centric understanding of humans as part of nature (Merchant 2012).

Drawing upon the insights of radical ecology and the feminist attention to social reproduction, contemporary intellectuals and activists are tackling the impact of the bio- and finance economy's new forms of value and developing materialist analyses capable of explaining the structures they depend on and the realities they provoke (Merchant 2012). Some of these responses aim to account for the value increasingly attached to workers' embodied potential rather than to their accumulated skills. As capital accumulation from "immediate life" advances, social reproduction is being eviscerated and value is becoming increasingly dissociated from surplus labor. One example is surrogacy; as opportunities to perform wage labor evaporate, increasing numbers of women are compelled to sell their bodies' vital energy and reproductive capacities directly to the consumer. According to Kalindi Vora, these new forms of labor "contribute to the unquantifiable ability of consuming classes to thrive" while "disenfranchising the humanity of those whose productivity allows for this investment" (2012, 697).

Another point of contemporary engagement for materialist analysis concerns the harvesting of reproductive tissue from stem cells. Here the body's value lies in its promissory potential. For Melinda Cooper and Catherine Waldby, such "clinical labor" is best understood as a relocation of the labor process such that the abstract, temporal imperatives of accumulation come to operate at the level of the body itself. Meanwhile, through a process of material abstraction, "the biological is being rendered newly pliable to the exigencies of abstract, statistical time" (2014, 12). As Kevin Floyd (2015) explains, the "biomedical mode of reproduction," facilitated by the conjuncture of finance and biotechnology, is best understood as "an emergent, gendered variation on a very old story of financial plunder" through which capital reduces the feminized body to a condition of value-dissociated abstract life.

In response, women in the Global North and South currently developing alternative forms of political organization are framing more robust analyses of formerly unrecognized components of material life, including emotional labor, sex, care, and attention. The Madrid collective *Precarias a la deriva* is one example. Started in 2002 when several unions in Spain called a general strike and many women workers were not in a position to participate, the collective developed a practice of "militant research" to uncover "the physiognomy of the crisis of care" while expanding the materialist analysis of caring and precarious labor more generally (*Precarias a la deriva* 2005). For their part, feminists in the radical ecology movement have highlighted the material relation between time and value encoded in capital's speed-up of the regenerative time required by humans, plants, and animals. Others, like Teresa Brennan (2003), have drawn out the impact of neoliberal globalization on the "bioderegulation" of everyday life in the West, in which the time constraints imposed by capital have created a culture of rushing that erodes the material requirements of reproducing human and nonhuman life. Some of the best accounts draw from the wisdom of indigenous and grassroots community organizing efforts that target capital's impact on the reproduction of life across marketplaces and communities (Hale 2008; Hennessy 2013).

As this overview suggests, one of the historical tensions in the genealogy of materialism turns on the question of what constitutes the scope and substance of "the material." Major theoretical shifts in the twentieth and early twenty-first centuries have broken from Marxism to advance analyses of the materiality of culture and of matter. Similarly, emergent commodity markets and technological developments have summoned more robust materialist accounts of expanding capital investments in culture, bodies, and matter.

Questions persist as to whether materialisms that aim to address these urgencies by prioritizing culture ("what matters") or ontology (matter) actually depart from the materialist problematic and thus become compatible with neoliberal hegemony. Nevertheless, in its aspiration to provide an integrated historical account of capitalism as a brutally destructive means of organizing social and natural life, historical materialism remains a valuable primer for explaining and confronting reified forms of consciousness, exploited labor, and a global crisis of dwindling resources. While acknowledging that capitalism sets limits upon the conditions for meeting survival needs, historical materialism also directs attention to the living material that capital cannot harvest—the human potential to impact the conditions we inherit through collaborative action. This potential is a crucial asset for those resisting capitalism's systemic depletion of life while striving to forge alternatives.

SEE ALSO: Class; History; Ideology; Labor; Nature; Politics; Reproduction; Sustainable

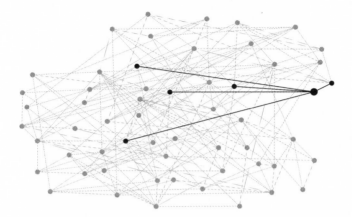

MISOGYNY

Eliza Steinbock

THE TERM "MISOGYNY" DERIVES FROM THE MODERN Latin, "*misogynia*" and from the Greek, "*misogynes*." Both contain the etymological root "*miso*," meaning "hatred, hater." For its part, "*gyne*" refers to "woman" or to "wife." Thus, "misogyny" sometimes slips into common usage as "woman-hater." This etymology does not specify who is to be considered a woman (e.g., on the basis of primary or secondary sex characteristics); instead it refers to the feminine gender role of "wife" and, in particular, the wife of the king—the "queen" (Old English "*cwen*," "*quean*," or honored woman "*gwen*"). Woman's nomination as queen then split from a sovereign reference to assume the more wide-ranging meaning of "powerful, young woman" while also describing the class of servitude performed by a "female serf." During the sixteenth and seventeenth centuries, the meaning of the cognates of "*gyne*" in woman-wife-queen mutated again to capture the threatening female sexuality attributed to the prostitute ("*portcwene*" for "public woman") and hussy (an ironic use of "*quean*").

The first recorded usage of "queen" to denote an effeminate male homosexual was in 1924, and the term gained popularity in Australia during the 1930s. Since then, "queen" has acquired specific ethnic and racialized dimensions through compound forms including "drag queen," "size queen," "snow queen," and "butch queen," which gives expression to the assumption of blackness in ballroom culture (Kulick 2000). The trans exploitation film *Queens at Heart* (1965) documents four pre-Stonewall trans women who, as "queens," are depicted as threatening on account of their male-assigned bodies' performances of nonwhite or nonheterosexual femininity (or both).

For second-wave feminists, "misogyny" became a critical term for illuminating the entrenched subjugation of women, otherwise described through reference to patriarchy or sexism. Accounting for both historical and contemporary misogynist practices remains a key feature of feminist writings, which have considered issues including property and voting laws that exclude women, the burning of "witches," the eradication of matriarchal kinship systems, the use of disciplinary instruments like chastity belts, and the struggle for sexual rights including access to birth control and abortion. Mary Daly's *Gyn/ecology: The Metaethics of Radical Feminism* (1978) typifies feminist usages of "misogyny" between the late sixties to early eighties:

> The fact is that we live in a profoundly anti-female society, a misogynistic "civilization" in which men collectively victimize women, attacking us as personifications of their own paranoid fears, as The Enemy. Within this society it is men who rape, who sap women's energy, who deny women economic and

political power. To allow oneself to know and name
these facts is to commit anti-gynocidal acts. (24)

The Women's Liberation movement of the 1960s and 1970s
emerged from these types of committed critiques of masculinist
social institutions and gynophobic cultural production. However,
it also further involved the identification of a female essence and
a celebration of femaleness as such. As with Daly, feminist author
Adrienne Rich maintained that the ultimate ontological difference was sex. In her view, the distinctness of "female consciousness" arose from an "intense, diffuse sensuality radiating out from
clitoris, breasts, uterus, vagina" (1979, 290). From this biological
ontology, Rich explains misogyny as arising from "the ancient,
continuing envy, awe and dread of the male for the female capacity to create life" (1979, 21). For Linda Alcoff, the contemporary
"identity crisis" in cultural and poststructuralist feminism arises
from the fact that the "category of woman is the necessary point
of departure for any feminist theory and feminist politics" (1988,
405). However, "in attempting to speak for women, feminism often
seems to presuppose that it knows what women truly are, but such
an assumption is foolhardy given that every source of knowledge
about women has been contaminated with misogyny and sexism"
(405–6). Indeed, the mediation of female bodies into the socially
constructed category "woman" is a process "dominated by misogynist discourse." And the problem is not resolved by positing female
anatomy as the basis for identity, since such an approach demands
the mobilization of criteria for inclusion and exclusion that are
themselves misogynist (406).

Writing about the institutionalization of Women's Studies as
an academic discipline, Wendy Brown recalls how the "women's
movements challenged the ubiquitous misogyny, masculinism, and
sexism in academic research, curricula, canons, and pedagogies"
(2008, 21). However, this led to incoherence because, "by definition," the field of Women's Studies "circumscribes uncircumscrib-
able 'women' as an object of study" (ibid.). The result has been an
interminable series of theory wars in which disciplinary adherents

have conservatively rebuked objections to their attempts at circumscription. In a 2015 *New York Times* op-ed, Elinor Burkett pushed back against trans perspectives that she claims go too far by infringing on cisgender women's right to self-definition. In her account, "the trans movement" oversteps its bounds by "demanding that women reconceptualize ourselves" (8). In one transphobic moment, Burkett claimed that Caitlyn Jenner was simply a man who wears nail polish and falsely concludes that this experience makes her a woman. For Burkett, this position made Jenner no better than other "women-hating" men. Today's stark division between trans-misogynist radical feminists and trans-feminisms reiterates the racist divisions carved by white women's liberation movements that spoke for all women on the presupposition that they knew who and what women truly were.

Trans women have been at the forefront of contemporary feminist deployments of "misogyny" as a key term. "Trans-misogyny" conceptualizes injured feminine subjects beyond those marked as "female" at birth. Writer and activist Julia Serano elaborates the concept in *Whipping Girl: A Transsexual Woman on Sexism and the Scapegoating of Femininity* (2007). In her view, "trans-misogyny is steeped in the assumption that femaleness and femininity are inferior to, and exist primarily for the benefit of, maleness and masculinity." As a result, trans women are the target of most of the violent attacks and the butt of most jokes aimed at gender-variant people (2012, 1). As a result of trans-misogyny, "trans women and others on the trans female/feminine spectrum are routinely sexualized in the media, within psychological, social science and feminist discourses, and in society at large" (ibid.). Peggy Phelan's famous joke about misogyny in the media bears repeating in an age when Laverne Cox and Caitlyn Jenner have graced the covers of *Time Magazine* and *Vanity Fair*: "If representational visibility equals power, then almost-naked young white [cisgender] women should be running Western culture" (1993, 10).

Both Serano and Phelan understand that misogyny is wedded to essentialist notions concerning femininity. This makes it all the more hypocritical when trans-exclusionary radical feminists

(TERFs) participate in trans-misogynist smear campaigns that sexualize trans-women as predators. They become "feminist misogynists," to use Susan Gubar's term (1994) for when feminists paradoxically reinforce what they would otherwise denounce by invoking the same restrictive logic of womanhood and manhood marshaled by patriarchal misogynists. In this case, TERFs draw on feminist critiques of misogynist practices that target females exclusively while denying that the "sex/gender system" is itself a changing "sets of arrangements" that create hierarchical divisions between the sexes (Rubin 1975, 159).

Trans-feminism builds on the insight that femininity is disparaged in patriarchal societies, but it sheds the essentialist notion that it is solely attributable to female-assigned persons. Expanding the circumference of femininity prevents misogyny from being seen as a problem solely for women who have "female" life experience, vulvas, XX-chromosomes, or who can biologically reproduce and are therefore enslaved to patriarchy in some special sense.

In her trans-feminist manifesto, Emi Koyama calls attention to shared and differential experiences of misogyny: "trans women are targeted because we live as women. Being a woman in this misogynist society is dangerous, but there are some factors that make us much more vulnerable when we are the targets of sexual and domestic violence" (2003, 7). On *Feminist Wire*, Nick Artrip recounts the impact of misogyny on the gay hook-up application Grindr, claiming that "misogyny has crept so greatly into our culture that even sexual positions within the gay community have become politicized" (2013). "No Fat, No Femme" tags reflect current strictures concerning the admission of a preference for being a bottom. In this context "Vers" (for versatile) becomes code to cover the shame of being a bottom in a scene where it is perceived as feminine. In both cases, discrimination is aimed at feminine male-assigned subjects (trans women and gay men), though those subjects identify with femininity from different gender positions. Similarly, femme queer women face misogyny from lesbians who question their identification with femininity or perceive them as passive and weak (Brushwood Rose and Camilleri 2003).

How to best combat misogynist practices has become a key question in workplace and street harassment activism (e.g., the "Lean In" and "hollaback!" movements). It has also been explored in popular hashtag campaigns like "whatafeministlookslike" on Tumblr. The circulation of photographs of all kinds of people— but especially of A-list celebrities—wearing T-shirts or holding signs bearing the slogan sought to challenge the notion that only man-hating white women were feminists. Like the "I'm a feminist because" campaign, the strategy aims to challenge the "f-word" phenomenon in which feminism is considered either a curse word or an obsolete political position. As Andrea Dworkin remarked, "Feminism is hated because women are hated. Antifeminism is a direct expression of misogyny; it is the political defense of women hating" (1978, 195). In response, the UK-based website F-word (thefword.org.uk) has embraced this condemnation, while Kristin Anderson's *Modern Misogyny: Anti-Feminism in a Post-Feminist Era* (2015) recounts how women's perceived gains have revitalized invocations of the "male-bashing feminist" who complains because she just doesn't like men.

Meanwhile, a new crop of terms has emerged to describe the misogynist behaviors that occur when a masculine person actively disparages the intellectual capacities of feminine people or invades their physical space. These misogynist behaviors are hardly new. However, like the bullying behaviors of "trolling" or "flaming" online, "mansplaining" and "manspreading" are neologisms that qualify how masculinity finds expression through unwarranted intellectual confidence and a sense of entitlement to space. "Mansplaining," writes Sarah Seltzer, "describes the phenomenon of someone (usually a man, but not always) behaving as though he has superior knowledge to someone else (often a woman) who actually knows more about the topic in question than he does" (2015). Similarly, "manspreading" describes the physical entitlement felt by men to treat public space as their own private domain. As Emma Fitzsimmons (2014) notes, the problem is so acute that New York's Metropolitan Transportation Authority has launched a campaign to shame men into closing their legs while riding trains and buses. These novel additions to the lexicon of misogyny reveal fresh anger and frustration at everyday sexism. A similar term, "manslamming" names a resistance tactic. In an effort to confront the mentality that a feminine person should give way to a masculine pedestrian, manslammers hold their line, refuse to yield, and "slam" back (Roy 2015).

Activists today must consider analytics beyond the two neat camps of "perpetrator" and "victim," which are aligned respectively with "men" and "women." Misogyny's critical purchase arises from its ability to identify the injustices endured as a result of disparaged femininity and to acknowledge how these injustices are experienced differentially by white women, women of color, homosexual men, trans women, femmes, queens, and sissy-, faerie-, or fag-identified people. In contrast, popular usages of "misogyny" continue their struggle to determine what a woman is. This tension makes "misogyny" a key term for radicals to consider as we respond to the hate coursing through patriarchal, racist, and capitalist relations.

SEE ALSO: Experience; Gender; Oppression; Representation; Trans*/-

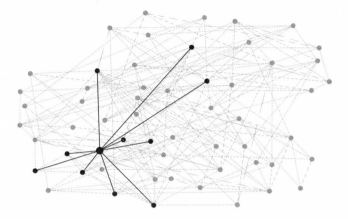

NATION

Sunera Thobani

DEFINED BY THE *OXFORD ENGLISH DICTIONARY* AS "A large body of people united by common descent, history, culture or language, inhabiting a particular state or territory," the English word "nation" has been traced to the French "*nacion*" ("birth, rank; descendants, relatives; country, homeland"), which in turn came from the Latin "*natio*" ("birth, origin; breed, stock, kind, species"). "Nation" was thus historically associated with biological understandings of birth, stock, and breed. Additionally, many of the meanings attached to "nation" during the modern era were rooted in classical and biblical antiquity (Geary 2003). Some scholars in fields like History and Religious Studies have pointed to the existence of ancient

(Egyptian, Israeli) and medieval (Anglo-Saxon, Viking, Norse) nations to argue for the longevity of the entity. Others, however, have argued that the meanings associated with the term in the past were significantly different from those that are current today (Geary 2003; Brubaker 1996).

Until the mid-twentieth century, most Western theorists saw the nation as a modern invention that first appeared in Europe during the eighteenth century. As Geary explains, the most common definitions of "nation" tended to argue that "there were two sorts of 'peoples.' The one was constitutional, based on law, allegiance, and created by a historical process. The other, standing largely outside the process of historical change, was biological, based on descent, custom and geography" (Geary 2003, 42). Whereas the former were designated "civilized," the latter were considered "barbarian" (ibid.).

Liberals drew on social contract theory to define the modern nation as a distinct and unique fraternity, based on shared citizenship status (Rousseau 2002). The social pact, explained Rousseau, "substitutes a moral and lawful equality for the physical inequality that nature imposed upon men, so that, although unequal in strength and intellect, they all become equal by convention and legal right" (Rousseau 2002, 169). By subsuming internal hierarchies, "nation" was presented as a form of horizontal association based on the mutual consent of self-determining individuals and identifiable by a distinct set of characteristics considered immanent to the community itself (Balibar and Wallerstein 1991). As Rousseau explained, "Born a citizen of a free State, and a member of that sovereign body, however feeble an influence my voice may have in public affairs, the right to vote on them is sufficient to impose on me the duty of informing myself about them; and I feel happy, whenever I meditate on governments, always to discover in my research new reasons for loving that of my own country" (Rousseau 2002, 155). In contrast to uncivilized populations who lived under the tyranny of brutal chieftains and Oriental despots, European conservatives and liberals believed that they had developed the modern state based on democratic representation and equal treatment before the law.

In contrast to these liberal claims, critical thinkers influenced by Marxism defined the nation-state as a materially grounded relation that was indispensable to the vertical organization of capitalist inequalities (Benedict Anderson 1991; Marshall 1992). According to Benedict Anderson, the nation was an "imagined community" that came into being during the late-eighteenth century through the "confluence" of a number of historical forces. In his account, the nation "is *imagined* because the members of even the smallest nation will never know most of their fellow-members, meet them, or even hear of them, yet in the minds of each lives the image of their communion" (Anderson 1991, 6). Highlighting the importance of print capitalism to the creation of such bonds, Anderson analyzed how the development of this media helped to create a sense of shared daily life even as it enabled the dissemination of elite class interests as "national interests" among the general population. The emergence of the modern nation thus led to a profound transformation in social consciousness, particularly since "nation" could not be imagined without "state." Indeed, it was in the state that the sovereignty of the nation was believed to reside.

In addition to Anderson's work, contemporary critical approaches to "nation" are also indebted to the work of Étienne Balibar, who—like Anderson—identified the conjunction of nation and state formation as being crucial to the development of capitalism. In this view, the rise of the nation-state corresponded with "the development of the market structures and class relations" that enabled proletarianization through "a process which gradually extracts its members from feudal and corporatist relations" (Balibar 1991, 89). Further, Balibar drew attention to the role played by "retrospectivity" in the production of the nation. Here myths of common origin and shared destiny ground national narratives, thereby constructing historical pasts as the basis for shared futures. Such myths draw on "prehistory" to produce an ideologically derived community in the "form of a narrative which attributes to these entities the continuity of a subject" (Balibar 1991, 86). Important events and personalities from this "prehistory" are subsequently integrated into "new political structures" (Balibar 1991, 88). As these structures get "nationalized," they become crucial markers in the nation's life. For Balibar, the production and management of the social and political institutions that "nationalize society" are a major function of the state (Balibar 1991, 88).

From Balibar's perspective, imperialism and colonialism were "decisive" to the emergence of the nation-state system. Although various state forms had emerged prior to the consolidation of the nation state, the "national" bourgeoisie became dominant by controlling the state's armed forces in the external sphere while internally subjugating the peasantry through market extension into rural areas (Balibar 1991). With the subsequent development of the welfare state, the nation also began to serve capitalist interests in more mundane ways—for example, through the organization of the "national debt," which "becomes everywhere the means to socialize the costs of private capitalism's crisis" (Wolff 2010).

Although it has been influential, Anderson's perspective has been critiqued for presupposing that there is a universal "underlying form for thinking the nation" that would allow for comparative approaches (Mongia 2007, 388). According to Radhika Mongia, such an approach obscures the asymmetrical status of—and relationships between—nations. Moreover, as Balibar makes clear, defining the nation in abstract terms fails to reveal exactly *how* it is related to capitalism. Historical studies of the nation-state reveal it to be co-constitutive with modernity, European expansion, racial slavery, and colonial conquest. From the eighteenth to the nineteenth centuries, Western philosophical and political thought presupposed that Europeans (having successfully established modern nation-states) were themselves modern historical subjects, whereas non-Europeans (trapped in the primitive stage of tribalism or by the savage rule of tyrannical despots) remained outside of history and modernity. "It is, I believe, no exaggeration to say that all the historical information which has been collected from all the books written in the Sanscrit language is less valuable than what may be found in the most paltry abridgements used at preparatory schools in England. In every branch of physical or moral philosophy, the relative position of the two nations is nearly the same," intoned the Honorable T. B. Macauley in his famous minute on education (1835).

After Haitian Revolution of 1791 to 1804, however, this wisdom began to be challenged by antislavery and anticolonial movements. These movements gave rise to revolutionary thinkers who argued that race and nation were inseparably bound in the making of the West (Douglass 1845; James 2001). Debunking the notion that race was a natural condition that partitioned the world and its peoples into discrete nations, thinkers like Toussaint Louverture, Frederick Douglass, and Sojourner Truth challenged Eurocentric understandings that delinked the capitalism and the nation from histories of slavery and colonization. Instead, and along with intellectual descendants including W. E. B. Du Bois (1903) and Frantz Fanon (1963), they argued that the racial and colonial logic at work in the production of the nation made it a racially exclusive and culturally bounded community. Between the late nineteenth and early twentieth century, this colonial and racial logic underwrote the imposition of the modern nation-state system in the colonized world through genocide, massacre, and partitions including the "scramble for Africa," the carving up of the Ottoman Empire, and the partitions of Palestine by the Balfour Declaration and of the South Asian subcontinent following the decline of the British Raj.

The emergent nationalist elites of the previously colonized world also came under fire from anticolonial revolutionaries, who pointed out how the former group collaborated with—and continued to further the interests of—colonial rulers. An early critic of the nation form in the Third World, Fanon's warnings against the "pitfalls of national consciousness" remain prescient even now. Nationalism in this context, he argued, fostered the ambitions of a native elite embedded in colonial institutions and logics. "In its narcissistic monologue," wrote Fanon, "the colonialist bourgeoisie, by way of its academics, had implanted in the minds of the colonized that the essential values—meaning Western values—remain eternal despite all errors attributable to man." (1963, 10–11). As a result, rather than embracing its "historical vocation" to "repudiate its status as bourgeois" and "become entirely subservient to . . . the people" while acknowledging that accumulating capital under the colonial system would be "in the realm of the impossible" Fanon noted that the aspiration guiding the national bourgeoisie was in fact to displace colonial rulers in order to assume their position (1963, 98–99). Small in number, largely urban, and culturally cut off from the revolutionary energies of the masses, this elite was likely to advance chauvinist and counterrevolutionary expressions of "national" culture in the pursuit of its aims.

Following on the heels of the anticolonial revolutionary thinkers of the mid-twentieth century, postcolonial theorists in the second half of the twentieth century traced how the "pitfalls" flagged by Fanon and his counterparts arose from the elite nationalists' tendency to suppress the experiences and consciousness of subaltern groups. For his part, Partha Chatterjee (1993) argued that nationalist thought in South Asia does not derive from the Western form and ought to be engaged on its own terms. Although political nationalism is generally considered a Western phenomenon, Chatterjee drew on Indian history to show that, in this context, the nationalist imaginary developed through claims to sovereignty in the "inner" realms of culture, spirituality, and tradition: "In the entire phase of national struggle, the crucial need was to protect, preserve and strengthen the inner core of the national culture, its spiritual essence. No encroachments by the colonizer must be allowed in that inner sanctum" (quoted in Taneja 2005, 36). According to Chatterjee, this sphere was delineated from the material-political "outer" realm *prior* to the emergence of anticolonial movements. By this account, making sense of nationalist thought in the postcolonial world needs to be historicized within the specificities of its own trajectory.

Despite these interventions, liberal notions of "nation" continue to dominate the intellectual and political field. Consequently, "nation" is regularly enacted—and experienced—as being as intimate to selfhood as the blood flowing in one's veins, as affective as the color of one's skin, or as communal as everyday cultural practice. In his commemoration of the fiftieth anniversary of Martin Luther King's march for voter registration in Selma,

Barack Obama celebrated "the American instinct that led these young men and women to . . . cross this bridge." In his view, it was "the same instinct that moved patriots to choose revolution over tyranny" and "the same instinct that drew immigrants from across oceans and the Rio Grande; the same instinct that led women to reach for the ballot and workers to organize against an unjust status quo; the same instinct that led us to plant a flag at Iwo Jima and on the surface of the moon" (quoted in Rhodan 2015). Obama's comments demonstrate how, within the liberal paradigm, national attributes become innate and unchanging even if the constituencies thought to embody them shift over time.

Although social movements in the West tend to be critical of nationalism on account of its tendency to foster nativist bigotry, they often leave the nation form itself unquestioned. Indeed, as Anderson pointed out, even "Marxist movements and states have tended to become national not only in form but in substance, i.e., nationalist" (Anderson 1991, 2). The labor movement's historical commitment to internationalism, for example, has done little to prevent unions in North America and Europe from supporting the imperialist ambitions of their respective states (e.g., as during WWI) or from seeking to protect "their" members from the claims of "foreign" and "immigrant" workers (Bolaria and Li 1985; Lowe 1998). Even today, the histories of such national compromises remain embedded in labor politics. For example, the Canadian Labour Congress (2015) describes itself as "the national voice of the labour movement, representing 3.3 million Canadian workers" despite decades of anti-racist activism that has highlighted how "Canadian" becomes equated with whiteness. For these movements, self-characterizations of this kind implicitly construct migrant workers as alien to organized labor's "natural"—that is, "national"—constituency.

Recently, the nation has also been implicitly buttressed in activism against Bill C-51, the new anti-terrorism legislation in Canada. Passed into law in June 2015, the bill enables the Canadian Security Intelligence Service to operate as a "secret police" force, with little civilian oversight (Woo 2015). The community-based group Open

Media played a key role in organizing demonstrations against the legislation. According to their website, passage of the bill would result in "violations of our Charter Rights." This appeal to the national charter did little to highlight the bill's criminalization of Muslims, who are presently the primary target of the legislation. Activists can thus reinforce the nation even as they challenge the power of the state.

Considered an important platform for progressive politics in the United States, long-running magazine *The Nation* recently asked how "American capitalism" might be reformed. "Imagine you have the ability to reinvent American capitalism," invited the editors. "Where would you start? What would you change to make it less destructive and domineering, more focused on what people need for fulfilling lives?" According to the *Nation*, the answers it received "demonstrate that the nation is alive with fresh thinking and bold outlines for big change." However, while the questions sparked inspired suggestions for reinventing "American" capitalism, they did nothing to question the concept of nation itself.

SEE ALSO: Bodies; Colonialism; Community; Liberal; Occupation; Race; Representation; Sovereignty; War; Zionism

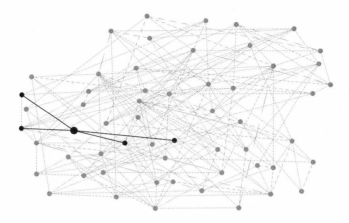

NATURE

John Bellamy Foster

"Nature," wrote Raymond Williams in *Keywords*, "is perhaps the most complex word in the language" (1983, 219). It is derived from the Latin "*natura*," as exemplified by Lucretius' great didactic poem "*De rerum natura*" ("On the Nature of Things") from the first century BC. The word "nature" has three primary, interrelated meanings: (1) the intrinsic properties or essence of things or processes; (2) an inherent force that directs or determines the world; and (3) the material world or universe, the object of our sense perceptions—both in its entirety and variously understood as including or excluding God, spirit, mind, human beings, society, history, culture, et cetera.

In his *Critique of Stammler*, Max Weber (1977, 96) suggested that the intrinsic difficulty of nature as a concept could be attributed to the fact that the word was most often used to refer to "a complex of certain kinds of *objects*" from which "another complex of *objects*" having "different properties" were excluded; however, the objects on each side of the bifurcation could vary widely, and this might only become apparent in a given usage. Thus, we commonly contrast humanity or society to nature while, at the same time, recognizing that human beings are themselves part of nature. From this problem arise such distinctions as "external nature" or "the environment." At other times, we may exclude only the mind/spirit from nature.

Science and art are two of the preeminent fields of inquiry into nature, with each operating according to its own distinct principles. As Alfred North Whitehead (1920) noted in *The Concept of Nature*, natural science depicts nature as the entire field of things, which are objects of human sensory perception mediated by concepts of our understanding (such as space and time). Consequently, one of the two leading scientific periodicals carries the title *Nature* (the other is *Science*). Within the Romantic tradition in art (a direct influence on modern environmentalism), nature is often perceived in accordance with notions of "natural beauty" (Percy Bysshe Shelley's skylark and William Wordsworth's Lake District). However, the validity of this concept has frequently been challenged within the field of aesthetics.

As a concept, nature gives rise to serious difficulties for philosophy, encompassing both ontology (the nature of being) and epistemology (the nature of thought). Since Immanuel Kant, philosophers have emphasized that human beings cannot perceive "things in themselves" (*noumena*). Consequently, they remain dependent on *a priori* knowledge, which is logically independent of experience. Within academic philosophy today, it is therefore customary either to take an outright idealist stance and thus to give ontological priority to the mind and ideas, or to subsume ontology within epistemology in such a way that the nature (including the limits) of knowledge takes precedence over the nature of being.

In contrast, natural scientists generally adopt a materialist/realist standpoint by emphasizing our ability to comprehend the physical world directly. Concerned with growing ecological crises, most ecological activists today take a similar stance and implicitly stress a kind of "critical realism" (Bhaskar 1975, 1979) that rejects both mechanical materialism (e.g., positivism) and idealism.

Reflecting a similar division of views, many contemporary social scientists (particularly postmodernists) emphasize the fact that our understanding of nature is socially or discursively constructed and that there is no nature independent of human thought and actions. For example, according to Keith Tester (1991, 46), "A fish is only a fish if it is socially classified as one, and that classification is only concerned with fish to the extent that scaly things living in the sea help society to define itself. . . . Animals are indeed a blank paper which can be inscribed with any message, and symbolic meaning, that society wishes." In contrast, while recognizing the role of thought in mediating the human relation to nature, most ecological thinkers and activists gravitate toward a critical materialism/ realism, in which nature (apart from humanity) is seen as existing prior to the social world, is open to comprehension, and is something to defend.

With the advent of nuclear weapons in the 1940s, the world came to the sudden realization that the relation between human beings and the environment had forever changed. The human impact on nature was no longer restricted to local or regional effects; conceivably, it extended to the destruction of the entire planet as a safe home for humanity. Subsequently, modern synthetic chemicals (with their capacity to biomagnify and bioaccumulate) and anthropogenic climate change brought the human degradation of nature to the forefront of society's concerns. Book titles like *Silent Spring* (Carson 1962), *The Closing Circle* (Commoner 1971), *The Domination of Nature* (Leiss 1972), *The Death of Nature* (Merchant 1980), *The End of Nature* (McKibben 1989), *The Sixth Extinction* (Leakey and Lewin 1995), and *This Changes Everything* (Klein 2014) reflect a growing state of alarm about ecological sustainability and the conditions required for human survival.

Compared to earlier centuries, the question of nature in the twentieth and twenty-first centuries has been radically transformed. No longer is nature seen as a *direct* external threat to humanity through forces like famines and disease. Instead, emerging or threatened global natural catastrophes are viewed as the *indirect* products of human action itself. We now live in what scientists have provisionally designated the Anthropocene, a new geological epoch in which humanity itself has become the dominant geological force. This new reality has compelled a growing recognition of the limits of nature, of planetary boundaries, and of economic growth within a finite environment.

The meteoric rise of "ecology" (along with derivatives like "ecosystem," "ecosphere," "eco-development," "ecosocialism," and "ecofeminism") stems from these rapidly changing interactions between capitalism and its natural environment. The concepts of "ecology," "ecosystem," and "earth system" have become central both to science and to popular struggle. At times they even displace the concept of nature itself.

Attempts to address the enormity of the ecological problem have, however, been complicated by a resurrection of essentialist conceptions of "human nature." By subsuming the social under the "natural," such views often downplay or altogether deny the importance of the social-historical dimension of human interactions with nature. This outlook has recently gained ground through the social Darwinist pronouncements of sociobiologists and evolutionary psychologists. E. O. Wilson's *On Human Nature* (1978), for instance, professes "simply" to be "the extension of population biology and evolutionary theory to social organization." An inevitable struggle thus arises between ecological radicals who demand that society be historically transformed to create a sustainable relation to nature and thinkers who insist that possessive individualism, the Hobbesian war of all against all, and a tendency to overpopulate are all inscribed in the human DNA.[1] Accompanying this revival of biological determinism has been the

---

1.   On the possessive individualism of capitalist society and its conception of natural-social relations, see Macpherson 1962.

presumption that capitalism itself is a product not only of human nature but of the natural world as a whole. Such views deny the historical origins of alienation. In contrast, most radicals view the alienation of nature and the alienation of society as interconnected and interdependent phenomena requiring a new co-evolutionary social metabolism if world ecology as we know it is to be sustained.

Contemporary conflicts over the relationship between nature and society can be traced to the rise of capitalism and modern science during the sixteenth and seventeenth centuries. The seventeenth-century scientific revolution witnessed the emergence—most notably in Francis Bacon, but also in René Descartes—of calls for the "conquest," "mastery," or "domination" of nature. In *The Masculine Birth of Time*, Bacon metaphorically declared: "I am come in very truth leading to you Nature with all her children to bind her to your service and make her your slave" (1964, 62). In *The New Atlantis* (1991), this ambition became tied to a program for the institutionalization of science as the basis of knowledge and power. Descartes also linked it to a mechanistic worldview in which animals were reduced to machines. Following Bacon, the conquest of nature became a universal trope to signify a vague mechanical progress achieved through the development of science. Nevertheless, as Bacon himself made clear in a famous statement from his *Novum Organum*, "nature is only overcome by obeying her." In this view, "nature" could only be subjected by following "her" laws (1994, 29, 43).

The domination of nature espoused by Bacon was subjected to critique during the nineteenth century through the dialectical perspectives associated with Hegel and Marx. In his *Philosophy of Nature* (1970, 195–96), Hegel insisted that—while Bacon's strategy of pitting nature against itself could yield a limited mastery—total mastery of the natural world would forever remain beyond humanity's reach. "Need and ingenuity have enabled man to discover endlessly varied ways of mastering and making use of nature," he wrote. Nevertheless, "Nature itself, as it is in its universality, cannot be mastered in this manner . . . nor bent to the purposes of man." For Hegel, the drive to master nature generated wider contradictions that were beyond human control. In *Grundrisse*, Marx (1973, 409–10) treated Bacon's strategy as a "ruse" introduced by bourgeois society. In his *Theses on Feuerbach*, he rejected essentialist views of human nature outright. Human nature, he argued, was nothing but "the ensemble of the social relations" (1974, 423). Similarly, in *The Poverty of Philosophy*, he declared that history itself was "nothing but a continuous transformation of human nature" (1963, 147).

In his later economic writings, Marx developed an analysis in which the human relation to nature was conceived as a form of "social metabolism." In this view, the social metabolism was part of the "universal metabolism of nature," which found itself increasingly in contradiction with industrial capitalist development. During this period, the soil was being robbed of essential nutrients (e.g., nitrogen, phosphorous, and potassium), which were being shipped hundreds and sometimes thousands of miles to the new urban centers. "Instead of a conscious rational treatment of the land as permanent communal property," Marx charged, "we have the exploitation and squandering of the powers of the earth" (1981, 949). In response, he pointed to the "irreparable rift in the interdependent process of social metabolism" arising from the very nature of accumulation under capitalism. This break with the "eternal natural condition" underlying human-social existence, he argued, demanded a "restoration" through the rational regulation of the metabolism between humanity and nature (1976, 637–38; 1981, 959). In *Capital*, Marx advanced what remains perhaps the most radical conception of ecological sustainability yet propounded: "From the standpoint of a higher socio-economic formation, the private property of particular individuals in the earth will appear just as absurd as the private property of one man in other men. Even an entire society, a nation, or all simultaneously existing societies taken together, are not the owners of the earth. They are simply its possessors, its beneficiaries, and have to bequeath it in an improved state to succeeding generations, as *boni patres familias*" (Marx 1981, 911).

Today, radical ecologists tend to fall into two broad camps. The first consists of those who—from a deep ecology, radical-green, or "ecologism" perspective—simply counter Baconian anthropocentrism with ecocentric philosophies.[2] Such views retain the society-nature dualism but approach it from the side of external nature, life, or some kind of spiritualized nature. This general perspective has played an important role within the ecological movement. Ecofeminist thinkers, for instance, have highlighted the link between the mastery of nature and the subordination of women (often by taking the critique of Bacon as their starting point). Nevertheless, the one-sidedness of radical-green or deep ecology perspectives has often encouraged misanthropic views (especially when human population growth is seen as the principal problem) as well as anti-science stances, in which the critical role of science in understanding ecology is misunderstood.

The second broad camp consists of those who have adopted more dialectical perspectives.[3] Here the problem of nature and ecology is conceived as one of social metabolism. From this vantage, the goal is to transcend "the rift in the interdependent process of social metabolism" (Marx 1981, 949) and thus create a more sustainable form of human development inseparable from the struggle for human equality. This outlook critically builds on ecological science with its emphasis on the ontological interconnection of all living and nonliving things. From this perspective, conflict arises between a social system geared toward endless growth and everlasting, nature-imposed conditions of ecological sustainability and substantive equality. It is along these lines that critical scientists, ecosocialists, socialist ecofeminists, anarchist social ecologists, and many Indigenous activists have coalesced to take a stand in defense of the earth. As Frederich Engels wrote in the *Dialectics of Nature*, "Let us not . . . flatter ourselves overmuch on account of our human victories over nature. For each such victory nature takes its revenge on us. . . . Thus at every step we are reminded that we by no means rule over nature like a conqueror over a foreign people, like someone standing outside nature—but that we, with

2.   Representative works include Dobson 1995; Eckersley 1992; Nicholas Smith 1998; Devall and Sessions 1985.
3.   See, for example, Bookchin 1995; Paul Burkett 2014; Longo, Clausen, and Clark 2015; Salleh, 2009; Klein, 2014.

flesh, blood, and brain, belong to nature, and exist in its midst, and that all of our mastery of it consists in the fact that we have the advantage over all other creatures of being able to learn its laws and apply them correctly" (1934, 180).

SEE ALSO: Domination; Materialism; Representation; Sustainable

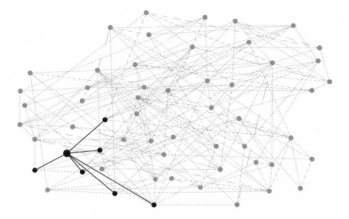

OCCUPATION

Sara Matthews

ACCORDING TO THE *OXFORD ENGLISH DICTIONARY*, THE word "occupation" can be traced back to the twelfth-century Anglo-Norman and Old French "*occupacion*" and first appeared in English as a noun denoting employable activity. During the thirteenth century, it came into usage as a verb denoting the *action* of taking possession of land or space, as in a tenancy or holding. As contemporary debates concerning the concept's usefulness for social and political struggle make clear, "occupation" has the power to expose and reconcile but also to repeat the traumatic legacies of our colonial past and present.

In its widest sense, "occupation" is a dynamic of power and spatiality. According to the *OED*, "occupation" corresponds to "the action of taking or maintaining possession or control of a country, building or land, especially by military force; an instance of this or period of such action; the state of being subject to such an action." Key to this formulation is the slippage between "occupation" as an *action* and as a *subjective experience*. For radicals, the hope is that the subjective experience and objective dynamics of occupation by hostile powers might be exposed and then transformed by means of radical occupations carried out by the people themselves. For contemporary radicals, perhaps one of the most familiar instances of this kind was the Occupy Wall Street movement. Before considering the veracity of occupation as a practice of resistance, however, it is important to consider its historical legacy as an instrument of state building.

Often a mechanism of state violence, occupation signals the installation of a sovereign presence through organized campaigns that aim to subjugate the target group physically, socially, and psychically. The first recognized iteration of occupation as a military tactic was coded into international law via the United Nations 1907 Hague Convention resolution concerning "Laws and Customs of War on Land." Considered a temporary rather than permanent solution to conflict, military occupations have nevertheless tended to strip citizens of their sovereign rights and expose them to political and social exploitation. Given that the United Nations endorses the Westphalian system—which presupposes the territorial integrity of sovereign nations—occupation has become an important problem of geopolitics and international law.

The phrase "territories occupied" first appeared in United Nations Resolution 242, which called for "withdrawal of Israel armed forces from territories occupied" during the Six-Day War. Nevertheless, the longest-standing military occupation in contemporary times remains the Israeli occupation of Gaza, the West Bank, the Golan Heights, and East Jerusalem. Since 1967, Israel has unilaterally occupied Palestinian territory and systematically denied Palestinian residents their right to return to confiscated lands, to access the economic and physical resources necessary for survival, and freedom of movement and self-determination.

Cartographies of the region produced over the past forty years reflect these geopolitics. Maps that label the area "Palestine" rather than "Occupied Territories," for instance, suggest a resistant sovereignty that refuses ongoing Israeli occupation. Indeed, the iconic "disappearing map" of Palestine used by groups like the Toronto-based Queers Against Israeli Apartheid has become an important pedagogical tool in campaigns aimed at revealing the geography of occupation. The disappearing map exemplifies the ambivalent nature of occupation (see Figure I): it announces Palestinian resistance *at the same time* as declaring the colonizing threat of the Israeli intervention.

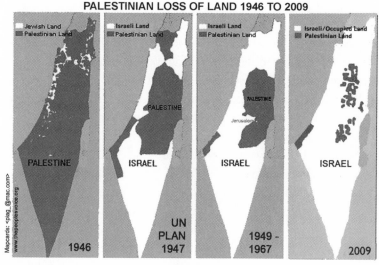

Figure I

References to Israeli "occupation" have also appeared more broadly in discourses concerning human rights abuses. For instance, Amnesty International's "Enduring Occupation" report (2007) details the subjective experience of life under occupation, including the impacts of the illegal apartheid wall, the unlawful procurement of lands and natural resources, the destruction of Palestinian homes and olive groves, and growing restrictions on physical movement. Although Israel officially disengaged from Gaza in 2005 and declared itself no longer to be an occupying force, it has continued to retain control of Gaza's airspace and coastline, effectively sustaining sovereign pressure through military occupation of the air and sea.

In addition to being a tool of belligerent nation-states, however, occupation has also historically been a tool of opposition and resistance. This approach involves attempts to reconfigure the spatial formations that uphold repressive regimes. In opposition to spatial restrictions, radical acts of occupation contest restrictions on psychic and physical survival through efforts to reassert claims on public space. In the context of the Israeli occupation of Palestine, groups like the International Solidarity Movement (ISM), formed in 2001, act in solidarity with those forced to confront the experience of occupation. With their campaign to "End the Occupation," ISM has made use of nonviolent and direct-action tactics including accompaniment, physical removal of IDF roadblocks, organized violation of curfew orders, blocking tanks and bulldozers, and interference with the Apartheid Wall through political graffiti. While such tactics disrupt the mechanisms of Israeli occupation, they also provide opportunities for Palestinians and their international allies to reclaim or reoccupy public space as a political act of resistance. The *Electronic Intifada* provides a further example of how the tactic of occupation might be reconfigured for emancipatory ends. Started in 2001 by writers and reporters from Palestine and beyond, the publication challenges occupation by providing an alternative space for digital information and popular education.

These strategies intend a reconfiguration of the act of possession upon which military occupations rely. However, they also demonstrate how occupation itself can be galvanized as resistance. Arising from political struggles in Palestine and elsewhere, the demand to "end the occupation" stands at odds with the concurrent injunction to "occupy everything" advanced by those for whom "occupation" is first and foremost a strategy of resistance. Bady and Konczal (2012) trace the slogan "Occupy Everything, Demand Nothing" to the California student movement of 2009, in which students protested the neoliberalization of the university—as well as their experience of scholastic alienation—by occupying campus buildings.

As a form of public dissent and protest, occupation has a long history in social movements. In "Tactic: Occupation," Russell and Gupta (2015) describe occupation as a method "to hold public space; to pressure a target; to reclaim or squat property; to defend against 'development' and to assert Indigenous sovereignty." In this context, they highlight the example of the labor strike. By mobilizing labor (i.e., practical human activity) against its everyday "occupation" within capitalism, a strike can seize hold of the workplace and interrupt the relations that alienate workers from their own subjectivity. Normally cast as what Marx in *The Communist Manifesto* (1848) called "an appendage of the machine," striking workers marshal their "occupation," which has value on the market, against their own alienation. Russell and Gupta provide the following short history of actions that have resisted labor as capitalist occupation:

> In seventeenth-century England . . . the Diggers formed a utopian agrarian community on common land. Workers, soldiers and citizens established the Paris Commune in 1871. In the United States, in the Great Upheaval of 1877, striking railway workers and their supporters occupied train yards across the land. A wave of plant occupations in the mid-1930s led to the justly famous Flint sit-down strikes of 1936, which won union recognition for hundreds of thousands of auto workers. (2015)

Seizing public space or repurposing privatized space in this way distinguishes radical occupations from those that are sanctioned by—and reproduce—normative standards of sovereign power. As an oppositional act, occupation seeks to expose and unsettle the boundaries maintained by sovereign rule. According to London-based writer and activist Anindya Bhattacharyya (2012), "We live our lives surrounded by a field of invisible regulations that tell us where we can or must go, and what we are and aren't allowed to do there. Occupation makes these regulations of bodies in space visible."

As a radical practice, occupation refuses the enclosure of what would otherwise be common and challenges sovereign power's partitioning of space in the interest of mastery and knowability. For Michel Foucault, such regulated "disciplinary space" aims to "establish presences and absences, to know where and how to locate individuals, to set up useful communications, to interrupt others, to be able at each moment to supervise the conduct of each individual, to assess it, to judge it, to calculate its qualities or merits" (1975, 143).[1] If, as a dimension of sovereign rule, "occupation" is also a project of what Foucault called "power/knowledge," then "occupation" as a radical tactic creates new opportunities for self-knowledge and self-determination while challenging disciplinary regimes. Consider, for instance, Hakim Bey's (1991) Temporary Autonomous Zone, which he viewed as a moment of festive non-hierarchical gathering that could foster collective conviviality in the face of state control.

> The TAZ is like an uprising which does not engage directly with the State, a guerilla operation which liberates an area (of land, of time, of imagination) and then dissolves itself to re-form elsewhere/elsewhen, *before* the State can crush it. Because the State is concerned primarily with Simulation rather than substance, the TAZ can "occupy" these areas clandestinely and carry on its festal purposes for quite a while in relative peace.

By this account, the TAZ provokes momentary utopias that challenge the normative order and transcend the ordinary by creating subjective experiences of convivial intensity. Out of these

---

1. Indeed, the various meanings of "occupation" recounted above are each given practical expression in Foucault's *Discipline and Punish*. (i) As knowability: "to each bed was attached the name of its occupant" (1975, 144). (ii) As territorial encroachment: "the Chassaud ironworks occupied almost the whole of the Médine Peninsula (1975, 142). (iii) As form of labor and as psychic imposition: "there was compulsory work in workshops; the prisoners were kept constantly occupied" (1975, 122).

moments, difference can be imagined and then made. Other forms of collaborative resistance to enclosure that claim space for the expression of alternative visions include Reclaim the Streets and Critical Mass, both of which have mobilized occupation as a physical and psychic strategy.

Reclaim the Streets is a direct action network with roots in the United Kingdom whose tactics of creative festivity have spread to cities around the world. Calling for the creation of "collective daydreams" that challenge normative life under capital, Reclaim the Streets argues that "ultimately it is in the streets that power must be dissolved: for the streets where daily life is endured, suffered and eroded, and where power is confronted and fought, must be turned into domain where daily life is *enjoyed, created and nourished.*" Writing in the *Guardian*, journalist Jay Griffiths (1996) described the seven-thousand-strong occupation by Reclaim the Streets of the M41 in West London as a carnival aimed at reclaiming the urban commons from car culture. For its part, the Earth First!-inspired periodical *Do Or Die* summed up movement sensibilities when it recounted how Reclaim the Streets was "not going to demand anything. . . . We are going to occupy" ("Reclaim the Streets" 1997). Formed in San Francisco during the early 1990s and now used in different cities around the world, Critical Mass similarly reclaims urban space by using bicycles to occupy roadways that predominantly serve cars.

An understanding of this approach would be incomplete, however, without a discussion of Occupy Wall Street. Prompted by Micah White's July 2011 call for "a worldwide shift in revolutionary tactics" published in *Adbusters*, the movement revitalized interest in occupation's meaning and possibilities. "What makes this novel tactic exciting," White wrote, was "its pragmatic simplicity":

> We talk to each other in various physical gatherings and virtual people's assemblies . . . we zero in on what our one demand will be, a demand that awakens the imagination and, if achieved, would propel us toward the radical democracy of the future . . . and then we

go out and seize a square of singular symbolic significance and put our asses on the line to make it happen.

Approximately one thousand people coalesced in Manhattan's
Financial District on September 17, 2011 in response to White's call
for people to occupy Wall Street, which he identified as the "financial Gomorrah of America" (White 2011). Many stayed on to establish a tent city in Zuccotti Park, which they occupied for about two
months. Occupy Wall Street inspired hundreds of similar actions in
cities around the world. In his brief history of the movement, Willie
Osterweil (2011) notes how the activists in Lower Manhattan bor-
rowed a page from sources as varied as the *Indignado* Movement in
Spain, the Egyptian revolution, and struggles for workers' and veterans' rights in the United States. The power of occupation, Osterweil
writes, is that "it foregrounds the political issues of everyday life and
public space, it produces a positive communitarian solution to the
problems it critiques, it is highly visible and struggle is continuous in
a way that radicalizes its participants" (2011).

However, given occupation's legacy as a practice of sovereign
rule imposed from without, it is not surprising that the movement's use of the term and tactic prompted criticism. What are
the ethics and politics of occupation as radical practice when the
concept remains closely bound to colonial and settler relations?
Activist Harsha Walia (2014) raised this dilemma when she noted
how "one of our most common rally slogans" remains "from Turtle
Island to Palestine, occupation is a crime." Matt Mulberry (2014)
considered the problem from a slightly different angle when he
asked whether the term "occupation delegitimize[s] movements by
casting participants as short-term guests, instead of representatives
communicating grievances held by a wider society within a public
forum that is theirs?" Whatever the case, "occupation" as an exercise in creative resistance remains haunted by the term's concurrent history as an oppressive force. We must therefore recognize its
limits as well as its possibilities.

SEE ALSO: Colonialism; Nation; Sovereignty; Space; War; Zionism

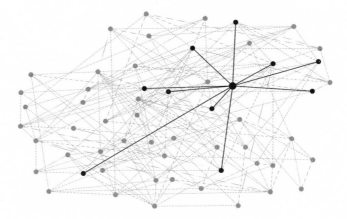

OPPRESSION

Justin Podur

DERIVED FROM THE LATIN *OPPRIMERE* (*OB-* "AGAINST" +
premere "to press, push"), the word "oppression" entered
English in the fifteenth century and denoted "pressure
(*c*1430), fact of overcoming by violence, state of being
overcome (1487)" (*OED*). Its contemporary mainstream
definition recounts "prolonged cruel or unjust treatment
or exercise of authority, control, or power." However,
two alternate contemporary definitions of "oppression"
circulate within the political left. The first arises in traditional, revolutionary political theory and builds on
a fundamental distinction between oppressor and oppressed. The second, activist, definition refers to the use
of power to maintain privilege.

Each variation is based on specific conceptions of power, privilege, authority, and leadership. The mainstream definition of "oppression" implies the possibility of a just exercise of power. The definition within revolutionary political theory implies the same, although writers in this tradition have long debated the terms on which legitimate power might be established. In current activist usage, however, virtually all exercise of power is understood to be oppressive. Driven by theories of intersectionality, this usage is popularized by professional organizers and anti-oppression workshops. The provenance of the term, however, is much older.

In *The German Constitution* (1802), Hegel used the oppressor-oppressed dialectic to describe historical tensions between Catholics and Protestants. "The outward appearances are the same: civil rights are denied to Protestants in Catholic territories, and to Catholics in Protestant territories." Nevertheless, he noted, "the basis seems to be different."

> The Catholics had been in the position of oppressors, and the Protestants of the oppressed. The Catholics had treated the Protestants as criminals, and denied them the free exercise of their religion in their midst; but where the Protestant Church was dominant, this basis was removed, along with the fear of oppression.

Several decades later, Marx adopted Hegel's usage, most famously in the opening lines of *The Communist Manifesto*, where—along with Engels—he wrote: "The history of all hitherto existing society is the history of class struggles."

> Freeman and slave, patrician and plebeian, lord and serf, guild-master and journeyman, in a word, oppressor and oppressed, stood in constant opposition to one another, carried on an uninterrupted, now hidden, now open fight, a fight that each time ended, either in a revolutionary reconstitution of society

at large, or in the common ruin of the contending classes. (1976b)

A critic within the revolutionary socialist tradition, Bakunin challenged what he viewed to be Marx's inadequate understanding of the state's oppressive function. In Bakunin's view, states were "internally oppressors and outwardly despoilers, i.e., enemies to each other. The State, since it involves this division, oppression, and despoliation of humanity, must represent the . . . destruction of human society" (1869). Condemning both church and state as institutions that "exist exclusively to conserve the interests of the privileged classes," Bakunin also conveyed a shifting conception of privilege that corresponded to shifts in organized power.

While Engels (1845) maintained that "before the privilege of property all other privileges vanish," others considered the power relations within revolutionary organizations to be another front of struggle against oppression. Disagreement about what constituted a just use of power thus came to inform use of the term. In *The State and Revolution*, for example, Lenin defined the dictatorship of the proletariat as "the organization of the vanguard of the oppressed as the ruling class for the purpose of suppressing the oppressors" (1932) while, in *The Unknown Revolution, 1917–1921*, Russian anarchist Voline (whom the Bolsheviks exiled in 1921) decried the vanguard organization for imitating "the old society of oppression and exploitation."

> Opposed to a large extent to oppression, animated by a powerful breath of liberty, and proclaiming liberty as their essential purpose, why did [the revolutions of 1789 and 1917] go down under a new dictatorship, exercised by a new dominating and privileged group, in a new slavery for the mass of the people involved? (1947)

These debates persisted throughout the twentieth century. In *Oppression and Liberty* (1955), philosopher Simone Weil credited

Marx with identifying the social causes of oppression in the system of production. Consequently, oppression was "no longer considered the usurpation of privilege, but as the organ of a social function" (55). However, Weil also argued that Marx failed "to explain . . . why the oppressed in revolt have never succeeded in founding a non-oppressive society." As a result, "he leaves completely in the dark the principles . . . by which a given form of oppression is replaced by another" (55). Linking oppression to the privileges of arms and money and to the struggle for power, Weil concluded that, in a society with a complex economy and division of labor, oppression arises inevitably.

In *Pedagogy of the Oppressed* (1970), Paolo Freire elaborated upon the conceptual link between oppression and privilege underlying current activist usage. Describing "humanization" as the people's vocation despite "injustice, exploitation, oppression, and the violence of the oppressors," Freire found it to be "affirmed by the yearning of the oppressed for freedom and justice" (44). Like the philosophers who preceded him, Freire did not define "oppression." However, through his usage, it becomes clear that oppression is something an oppressor does to deny the full humanity of the oppressed. Influenced by Frantz Fanon, who decried the settler's "rule of oppression" (1963, 5) and the dehumanization it yielded (Horton and Freire 1990, 36), Freire helped design models of popular education to empower the oppressed.

With the turn to intersectionality during the 1980s, the project of reclaiming humanity became explicitly linked to the work of discerning distinct but intersecting forms of oppression. Although the term was only introduced later, intersectional forms of analysis were devised by anti-racist feminists in the 1970s women's movement and gradually popularized by the academic field of Women's Studies. The influential 1982 book *Some of Us are Brave* confronted the "multilayered oppression" of Black women in the feminist movement. The book included "A Black Feminist Statement" written in 1977 in which members of the Combahee River Collective described how conditions of multilayered oppression shaped their organizing:

> The major source of difficulty in our political work is that we are not just trying to fight oppression on one front or even two, but instead to address a whole range of oppressions. We do not have racial, sexual, heterosexual, or class privilege to rely upon, nor do we have even the minimal access to resources and power that groups who possess even one of these types of privilege have. ("Some of Us are Brave" 2005, 18)

In response to these conditions, the Collective found that, "in the process of consciousness-raising . . . we began to recognize the commonality of our experiences and, from the sharing and growing consciousness, to build a politics that will change our lives and inevitably end our oppression" ("Some of Us are Brave" 2005, 15). Although it is difficult to trace the origins of contemporary "anti-oppression politics," the widely circulated Combahee River Collective statement is certainly an early and foundational text.

Citing this statement in her 1988 essay "White Privilege and Male Privilege," Peggy McIntosh reiterated its conclusions with a larger catalogue of oppressions: "it is hard to isolate aspects of unearned advantage that derive chiefly from social class, economic class, race, religion, region, sex, or ethnic identity. The oppressions are both distinct and interlocking." That same year, McIntosh published "White Privilege: Unpacking the Invisible Knapsack," an essay that offered a list of fifty examples of personal privilege intended to demonstrate that racism is not "only in individual acts of meanness" but also in "invisible systems conferring dominance."

Subsequent anti-oppression tools followed this more technical model, identifying groups or categories of oppression and encouraging activists to consider the ways in which they have privilege and are oppressed. In practice, this has typically taken place in the context of anti-oppression workshops—a contemporary iteration of consciousness-raising (and methodologically related to Freire's popular education model). Once activists have learned how to identify their personal privileges and oppressions, they can attempt to "check their privilege." For anti-oppression trainers, workshops are intended to provide "space for participants to reflect on or acknowledge their privilege, or 'see' the systemic discrimination and oppression marginalized groups experience" (Desil, Kaur and Kinsman 2005). Anti-oppression trainings and workshops have become common in radical activist groups. SOA Watch, for instance, provides an extensive list of training groups in every state of the US on their website, and the list is almost certainly not exhaustive.

Many activist groups, NGOs, and church groups also now have anti-oppression policies. Sistering's "Anti-Oppression and Diversity Policy," for example, contains an implementation plan and outlines a formal complaints procedure (2007). The Wild Roots Feral Futures Collective describes oppressive behavior as "*any* conduct (typically along lines of institutionalized power and privilege) that demeans, marginalizes, rejects, threatens or harms any living being on the basis of ability, activist experience, age, class/ income level, cultural background, education, ethnicity, gender, immigration status, language, nationality, physical appearance, race, religion, self-expression, sexual orientation, species, status as a parent or other such factors" (Anti-Oppression Policy). Many activist and NGO definitions strive to delineate the maximum number of possible axes of oppression (Global Exchange 2006). As policy, anti-oppression is about having structures within organizations to stop oppressive behavior.

In the current activist usage, "oppression" takes on the implied meaning of "the opposite of privilege." If, for example, white people enjoy white privilege, non-white people are by definition oppressed. This meaning is implied in activist definitions, such as this one: "the use of power to disempower, marginalize, silence or otherwise subordinate one social group or category, often in order to further empower and/or privilege the oppressor" (Free Geek 2013). However, despite its prominence, it remains to be seen whether this current activist usage will retain its political power.

The primary threat to its viability is co-optation as a professionalized concept, where a tension arises between its usage as a central political distinction and its usage as a technical term. The latter usage implies that oppression can be resolved through professional competency. Anti-oppression analysis has found greatest traction in the academic field and profession of social work. As a result, social workers have generated some of the most sophisticated challenges to the anti-oppression framework. In "'Anti-oppressive practice': emancipation or appropriation?" Wilson and Beresford describe anti-oppression practice (AOP) in social work as an outgrowth of "broader struggles . . . by the women's, black and minority ethnic, gay men's and lesbian movements" (2000, 563). Aside from a handful of exceptions, they state that, most of the social work literature "seems to view anti-oppressive practice as essentially benign and is concerned with promoting its tenets as widely as possible" (559).

Wilson and Beresford describe the "somewhat grandiose" stated purposes of anti-oppressive practice as being about "minimizing the power differences in society" and even "transforming society" (2000, 558). They cite proponent Lena Dominelli, for whom "anti-oppressive practice is a specialism with specialist knowledge which, as in other specialisms must be learnt fully" (1998, 15). For Wilson and Beresford, treating anti-oppression as a specialist competency circumvents possibly painful personal and political discussions: "anti-oppressive practice can arouse fears and anxieties for students, tutors and practice teachers who are required to work within its precepts, not least because it can entail examining our own deep-seated biases and prejudices—something which none of us finds easy." It is hardly surprising, then, that "There can be a temptation . . . to focus on the pragmatics or skills of practice—how we should do AOP; what we should do to/for/with services users rather than questioning . . . why it is we have chosen to focus on such practice precepts" (2000, 559).

Although activists insist that "anti-oppression education is a lifelong commitment" and that "no amount of workshops will make one an expert" (Desil, Kaur and Kinsman 2005), in both social work and in activist trainings and workshops, anti-oppressive practice is regularly treated as a competency. This competency approach produces what Wilson and Beresford refer to as the "machine" of anti-oppressive practice. As political concepts, "oppression" and "anti-oppression" could help people think about forms of social subordination and ways to resist. However the creation of specialized academic and professional machines has the potential to disempower non-specialists looking for ways to understand and change their condition.

The logic underlying current activist usage of "oppression" seems to be the following: (i) oppression is systemic, (ii) oppressions can be catalogued, (iii) the catalogue ought to be exhaustive, (iv) confronting oppressions requires focus on oppressive behavior, and (v) oppressive behavior can be undermined through workshops and trainings. This might suggest that activists are sensibly focusing on what they can control. However, if it leads to a de-emphasis on the original, society-wide, structural problem of oppression, it can also lead to narrowed horizons with respect to thinking and action. For instance, although activists oppose oppression because it disempowers, activist conceptions of "oppression" leave little room for the non-oppressive use of power. In other words, the activist definition of oppression leaves little room for empowerment.

In the mainstream definition, "oppression" is clearly immoral and resistance to it is clearly justified. In the activist definition, everyone with privilege is an oppressor, a competently trained "ally," or something somewhere in between. Not only does this usage shift conceptions of resistance and opposition, it also prevents activists from communicating with non-activists. Although the activist definition of oppression yields important insights and should not be discarded, these insights become imperilled if the word's context and relationship to the mainstream definition are lost.

SEE ALSO: Allies; Authority; Bodies; Class; Colonialism; Experience; Misogyny; Privilege; Queer; Rights

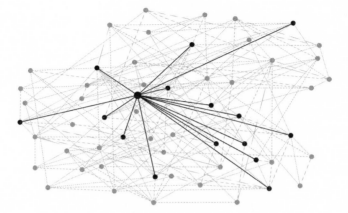

POLITICS

Deborah Gould

THE WORD "POLITICS" DERIVES FROM THE ANCIENT Greek meaning "public matters," "civic affairs," and "of or relating to citizens." "Politics" thus refers to the affairs of a social grouping and to the running of those affairs. The word signals a recognition that life is always lived *together* and that the arrangements for living together are an open question. "Politics" thus concerns a collective's guiding principles, the social expectations when guidelines are breached, the establishment and preservation of members' rights, and the navigation of conflict.

But prior questions arise immediately— and necessarily so, given the term's derivation from the concept of citizen, which entails exclusions and hierarchy. Who is part of the collective and who is not? Who can and should govern? What issues are "public" and thus political? Where is the site of politics? Many activists and theorists place such questions at the heart of politics.

Hannah Arendt elevated the question of belonging with her phrase "the right to have rights" (1951). For Jacques Rancière, "[p]olitics is first and foremost an intervention upon the visible and the sayable" (2001). Activists contest the status quo in part by challenging who gets seen as a political subject, whose demands get heard, and whose lives matter. When Black Lives Matter forces police killings of African Americans onto the political stage, they are "re-partitioning the political from the non-political" (Rancière 2011, 4). Politics occurs, Rancière notes, "when there is a disagreement about what is politics, when the boundary separating the political from the [social or the public from the domestic] . . . is put into question" (2011, 4).

AIDS activism provides another example of activists challenging existing conceptions of who and what are matters of public concern. President Reagan made no public mention of AIDS during the first four years of the epidemic during which thousands of mostly gay men died. In response to this willful erasure, ACT UP used direct action to force the epidemic onto the political stage. Today immigrants' rights activists contest the nation-state's dehumanizing exclusions by declaring "No One Is Illegal." The late 1960s feminist declaration that "the personal is political" is perhaps the most iconic example of an activist challenge to the boundaries of politics. This insertion of people's everyday lives into the sphere of politics resonated across the New Left.

Although nothing in its etymology confines "politics" to politicians and states, dominant meanings of the word tend to designate those as its proper agents and sites. Contemporary democratic rhetoric notwithstanding, Joseph Schumpeter's mid-twentieth-century view endures today. "Democracy is the rule of the politician," he claimed. Practically speaking, this meant that "voters . . . must understand that, once they have elected an individual, political action is his [*sic*] business and not theirs" (quoted in Azzellini and Sitrin

2014, 46–47). Grasping that politicians and their technocrats have delegated the business of politics to themselves, many see politics as "out of reach to ordinary people," "something distant," "made by a few and . . . done in a palace" (Colombo and Mascarenhas 2003, 461). With "politics" thus cordoned off, many people have become cynical, seeing politics as a corrupt business controlled by elites and populated with deceitful individuals who hold little concern for the populace.

The bourgeois revolutions of the late eighteenth and nineteenth centuries shifted the foundation of political rule from birth to wealth, and opened ideas about who could be a political actor—a question that remains contested and fundamentally undecided. Pulling from the Zapatistas' rebellion beginning in 1994, the demand of protesters in Argentina for all politicians to leave ("*que se vayan todos!*"), and the global wave of protests of 2011–13—contemporary radicals have manifested an alternative view of "politics" that moves it from cabinets, legislatures, and back rooms to the streets and public squares, and puts ordinary people and their collective decision-making at the helm. In this way, they have challenged a liberal conception of sovereignty that in practice upholds a split between rulers and ruled, experimenting instead with collective decision-making that takes form in relation to specific situations.

This non-elite understanding of politics prompts today's radicals to pay careful attention to the forms of governance used in organizing. Contending that hierarchical modes (including representational ones) can reproduce unjust social relations, contemporary movements often reject organizational forms like political parties and elected leaderships that dominated the Old and New Left alike. Anarchist activist and theorist David Graeber contends that non-hierarchical, horizontal modes of internal governance now dominate the activist left. "After the Global Justice Movement" that arose at the turn of the century, he writes, "the old days of steering committees and the like were basically over." Indeed, "pretty much everyone in the activist community ha[s] come around to the idea of prefigurative politics: the idea that the organizational form that an activist group takes should embody the kind of society we wish to create" (2013, 23). To be sure, Graeber may be overstating the case. He seems to ignore, for example, the more traditional organizing models that—according to Manuel Pastor (2015)—have brought important successes to today's resurgent immigrants' rights movement. Nevertheless, it remains true that many current activist formations reject hierarchy and embrace "leaderless" or "leader-ful" models (Starhawk 2011, 264). According to Black Lives Matter founders Garza and Tometi, "We resist the urge to consolidate our power and efforts behind one charismatic leader." Instead they "center the leadership of the many who exist at the margins" (Tometi et al. 2015). This style echoes the bottom-up form of leadership that Ella Baker cultivated throughout her life and is premised on a non-elite, grassroots notion of politics—what Black freedom activist and historian Barbara Ransby describes as "a confidence in the wisdom of ordinary people to define their problems and imagine solution" (Ransby 2015). Here, politics is people forming collectivities, discussing and analyzing the conditions they together are facing and what they want and need, and figuring out what then to do. Radical activists have experimented with egalitarian organization models that amplify participants' political capacities, their abilities to act collectively. "Another world is possible," activists declare, and "another politics"—grassroots, non-hierarchical, and prefigurative—will help us get there (Dixon 2014).

Much recent radical activism is territorial, taking the form of squats, occupations of factories and public spaces, and neighborhood assemblies that become new sites of politics in which people can think together, experiment, develop new capacities, and try to build new social relations. In providing the means for survival (food, shelter, health care, child care, knowledge-sharing, fun, sociality), they are spaces where love and care come to be viewed as political acts. They are sites for forming trust and practicing solidarity, collectivist sentiments that challenge capitalist imperatives. Characterizing solidarity as "sharing risk," artist and organizer Dan Wang describes how doctors made known their willingness to sign illness excuse forms for teachers occupying the State Capitol in Madison, Wisconsin, in protest of Governor Scott Walker's efforts to curb public workers' collective bargaining rights (Wang 2011). In a world where differences are often used to divide, reclaimed activist spaces become sites to "find each other" as proposed by both the Invisible Committee (2009) and Comrades from Cairo (2011).

Finding one another holds the potential of forming new collectivities and is thus both profoundly political and ever more important as identity divisions intensify under economic conditions in which increasing numbers of people are threatened with becoming part of the surplus population. As the Marxist collaborative Endnotes write, "the occupiers came together by sidestepping the composition problem," and proclaiming unity—"we are the 99%" (Endnotes 2013). Even so, finding one another and working across differences is an essential part of the long process of composing a class that can dismantle capitalist society.

Activists often describe the euphoria and expanding sense of political possibility that accompany finding one another. Ayelen Lozada, a participant in the Puerta del Sol encampment in Madrid, noted the powerful pull of collectivity: "We all stayed and talked about things we had been thinking alone in our bedrooms, individually." Coming together generated new political doings and opening horizons: "Suddenly we were creating a new reality, something that we couldn't have imagined before. . . . *When the encampment shows* as possible something we haven't imagined before, an infinite field opens for things to imagine and then, suddenly, you join with others to say: 'And now what can we do?'" (quoted in Azzellini and Sitrin 2014, 132–33).

This aligning of politics with collective imagining, beyond *what is*, is a far cry from Otto von Bismarck's famous declaration that politics was "the art of the possible." It is also distinct from the current version of this tyranny of pragmatism, which Slavoj Žižek has disparaged as "the art of expert administration" and even "politics without politics" (2014). Indeed, deliberation and decision-making, not to mention imagining other worlds, disappear in an era when experts decree the only possible course of action: "there is no alternative!" Radical activist sites reject this reduced form of politics, as Graeber suggests when describing what it was like to participate in Occupy: "watching a group of a thousand, or two thousand, people making collective decisions without a leadership structure, motivated only by principle and solidarity, can change one's most fundamental assumptions about what politics, or for that matter, human life, could actually be like" (2013, 89).

From this perspective, "politics" entails turning away from politicians, leaders, and experts and instead turning to one another, forming new bonds in a manner that both prefigures a changed world and can help bring it into being. It thus entails trying out a more collectivist relation to the world, echoing long-time activist Grace Lee Boggs' reminder that broader social transformation must be accompanied by self-transformation. "Politics," she says, requires a "two-sided transformation of ourselves and our institutions" (Boggs 2011, 101). Politics thus comes to be inseparably intertwined with people's affective lives, stemming from dissatisfaction with what is and a desire for something else. In generating new affinities, new political imaginaries, even a new human sensorium, activist sites of politics offer a potent affective challenge to a more common resignation, cynicism, and what Feel Tank Chicago (2015) has called "political depression."

Not knowing what is to be done, at least in any definitive sense, and following the words of the Zapatistas, who say, "Walking, we ask questions" (Notes from Nowhere 2003, 506), radical politics are often improvisational and experimental. Occupy Wall Street participant Matt Presto described the group's "prefigurative politics" as "an ongoing experiment to see what works and what doesn't, and how to constantly adapt to changing circumstances" (quoted in Azzellini and Sitrin 2014, 163). In this vein, and following Stefano Harney and Fred Moten, activists "study" in the sense of engaging in a "common intellectual practice" that prompts wonderment about the difference between what is and what could be. They ask: "How come we can't be together and think together in a way that feels good?" (2013, 110, 117). Rejecting both institutional politics and sectarian left formations with their blueprints for action, contemporary radicals enact what Chris Dixon has described as "another politics" (2014).

This approach to politics and activism is not without its left critics. Feminist theorist Nancy Fraser argues that "anarchist tactics are not themselves sufficient to effect fundamental structural change" and criticizes the strategy of non-engagement with existing governance institutions, stating that it "lets off scot-free the mammoth concentrations of private power whose interests now rule" (2013). For her part, theorist Jodi Dean acknowledges that Occupy was effective in making "the underlying division" between capitalists and everybody else "appear" (2012, 219). However, she criticizes the movement (and the left more generally) for being too focused on democracy, inclusivity, and participation, and insufficiently antagonistic toward capitalism and thus incapable of adopting a strong political stance in favor of fundamental social transformation (55–58). Dean also challenges the fetishization of horizontality, arguing that movements like Occupy can make a revolution only by becoming a new communist party, which—in order to have "structures of accountability and recall"—would require "vertical and diagonal components in addition to horizontal ones" (238). By Dean's account, a party can meet the chaos of revolution—which she describes as "a condition of constitutive non-knowledge"—with necessary "discipline and preparation." In contrast to contemporary horizontal movement formations, these qualities "enable the party to adapt to circumstances rather than be completely molded or determined by them" (241).

To be sure, uncertainty is a condition of radical politics. The way forward is an open question requiring experimentation and learning from mistakes. No one knows definitively what is to be done. Recent conceptions of politics, which embrace prefiguration and direct democracy (in a phrase, turning toward one another), combined with an agonistic orientation toward the world and its institutions, offers one impure way forward.

SEE ALSO: Accountability; Bodies; Conspiracy; Democracy; Experience; Liberal; Materialism; Prefiguration; Privilege; Representation; Revolution; Solidarity; Space; Utopia; Violence

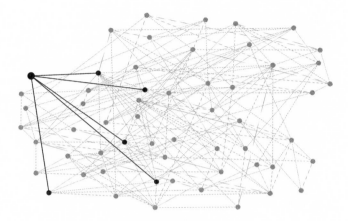

POPULISM

Stefan Kipfer

As a phenomenon, "populism" is as omnipresent as it is conceptually vague. This, at least, is the case with understandings that posit "populism" as a form of political engagement that mobilizes a de-differentiated "people" ("*populus*" or "*plebs*" in Latin) against an equally amorphous elite or establishment. Indeed, the ambiguity of populism alerts us to the challenge of pinning down the meaning of the "popular" in social life and political discourse. Movements and parties seeking to speak to the majority of the population like Occupy, *Indignados*, and Podemos did face this challenge too.

In societies that view themselves as "democratic" (at least nominally, based on that other Greek notion of the people, the "*demos*"), populism should be uncontroversial. Why, then, the anxiety about populism among the self-proclaimed guardians of democracy in Euro-America? Editorialists from the *Financial Times* to *Le Monde* have deployed "populism" as an insult to label divergent political phenomena—the Tea Party and the Campaign for America's Future in the United States, the *Front National* and the *Front de Gauche* in France, and Golden Dawn and Syriza in Greece (Dion 2012; Seguin 2014). Associating left-wing projects with hard-right ones in this way discredits challenges to neoliberal orthodoxy while minimizing the genuine threat of far-right populism and fascism.

According to radical French philosopher and May 1968 alumnus Daniel Bensaïd, editorial anxieties about populism reveal that genuine democracy represents a "permanent scandal" for the bourgeoisie (2011). Indeed, such anxieties attest to the difference between defending liberal, representative democracy and support-ing democracy in the original sense, in which the people (*demos*) run their own affairs (Wood 1995). At an even deeper level, bourgeois distrust of democracy is often rooted in a fear of "the people," un-derstood as an unsophisticated, irrational, and irresponsible mass. The growing acceptance of "popular culture" as a legitimate field of Euro-American capitalist development has reoriented but not done away with bourgeois fears of the popular (Williams 1976). In an age of acute social polarization, intermittent revolt, and imperial war, dominant critiques of populism attest to the ongoing fear of the "dangerous" classes and "races." In turn, this fear fuels the very populist anti-elitism it opposes.

Between the early twentieth century and the 1970s, many on the revolutionary left—including Lenin—associated populist cross-class claims with middle-peasant strata in peripheral or semi-peripheral regions, and with small farmers, artisans, and shopkeep-ers in the so-called advanced capitalist world. However, populism can radiate beyond its primary social bases, and its techniques, styles, and sensibilities can be translated into different historical sit-uations and political strategies. This, at least, was Ernesto Laclau's point about the relationship between Peronism and socialism in

Argentina (1977). The fact that populism can flourish in different contexts and guises makes it necessary to analyze the determinate social and political forces that produce it in any given situation.

Since the late 1970s, radicals have had to grapple with what Stuart Hall described as an "authoritarian" form of populism (1988). This brand of populism established itself as a form of elite bourgeois rule (by winning elections) or exerted significant influence on politics (by operating as a force of opposition). Key examples include Thatcher and the Independence Party (UKIP) in Britain, Ronald Reagan's Republicans and the Tea Party in the United States, the Reform and Conservative Parties in Canada, Narendra Modi's Bharatiya Janata Party (BJP) in India, and Recep Tayyip Erdogan's AK Party in Turkey. Authoritarian populism operates with a profoundly anti-democratic conception of the people (*ethnos*). In this iteration, an inert mass of taxpayers, families, nationals, or believers are invoked from above by folksy or fiery leaders and mobilized by demagogy and fear-mongering directed against internal or external enemies (Rancière 2013). When authoritarian populists claim a direct line to the people, they typically do so by exploiting resentment against existing establishments but symbolically stacking it with subaltern figures.

One of the distinct features of recent right-wing populism is its close connection to economic liberalism. At the forefront of the neoliberal turn, new populists like Thatcher also had intimate links to aggressive segments of finance capital. More recently, figures like Erdogan, Modi, and Nicolas Sarkozy played a key role in radicalizing neoliberalism. Nevertheless, authoritarian populism has never been solely about liberalization, privatization, and class struggle from above. As Stuart Hall pointed out, authoritarian populists raised the stakes for the left by articulating economic liberalism to a wide variety of gendered and racialized projects (1988). In this, they have tried—quite successfully—to reorganize the terrain of struggle and the very meaning of "class." In fact, today's right-wing populisms remind us that liberalism has a long history of complex imbrication with nationalism, patriarchy, and colonialism (Losurdo 2011).

What explains the rise of today's right-wing populisms? Formative for the Anglo-American world, discussions about Thatcherism have underscored the need to explain populism with reference to the complex relationships between economic restructuring, sociopolitical struggle, and ideology. Useful references for such approaches have included Karl Marx's analysis of the Second Empire and Napoleon III in France (2010a; 2010b), Antonio Gramsci's writing about Mussolini (1971), and Frantz Fanon's critique of newly independent regimes in North and West Africa (1967). According to these perspectives, conservative populism is a particular response to the inability of states to govern in the face of challenges from below or tensions among ruling circles magnified by economic crises, war, or imperial intervention. From this perspective, the rise of right-wing populism in the late 1970s was a reply to the impasse of the postwar imperial world order and the challenges emanating from the "long 1968" in both the global South and North. While populism has become a self-reproducing technology of rule (e.g., through the deployment of "wedge issues" during elections), the current resurgence of right populism also arises from the inability of either existing regimes or the left to organize a credible response to the economic and ecological crisis (Solty 2013).

What might be done about authoritarian populism? The fact that it arises from instability is hardly comforting since it is bent on exploiting and intensifying—not managing—crisis. From Hungary to India, explicitly fascist elements have asserted themselves within right populism or outflanked populist parties outright (Löwy 2014; Bannerji 2014). Left responses therefore need to come to terms with the thorny question of subaltern support for populism and fascism. Many authoritarian populist and fascist parties are built with support from ruling-class fractions (e.g., the Tea Party, the AKP, and BJP) and resonate most strongly with the old or new middle classes. In various cases, however, they have managed to garner support from among the dominated classes—workers, the unemployed, and even immigrants and minorities. Ascertaining the precise extent and nature of bottom-up support is thus vital.

Does authoritarian populism require a left-populist response? Certainly, the prospects of left or socialist populism have been debated fervently in those parts of the global South—especially Latin America—where older left-leaning anti-imperialist and anti-colonial populist traditions have been reactivated. These debates had to come to terms with the left-wing populist elements (e.g., charismatic leadership and heterodox economic policies) of Hugo Chavez's Venezuela, Evo Morales' Boliva, and Néstor and Cristina Kirchner's Argentina (Spronk and Webber 2014). In South Africa, meanwhile, debates about ANC rule under Jacob Zuma and the challenge posed by Julius Malema's Economic Freedom Fighters have shown that one cannot always draw a clear line between left- and right-wing populisms (Hart 2014).

In Euro-America, the *Indignado* and Occupy movements exemplified populism by counterpositioning "the people" to the power bloc. By stressing the common interests of the majority ("the 99 percent") against a small minority ("the 1 percent"), these movements highlighted existing social polarization. In promoting such an analysis, some—like Podemos leader Pablo Iglesias—have expressed interest in replacing class categories with a "plebeian" politics (2015). In contrast, others want to redirect the language of right populism. Comparing Occupy Wall Street to the Tea Party and early-twentieth-century progressive US populism, Dorian Warren claimed that Occupy was "the first anti-authoritarian populist movement in this country" because it prioritized direct-democratic assembly-based decision making over charismatic leadership (quoted in Goodman 2011). Similarly, Paolo Gerbaudo (2013) described Occupy as "anarcho-populist" for its attempt to fuse anarchist sensibilities with majoritarian ambitions.

Attempts to sustain these amorphous mobilizations have confronted various obstacles. In English-speaking North America, left populisms face popular disorganization. As a result, they tend to fall back on existing party machines (like New York mayor Bill de Blasio's Democratic Party) or succumb to the allure of "great men" (like Jack Layton of the Canadian New Democratic Party). Meanwhile, the European situation demonstrates the difficulty of reclaiming national politics from conservatives and fascists. In France, the experience of the Front de Gauche under Jean-Luc Mélenchon showed that making appeals to "the people" risks legitimizing ethno-nationalist forms of populism despite advocating for a *political* rather than an *ethnic* conception of national citizenship.

Ultimately, a populist response to the fragmentation of subaltern life may not always be advisable—or even possible. Indeed, it may represent a dangerously voluntarist effort to find a shortcut to substantial alternatives to neoliberalism and right-wing populism (Kraniauskas 2014, 33). Still, any radical politics that aspires to become majoritarian cannot do without appeals to "the people." Socialist politics can only become hegemonic by linking particular dominated and exploited groups—workers, the unemployed, peasants, and others—to whole social formations. Various strategic thinkers, including Antonio Gramsci and Frantz Fanon, have insisted that building such a bloc entails a transformation of the very social bases of opposition. Because of their dialectical and differentiated understanding of "the people" and its component parts, however, such projects are better called "popular-democratic" than "populist" (Hall 1988, 146; Hart 2013).

While radical attempts to make claims to "the people" cannot avoid a measure of ambiguity, these claims cannot be indeterminate. This is well illustrated by the experiences of Syriza in Greece and the electoral coalitions that won municipal elections in Spain in 2015 (Barcelona en Comù and Ahora Madrid, which include Podemos). Originally energized by base-democratic movements (the *Indignados* and the Movement of the Squares), they had to articulate multiple projects with heterogeneous social bases in collective terms (Candeias 2015; Rehmann 2013). For organizational and programmatic reasons, they therefore needed to combine claims to "the people" with concrete references to movements (e.g., labor, feminist, ecology) and social groups (e.g., workers, students, the unemployed, migrants, the oppressed) (Syriza 2015).

These examples allow us to identify two basic conditions for a popular democratic politics. The first means working with a notion of "the people" that is diametrically opposed to the one championed by authoritarian populists: a people that, as "*demos*," is not a pre-given "*ethnos*" defined from above but rather organized from below through open-ended forms of egalitarian decision-making (Rancière 2013). The planning processes in the *barrios* of Caracas, the movements of the squares in Greece, and the neighborhood committees of the *Indignados* all show how "the people" come into existence through political mobilization and democratic experiments. Rather than expressing the fully formed views of a preexisting entity called "the people," radicals strive to make "the people" into a political subject.

The second condition involves refusing to overlook the socially differentiated dimensions of popular democratic politics. Desocializing claims about the political makes it easier for "the people" to be invoked in the abstract, homogenizing, and even paternalist formulations of populism—authoritarian or otherwise (Kipfer and Hart 2013). Such invocations make light of class and gender divides and ignore the fact that, in an imperial world, "the people" are often counterposed to those effectively deemed non-people for being on the wrong side of neocolonial divides, national borders, and twenty-first-century color lines (Khiari 2013). A popular democratic project must therefore account for the differentiated and uneven relations among dominated groups by, for example, combining moments of autonomy with moments of alliance.

SEE ALSO: Class; Democracy; Leadership; Liberal; Representation

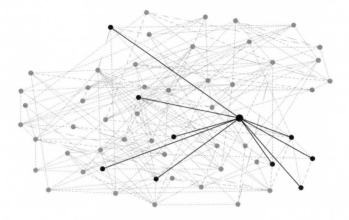

PREFIGURATION

Christian Scholl[1]

WHEN FACED WITH QUESTIONS CONCERNING THE ultimate goal of their encampments, many Occupy activists responded with variations on what is by now an established truism: "*We are the change!*" This answer symptomatically expresses the prefigurative orientation embraced by contemporary activists. For many Occupy activists, social change was *immanent to the process* unfolding in the encampments. By locating the goal within the action itself, means and ends melted together.

---

1. This entry is highly indebted to ongoing exchange with AK Thompson—so much so that, at the end of writing, I am no longer sure whether the words are his or mine.

As in other contemporary radical movements, this focus on "process" coincided with an inclination toward participatory democracy. Drawing on elements from previous waves of protest (including standardized procedures for "horizontal" and "inclusive" decision-making), Occupy Wall Street's General Assembly became the central image suggesting that Occupy was a prefiguration of "real democracy." In order to understand how this situation arose, it is necessary to contextualize the bifurcated historical development of "prefiguration" as both political concept and practice.

As a concept elaborated to guide activist practice, "prefiguration" emerged in the 1960s along with the North American New Left. Among the concept's various and sometimes-vague deployments since then, two distinct inflections can be distinguished (Yates 2015). The first sees prefigurative politics as an ethical approach to conducting protest. Here means must be consistent with and inherently reflect the desired end (Honeywell 2007). In the second iteration, "prefiguration" implies the active creation of counter-institutions designed to foster individuals' and communities' power (Murray 2014). Whereas the first conception prioritizes the symbolic value of exemplary gestures, the second sees prefigurative politics as an additional aspect of social movement activity focused on self-organization. Despite their equivalent strategic importance, however, the first conception is currently prevalent within radical scenes in the global North.

Although the codification of prefigurative politics is strongly associated with the radicalism of the '60s, it is hard to determine the historical roots of this approach. Throughout the nearly two thousand years leading up to the rise of the New Left, heretical religious movements formed exemplary communities to enact belief outside of established doctrine. Although contemporary activist accounts often obscure the religious origins of "prefiguration," the *Oxford English Dictionary* raises them implicitly through its indication that the concept refers to the "foreshadowing of a person or thing." Such foreshadowing can be seen in John's millenarian vision of the New Jerusalem in Revelations, where the revelation of Jesus Christ is foreshadowed to John of Patmos through prophetic visions. Later, in *City of God*, Saint Augustine (1962) proposed that Christianity involved an awareness that two worlds—distinct but overlapping—existed within this one. Although Christians could not remain aloof to earthly affairs, it was necessary for them to stay alert to the work of providence that animated them. Whereas the actualization of the divine was projected into the future, some glimpses could—through devotion—be lived in the present. In this way, Augustine bound the conception of prefiguration to the messianic promise.

Later, without ever advancing the term "prefigurative politics" themselves, early-nineteenth-century socialist and anarchist thinkers like Fourier, Saint-Simon, and Proudhon advocated the creation of alternative institutions as a means of overcoming existing social relations. Mostly stripped of religious content, these proposals were nevertheless inflected with messianism. As intentional communities established to prefigure a society based on cooperation and striving toward harmony, the Fourier-inspired Phalansteries are a case in point. Social movements of these times were determined to contribute to the moral renewal of industrial society. The implicit assumption underlying these prefigurative experiments was that the good example would lead. According to Michael P. Young (2006), the moral underpinnings of early-nineteenth-century social movements in the United States was directly attributable to their evangelical character and their emphasis on personal responsibility.

Criticizing the "purely utopian character" of these early socialist experiments, which he thought were "necessarily doomed to failure" (Marx and Engels 2012, 74), Marx proposed in a letter to Arnold Ruge (1843) that the task was not to create a new, alternate content but rather to actualize the content of the existing world through conscious engagement so that it might accord with revolutionary desires. This dialectical approach encouraged a strategic orientation to the contradictions of capitalism. Conventional ethics in the present became superfluous in the face of an unswervingly instrumental orientation toward the future. The inevitable subsequent conflict between Marxist and anarchist tendencies within the International Workingmen's Association seems in retrospect to foreshadow the tensions between "prefigurative" and "strategic" approaches that would emerge in social movements in the 1960s and 1970s.

In the first decades of the twentieth century, anarchist and anarcho-communist thinkers like Voltairine de Cleyre, Rudolf Rocker, and Gustav Landauer strongly influenced the prefigurative approach devoted to the formation of counter-institutions. As the autonomous action of workers became increasingly opposed to hierarchical, centralized, and statist socialist organizations, anarchists and other libertarian communists encouraged decentralized forms of self-organization, including production and consumption cooperatives (Azzelini 2015; Cleaver 2000) In their preamble, the Industrial Workers of the World refer to this process as "forming the structure of the new society within the shell of the old." Radical communists picked up this prefigurative practice and carried out important experiments in council communism.

In contrast to prefiguration's ethical inflection, the focus on alternative institutions is viewed less as a pedagogically conceived exodus than as a direct part of the challenge to existing power relations. Although process still matters, it is seen less as an aim in itself (a signature of the ethical) than as a means of organizing movements for justice. Considering Occupy's orientation toward immanence, such a prefigurative orientation forces us to ask: how does consensus-based decision-making in General Assemblies concretely serve the goal toward which it aspires?

During the 1960s, with the rise of the counterculture, a broader "cultural turn" in the social sciences, and the emergence of the New Left, the ethical dimensions of prefiguration were rediscovered, and the idea (if not yet the term) became implanted in the radical imagination. Already in 1962, members of SDS could lament that American society had become witness to a "democracy apathetic and manipulated when it should be dynamic and participative." Recounted in *The Port Huron Statement*, this perspective heralded the rise of what Christopher Lasch (1979) would later decry as a "cult of participation," in which the *experience* of protesting was tantamount to protest itself. For their part, although the Student Nonviolent Coordinating Committee (SNCC) did not make mention of "prefiguration," they did invoke "beloved community" to "define both how we related to one another within the organization and what we sought to build 'out there' in the world we sought to transform" (Miller 2014).

Carl Boggs (1977) coined the term "prefigurative politics" in the context of his work on revolutionary movements in Russia, Italy, and Spain, as well as on the New Left in the United States. The sociologist Wini Breines (1980; 1988; 1989) later popularized the term through her writing on the US New Left. For Boggs (1977, 100), such politics were "the embodiment, within the ongoing political practice of a movement, of those forms of social relations, decision-making, culture, and human experience that are the ultimate goal." Conceptually, prefiguration marked a rejection of both centrism and vanguardism. For her part, Breines (1989, 6–7) distinguished between "strategic politics" aimed at structural changes, and "prefigurative politics" aimed at creating communal embodiments of the desired society. In this view, "prefigurative politics" offered a means of moving beyond a demand-based politics focused primarily on socio-economic issues.

Inspired by these discussions, radicals began adopting "prefigurative politics" to describe their own practices and mark their distance from the bureaucratic and hierarchical "old" left. Strong critiques of both technocratic liberal democracy and of Soviet state bureaucracy resulted in a widespread preference for horizontal forms of organizing. Meanwhile, the cultural turn in social movements created more space for identity as well as for emotional and personal issues—what has been called "the democratization of everyday life" (Melucci 1989). Finally, the politicization of subjectivity and interpersonal relations has politicized integrity: people are now called upon to have their daily practice fully reflect their political values.

This politicization of personal experience became especially prominent in the consciousness-raising groups of the 1960s. Organizational hierarchies were decried not solely as part of an "old" bureaucratic left, but also as expressions of a "male left" with its "perpetuation of patriarchal, and. . . capitalist values" (Cathy Levine 2002). In her famous essay "The Tyranny of Structurelessness," feminist organizer Jo Freeman (2002) criticized this position for having fostered informal hierarchies that were even harder to address. Prefiguration began to be critiqued as a sub-cultural tendency as the New Left's commitment to the "beloved community" began erring toward self-marginalization. As Engler and Engler (2014a) put it, "If the project of building alternative community totally eclipses attempts to communicate with the wider public and win broad support, it risks becoming a very limiting type of self-isolation."

By the late 1970s, the US antinuclear movement had adopted a number of Quaker principles to advocate for participatory democracy, decentralized affinity groups, and planned violations of legal boundaries. These groups added a propositional dimension to the oppositional direct action approach deployed by late-nineteenth-century anarchists. According to Epstein, what was new about these groups was that "the opportunity to act out a vision and build community was at least as important as the immediate objective of stopping nuclear power" (1991, 123). The combination of opposition and proposition through "nonviolent direct action" subsequently influenced many counter-globalization groups during the late 1990s (see Graeber 2009).

The rise of the counter-globalization movement triggered renewed interest in prefiguration. Several activist scholars consider the counter-globalization movement to be the ultimate movement-based expression of prefigurative politics (Graeber 2002). Picking up on the heritage of the antinuclear Clamshell Alliance and supported by anarchist writers like David Graeber, Paul Goodman, and Colin Ward, activist collectives like the Direct Action Network (DAN) aimed to make their non-violent direct action a perfect reflection of the prefigurative ethics. Reflecting on the 1999 anti-WTO blockade in Seattle, Rebecca Solnit (2007, 8) summarized prefiguration when she insisted that "you can and perhaps ought to embody what you avow."

Today the context for discussions about prefiguration has changed. Global capitalism rather than the Old Left is now the reference point. As Farber (2014) points out, "The contemporary supporters of this perspective are no longer reacting to an Old Left but to . . . the rituals of a political democracy increasingly devoid of content." In *Beautiful Trouble*, we learn that "the goal of a prefigurative intervention is twofold: to offer a compelling glimpse of a possible, and better, future, and also—slyly or baldly—to point up the poverty of imagination of the world we actually do live in" (Boyd 2012).

The ethical reading of prefiguration emphasizes immanence and immediate experience. In this way, it echoes Hakim Bey's (2004) account of the "temporary autonomous zone," where "we concentrate our force on temporary 'power surges', avoiding all entanglements 'with permanent solutions.'" At its threshold, this orientation declares the present to be the future; however, if our organization *is* our strategy, then strategy and organization become blurred, and instrumental reckoning about objectives becomes impossible.

Surely, where it designates an experimental approach to the creation of counter-institutions while organizing with explicit goals, there is nothing wrong with prefiguration. However, if it comes to mean experiments without goals, it may deprive radical movements of one of their most powerful weapons—the idea that current acts have future consequences. If "prefiguration" as experimentation with counter-institutions is to maintain its teleological focus, it is necessary for radicals to determine whether a division between community-builders and strategy-builders is actually possible.

SEE ALSO: Demand; Democracy; Domination; Friend; Future; Hegemony; Hope; Politics; Utopia

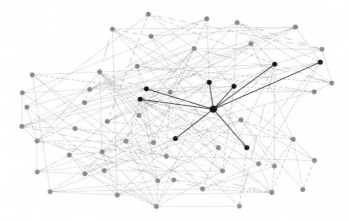

PRIVILEGE

Douglas Williams

BOTH A NOUN AND A VERB, THE WORD "PRIVILEGE" originates in Roman politics, where the Latin *"privile-gium"* was used to describe a bill that afforded a special right or prerogative to an individual. While later versions of the word in Anglo-Norman, Old French, and Middle French eliminated the term's specific policy-procedural definition (and, with it, its ad hoc conceptualization), they preserved the basic connotation of "a special right, advantage, or immunity granted or available only to a particular person or group of people." This remains the common meaning of privilege today. However, while "privilege" orients us to the exception in mainstream usage—the boss giving a job to a family member, the opportunity to meet someone we admire ("it's a privilege")—radicals have come to use the term to describe the rule: general power differentials between social groups.

In North America, this latter conception can be traced to W. E. B. Du Bois' 1935 book *Black Reconstruction in America*. Though Du Bois did not use the concept of "privilege" itself, his reference to the "psychological wage" laid the foundation for contemporary radical use of the word—particularly its best-known variant, "white privilege." He explained that although the white worker and the Black worker were similarly underpaid and undervalued, Du Bois argued that the former were "compensated in part by a sort of public and psychological wage" that included social deference, preferential media treatment, and access to preferential treatment by state actors including politicians and law enforcement (2013, 700).

By the 1960s, this use of "privilege" entered radical discourse through the work of social theorists like Theodore Allen and Noel Ignatiev. Drawing explicitly on Du Bois, Allen and Ignatiev wrote a series of open letters, titled "White Blindspot" (1967), in which they criticized the Progressive Labor Party for positing that the white working class and the Black working class had distinct economic demands, that Black liberation could be boiled down to "more jobs, housing, and full political rights," and that the white working class did not have to fully engage in a fight against white supremacy. In contrast, and according to Allen and Ignatiev, white supremacy was the "greatest ideological barrier to the achievement of proletarian class consciousness, solidarity and political action" and "the greatest political, social and ideological bulwark of the imperialist war makers and colonial oppressors" (Davidson 2011, 149). They therefore advocated for white working-class engagement in the fight against white supremacy, using the concept of "white skin privilege" to advance their argument.[1] "The U.S. ruling class has made a deal with

---

1.   Allen would go on to write several more books on this topic, including the influential *Class Struggle and the Origin of Racial Slavery: The Invention of the White Race* (1994). Ignatiev published *How the Irish Became White* (1995) on the same topic.

the mis-leaders of American labor, and through them with the masses of white workers," they lamented.

> The terms of the deal, worked out over the three-hundred-year history of the development of capitalism in our country, are these: you white workers help us conquer the world and enslave the nonwhite majority of the earth's laboring force, and we will repay you with a monopoly of the skilled jobs. We will cushion you against the most severe shocks of the economic cycle, provide you with health and education facilities superior to those of the nonwhite population, grant you the freedom to spend your money and leisure time as you wish without social restrictions, enable you on occasion to promote one of your number out of the ranks of the laboring class, and in general confer on you the material and spiritual privileges befitting your white skin. (Davidson 2011, 149–50)

Around this time, the precursors of "privilege theory" began to gain traction within the academy. In *Pedagogy of the Oppressed*, Paulo Friere noted that "The oppressors do not perceive their monopoly on *having more* as a privilege which dehumanizes others and themselves" (1970, 59). The problem with this monopoly became apparent throughout the late 1960s and early 1970s as students of color and female students began to occupy university administration buildings across the country, demanding increased diversity in higher education. As pedagogical frameworks and curricula became more inclusive with the formation of race and gender specific programs and Departments, the theorizing about privilege began to quicken.

Peggy McIntosh's influential 1988 article "White Privilege: Unpacking the Invisible Knapsack" drew from these radical Left deliberations and introduced "privilege" as a central concept to activist discussions about power. To do this, McIntosh provided fifty examples of white privilege, presented as personal statements: "I can if I wish arrange to be in the company of people of my race most of the time. . . . I can criticize our government and talk about how much I fear its policies and behavior without being seen as a cultural outsider. . . . I can remain oblivious of the language and customs of persons of color who constitute the world's majority without feeling in my culture any penalty for such oblivion" (quoted in Andersen and Hill Collins 2013, 98–103). McIntosh's use of "privilege" differed from previous radical uses; whereas Du Bois, Allen, and Ignatiev focused on the ways in which the state and capital afforded privileges to break intra-class solidarity, McIntosh focused on micro-level manifestations.

It is this micro-level conception that has come to dominate contemporary social movements, particularly with respect to "anti-oppression" politics. In a discussion of these politics, the organization SOA Watch describes "privilege" as something that "play[s] out in our group dynamics." They further note that privileged individuals must "be honest and open and take risks to address oppression head on" (SOA Watch). Similarly, in *White Anti-Racist Activism: A Personal Roadmap*, for example, Jennifer Holladay echoes many of McIntosh's points, while adding to the original list of individual privileges: "I can purchase travel size bottles of my hair care products at most grocery or drug stores," she notes (Teaching Tolerance). Meanwhile, "privilege" has come to be used not solely in reference to race (although it still arises most often in this context). An article on *Everyday Feminism*, for instance, lists privileges based on physical abilities in a fashion reminiscent of McIntosh's article: "Public transportation is easy for you. . . . You can expect to be included in group activities. . . . You can go about your day without planning every task, like getting dressed or going to the bathroom" (Teaching Tolerance).

In activist usage, "privilege" gradually came to denote something that people either did or did not possess. The question thus became: since it is dishonest for people to hide their privilege (though there has surely been some of that), how should people use their privilege? This question has generated two dominant responses. The first is associated with the idea and practice of "accountability" (a position that finds emblematic expression in calls to "check your privilege.") This response reinforces the micro-level conception by placing the burden on individuals rather than institutions.

The second response is associated with the politics of becoming an "ally." There, the aim is to politically mobilize privilege in the service of its elimination. Typical of this position, bell hooks wrote that "Privilege is not in and of itself bad; what matters is what we do with privilege. I want to live in a world where all women have access to education, and all women can earn PhDs, if they so desire. Privilege does not have to be negative, but we have to share our resources and take direction about how to use our privilege in ways that empower those who lack it" (hooks and Mesa-Bains 2006, 73).

Conversations about privilege and allies have recently gained traction in some more mainstream arenas. For instance, talk show host and Wake Forest University professor Melissa Harris-Perry has focused on privilege on several occasions. In one episode of her self-titled MSNBC program, she quoted anti-racism activist and author Tim Wise in a discussion about being an ally: "Whenever people are in a position of privilege, and that can be skin privilege, it can be gender and sex privilege, money privilege, or celebrity privilege, there is a responsibility, I think, to use that privilege as responsibly as possible. And most all of us have some of it in some way, shape, or form; it's about how we use it. And so for those of us who are white trying to be allies in the struggle against racism, we are trying to use that in a responsible way. Men fighting sexism are doing the same thing" (Clark 2013).

However, this popular use of "privilege" has not been without its detractors. Writing in the *Socialist Worker*, Candace Cohn encapsulates most of these critiques in her 2015 article "Privilege and the Working Class," in which she focuses specifically on white skin privilege. Cohn attributes the dissolution of Students for a Democratic Society (SDS) to the publication of "White Blindspot," stating that the resulting sectarian splintering initiated the decline in credibility of revolutionary socialist organizations among the broader Left. In addition to these institutional effects, Cohn critiques "privilege theory" itself as being at odds with the fight for working-class liberation. This, she explains, is because privilege theory holds that *all* white people benefit from white supremacy and are thus complicit in its maintenance. For Cohn, this notion is absurd: "In holding white workers co-responsible for systemic racism, the privilege model attributed a power to white workers they manifestly do not have: control over the institutions of American capitalism—schools, jobs, housing, factories, banks, police, courts, prisons, legislatures, media, elections, universities, armed services, hospitals, sports, political parties—all of which function in a racist manner." In opposition to this perspective, Cohn points out that "These institutions are owned and controlled by the capitalist class. They engineer, manage and enforce the social, economic and political racism that serves the social relations of American capitalism. It is these institutions that make racism such a powerful and inescapable part of American daily life" (Cohn 2015).

Pushing her argument to its logical conclusion, Cohn challenges the very notion that white workers have privilege at all. Instead, she states that the things that are seen as privileges are, in fact "reforms won by the working class through bitter struggle. These class gains represented the return of a small part of the great wealth held by capitalists that workers had produced. Privilege theory—on the basis of unequal access to these gains under racist American capitalism—converted hard-won class victories, reforms, and rights into 'undeserved' workers' 'privileges'" (Cohn 2015).

In addition to political and class critiques of deployments of "privilege," there have also been critiques of the way that the use of such language can mask insufficient theorizing on issues that are important to radicals. In this view, radicals run the risk of debating the packaging of ideas rather than the ideas themselves. In an article titled "Anarchism and the English Language," Kristian Williams writes:

> The effect on readers is certainly bad enough, but the implications for writers are more serious still.

Sometimes, of course, vague and shoddy prose—and the readiness with which such is accepted—makes it possible for a writer to deliberately pass off one thing as another, or to hide bad reasoning in a rhetorical fog. More often, however, a well-meaning writer just accepts the standard currently in use and out of witless habit uses language that alters, obscures, or nullifies his own meaning. In such cases, the writer, too, is the victim: he means to say one thing, and says another; or, he means to say something, but says nothing instead.

Our use of "privilege" has the power to shape not only the way we understand the underlying issues causing social ills but also the solutions we put forth to eradicate them. Whether we adopt Allen and Ignatiev's use of privilege to denote a tool of imperialism and capitalism, McIntosh's use of privilege to denote lived everyday advantages, or Cohn's conception of "privilege" as a word that has obscured the actual conditions of struggle, we must be deliberate in our usage and prepared to defend the meaning we choose.

SEE ALSO: Accountability; Allies; Class; Community; Domination; Oppression; Politics; Rights

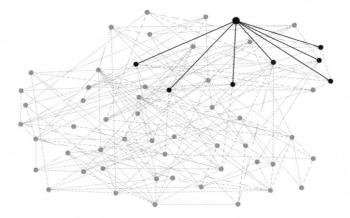

QUEER

Natalie Kouri-Towe

"WE'RE HERE, WE'RE QUEER, GET USED TO IT!"
Popularized by Queer Nation, a US-based direct-action
organization formed in 1990, this now-canonical chant
remains one of the most recognizable instances of queer
political speech. Issued as a rallying cry for political confrontation, "we're here, we're queer, get used to it!" called
upon queers and their allies to take action against the "es-
calation of violence against LGBT people in the streets
of New York, and the ongoing existence of anti-gay discrimination in the culture at large" (Queer Nation New
York 2013). More than two decades later, however, the
social and political landscape concerning sexuality in
North America has changed substantially. On the heels of

same-sex marriage legislation in places like Canada and the United States, the repeal of the US military "don't ask don't tell policy, and the proliferation of LGBTQ figures in media and popular culture, we must ask: what happens to "queer" when it appears that people have indeed *gotten used to it*?

Although its precise origins remain unknown, the word "queer" was first used in the English language as an adjective, and as a synonym for the strange, odd, or peculiar. Between the late nineteenth century and early twentieth century, as modern discourses concerning sex proliferated (Foucault 1978, 18) and introduced the terms "homosexual" and "heterosexual" into the English language, "queer" became a derogatory reference to homosexuality. Almost a century later, between the late 1980s and early '90s, activists and others reclaimed "queer" as a form of identification (as a noun), a celebration of maligned sexuality (as an adjective), and an intervention into the increasingly normalized discourses of sexuality and sexual rights (as a verb) in the mainstreaming of gay, lesbian, and bisexual lifestyle through the call for marriage equality. Most notably, New York–based Queer Nation popularized the reclamation of "queer" as an act of resistance in the early nineties. During this period, "queer" simultaneously helped to expand categories of sexual identification beyond "lesbian," "gay," and "bisexual" while foregrounding an emergent practice of self-identification and desire that rejected gender binaries. In other words, even as "queer" became an established identity in the LGBTQ rainbow acronym, it also worked against the normalization of gender and sexuality by challenging the presumption of a two-gender system.

Despite the new opportunities for self-expression and self-identification that the reclamation of "queer" has facilitated, tensions between the normalizing impulse to make "queer" a stable identity category on the one hand, and the queer political critique of normalization on the other have led to contradictory and contested mobilizations of "queer" in the twenty-first century. Indeed, the term has been variously critiqued by trans activists for appropriating and erasing transgender and transsexual subjectivities and politics (Namaste 2000; Stryker 2008), celebrated as the unifying front for the rainbow of sexual and gender diversity (e.g., the "queer" community), institutionalized in community and campus-based service organizations (e.g., the establishment of university sexual diversity offices), and co-opted by TV shows like *Queer Eye for the Straight Guy* (2003–7) to facilitate the marketing of queerness as a consumer lifestyle.

The conflict over what constitutes queerness can ultimately be distilled to a fundamental tension between the assumption that "queer" denotes an inherently radical political subjectivity, on the one hand, and its contemporary normalization in consumer culture and mainstream society on the other. In part, this is a tension between perspectives that view queer identity as a celebration of sexual and gender diversity and those that view it as a political orientation against normalization. The addition of "queer" in the expansion of LGBT to LGBTTIQQ2SAAP (Lesbian, Gay, Bisexual, Transsexual, Transgender, Intersex, Queer, Questioning, 2-Spirit, Asexual, Allies, and Pansexual) is generally heralded as a sign of radical inclusion. However, this inclusion is politically at odds with queer activist critiques of the politics of inclusion. These politics are critiqued due to their tendency to replace the political project of social transformation with a heightened focus on the representation of sexual and gender diversity and the recognition of "queer" as an identity. For instance, Against Equality, which formed in 2009, writes, "As queer thinkers, writers and artists, we are committed to dislodging the centrality of equality rhetoric and challenging the demand for inclusion in the institution of marriage, the US military, and the prison industrial complex via hate crimes legislation."

Although queer politics and queer identity share a fundamental rejection of homophobia and heteronormativity, what this means in practice is often different depending on whether politics or identity is foregrounded. In its radical forms, queer politics is often envisioned as being distinct from assimilationist gay rights movements that aim to normalize homosexuality and expand state recognition. In reality, however, the relationship between queer radicalism and queer assimilation is often much closer than activists tend to think. The history of pride parades is one of the clearest examples of this tension.

Emerging from the riots, marches, and demonstrations that followed the 1969 police raid of the Stonewall Tavern in New York City, the early pride parades were rallies against police brutality, criminalization, and repression. As pride marches spread internationally and gay rights began entering the mainstream between the mid-1980s and 1990s, however, the meaning of "pride" shifted from liberation to celebration. Now largely institutionalized in countries where sexual rights are legislated, pride parades have become large-scale festivals celebrating acceptance and inclusion within mainstream society. Unsurprisingly, the events have also become increasingly corporatized, with many festivals now featuring corporate sponsorship and heavy corporate participation in the parade.

Despite this turn toward normalization and assimilation, however, political contestation persists through public debates about whether pride parades are political events or festive celebrations of sexual inclusivity. In Toronto, such political contestations have included fights against attempts to "cover up" public nudity (as when Toronto District School Board trustees asked police to enforce public nudity laws at Toronto World Pride in 2014) and censorship of contentious political speech (like the temporary 2010 ban on the term "Israeli apartheid"). The past few years have also witnessed a resurgence of direct political interventions including the 2010 Take Back the Dyke march and the now-annual Night March, which was first organized by Queers for Social Justice in 2012. Beyond Toronto, other radical queer interventions into pride celebrations have included the annual Pervers/Cité events organized in Montreal since 2007 and the international Queeruption gatherings (DIY anticapitalist events frequently organized as alternatives to WorldPride celebrations) that took place between 1998–2010.

Radical queer organizing generally uses varied approaches (from direct action to public education) to critique consumerism and normalization—especially the normalization of gay sexuality as lifestyle. The US-based "Put a Rainbow on It" campaign is a queer intervention into practices of assimilation and normalization that parodies the association of the rainbow pride flag with "some things that are just not that awesome." The campaign website includes a toolkit that critiques the way that sexual rights frameworks have provided cover for and helped to foster gentrification, labor exploitation, and normalized family and marriage regimes as well as expansions of police surveillance, the prison and military industrial complexes, and zero-tolerance policies in education.

The assimilation of "queer" into mainstream society, the role that sexual rights now play in twenty-first-century civilizational discourses, and radical interventions like the "Put a Rainbow on It" campaign are emblematic of the ambivalence today surrounding the term "queer." For many critical thinkers engaged in queer politics and theory, "queer" is an explicitly ambivalent concept. Indeed, "part of queer's semantic clout, part of its political efficacy," argues Annamarie Jagose, "depends on its resistance to definition" (1996, 1). But if "queer" never attains lexical coherence or stability for itself, for subjectivity, or for society, then its strength lies in its ability to foster orientations, approaches, and embodiments that run counter to the mainstream, the dominant, and the normative.

As with many resistant frameworks, however, "queer" too has its limits. Under the conditions of globalization, "queer" has shown signs of being at risk of universalizing sexual and gender identities and politics by applying uniform global sexual rights across the international context. According to Jasbir Puar, such "rights discourses produce narratives of progress and modernity that continue to accord some populations access to citizenship—cultural and legal—at the expense of the delimitation and expulsion of other populations" (2013, 337). Critics of gay internationalism and WorldPride have argued that global gay rights conform to Western imperial practices of international development and aid, military intervention, and globalized mobility elitism through gay tourism (Massad 2007; Puar 2007). Such practices reinforce rather than transform global inequalities, Puar charges, and "queer" (envisioned as inherently transgressive) becomes "precisely the term by which queerness narrates its own sexual exceptionalism" (Puar 2007, 22). For Puar, queer activists must reconcile the alluring promise of queerness as an open-ended anti-normative project with the harsh reality that the mechanisms of power do not prevent queer subjects from acting as "accomplices of certain normativizing violences" (ibid., 24). Thus, if "queer" is radical because it opens to radical self-identification, at what point does it risk reinstating a new set of rigid (albeit expanded) norms?

Contemporary radical queer activism must contend with the normalization and co-optation of queer struggles. This is especially true in light of neoliberalism's seductive regime of extended sexual rights and inclusion for those who previously went unrepresented. Although the rallying cry "we're here, we're queer, get used to it" symbolizes a radical intervention in one context, the moment that people do in fact get used to it signals the point at which "queerness," as previously conceived, already exceeds its frame. Once we've gotten used to it, the queer intervention is normalized. Does this mean that "queer" must therefore entail a continual return to ambivalence? If "queer" is only oppositional, then how might we productively negotiate justice through queerness? Perhaps this is the limit of the term. Perhaps, in the end, "queer" fails to provide the material for building stable lives even as it announces an effective intervention into the status quo.

If the strength of "queer" lies in disruption, discomfort, and the failure to properly fit, is it a failure to model "queer" as something that—as queer scholar José Muñoz has suggested—always remains "not yet here" (2009)? Although "queer" offers a useful expansion of sexual identity categories (e.g., by enabling new and diverse forms of sexuality and gender-based identification), a significant current of radical queer activism diverges from identity-based organizing. Radical queer activist groups are increasingly focusing their efforts on countering state practices (including the criminalization of HIV/AIDS, immigration and asylum policies, incarceration, and pinkwashing), as well as consumerism and the mainstreaming of queer sexuality as lifestyle. It is therefore important to highlight that despite the ambivalence underlying the relationship between identity-based and radical interventionist streams in queer activism today, normalizing projects might very well be effectively queer. For instance, expanding the categories of sexuality and gender identity remains vital to mobilizations against hegemonic social structures like the hetero-patriarchal family and the pathologization of inter-sexed, trans, and disabled subjects. Such struggles include the fight against structural heteronormativity, homophobic and transphobic violence, as well as the fight against criminalization (e.g., through colonial sodomy laws), and colonization (e.g., queer solidarity with indigenous struggles or the Palestinian liberation movement). They also include demands for access to health care and social services from local governments and the nation-state. From this vantage, "queer" remains a viable framework for articulating justice because it is capable of adapting to the shifting conditions of power once we have *gotten used to it*.

SEE ALSO: Allies; Crip; Experience; Gender; Oppression; Rights; Trans*/-

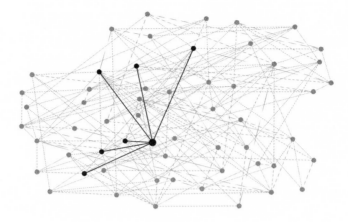

RACE

Conor Tomás Reed

RACE IS A VOLATILE METONYM. ITS ETYMOLOGICAL formation spans several languages: sixteenth-century Middle French *"race"* (common descent), Italian *"razza"* (lineage), Spanish and Portuguese *"raza"* (family), Arabic *"ra's"* (origin), Hebrew *"rosh"* (first), fourteenth-century Old Norse *"ras"* (rush), Old English *"ræs"* (attack), and Middle Dutch *"rasen"* (rage). As these origins suggest, the word "race" is historically inseparable from "racecraft," that "mental trick that turns racism into race" (Fields and Fields 2014). As Ta-Nehisi Coates has recently argued, "Our notion of what constitutes 'white' and what constitutes 'black' is a product of social context. It is utterly impossible to look at the delineation of a 'Southern race'

343

and not see the Civil War, the creation of an 'Irish race' and not think of Cromwell's ethnic cleansing, the creation of a 'Jewish race' and not see anti-Semitism" (2013).

Contemporary conceptions of "race" can be traced to two fifteenth-century religious colonization campaigns: the Protestant takeover of Ireland (Robinson 2000, 36–43) and the Christian Crusades in what is now the Iberian Peninsula and North Africa, which yielded the law of *limpieza de sangre* (cleanliness of blood, an early progenitor to the "one-drop rule"). According to Roxanne Dunbar-Ortiz, "Before this time the concept of biological race based on 'blood' is not known to have existed . . . in Christian Europe or anywhere else in the world" (2014, 36–7). Nevertheless, through the sixteenth and seventeenth centuries, Spanish Inquisition interrogators would demand that citizens be "Old Christians, of clean blood, without the race, stain, or descent from Jews, Moors, or conversos, or from any other recently converted sect" (Martínez 2011, 67).

During the Enlightenment, philosophers, scientists, explorers, and politicians devised racial classifications that perpetuated the Spanish empire's fixation on purity. In 1733, Voltaire surmised: "The Negro race is a species of men different from ours as the breed of spaniels is from that of greyhounds" (quoted in West 1999, 83). In his 1775 work *On the Different Races of Man*, Immanuel Kant defined "the white race, the Negro race, the Hun race (Mongol or Kalmuck), and the Hindu or Hindustani race" as belonging to the same species (Goldner 1997). After traveling from France to help colonize North America, J. Hector St. John de Crèvecœur wrote in his *Letters from an American Farmer* of 1782 that "Here individuals of all races are melted into a new race of man," an "American race" formed by a "mixture of English, Scotch, Irish, French, Dutch, Germans, and Swedes" (Singh 2004, 21). Christoph Meiners, who coined the term "Caucasian race" in his 1785 work *The Outline of History of Mankind*, whittled humanity down further into two types: the "beautiful White race" and the "ugly Black race" (Isaac 2006, 105).

Although US settler-colonial expansion and capital accumulation during the early seventeenth century was made possible by enslaved and indentured labor, the distinction between "free" and "slave" people was not yet legally designated by race. Resistance strategies between Africans, Europeans, and Native Americans disrupted racial categories and precipitated colonial policing methods. By 1661, a law forbade "English servants" from running away "in the company of Negroes." Similarly, a 1691 law banished any "white man or woman being free who shall intermarry with a negro, mulatto, or Indian man or woman bond or free" (Rose 1976, 17; 21). Europeans and Native Americans were designated "mulattos" not for having African ancestry but simply for communing with them (Forbes 1993, 2; 199). The response was clear. By 1811, after fellow Native Americans were forced to cede a large tract of land to the US government, the Shawnee leader Tecumseh gathered five thousand in Alabama to announce: "Let the white race perish. . . . Back whence they came, upon a trail of blood, they must be driven" (Zinn 1980).

By the time of the U.S. Civil War, claims to the mantle of "master race" were being hotly contested amongst Euro-descended elite men. Southern slave-owning settlers who identified as "Cavaliers, Jacobites, and Huguenots naturally hate[d], condemn[ed], and despise[d] the Puritans who settled the North," since "the former [were] a master race—the latter a slave race, the descendants of Saxon serfs" (cited in McPherson 1999, 6). After Reconstruction, further legal and labor divisions were introduced to suppress affinities between poor Africans, Europeans, and Native Americans. According to W.E.B. Du Bois, "the theory of race was supplemented by a carefully planned and slowly evolved method, which drove . . . a wedge between the white and black workers." As a result, "there probably are not today two groups of workers anywhere in the world with practically identical interests who hate and fear each other so deeply and persistently" (Du Bois 1992, 700). By the "late-nineteenth-century heyday of the Jim Crow regime," Karen and Barbara Fields add, "the term 'race relations'" had been introduced to finesse "the abrogation of democracy and the bloody vigilantism that enforced it" (2014, 39–40).

In the early twentieth century, women's liberation advocates and eugenicists alike sought to augment women's position by connecting it to the improvement of the race. In this moment, the concept became divided between its universal, human scope and its particular, hierarchical, and exclusionary one. In his labor anthem "Bread and Roses," James Oppenheim proclaimed that "The rising of the women means the rising of the race" (Oppenheim 1911). A year later, however, Myre Iseman warned in *Race Suicide* that waning birth rates would signal the "passing of this great Anglo-Teuton people" (Iseman 2010, 5). In 1914, Margaret Sanger (who would later found Planned Parenthood) began promoting contraception in the pages of *The Woman Rebel*, which bore the slogan "No Gods, No Masters" on its masthead. By 1920, however, she was arguing that, "If we are to develop in America a new race with a racial soul . . . we must not encourage reproduction beyond our capacity to assimilate our numbers so as to make the coming generation into such physically fit, mentally capable, socially alert individuals as are the ideal of a democracy" (Sanger 1920, 44). In contrast to this narrow vision, José Vasconcelos' 1925 publication *La Raza Cósmica* (The Cosmic Race) surpassed Kant's four racial types to advocate for a "fifth universal race, the fruit of all the previous ones and amelioration of everything past" (Vasconcelos 1979, 9).

Around this time, distinct forms of "race pride" also began coalescing among African Americans and Afro-Caribbean, European, and Levantine immigrants. In a 1920 *Negro World* article entitled "Race First versus Class First," Caribbean socialist Hubert Harrison wrote: "We can respect the Socialists of Scandinavia, France, Germany, or England . . . [but] we say Race First, because you have all along insisted Race First and class after when you didn't need our help" (Harrison 2001, 109). Across the Atlantic, and on the eve of the 1916 Easter Uprising, James Connolly similarly declared: "no agency less potent than the red tide of war on Irish soil will ever be able to enable the Irish race to recover its self-respect" (Connolly 1916).

Harrison tactically moved from his "race first" position toward one of "race consciousness" as race riots engulfed the United States between 1917 and 1921. During this period, the Universal Negro Improvement Association (UNIA) coordinated over a thousands divisions, and their newspaper *Negro World* circulated worldwide via Black dockworkers, sailors, and soldiers (Hahn 2009, 124–5). The UNIA embraced Ireland's anti-colonial nationalist struggle, and Marcus Garvey even named Liberty Hall Harlem and *Negro World* after their Irish comrades' Dublin Liberty Hall and *Irish World* (Hahn 2009, 220). Meanwhile, straddling the line between universal and particular conceptions of race, Zora Neale Hurston revealed in 1928 that, "At certain times I have no race, I am me." However, "when I set my hat at a certain angle and saunter down Seventh Avenue, Harlem City, feeling as snooty as the lions in front of the Forty Second Street Library. . . .The cosmic Zora emerges" (Hurston 1979, 154–5)

Aware of the dangers posed by inter-ethnic solidarity between Chinese, Filipin@, Indian, Japanese, Korean, Mexican, Portuguese, and Puerto Rican workers, the California Department of Industrial Relations reported in 1930 that owners preferred to employ "a mixture of laborers of various races, speaking diverse languages, and not accustomed to mingling with each other," with the hope that this would prevent them from arriving at "a mutual understanding which would lead to strikes" (Takaki 1989, 30). Later, the 1964 Civil Rights Act aimed to quell protests by further enshrining both racial difference and nominal recognition within the national culture and legal order. Still, the typical Newark and Detroit rioter circa 1967 could be characterized as a young, educated, unemployed or underemployed Black man, "proud of his race, extremely hostile to both whites and middle-class Negroes and, although informed about politics, highly distrustful of the political system" (quoted in Zinn 1980, 460). In 1969, an emerging Chican@ movement adopted *El Plan de Aztlán*, claiming "the call of our blood is our power, our responsibility, and our inevitable destiny... Por La Raza todo. Fuera del La Raza nada (For the race everything. Outside of the race nothing.)" (Anaya and Lomeli 1998, 1–5). For its part, The Nation of Islam (NOI) condemned the "white devil race" and prohibited "race-mixing" (Malcolm X 1999, 167).

In contrast to these particularistic orientations, the Chicago-based Rainbow Coalition of the late 1960s and early 1970s aligned the Black Panthers, Brown Berets, Rising Up Angry, Young Lords, and Young Patriots to organize across race lines against police violence, urban poverty, prison conditions, and more (Sonnie and Tracy 2011). According to Rainbow Coalition leader Fred Hampton, "when I talk about the masses, I'm talking about the white masses, I'm talking about the black masses, and the brown masses, and the yellow masses, too. . . . We say you don't fight racism with racism. We're gonna fight racism with solidarity" (Hampton 1969). However, as the movements of the sixties and seventies were smashed, a politics of identity arose, which maintained that only the most immediate alliances were possible under conditions of embattled retreat (Springer 2005).

Under Ronald Reagan, the creation of a "color-blind" society meant confronting racism (purportedly directed against whites) by eroding affirmative action policies and racializing social programs like Open Admissions, affordable housing, and food aid (Omi and Winant 1994, 135). Some Black and Third World feminists sought to reverse these trends by deepening their critiques of racism: "we understand the importance, yet limitations of race ideology to describe our total experience. Culture differences get subsumed when we speak of 'race' as an isolated issue" (Anzaldúa and Moraga 1981, 101). Meanwhile, by the late 1980s and early 1990s, formations like Anti-Racist Action (ARA), the *Race Traitor* journal, and the scholarship of figures like Theodore Allen, Noel Ignatiev, and David Roediger (who adopted an abolitionist perspective calling for "treason to whiteness") set the stage for subsequent coalitions like Showing Up for Racial Justice (SURJ) and White Noise to organize self-identified white people against racism.

Much radical left dialogue in the US today invokes "race" as part of a rehearsed list of intersecting oppressions with scant historical explanation. Consequently, there is considerable skepticism regarding the possibility of multi-ethnic coalitions against racial capitalism. Part of the dilemma arises from race's elusive role in language. While race has become more veiled, other terms have become race-encoded: "diversity," "good neighborhood," "outside agitator," "riot." Poet Claudia Rankine dissects this daily racecraft: "Then flashes, a siren, a stretched-out roar—and you are not the guy and still you fit the description because there is only one guy who is always the guy fitting the description" (Rankine 2014,160). Meanwhile, the proliferation of terms coined by anti-racist discourse may obscure more than they explain, as when the intricate process of disinvestment from multi-ethnic urban centers, the creation of segregated middle-class Euro-American suburban outposts, and systematic rezoning get whittled down to the term "white flight."

As many have come to view "race" as a "historically emergent lived experience, variegated, changing, and changeable" (Alcoff 2015, 7–8), some have warned that organizing movements "after race" may risk association with the neoconservative "colorblindness" that keeps racism intact (Darder and Torres 2004; Bonilla-Silva 2006). Major questions persist: How can anti-racists engage race without reaffirming raciology? (Gilroy 2002). How can revolutionary solidarity surpass allyship sensitivity trainings and potentially opportunistic claims to race-based leadership? Would the abolition of whiteness necessarily entail the abolition, or transformation, of blackness? As anarchist Black Panther Ashanti Alston offers, "I think of being black not so much as an ethnic category but as an oppositional force or touchstone for looking at situations differently" (quoted in Milstein 2015, 100).

For now, radical coalitions of different descents can begin to rupture hardened notions of "race" and racial pessimisms by learning to trust each other through action and reflection. Inspiring examples include the December 2014 Oakland Police Department blockade by The Blackout Collective, #BlackBrunch, #BlackLivesMatter, #Asians4BlackLives, and the Bay Area Solidarity Action Team, as well as the October 2015 "Black and Palestinian Struggle for Liberation" convergence organized by The Campaign To Bring Mumia Home, NYC Solidarity with Palestine/Direct Action Front for Palestine, Jews for Palestinian Right of Return, and Black-Palestinian Solidarity. Together, such divergent compositions of old lineages and new families can rush, rage against, and attack racism, armed with the promise of transmuted lives and unfettered vocabularies.

SEE ALSO: Bodies; Colonialism; Gender; Liberal; Nation; Representation

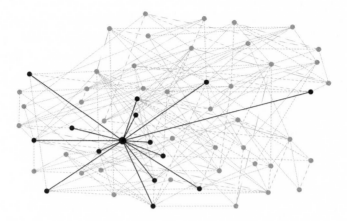

REPRESENTATION

Jaleh Mansoor

SINCE THE TWIN BOURGEOIS REVOLUTIONS OF THE eighteenth century—first the American and then the French—"representation" has been viewed as a path to social justice. In this formulation, the body politic renders itself knowable through communication with a sovereign whose consciousness it purportedly forms in turn (Habermas 1991). The cry of the Boston Tea Party, "No Taxation without Representation," crystallized a presumed symmetry between government and governed.

Outside of the electoral system, "representation" is frequently associated with "visibility." According to Jacques Rancière (1999), it is in this arena that popular movements have struggled to attain recognition in order to direct or supplement electoral campaigns. The tacit hope underlying these efforts is that visibility might help to influence electoral results or compel systemic changes. During the nineteenth and twentieth centuries, both the Civil Rights and Feminist movements made the case that traditional representational politics both excluded and *misrepresented* the people by devising and projecting a false image of universal interests. Within these movements, political survival often seemed to depend upon achieving visibility or, in some cases, audibility. As the French anarchist Auguste Vaillant proclaimed after throwing a bomb in the French National Assembly in 1893, "the more they are deaf, the more your voice must thunder out so that they will understand you" (quoted in Thompson 2010, 159). In the context of the AIDS epidemic of the 1980s and 1990s, ACT UP summarized the problem as follows: "Silence = Death."

By the end of the twentieth century, however, "representation" had begun to lose its emancipatory purchase. The term's ubiquity in 1990s rap and hip-hop elegantly conveyed the problem. On the one hand, calls to "represent" stood as assertions of individual and collective self-determination. On the other, they amounted to little more than a meaningless slogan. In Nas's "Represent" (1994), the term seems both to be a watchword for survival in a police state and a symptom of struggle's futility:

> Somehow the rap game reminds me of the crack game
> Used to sport Bally's and Gazelle's with black frames
> Now I'm into fat chains, sex and Tecs
> Fly new chicks and new kicks, Heine's and Beck's
> Represent, represent!

Despite the word's association with autonomy, Nas made clear that the best one could hope for was to take a few steps forward on the logos-and-brands game board. Around the same time, various social movement currents began to turn away from representation, seeking instead to elaborate tactics of interruption and withdrawal. From anticapitalist protests at global summits to the struggles of indigenous people to reassert sovereign control over territory and

from the Zapatistas to the recent American riots against racist policing, these movements show signs of edging beyond representation's political horizon.

Asserting that "to be heard, we march in silence," twenty thousand masked Zapatistas descended upon San Cristóbal, Mexico,
on December 21, 2012. The gesture evoked Nanni Balestrini's
Vogliamo Tutto (1971) and *Gli Invisibili* (1986), semi-fictional accounts of civil unrest set in workerist Italy during the 1960s and
1970s. Anonymity, horizontal organization, assemblies, and the
refusal to advance demands for fear of legitimating the state gave
these movements their specific character. Like the Zapatistas, such
movements refuse not only the vote but visual identification as
well. This rejection is symptomatic of capitalism's failure to ensure
a future for broad sectors of the population—a global underclass
that cannot be made to fit into the representational universe that
came into being at the end of the eighteenth century. As one commentator observed:

> In order for capitalist society to continue its course,
> the growing mass of surplus humanity must some-
> how be "integrated" into class society even despite
> being socially "unnecessary" to its reproduction. In
> the absence of any wider social resolution to growing
> immiseration, the predicament is for now resolved
> ideologically through criminalisation and practically
> through punishment. Increasing immiseration, and
> subsequently exclusion, must therefore be justified
> and normalised. Rising social inequality becomes
> framed as a problem of containment and the solution
> one of increasing control. (R. L. 2014)

The historical elaboration of the word "representation" over the
long term affords not only a sense of its contingency, but also clues
to the conditions of its dissolution. Notable here is the way in which
the *Oxford English Dictionary* entry on "representation" frames
the historical period wherein the term's meaning in aesthetics (as

likeness, imitation, substitution) converges with its political connotations of standing in for another—as an elected official stands
for a body politic in whose interest she or he acts—to provide an
anticipatory sketch of the regime we currently inhabit. While in
late Middle English it indicated the act of drawing something to
consciousness through a range of strategies (e.g., description, per-
suasion, argumentation, various forms of symbolization), by the
mid-seventeenth century it had crystallized into its association with
parliamentary government, as "a substitute for a number of people
in a legislative assembly." During the nineteenth century, "equivalent" and "counterpart" had come to act as synonyms. The transition in meaning from disparate forms of designation to equivalence
and substitution coincides with the rise of mimetic illusionism and
the Renaissance era's single-point perspective. Here "representation" comes to assume the burden once reserved for mimesis.

With mimesis, an image was charged with resembling a thing
while affirming that the pictorial resemblance was nothing more
than a visual copy of its referent. The passage from the late-
medieval to early-modern period witnessed the extension of this
new logic of representation to include text. By the early seventeenth
century, "representation" had come to mean "the fact of standing
for, or in place of, another, especially with authority to act on that
other's account" (*OED*), as in the legal function of the signature.
Concurrently, "representation" entered the juridical realm, where it
became associated with property assignation and guarantee. Here
a document was said to "represent" the interests of its signatory.
During this period, representation also came to denote a presentation of facts aimed at conveying a particular view in order "to influence opinion and action." This new meaning became entwined
with modern democratic politics during the mid-eighteenth
century, when "representation" became "the fact of representing or
being represented in a legislative or deliberative assembly."

By the mid-to-late-eighteenth century, sovereignty had ceased
emanating from an external agent (e.g., God or a king thought to
possess divine right) and came to be located in the body politic itself.
Conceived as sharing homogenous "universal" interests, despite

being dispersed across the nation, a sovereign people thus came into being by reflecting itself to itself. Through representation, this "people" arrived to prove the identity of model and copy. The question of who or what constituted the "people," however, would haunt democratic politics over the coming centuries (Habermas 1991). Meanwhile, the putative identity between political representation and social order was interrupted by the dynamics of capitalism.

According to Georg Lukács (1971), an early theorist of the relation between the capitalist mode of production and the phenomenon of consciousness to which representation is oriented, the forms of cognition that enabled bourgeois ascent had become inoperative by the advent of the twentieth century. At the level of consciousness, transparency was no longer possible since the new relations of production obscured the human labor upon which they relied. In this view, capitalism introduces a rift between object and process and—with that—a tendency toward abstraction. The resulting disarticulation of fragment and whole yielded what Lukács called "reification."

As a mode of value extraction founded on what Karl Marx in *Capital* called "the hidden abode of production," capitalism undermines representation by undoing its nominal transparency. Meanwhile, because capitalism yields a contradictory situation in which value production simultaneously impoverishes the workforce, the presumption of self-interest underlying the concept of representation becomes increasingly untenable under capitalism. Additionally, because "the people" to be represented encapsulates both worker and capitalist, an antagonistic relationship arises within (and becomes simultaneously concealed by) the representational category itself. Not only does this antagonism find expression between class enemies, however, it also leaves each of them internally riven. The worker works against herself and in opposition to the principles of equality, liberty, and property. Meanwhile, the capitalist presumes to exercise choice while remaining a cipher in a machine that may well render him obsolete.

Between reification and the social reproduction necessary for capitalism's perpetuation, there no longer appears to be any correlation between an image and the thing it was said to represent—and still less between an elected individual and people's actual interests. The mythic transparency upon which democracy is founded is further undermined by capitalist globalization, where the national framework upon which representation depended during the Enlightenment becomes undermined by unfettered capital accumulation.

Art historians have noted that the rise, elaboration, and decline of *aesthetic* abstraction roughly coincided with capitalism's entry into and saturation of social consciousness between the 1860s and 1940s. This period is marked by the failures of the nineteenth-century revolutionary left (including the fall of the Paris Commune) and the intensification of proletarianization. In high culture, the period is bookmarked by the works of Manet and Mondrian. The temporal coincidence of aesthetic abstraction and the systematization of what Marx called "real abstraction" (e.g., money) signals the difficulty of forging representational correlations.

What does the representation of real abstraction look like today? According to Rosalind Krauss, full-blown *aesthetic* abstraction dialectically signaled the loss of the object it wished to represent. "This grounding of the terms of representation on absence—the making of absence the very condition of the representability of the sign—alerts us to the way the sign-as-label is a perversion of the law of the sign" (1994). Today, the passage from sign as authority (law) to sign as a gesture toward presence that serves ultimately to highlight the absence it conceals is fully accomplished. Nevertheless, the fight over representation continues. What will these signs mean? In *The Coming Insurrection*, the anonymous authors remind us that "certain words are like battlegrounds: their meaning, revolutionary or reactionary, is a victory to be torn from the jaws of struggle" (Invisible Committee 2009).

Within political and theoretical discourse, a range of positions now question the "politics of recognition" upon which democratic representation depends—not to mention the representational logic that holds transparency and justice to somehow be synonymous. Similarly, social movements operating on a variety of terrains have ceased calling for "representation" as though it were a self-evident good. It's as though a politics founded on a refusal to be represented has become the only way to demonstrate, once and for all, the structural impossibility of representation itself.

SEE ALSO: Agency; Community; Democracy; History; Ideology; Leadership; Misogyny; Nation; Nature; Politics; Populism; Race; Sovereignty; Vanguard

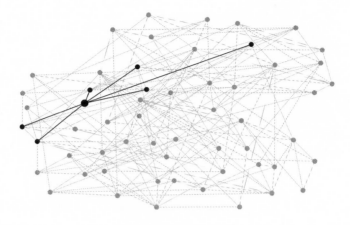

REPRODUCTION

Silvia Federici

ORIGINATING IN THE EIGHTEENTH CENTURY IN THE natural sciences to signify the processes by which organisms regenerate themselves and produce new life, the term "reproduction" was soon adopted by the French economist François Quesnay (1694–1774) and other Enlightenment-era Physiocrats. Although operating within a bourgeois horizon that made capital appear natural (Marx 1863),[1] the Physiocrats were the first economists to try to understand how capitalist production functioned. According to David McNally, in order to "establish political economy as a science of society," they "constructed . . . a general

---

1.   In *Capital*, vol. 2, Marx also speaks of the Physiocratic system as "the first systematic conception of capitalist production" (1993, 436).

model of economic interdependence organized around a circular flow," which they described as the "reproduction" of economic life (1988, 85). Thus, in his 1759 "Tableau Économique," Quesnay spoke of "reproductive expenditures" and "the annual reproduction of revenue" while lamenting that the excessive taxation of farmers reduced "the annual reproduction of wealth." Similarly, he distinguished between "circulation, distribution and reproduction," with the latter clearly referring to the process whereby a country's wealth was not only maintained but expanded.

Marx subsequently used this meaning of "reproduction" in *Capital*. In particular, he showed that "simple reproduction" (i.e., the process whereby capital "reconverts parts of the product into means of production and labor power") was not an option for capitalists, since capital must expand or perish. He also established that the only source of capital's valorization was the exploitation of labor and that the production of labor power was essential to the accumulation process. Finally, Marx demonstrated that capital accumulation was besieged by crises because the relations between production, circulation, and reproduction were in constant danger of breaking down.

"Reproduction" thus signified a crucial process that helped to reveal capitalism's "laws" as well as its vulnerabilities. Nevertheless, in *The Accumulation of Capital* (1968), Rosa Luxemburg argued that Marx could not explain how capital reproduced itself on an expanded scale since his model assumed the existence of only two classes and the universal dominance of capitalist relations (348). Rejecting the hypothesis that the "natural increase of population" might be a sufficient factor in explaining capital's expansion, Luxemburg theorized the need for capitalism to constantly incorporate and thus destroy pre-capitalist economies—the need, that is, for colonial conquest to provide markets for capital's products and raw materials and labor power for its production (361).

Written during the heyday of European imperialism, Luxemburg's critique drew its power from its vivid description of the new colonial relations. At the same time, however, she missed Marx's main contribution to the analysis of capital's reproduction and internationalization. As L. Ferrari Bravo (1975) showed, Marx's methodology takes us beyond the formation of the world market and anticipates the development of a *world cycle of capital accumulation* in which all national capitals would become integrated. Here the destiny of the system becomes indexed to a general world rate of profit—the form of capitalist accumulation we confront today.

Theorists paid little attention to Marx's reproduction model during the five decades following the publication of Luxemburg's text. Only in the wake of May 1968 did "reproduction" reemerge as a key concept when it appeared in the work of Louis Althusser (1995). In *Sur la Reproduction*, a text written in the 1970s but published long after his death, Althusser argued that capital must reproduce not only its production cycle (as posited by Marx) but also its *relations* of production, since these were the guarantors of its domination. Inspired by the rising political force of students in the streets and of Gramsci's concept of "hegemony," Althusser aimed to demonstrate that capitalism reproduced itself not only through the exploitation of labor but also through a set of state "apparatuses" (law, religion, the media, and above all the school and the family) that turned ideology into a material force. This approach highlighted the political side of reproduction by reinterpreting it as a reproduction of class relations—a thesis that Marx had only implied.

Still, "reproduction" did not become an explicitly political category until the rise of the women's liberation movement of the seventies, which began as a revolt against both women's confinement to reproductive activities and the state's control of their reproductive capacity. "Reproductive rights" and "reproductive freedom" have since become the cornerstones of feminism, inspiring slogans like "my body, my choice," and "our right to decide." Though primarily identified with the struggle to secure unimpeded access to abortion, the call for "reproductive rights" also sparked a powerful "self-help movement" that by 1975 had founded thirty women-controlled health centers across the United States. These centers educated women about their bodies and placed health at the center of feminist politics. Thanks to their activism, thousands of women learned to practice "self-examination," and medical researchers were encouraged to study the specific effects of diseases on women. Feminists in the movement of women's health centers were also among the first to denounce population control and to form alliances to combat sterilization abuse.

By the late-1970s, however, a "pro-choice" movement emerged that reduced "reproductive rights" to birth control, ignoring that many women still could not have the children they wanted and, if on welfare, faced the threat of sterilization. It was in response to this narrow, market-place interpretation of "reproductive rights" that in the early 1980s various organizations of women of color launched a movement for "reproductive justice" that rejected the pro-choice terminology, stressing the constraints on the rights of communities of color to reproduce themselves and the close relation between reproductive rights and economic justice (Silliman et al. 2004).

First organized through the National Black Women's Health Project, the "reproductive justice" movement also fought against the politics of population control that in the 1980s led to massive sterilization campaigns in several regions of the "Third World" (ibid.). New reproductive technologies like in vitro fertilization and the "surrogacy" and "multiple parenting" arrangements they make possible have further polarized feminist reproduction politics. While some liberal feminists have claimed that these technologies expand women's rights, figures like Maria Mies (2014) and Angela Davis (1993) have denounced them as carriers of a new eugenicist project in which the right of better-off women to have children beyond biological limitations is extolled while pregnancy among the poor is penalized. In this context, "reproductive freedom" and "reproductive rights" have become contested concepts that accommodate opposing class interests. These range from the defense of women's right to decide whether or not to have children to the defense of "outsourced" procreation and the separation of mothering from gestation.

"Reproduction" has been the ground for another important debate among feminist activists and scholars. As in the early 1970s,

Marxist feminists began to seek the roots of women's oppression by focusing on the unpaid domestic labor they performed in capitalist society. A heated controversy soon developed around whether or not "reproductive work" should be waged. Written while she was part of *Lotta Femminista*, Mariarosa Dalla Costa's "Women and the Subversion of the Community" (1975) became a key theoretical contribution to the debate. Breaking with a socialist feminist tradition that portrayed domestic work as a "backward" legacy of pre-capitalist relations, Dalla Costa argued that "housework" was in fact a precondition to capitalist production since it reproduced labor power and thus enabled the very process of capital accumulation. However, this reproductive labor was made invisible as "work" in order to further devalue labor power and help to ensure capitalist control. Unpaid and performed in isolation, reproductive work has not only subordinated women to men within the family, it has also undermined their physical integrity; even sexual life is subordinated to the reproduction of the workforce.

The political program that issued from this insight demanded that capital pay for the unpaid reproductive labor that women did and that had already been stolen from them. With the formation of the International Feminist Collective in 1972, these became the objectives of the Wages for Housework (WFH) campaign. Inspired by the struggle for the Family Allowance in Great Britain and the US struggle for welfare rights, WFH broadened the scope of feminist theory and organizing by demanding state remuneration for housework on the grounds that employers benefited from this work. WFH feminists fought against welfare cuts and for sex workers' rights while lending support to lesbian struggles arguing that all women do housework.

Although the WFH campaign did not succeed in its main objective, it exercised a significant influence on social movements and state policy. In Venezuela, housewives are now recognized as workers and entitled to a pension. In some European countries, aspects of reproductive work—like elder care—are now partly remunerated through state subsidies given to caregivers or to the recipients of care work. WFH has also proven to be an important perspective from which to negotiate better conditions in the waged workplace. For instance, it has enabled workers to demand that social services like child care no longer be viewed solely as means for women "to go out to work" but as means of liberating their time and labor. When in rallies and demonstrations women began chanting "We can't afford to work for love," "No more free labor," "All women are house-workers," and "We have always worked, we have never been paid, we never retire; we want our money back!" a page was turned on a long history in which labor has been mystified as love (Federici 2015).

By the UN's Third World Conference on Women, held in Nairobi in 1985, increasing public acceptance of the WFH perspective prompted organizers to call on governments to acknowledge the contribution made by women's reproductive work. Since then, several feminist circles have proceeded with efforts to "count women's labor." However, by the 1980s "reproduction" was again being redefined—this time to extend the concept beyond the domestic sphere. Ecofeminism brought attention to the fact that—in much of the world—reproducing one's family included not only cooking, cleaning, and caring for children, but also producing food, collecting medicinal plants and herbs, and caring for the natural environment (rivers, lakes, forests) as the main source of sustenance. In *Ecofeminism* (2014), Maria Mies and Vandana Shiva articulated the principles inspiring the movement. Mies, however, has avoided the use of the term "reproduction" since, in her view, it negatively contrasts with "production" and obscures the life-creating characteristics of the work involved.

For their part, Marxist autonomists voiced a different critique by noting that, in the present phase of capitalist development (in which work spills out of the factories and every aspect of social life becomes a point of production), the production/-reproduction distinction no longer makes sense (Hardt and Negri 2009). However, to the extent that reproductive work remains unpaid labor performed primarily by women, it must be treated as a different sphere (Federici 2011). Indeed, only in societies where people control the means of their reproduction does the difference between production and reproduction cease to exist. In order to achieve this aim, we are now witnessing a re-appropriation of the means of subsistence as new forms of cooperation—new "reproductive commons"—begin to develop (Federici 2012). Still, we are a long way from witnessing the disappearance of a divide that—as feminists have shown—remains a constitutive feature of work under capitalism. In the same spirit, we must not attribute a lower political value to "reproduction" than is attributed to "production."

As the rich history of women's struggle has demonstrated, the reproduction of life under capitalism requires a constant invention. From this viewpoint, while the feminist concept of "reproduction" may appear to be a more modest category when compared to the Marxian one, the opposite is true. For Marx, "reproduction" was the process by which capital accumulates itself. In contrast, feminists conceive of "reproduction" as the process that reproduces both the true makers of capitalist accumulation and the struggle against it.

SEE ALSO: Class; Commons; Gender; Ideology; Labor; Materialism

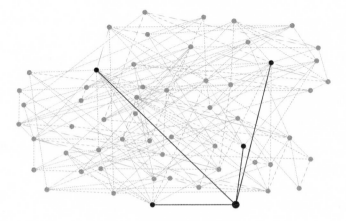

RESPONSIBILITY

Miranda Joseph

DEFINITIONS OF "RESPONSIBILITY" RANGE FROM THE positive quality of "capability," of being reliable or trustworthy (e.g., with regard to payment of a debt), to the status of "being in charge" and thus having "a duty" or "moral obligation" toward someone or to do something, to a state of potential or actual guilt, of "liability" (*OED;* Allan 2011–14). "Responsibility" is also a key term in neoliberal discourse and practice.[1] The concept of "personal

---

1. The naming of federal laws is one symptom of the neoliberal obsession with "responsibility" that has endured from Ronald Reagan to Barack Obama, including the 1982 Tax Equity and Fiscal Responsibility Act, the Personal Responsibility and Work Opportunity Reconciliation Act of 1996, the 1996 Illegal Immigration Reform and Immigrant Responsibility Act, and

responsibility" has been deployed to mobilize consent for shifting the burden of social welfare from the state onto families and individuals. And the rhetoric and practice of "corporate social responsibility" (CSR) has likewise become prominent in recent decades to legitimate free-market capitalism and often specifically the non-regulation of corporations.

These neoliberal deployments build on the conjunction of "rights and responsibilities" that is the common sense of liberal citizenship. For example, the pairing of "rights and responsibilities" is one rubric through which the US Department of Homeland Security Office of Citizenship and Immigration Services articulates US citizenship to "learners" (those considering applying for citizenship). The office lists "rights" to freedom of expression and worship, trial by jury, voting, eligibility for particular federal government jobs, and running for office, and "freedom to pursue 'life, liberty, and the pursuit of happiness'" and "responsibilities" to obey laws, pay taxes, serve on juries and "defend the country if the need should arise."[2]

Meanwhile, "responsibility" is freely deployed across the political spectrum to inspire ethical action and galvanize people to whatever action is being called "responsible" ("Drink responsibly"). "Responsibility" is a seductive term, calling upon us to voluntarily "do the right thing," as the Liberty Mutual Insurance Company's "Responsibility Project" would have it (Liberty Mutual Insurance). By contrast, "accountability" suggests a regime in which you will do the right thing or be punished (Joseph 2014, 12–13). Conversely, accusations of irresponsibility are also widely deployed to disparage the actions of the other in a political opposition, whether that other is the Wall Street financier or the pregnant teen of color.

---

the Credit Card Accountability Responsibility and Disclosure Act of 2009, among others (Joseph 2014, 161).

2. While the rights listed may not be the most urgent for immigrants seeking citizenship, the responsibilities may be daunting, precisely because they fall on individuals, understood to be sovereign willful subjects. See Lavin (2008) for a full discussion of this issue and an attempt to formulate what he calls "postliberal responsibility."

Lisa Duggan argues that "valorized concepts of *privatization* and *personal responsibility* travel widely across the rhetorics of contemporary policy debates, joining economic goals with cultural values" (2003, 14). Privatization and personal responsibilization are also practices that support upward redistribution of wealth; as Duggan says, "Social service functions are *privatized* through *personal responsibility* as the proper functions of the state are narrowed, tax and wage costs in the economy are cut and more social costs are absorbed by civil society and the family" (2003, 15–16). The Personal Responsibility and Work Opportunity Reconciliation Act of 1996, which Bill Clinton claimed would "end welfare as we know it" (quoted in Vobejda 1996) exemplifies this phenomenon. It linked intervention in kinship and gender relations (by requiring women to identify the biological fathers of their children who were to be held responsible for supporting those children, limiting the number of children eligible for benefits, and funding various programs promoting marriage) to the coercive promotion of "responsibility" through work (Anna Marie Smith 2002).

The discourse of personal responsibility has racial, class, and gender implications, building on "culture of poverty" discourse, which characterizes poor people of color as lacking both work ethic and ability to defer gratification, and thus as irresponsible. The 1965 "Moynihan Report," (officially titled *The Negro Family: The Case for National Action*), which described "the Negro Family" as trapped in a "tangle of pathology," is a persistent touchstone in popular and policy discourse in the US for the claim that people of color are poor because they do family wrong. But the idea that personal responsibility means the enactment of certain gender and life course norms and can cure all ills have come to seem obvious, at least on the right. On the anniversary of Hurricane Katrina, Juan Williams (2006)—in an op-ed in the *New York Times*—offered a "prescription" for curing poverty: "Finish high school, at least. Wait until your 20s before marrying, and wait until you're married before having children. Once you're in the workforce, stay in: take any job, because building on the experience will prepare you for a better job. Any American who follows that prescription will be at almost no risk of falling into extreme poverty."

And in a 2012 speech at the Republican National Convention, presidential candidate Rick Santorum used nearly identical language: "Graduate from high school, work hard, and get married before you have children and the chance you will ever be in poverty is just 2 percent" (quoted in Matthews 2012).

While this version of "responsibility" has been used to punish poor people of color (and distract us from critically assessing important economic policies, as per Brett Williams 1994), in fact, norms of responsible temporal/financial life management differ in conjunction with racial, gender, and class formation projects. While the *New York Times* performs this scolding of the poor for its (presumably more affluent) readers, it also offers them financial advice that treats those readers as entrepreneurs—responsible by virtue of taking and managing risk in financial markets, by investing for retirement, and leveraging (borrowing) for and against their homes (Joseph 2014, 71–72).

Meanwhile, financiers, who are financially liquid enough to reinvent themselves at the drop of a hat (or the stock market), are not building a life over time and are not held to the same standards of responsibility. This difference became a source of class conflict (or at least resentment) in the wake of the financial crisis. For instance, on August 1, 2012, the *New York Times* featured a story on the left side of the first business page headlined "Jury Clears Ex-Citigroup Manager of Charges" (Lattman 2012). It reported that an executive had been accused by the US Securities and Exchange Commission (SEC) of misrepresenting a deal to clients—a deal in which the bank put together a derivative financial instrument (a collateralized debt obligation) that it sold and simultaneously "bet against"—but had been acquitted. However, the article reported, the jury also offered a statement urging the SEC to continue "investigating the financial industry." The article then offered this interpretation: "The statement appears to echo frustration felt by many Americans that Wall Street executives had not been held responsible for its questionable actions leading up to the financial crisis." Meanwhile, on the right side of the same page, an article reported that the Federal Housing Finance Agency had once again rejected the idea of offering debt forgiveness to mortgage holders (Appelbaum 2012). The crux of the reasoning seemed to come at the end of the article, which reported that the head of the agency, Edward DeMarco, feared that doing so would provide an incentive for mortgage holders to default.

As law professor Brent White (2009) has argued, the social norm of financial "responsibility" involves a double standard in which individuals are morally obliged to keep paying, even when it is financially irrational because the value of the house is substantially less than the mortgage debt. This norm of "responsibility" is often reinforced through discourses of "moral hazard"—if one debtor is given a break then all others will expect the same.[3] By contrast, a corporation (or investment banker) has no such moral obligation but rather is expected to make a "rational" financial decision to "walk away" from unprofitable or unmanageable debts and contracts, to file for bankruptcy, get a fresh start, and thus fulfill their responsibilities to shareholders.

However, the one-dimensional view of corporate responsibility to financial goals, such as profit or so-called "shareholder value," expressed in this double standard has not gone entirely uncontested. The concept of corporate social responsibility has been deployed to suggest that corporations may have more diverse or complex responsibilities (Ghobadian et al. 2015; see also Garriga

---

3. "Moral hazard" has also been used to enforce the debts of the Greek nation. As Bloomberg reports, a new European Central Bank policy document dated July 2015 explicitly limits emergency liquidity assistance relative to "moral hazard" (Black 2015). In the context of the 2015 Greek debt crisis, the hazard is usually taken to be the possibility that other countries will follow Greece in expecting and demanding debt relief. But as Mackintosh (2015) points out in a *Financial Times* column, it is not only the borrowers that might be irresponsible: "There are two sets of moral hazard over Greece. First is the moral hazard of the lenders. Just like the criminally irresponsible banks in the run up to the 2007 subprime crisis, lenders took no account of Greece's ability to repay when advancing them ludicrously cheap loans." But in this context, as in the mortgage crisis, the standards of "responsibility" are not the same for the financial institution that lends as for the social entity that borrows (whether the homeowner or nation).

and Melé 2004). CSR has been understood to indicate moral or ethical obligations that must be met *in addition* to financial responsibility (profit, shareholder value). Corporations are sometimes conceived of as "citizens" and thus as bearing both "rights and responsibilities." Increasingly, social responsibility is cast as instrumental for, or even integral to, the financial goals of the corporation (Frederick 1994). And contemporary "social entrepreneurship" seeks to build enterprises from the ground up to pursue "social" goods in ways that are financially sustainable or even profitable within a capitalist economy. Of course, the limits of CSR are well recognized. Whether reactive to protest (McDonnell et al. 2015) or proactive, by promoting socially responsible efforts, especially with regard to the environment through "green" or "social" accounting as well as other marketing strategies, corporations seek to manage their "stakeholder relationships." Scholars on the left have critically assessed CSR as an effort to legitimate and thus preserve capitalism itself and thus as strategy for containing radical critique (Dunne 2007).

Left critics have become practiced at recognizing deployments of "responsibility" that create and reinforce social hierarchies by legitimating capitalism itself, forming race, gender, and class through differentiating standards and expectations, placing criminal blame and financial burden on individuals rather than systems and isms. Even so, we invoke "responsibility" ourselves to inspire and galvanize radical action in ourselves and to point to the failings, the "irresponsibility," of others. Esther Wang's (2011) review of *The Next American Revolution*, by renowned radical Grace Lee Boggs and Scott Kurashige, is entitled "The Responsibility of Radicals." This title suggests that the project of the book is to articulate that responsibility, a responsibility not merely to protest but to build alternative institutions. Others offer different views about the responsibilities of radicals.

Philosopher Jacques Derrida argues that "no justice . . . seems possible or thinkable without the principle of some *responsibility*, beyond all living present, within that which disjoins the living present, before the ghosts of those who are not yet born or who are already dead" (Derrida 1994, xix). And he argues that the disjuncture between justice and law imposes a "responsibility" to examine the boundaries of the law, "recalling the history, the origin and subsequent direction, thus the limits, of concepts of justice, the law and right, of values, norms, prescriptions that have been imposed and sedimented there" (Derrida 1992, 19) and pursue the ongoing effort to make the law fulfill "the classical emancipatory ideal" (ibid., 28; see also Joseph 2014, 54–55). Postcolonial theorist Gayatri Spivak learns from Derrida that "responsible action" requires accounting, requires deploying the "calculus" of "accountable reason," even while we keep "always in view" that "if responsible action is fully formulated or justified within the system of the calculus, it cannot retain its accountability to the trace of the other" (1994, 427–28; see also Joseph 2014, 141–42). Similarly, Angela Davis suggests that statistics showing the racial disparities in incarceration impose on us a "responsibility of understanding," specifically of understanding the "racist logic" (and the "encounter of gender and race") that determines this empirically documented, statistically represented result (Davis 64; see also Joseph 2014, 35).

These positive invocations of "responsibility" by those who are well aware of the violence to which it has contributed suggest that the critique of responsibility is not a call for chaos or a call to excuse all harmful acts as the results of (unaccountable) structures instead of people. Rather, as Lavin argues, citing Judith Butler's 1997 *Excitable Speech: A Politics of the Performative*, "drawing attention to the production and reproduction of conditions of unfreedom has the inciteful (and insightful) effect of enhancing our own responsibility for their perpetuation" (2008, 99). That is, while we should resist the dominant discourses of responsibility that are deployed to locate blame and debt in those already less powerful, we still must take responsibility for understanding and transformation.

SEE ALSO: Accountability; Liberal; Rights; Sovereignty

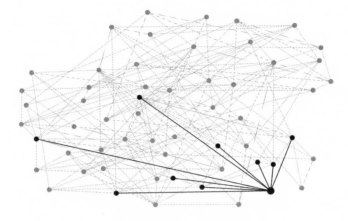

REVOLUTION

Thomas Nail

TODAY WE ARE WITNESSING THE RETURN OF REVOLU-
tion. This return, however, seems to be taking none of the
traditional forms: the capture of the state, the political representation of the party, the centrality of the proletariat, or
the leadership of the vanguard. The Zapatistas distinguish
between two types of revolution: an uppercase Revolution
and a lowercase revolution (Marcos 2004, 164). This distinction is emblematic of an indexical tension for radicals.
On the one hand, the two words are phonetically identical
and carry with them a unified history of social struggle.
On the other hand, the words are semantically distinct
and refer to two significantly different historical and political trajectories. For this reason, the idea of "R/revolution"

is less like an absolute signifier and more like a semantic Möbius strip that appears to be a continuous single-sided path and a discontinuous double-sided one at the same time (see Figure I).

Figure I

Radicals today thus find themselves both unified and divided by two intertwined trajectories of revolution: the uppercase and the lowercase. Lowercase revolution can be defined by at least four revolutionary strategies that have become increasingly prevalent over the last twenty years. The first of these concerns an intersectional analysis of power, in which revolution is not defined by a single axis of struggle (e.g., political, economic, cultural, or environmental). Accordingly, there should be no single privileged "subject of the revolution" (e.g., whites, the working class, heterosexuals, men). The second strategy concerns prefiguration. Here revolution is not aimed exclusively at creating counter-institutions to oppose state policies, modes of production, cultural norms, or environmental destruction. Instead, and in addition to these institutions, contemporary revolutionary strategy emphasizes the need to create alternatives that build (even if only locally) the kind of new social relations that revolutionaries would like to see "after" the revolution. Third, we find an emphasis on participatory politics, in which revolutionary strategy demands the direct participation of people in the decision-making processes that affect them. This strategy can be witnessed in the popular assemblies, consensus decision-making, and spokescouncils used around the world from the Zapatistas to the Occupy Movement. Finally, the strategic commitment to horizontalism has enabled revolutionary networks to link local popular assemblies without any central authority, program, or hierarchy. Examples of this strategy can be seen in the World Social Forum and the use of social media for decentralized local and global organizing.

Recent use of these tactics in the Alter-Globalization Movement, the World Social Forum, the *Indignados*, the Occupy Movement, and elsewhere can be traced back to the influence and inspiration of what many radicals now call "the first post-modern revolutionaries," the Zapatistas of Chiapas, Mexico (Burbach 1994, 113–24). Perhaps one explanation for the new prevalence of these tactics concerns global capitalism's increasingly financial and neoliberal "development" model. In many ways, Mexico was one of the first laboratories for neoliberalism. It is thus of no surprise that it was also one of the first laboratories for new revolutionary strategy. Of course, the Zapatistas were not the first to use the four strategies described above; indeed, anarchists, feminists, and some indigenous groups have used them in some form or another since the nineteenth century. The important difference—as David Graeber argues in "The New Anarchists"—is that, until the mid to late nineties, these strategies were not nearly as pervasive (Graeber 2002, 61–73). However, even as the synthesis and spread of these four revolutionary strategies increased during the rise and influence of Zapatismo, they have in no way eliminated the tension between upper- and lowercase "revolution" (Nail 2013, 20–35). If anything, and precisely because of the increased prevalence of lowercase strategies, radicals today confront this tension more than ever.

Furthermore, one can discern at least two kinds of lowercase revolutionary strategies: social strategies (like those listed above) and more individualist strategies (popularized by the Crimethinc. Ex-Workers' Collective and anti-civilization anarchists and historically preceded by anarchist theorists like Max Stirner, Ernest Coeurderoy, and Joseph Déjacque) (Landstreicher et al. 2014). Individualist revolutionary strategies are much less focused on building alternative institutions than on living revolutionary lives. If there is going to be any kind of revolution, they argue, it must be built from the ground up from our daily lives. As the CrimethInc. Ex-Workers' Collective writes in "Why We're Right and You're Wrong: Towards a Non-D(en)ominational Revolution": "Revolution . . . is not a single moment, but a way of living." Or, as Raoul Vaneigem put it: "People who talk about revolution and class struggle without referring explicitly to everyday life, without understanding what is subversive about love and what is positive in the refusal of constraints—such people have a corpse in their mouth" (2001, 26).

Despite their prominence in contemporary radical milieus, it is important to recall that such anarchistic "lowercase" strategies have not always defined "revolution." Historically, the etymology and idea of revolution has quite literally "revolved" around the state. Although Aristotle does not use the word "revolution" (contrary to common mistranslations of the word μεταβολή, "change," as "revolution"), his basic theory of political change remained the dominant one for thousands of years. For Aristotle, there were only two types of political change: change between types of state constitution (democracy, aristocracy, oligarchy, and monarchy) and change within a state constitution. Political theory from Machiavelli to Mao follows the kinetics of this basic statist definition of revolution: "a return to the state." According to Aristotle, the constitution (καθίστημι) is the "setting down" of a point of relative stasis (στάσις)—from the same root (*stā-) as the word "state." The stasis between conflicting forces produces a *polis* or city-state (πόλις)—from the same root (*pelə-, meaning "citadel" or "fortified high place") as the word "politics." Thus, for Aristotle, politics is the setting down of a walled city-state, and revolutions are constitutional changes of this centrally bounded point. People turn against and turn around its central axis. The political motion of revolution has thus been theoretically and practically one of rotation around the central point of the state. As Mao writes, "The seizure of power by armed force, the settlement of the issue by war, is the central task and the highest form of revolution" (1992, 548).

From the first usage of the English word "revolution" to describe political transformation in the sixteenth century to the twentieth-century socialist revolutions or near-revolutions in Russia, Germany, France, and China, Aristotle's cyclical kinetics remained dominant. As Hannah Arendt writes, "The fact that the word 'revolution' meant originally restoration, hence something which to us is its very opposite, is not a mere oddity of semantics. The revolutions of the seventeenth and eighteenth centuries, which to us appear to show all evidence of a new spirit, the spirit of the modern age, were intended to be restorations" (1963, 43).

This is not to say that there were no non-state theories and practices at the time, just that they were not the most prevalent ones. So far, however, twenty-first-century revolutionary struggles have tended to have more in common with the historically "lower-case" non-state or anti-statist tradition associated with indigenous struggles, slave revolts, peasant heretics, pirates, and anarchists than they have with the Aristotelian model.

Ironically, this recent shift can be attributed in part to the very "success" of the classical "uppercase" statist model. The more the revolutions of the nineteenth and twentieth century "returned to the state," the more they exposed the political limitations of both the state form and "the party," the dominant form for the revolutionary occupation of the state. Theoretically, the party was intended not solely to "abolish itself as the proletariat . . . and abolish also the state as state," as Engels wrote (Marx and Engels 1978, 713), but also to secure the "conditions under which the state can be abolished," as Lenin later added (1932, 94). Historically, however, the use of the state to abolish either itself or its conditions of possibility has failed. Consequently, the party has become perhaps the most widely discredited aspect of Marxism. It is accused of reducing revolutionary politics to state authoritarianism and bureaucracy, of recasting revolutionary theory as dogma, and of subordinating political imagination to disciplined order. In the name of the revolutionary party-state, all manner of the statist atrocities have been committed (political executions, labor camps, nationalist wars, propaganda campaigns, and so on). If radical activists today no longer talk about the class party, military-style discipline, the vanguard, or the capture of the state (or if they reject them explicitly as the Zapatistas do), it is precisely because these strategies have been so discredited by the revolutionary experiments of the twentieth century (Day 2005, 45).

The differences between the cyclical, uppercase definition of revolution and the lowercase one illuminate two important strategic and kinetic interpretations of the word "revolution" that are still in tension today. On the one hand, the uppercase definition is based on motion around a static center and the cyclical transformation of its state constitution. It is essentially a rotational and centrifugal theory of political motion. What returns in uppercase revolution is the *identity* of the state form—even if the constitution has changed. Revolution thus marks a difference internal to the identity of the state form. On the other hand, the lowercase definition of "revolution" is based on the motion of decentralized vectors assembled together in waves. Given their non-statist tendencies, these revolutionary movements behave more like trajectories or directions without static end points. They pursue their aims without a central command, vanguard, or program. Instead, their local movements are inspired or influenced by each other as by the common force of a wave that moves *through* them. In this case, what returns in revolution is not the identity of the circle but the differential *process of the returning itself.* Here revolution is not a difference internal to the identity of the state form but a differential process *external* to the state and thus capable of many other social forms. In this case, "revolution" returns not to its starting point (the state) but to somewhere else further along a decentralized trajectory. The definition of lowercase "revolution" proposed by many on today's radical left reveals a strategic decision to break with the political motion of the cycle and affirm the historically minor political motion of decentralized differentiation.

By engaging this etymological and historical difference, today's radicals might be in a better position to reinterpret other classical political institutions like the party, the constitution, and the state without falling prey to their cyclical dangers. After all, non-state or anti-state definitions of revolution must still grapple with existing party and state power at some point—as their Möbius doppelgänger. It is unlikely that the state will simply dissolve because alternative institutions have prefigured a future in which it does not exist. Under such conditions, it remains unclear how to reinterpret not only the concept of revolution but other political forms as well. Many theorists and activists have begun experimenting with such redefinitions, including Alain Badiou's anti-party, Daniel Bensaïd's New Anti-Capitalist Party, Hugo Chavez's revolutionary Bolivarianism, and the Zapatista's Other Campaign. Through this process, we are likely to uncover historical resources to facilitate the theoretical and practical return to forms of "revolution" that do not succumb to the traditional state form and its horrors. As these projects advance, the battle between lower- and uppercase definitions is likely to reach a zone of productive conflict.

SEE ALSO: Conspiracy; Demand; Ideology; Politics; Utopia; Vanguard; Victory; Violence; War

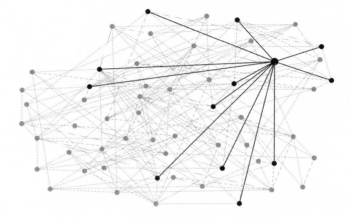

RIGHTS

Rebecca Schein

ACCORDING TO THE *OXFORD ENGLISH DICTIONARY*, THE word "right" derives from the Indo-European root "*reg–*," which referred to "movement in a straight line." It entered Old English in the eighth century as "*reht*" or "*riht*" (by way of the Proto-Germanic "*rekhtaz*"), denoting "fairness, justice, just claim." In the ninth century, "*reht*" generated the verb "*rihtan*," meaning "to straighten, rule, set up, set right," which evolved during the twelfth century into "*rigten*," "to correct, amend." During the thirteenth century, it emerged as a noun, a "legal entitlement or justifiable claim (on legal or moral grounds)," and corresponded closely to its concurrent adjectival form, "that which is considered proper, correct or consonant with justice."[1] Despite several transformations in the interim, this Middle English usage is largely consistent with the contemporary one.

With the emergence of right as "a moral quality, annexed to the person" came the establishment of our modern notion of "rights," both as intrinsic properties of individuals *as such*, and as an effect of a recognized relationship of moral obligation with others in a community. (Grotius 2001, 49). "Rights" are always signals of relationships, yet—especially in the case of "human" or "natural rights"—they often leave that relationship unnamed (or name only a relationship to god), as if the act of naming would undo the speech act carried out in the declaration of rights: namely, that they reside inalienably in individuals as such, and that their existence necessarily precedes the human acts of recognition through which we acknowledge their self-evident truth.

This conceptual tension has been a preoccupation for theorists on both the Left and the Right.[2] Edmund Burke famously declared that he would rather have the rights of an Englishman than a man, as only the relationship called "Englishness" could transform abstract "man" into a recognized citizen of a particular political community (2001). In her analysis of the "perplexities of the right of man," Hannah Arendt came to a similar conclusion: since all rights are effectively citizens' rights, the only meaningful "human right" is the right to be a citizen somewhere (1951, 290). In *On the Jewish Question*, Marx zeroed in on the relationship between the civil and political emancipation of the Jews and liberalism's impoverished vision of freedom, which rested on the "decomposition of man" into "Jew and citizen," "individual life," and "species-life"—a half-hearted vision that mistook the "rights of egoistic man, of man separated from other men and from the community" for "humanly emancipation" (1978, 40).

For Marx, "the rights of man" signaled the disavowal of the social relations he considered to be the substance of humanity. Echoes of

---

1. Around this time, it also came to denote the "right-hand side, part, or direction" where "right" was correct.
2. This political usage of right as opposed to left dates from 1825.

his skepticism still resound in contemporary radical circles despite the "rise and rise of human rights" as the framework for moral claims (Sellars 2002). One effect of that rise has been the increasing significance of law as a site for the realization of justice projects. Whether rights are being recognized or denied, proclaimed or violated, the idiom invokes legal experts and individual claimants as protagonists while the courtroom and legislature become scenes of defeat, compromise, or victory. While savvy participants in such battles may recognize a legal strategy's interdependence with popular struggle, the turn to "rights" nonetheless orients struggle toward the law and its experts. Although natural rights may be proclaimed in the streets, the pursuit of "rights" seems to end in the courts—the domain not of "the people" but of a lawyerly priesthood (Kennedy 2005). Legislative wins and legal precedents may signal substantive changes in the organization of social life. However, as David Rieff has observed, too often we mistake the advancement of human rights law for the advancement of human rights as such (2002). Meanwhile, as Marx observed, in the contest "between right and right, force decides," and "force" is not simply a matter for the courts (1976).

The ethical entanglements that give "rights" their social purchase are also their undoing—at least when it comes to human or natural rights, "the rights of man" rather than the "rights of citizens." The power of such rights stems from their putatively pre-political, trans-historical status, which enables those invoking them to question the legitimacy of particular laws in particular times and places. However, these pre-political, trans-historical rights are also predicated on a putatively trans-historical, pre-political human subject, which—for most of its history—has been the exclusive property of a small stratum of white men. But even when our declarations affirm the natural rights of all humans, irrespective of nationality, race, or other differences, the implicit attachment to a pre-political subjectivity remains a persistent point of tension between rights' moral power and their social effects. This tension raises a number of troubling questions.

First, what is the nature of this trans-historical subject as it has grown to include a wider swath of humanity? Genocide, slavery, expropriation: the costs of exclusion from the category "human" are well known. But are there costs associated with inclusion? According to Angela Davis, Frederick Douglass witnessed American chattel slavery transmute into the convict lease system; however, he was unable to identify their similarity, focused as he was on the recognition of former slaves as subjects of law whose freedom would be realized through the recognition of political rights (Davis 1998). Similarly, in the Seneca Falls Declaration, Elizabeth Cady Stanton made the case for women's inclusion among "the people" (the signatories of the Declaration of Independence), identifying women's exclusion as the substance of their grievance (1995). Both Douglass and Stanton leave unchallenged the character of rights' subject, asserting only the need to include more kinds of people within its reach. In these instances, rights claims yield a particular understanding of the nature of oppression, and thus a particular—arguably narrow—understanding of what it would mean to reverse it.

The putatively pre-political character of the rights-bearing subject also raises serious questions. Naming "biological humans" as its natural subjects, human rights sets the gears of procedural justice in motion and provides the foundation for all other rights. This is a substantial feature of human rights' power as an aspirational moral language, particularly for those in the process of demanding recognition. The ideal of pre-political rights usefully empowers individuals to make certain basic claims (e.g., "I am human"), which ostensibly insert them into the web of law and ethics. Such an account, however, represents an optimistic fantasy and presumes that the perfect execution of law represents the substance of justice itself.

For Wendy Brown, this fantasy is a symptom of human rights' anti-political character (2004). Do human rights help to provide the ethical grounding for collective deliberation, as Michael Ignatieff (2001) argues, or do they function instead as moral "trump cards" that shut down dialogue and shrink the ground of political negotiation? To what extent do human rights presume the substance of justice, generating consensus about its meaning only by taking it off the deliberation table? What use, then, would human rights have for radicals? Must we grapple with the power of rights only as a defensive response to their status as moral claim-making's hegemonic idiom (perhaps reason enough), or do rights also have something to offer us in our efforts to build meaningful equality, solidarity, or community?

Hannah Arendt famously refuted one of the most sacred principles of human rights in her attempt to divine their real social foundation. "We are not born equal," she wrote. "We become equal as members of a group on the strength of our decision to guarantee ourselves mutually equal rights" (1951, 301). This human rights heresy provides a useful foundation for a radical engagement with the rights tradition. Arendt concludes that "there is only one human right," the "right to have rights"—the right, in other words, to be recognized as a member of a political community, the parameters of which are not natural or god-given but the result of human deliberation. Although Arendt does not provide an escape hatch from what she identified as the paradox of human and citizens' rights, she helpfully locates the rights project at the point where radical political projects must begin and end—namely, by asking questions: Who counts as a subject of justice? (Fraser 2010). How are the parameters of membership morally justified? How will we (re)organize ourselves to ensure one another equality, and what form will that equality take? What, in other words, does our vision of a just society look like?

Whatever ambivalence radicals may feel about framing our claims within a rights framework, there are times when human rights inarguably serve as an important tool in our defensive arsenal. For instance, only the UN Convention on the Reduction of Statelessness served as a check on the ambitions of Canada's Conservative government, which introduced legislation in 2015 to strip dual citizens of their Canadian status when convicted of terrorism-related offenses. But can "rights" serve a more ambitious, politically radical vision? Two recent mobilizations of rights represent divergent attempts to repurpose rights language for justice projects radically at odds with the rights regime undergirding capitalist liberal democracies. In *Aboriginal Rights Are Not*

Human Rights, Peter Kulchyski (2013, 37) describes what he sees as a "conceptual confusion between human rights and aboriginal rights," a confusion evident not only among indigenous activists wary of any kind of rights language, but also in the United Nations Declaration on the Rights of Indigenous Peoples. For Kulchyski, aboriginal rights are not a special variety of human rights but a class of rights apart, invoking a moral logic that diverges from—and even conflicts with—the universalist individualism of the human rights tradition.

Although Kulchyski's language mirrors earlier claims that, for example, "human rights have not been women's rights," critics of the exclusion of women from human rights frameworks sought recognition of women as "representative humans," whose violation would constitute a violation of humanity as such (MacKinnon 2001, 526). In contrast, Kulchyski calls for the recognition of two distinct rights for indigenous peoples: their human rights and their indigenous peoples' rights. In a context where human rights have often been used to undermine indigenous rights, Kulchyski argues, the instances of legal and social recognition for indigenous rights—in both national and international foundational documents, however jumbled—can be wielded to advance indigenous peoples' collective rights to preserve distinct cultures and modes of production. We should not accept, Kulchyski urges, the subordination of indigenous rights to human rights, especially given the way universalist claims have justified the violation of both kinds of rights for indigenous people in Canada and elsewhere. Nor should indigenous organizations and activists abandon as dead letters the rights set out in the Canadian constitution and in the UNDRIP. When Marx wrote that "between right and right, force decides," he invoked the conflict between workers and capitalists, each as property owners demanding the "full value" of their property. The substance of that force, of course, was class struggle. Between human and indigenous peoples' rights, Kulchyski suggests, what might emerge are alternative "principles of social justice and democracy" that arise by "plac[ing] special value on meaningful difference" (MacKinnon 2001, 169).

Where Kulchyski distinguishes indigenous rights from human rights to distinguish the former from a liberal individualist heritage, David Harvey and other proponents of the "right to the city" opt rather to reclaim as "human" a right that is intrinsically collective and materialist. Not simply a right to access urban resources, Harvey presents the right to the city as "the right to change ourselves by changing the city more after our heart's desire"—a right, in other words, to remake the "humanity" that is the subject of human rights (2003, 939, 941). The right to the city has emerged as an organizing umbrella for a diverse array of urban struggles around the world. In contrast to the defensive, even minimalist political vision of conventional human rights, the right to the city offers an ambitious vision of humanity's collective capacity to transform itself by transforming the social world.

Many conventionally recognized rights claims can be made within the rubric of the right to the city. However, the right to the city *locates* rights through the simple but profound observation that rights cannot be exercised unless they literally *take place*. Jeremy Waldron makes this case when discussing the impact of privatization on the rights of homeless people simply to exist (1991). The evisceration of public space by property, Waldron observes, has a cataclysmic effect on people whose most basic human right—their right *to be*—is contingent on their right to be *somewhere*. Just as the division of the world into states means that statelessness is tantamount to rightlessness, the total division of the world into private property makes property the sine qua non of all other rights.

Right-to-the-city advocates foreground the material and relational substance of rights; the "who" and the "where" become the subjects of deliberation. Rights, they argue, are for the city's inhabitants rather than for its property owners. But who counts as an inhabitant? What are the spatial and temporal boundaries of membership, and what shared institutions are empowered to recognize or arbitrate membership? Finally, how will the city—and, by extension, its people—be created and re-created? These are the questions that go unasked when we focus on human rights, their answers presumed in the pre-political "human" that is the subject of rights. Although "the city" appears as its object, "the relation" (the "smallest unit of analysis") is the open question at the heart of the right to the city. It is also the invitation for radical political visioning.

SEE ALSO: Accessible; Authority; Crip; Demand; Democracy; Labor; Liberal; Oppression; Privilege; Queer; Responsibility; Trans*/-

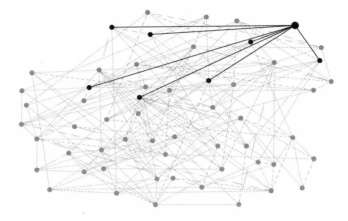

SOLIDARITY

Markus Kip

CONSIDERING ITS UBIQUITY, THERE HAVE BEEN RELATIVE-
ly few attempts by radicals to arrive at a common understanding of "solidarity." In addition to the confusion that
prevails with respect to the term's political commitments
and practical implications for radical forces, invocations
of "solidarity" can also be found among conservative trade
unions, within Catholic social teaching, and in nationalist and racist politics. As a result of these tensions, invocations of "solidarity" have been marked by ambiguity;
descriptive and prescriptive aspects blur together. Clearly,
radical uses of the term carry strong normative commitments and appeals. However, these are difficult to reconcile with its concurrent use as an analytical tool. At the

appellative level, "solidarity" is usually taken to be a self-evident concept that denotes the idea of supporting each other. Here the only problem arises from the question of how a moral insight is put into practice when it requires effort or renunciation. It is a different issue, however, to use solidarity analytically to understand social processes of collaboration and to analyze how current expressions and longings for solidarity could be strategically related for radical transformation.

In analytic treatments of "solidarity," ambiguity arises from the concept's implicit parceling of the world into zones of inclusion and exclusion. In view of the former, claims to solidarity are frequently made on the basis of asserted common objectives, values, or bonds. Simultaneously, in view of the latter, these assertions express shared opposition to a common, excluded enemy to whom solidarity cannot be extended. A related ambivalence concerns solidarity's character as both goal and instrument. As an end in itself, a "solidarity economy," for example, seeks to realize an alternative cooperative form of production inspired by experiments in places like Chiapas, Venezuela, or Argentina. In a similar vein, geographer and social theorist David Featherstone (2012, 186) has described the practices of the Counter-Globalization Movement as "prefigurative solidarities" motivated by commitment to the idea that "organizing spaces should bring into being the alternative worlds they seek to create." In contrast to such end-based views, other activists have foregrounded the value of "solidarity" as a means that might be deployed against an outside enemy or threat. Anarchist activist and author Cindy Milstein (2015), for instance, has conceived it as a "weapon . . . versus killer cops," while an Irish union vice-president declared that "the only effective weapon in our arsenal is worker and social solidarity" (Piaras Murphy 2002).

For its part, the scholarly literature on solidarity has tended to be less concerned with naming the enemy or establishing the concept's strategic dimension than with elaborating its inclusionary and end-based dimensions. This orientation highlights the role of sameness and difference as constitutive factors. With sameness, a collective identity is invoked regardless of whether it is based on political goals, social categories, a common threat, or a shared humanity. In contrast, radical movement–based thought often emphasizes difference as being among solidarity's distinctive features. Following poststructuralist critiques, many contemporary radicals find presuppositions of "human nature" or even of common interests based in shared identities to be untenable. Formalizing this perspective, philosopher Richard Rorty (1989) has argued that even seemingly objective commonalities like "humanity" are not sufficient to account for the ways that solidarities are—or are not—practically enacted. In Paulo Freire's *Pedagogy of the Oppressed*, "solidarity" bridges difference and allows oppressors to create liberatory relationships with the oppressed. According to Freire, "Solidarity requires that one enter into the situation of those with whom one is in solidarity." As such, "it is a radical posture" since "true solidarity with the oppressed means fighting at their side to transform the objective reality" (Freire 1970, 49).

For her part, Chandra Talpade Mohanty (2003) has critiqued invocations of solidarity in labor and feminist movements, where claims to universal solidarity based on likeness among "women" or "workers" have papered over conflicts between male and female workers and between women from the Global North and the Global South. Rejecting the idea that any particular form of oppression can be privileged as the basis for establishing commonality, feminist theorist Diane Elam (1994, 67) has suggested that solidarity is in fact "groundless." In his own work, Richard F. Day has elaborated this idea by noting how groundless solidarity means that "no particular form of inequality . . . can be postulated as the central axis of struggle" (Day 2005, 18). In this view, solidarity is not something for which a blueprint can exist. It requires open and honest communication between partners in solidarity. Describing "revolutionary solidarity" in a similar fashion, Milstein declares that "it looks like not jumping to conclusions about each other, especially based on perceived identity(ies)" (2015, 56). And for Mohanty "solidarity is always . . . the result of active struggle to construct the universal on the basis of particulars/differences" (Mohanty 2003, 6). Framing solidarity in this way implies the rejection of self-denial, which—according to the anonymous authors of "A Critique of Ally Politics"—"has repeatedly failed to equip would-be allies to do more than seek their own endlessly deferred salvation" (2015, 9). In opposition to ally politics, solidarity demands mutual aid, "the idea that we all have a stake in one another's liberation" (5). As Lilla Watson put it: "If you have come here to help me, you are wasting our time. But if you have come because your liberation is bound up with mine, then let us work together."

Solidarity, Elam notes, "is a stability but not an absolute one; it can be the object of conflict and need not mean consensus" (1994, 109). This emphasis on conflict underwrites the association between solidarity and commitment, which—for bell hooks—is what distinguishes solidarity from mere support. "Support can be occasional. It can be given and just as easily withdrawn. Solidarity requires sustained, ongoing commitment" (hooks 2000, 67). The question, then, is this: how can a radical commitment be fostered?

Earlier historical discussions reflect the tensions between exclusion and inclusion, ends and means, sameness and difference, and conflict and commitment that continue to inform debates about solidarity today. Solidarity's etymological roots can be traced back all the way to the Roman legal concept of "*obligatio in solidum*," which described shared liability for a financial debt. The significant historical advancement expressed by this juridical concept arises from the fact that it did not rely upon existing kinship ties; instead, it established shared liability among people who may have been strangers with heterogeneous interests.

As an explicitly political concept, however, "solidarity" only emerged during the French Revolution. Counterrevolutionaries were among the first to adopt the term when they linked the Roman legal formulation to a Christology of the sacrifice (Hoelzl 2004). In the early nineteenth century, ultraconservative Joseph de Maistre concluded that, since the crown was the divine representative, the people held collective liability for the maintenance of the Christian monarchy. In this view, "solidarity" became an individual's duty and involved the faithful preservation of order.

Rejecting such authoritarian interpretations, socialist philosopher Pierre Leroux devised a horizontalist conception of "*solidarité*." In his treatise "On Humanity" first published in 1840, Leroux proposed solidarity as a humanistic alternative to Christian duty that simultaneously challenged the idea that Christ's sacrifice was the necessary precondition for love. For Leroux, solidarity was an ethical virtue. A follower of Leroux, Louis Blanc later coined the phrase "From each according to his ability, to each according to his needs," which has widely been regarded as a foundation of radical solidarity—though one often falsely accredited to Marx.

It was within the revolutionary context of the mid-nineteenth century that "*solidarité*" became a competitor to "*fraternité*" and, at least within radical contexts, began to gain significant traction. *Solidarité* rejected the feudal connotations of *fraternité* and replaced them with a new form of bonding based on reason and fellowship rather than on kinship. After the failed revolutions of 1848, "solidarity" gained a Romantic inflection, which emphasized antagonism. The resulting splits within the radical socialist movements of France and Germany also helped to reveal differences between anarchist and communist uses of the term. Main points of contention concerned the relationship between movement and state, individual and collective, and duty and affect. Radical socialists approached the state as a terrain of struggle upon which concessions capable of fostering working-class solidarity could be won and institutionalized. In contrast, anarchists championed solidarity for its ability to prefigure alternative social possibilities in spaces liberated from the grip of the state. For Errico Malatesta and Peter Kropotkin, human evolution itself pointed toward solidarity's flourishing. For Malatesta, affect and feeling played a constitutive role in this development: "Solidarity, that is the harmony of interests and of feelings, the coming together of individuals for the wellbeing of all, and of all for the wellbeing of each, is the only environment in which man can express his personality and achieve his optimum development and enjoy the greatest possible wellbeing" (quoted in Wilde 2013, 30).

In contrast, communist thinkers emphasized solidarity's procedural and strategic character. Vladimir Lenin (1920), for example, posited solidarity as the discipline of the individual within the revolutionary party: "Without this solidarity, without this conscious discipline of the workers and peasants, our cause is hopeless. Without this, we shall be unable to vanquish the capitalists and landowners of the whole world. We shall not even consolidate the foundation, let alone build a new, communist society on that foundation."

In their endeavor to establish a science of socialism, German Marxists at the beginning of the twentieth century sought to rid solidarity of its Romantic character by eschewing references to affect. Socialist journalist and statesman Kurt Eisner, for example, insisted that there be "no more talk of love, pity, and compassion. The cold, steely word solidarity has been welded in the furnace of scientific thought. It does not appeal to floating, gliding, sweetly shining, perishing sentiments; it trains the mind, fortifies the character, and provides the whole of society with an iron foundation for the transformation and renewal of all human relations in their entire scope. Solidarity has its cradle in the minds of mankind, not in the feeling. Science has nurtured it, and it went to school in the big city, between the smokestacks and the streetcars. Its apprenticeship is not yet completed" (quoted in Wildt 1999, 215).

Despite differences in their inflection, however, both conceptions of solidarity have run into significant difficulties over the past century. The collapse of the Soviet bloc further delegitimized top-down approaches to solidarity among radicals, though this effect has been uneven on a global scale. Meanwhile, bottom-up approaches have not fared much better. Solidarity-based production cooperatives, self-help initiatives, or squatting collectives, for instance, have increasingly found themselves functioning as a revitalizing supplement to neoliberal capitalism (Ratner 2015; Mayer 2013).

One can also detect a disjuncture between appellative and analytical usages of "solidarity" among radicals. Internet searches reveal that, in the majority of cases, radicals invoke "solidarity" while writing letters, signing petitions, and attending rallies. Such activities tend on the whole to be insignificant when measured against the threatening realities they purport to engage. Although solidarity actions like consumer boycotts may sometimes yield enormous consequences (e.g., the campaign against apartheid South Africa), today's radicals are faced with the challenge of devising a strategy to overcome fragmented activism to produce a solidarity capable of defeating the enemy. Within this context, radicals have found it difficult to define boundaries (friends and enemies) and identify what members of the *"obligatio in solidum"* actually owe one another.

Having rejected metaphysics, contemporary advocates of radical solidarity struggle to establish stable ground. One current trend is to view solidarity as both the process and outcome of organizing or commoning. This procedural approach understands that solidarity is learned and may be stimulated by appeals to an individual's immediate concerns. Organizing around specific demands thereby promises to reveal the collective character of the problem and foster solidarity among those who recognize a common interest. According to food activist Martha Stiegmann, "Building meaningful solidarity is a political work-in-progress. Aligning ourselves with this global movement is, in a sense, an acknowledgement that we have much to learn from examples that lay bare the logic of the dominant system, about the ways our domestic challenges are rooted in the globalization project" (Stiegmann 2012, 270).

Despite this objective, however, short-term organizing doesn't always develop into long-term solidarity projects. Broadened commitment to other struggles is not inevitable. Recently labor activists Bill Fletcher Jr. and Fernando Gapasin have taken aim at the predominant approach to organizing solidarity in the US labor movement, where "each side cooperates on the basis of its immediate material interests. No larger view informs this type of solidarity; it forms around the needs of the moment. Both sides treat each agreement akin to a business decision, rather than see their activities as part of a larger struggle for power and against a common opponent" (Fletcher and Gapasin 2008, 195).

Such an account neatly summarizes the challenges that arise from solidarity's ambiguity with respect to inclusion and exclusion and its ambivalent character as both goal and instrument. As philosopher Kurt Bayertz argues, "the agreement of interests . . . may represent an explanation for solidary activity." However, solidarity necessarily goes beyond such commonality, since it also "contains a genuinely moral dimension" (Bayertz 1999, 17–18) In a post-metaphysical era, determining how to justify the suspension of immediate concerns in the interest of pursuing a collective future has become a key question. Despite its significant development since the eighteenth century, "solidarity" continues to be haunted by sacrifice.

SEE ALSO: Allies; Commons; Community; Friend; Love; Politics

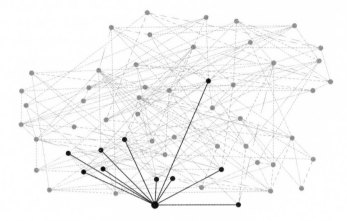

SOVEREIGNTY

Stacy Douglas

ALTHOUGH THE WORD "SOVEREIGNTY" DID NOT COME INTO popular usage until approximately the sixteenth century, debates over what constitutes legitimate political authority can be traced back as far as Ancient Greek. As a noun, "sovereignty" first appears in English in the mid-fourteenth century and was associated with "pre-eminence." It stems from the Anglo-French "*sovereynete*" and Old French "*souverainete*," which derived from the French adjective "*soverain*," which in term derived from the Latin "*super*" (*OED*). The shift in the term's meaning in the early 1700s from "authority," "rule," and "supremacy of power or rank" to existence as an independent state coincided with the advent of the modern nation-state and its corresponding political philosophy.

Today activists use the term in numerous overlapping social movement contexts to claim national, indigenous, and food sovereignty. Within these movements, the term "sovereignty" is typically invoked as a self-evident good. It represents the possibility of liberation through autonomy. However, while these struggles stand as crucial rejoinders to colonial and imperialist legacies, the Enlightenment-inspired principles that undergird the concept pose challenges. "Sovereignty," as it is imagined in Western political and legal thought, presupposes a liberal individual contractualism that yields corresponding images of justice. Social movements that wish to contest these parameters may want to resist the framework of sovereignty and the narrow conception of autonomy upon which it is built.

The modern Western conception of sovereignty derives from medieval Christian theology. In *The King's Two Bodies* (1957), Ernst Kantorowicz traces the concept's emergence. He shows how, just as Christ is manifested through the mortal body and the mystical body, the king is also represented in this dual fashion. The monarch is both a physical person (*"corpus verum"* or *"corpus naturale"*) and an institution that lives on regardless of bodily mortality (*"corpus mysticum"*). This duality is best exemplified in the phrase "The king is dead! Long live the king!" (Kantorowicz 1957, 412). Whereas medieval theology conceived only God and the heavens to be permanent, secularization extended this legacy to the state. As James Martel summarizes, "The idea of a Church that would last until the day of judgment was readily transferred to the courts, to the state's fiscal holdings and to the dignity and crown of the monarchy" (2012, 21). In this way, "sovereignty" came to be associated with the state and its enduring claim to political authority.

Published in 1922 (a decade before he became a member of the German National Socialist Party), Carl Schmitt's *Political Theology: Four Theses on the Concept of Sovereignty* grappled with this theological inheritance. In this work, Schmitt condemned the legal positivists and liberal constitutional thinkers of his time, who— in their attempt to write legal code for all eventualities—failed to realize that "all law is situational law" (2005, 13). The presumed protection of law, Schmitt argued, disguised the need for human decision-making outside of the legal code. This role, he argued, mirrored that of God in theology; sovereignty required an ultimate decider for situations that exceeded legal parameters, or—as Schmitt put it—"sovereign is he who decides on the exception" (2005, 5). Despite these efforts to excavate law's theological hangover, however, Schmitt failed to displace the liberal constitutional conception of sovereignty or its God-function cover-up.

This liberal constitutional conception, which generated the idea of the "social contract," had been central to republican struggles against authoritarian rule. An early theorist of the social contract, Thomas Hobbes, based his treatise on his experience of the English Civil War (mid-1600s), during which parliamentarians attacked the monarch for what they perceived to be arbitrary uses of power. Alongside their arguments for equality, these parliamentarians were interested in preventing the monarch from suffocating free market trade in London (Tomkins 2005; Yandle 1993). In this way, they helped fuel the idea of the liberal individual (operating under contractual protections) that now lies at the heart of Western juridical thinking. For his part, Hobbes concluded that security required individuals to give up some of their rights for collective protection under "a strong sovereign" (1992, 641). Because humans are naturally selfish and vengeful, and since power distributed through a democracy or an aristocracy was bound to be fickle, weak, and easily corruptible, Hobbes concluded that the best form of commonwealth was monarchy.

Writing approximately fifty years after Hobbes, John Locke also advocated establishing sovereignty by social contract. Although he was less pessimistic about human nature, he worried that those who lived by force and violence rather than reason would infringe upon the land and resources of others. Consequently, Locke's concept of sovereignty hinged on the self-contained individual's rationality and the moral imperative to cultivate land. Here the sovereign is no absolute monarch but a figure checked by a division of powers and who can be overthrown by the people.

This conception of "general will" (an idea that today finds expression in slogans like "the power of the people") was subsequently developed by Jean-Jacques Rousseau. Writing in the mid-eighteenth century, Rousseau claimed that earlier philosophers justified enslavement by legitimizing the sovereign's hierarchical authority. While Rousseau felt that the state benefited the collective, he wanted it to be managed by a legislator charged solely with executing the general will. Rousseau's ideas influenced key figures in the French and Haitian Revolutions almost fifty years later, including Maximilien de Robespierre, Louis Antoine Leon de Saint-Just, and François-Dominique Toussaint L'Ouverture (C. L. R. James 2001). Indeed, modern sovereignty's republicanism continues to resonate today.

In the United States and Canada, indigenous peoples have advanced claims to sovereignty to resist assimilation and oppression by settler-colonial governments. The American Indian Movement (AIM) began explicitly mobilizing around "sovereignty" in the late 1960s. Speaking at a meeting in Minneapolis, Dennis Banks argued that, "only by re-establishing our rights as sovereign nations, including our right to control our own territories and resources, and our right to genuine self-governance . . . can we hope to successfully address the conditions currently experienced by our people" (Ward Churchill 2003, 153). From 1968 onward, AIM used both direct action and legislative tactics to force the government into recognizing indigenous sovereignty (Harring 1994; Means and Wolf 1995; Sanchez and Stuckey 2000).

In 2008, the Kitchenuhmaykoosib Inninuwug (KI), Grassy Narrows, and Ardoch First Nations held a "sovereignty sleepover" in Toronto's Queen's Park to protest the unsanctioned actions of extractive industry companies operating on the communities' land (Peerla 2012, 4). In 2013, Chief Theresa Spence and the Attawapiskat First Nation filed a successful judicial review of the federal government's decision to appoint a third-party manager of their monetary affairs, thereby breaching their financial sovereignty (*Attawapiskat First Nation v. Canada*, 2012 FC 948). In 2014, the Supreme Court of Canada released a decision in the case of

Tsilhqot'in First Nation v. British Columbia (2014) asserting that the First Nation had title to their land and that the provincial government needed to obtain consent before using it (para. 76).

In India, activists have also deployed "sovereignty" when fighting corporate giants like Monsanto for control of food crops and seeds (Navdanya 2015; Shiva 2012). This movement has popularized the term "food sovereignty" and encouraged communities to collect seeds after harvest—a practice made illegal by the conjunction of genetic modification and property law (Democracy Now 2010; Shiva 2012). Food sovereignty activists have since broadened this language through campaigns against "food deserts" and diminished food access (Block et al. 2011). Feminist movements have also taken up the language of food sovereignty. According to Mariarosa Dalla Costa (2008), by viewing food as a common good rather than as a commodity, "food sovereignty is an affirmation of the right of populations to decide what to eat and how to produce it."

In movement contexts, invocations of "sovereignty" typically coincide with demands for control by the people in opposition to that of the state or of corporations. Within the current global configuration, however, such articulations often end by underscoring these movements' subordinate status. The American Indian Movement, for instance, was met with militarized repression (Churchill 2003). And, while the victory of the Tsilhqot'in Nation has broadened the legal determination of title in Canada, it concedes that territorial sovereignty emanates from the settler-colonial state. Indeed, title can be "given" or "taken away" by the occupying government, which continues to hold legal superiority—including the ability to infringe on titled lands, without consent, if its actions have a compelling and substantial objective (para. 77). Meanwhile, advocates of "food sovereignty" demand their right to food, a demand beholden to legitimation by a superior legal authority. Not only do such claims emphasize the subordinate status of the claimant, they also lend power to the existing sovereign by extending recognition.

This is not the only dilemma presented by sovereignty. At the beginning of the Weimar Republic, Walter Benjamin (1978) recounted the intrinsic role of violence in the pursuit of sovereignty.

Having witnessed the Social Democratic Party's military suppression of communist uprisings across Germany, Benjamin argued that sovereign power was inseparable from violence since those in power and those who seek to be in power will always justify the suppression of dissent. Antonio Negri (1999) has also weighed in on the perils of sovereignty, and especially the form associated with the social contract articulated by Hobbes, Locke, and Rousseau. Instead of calling for and perpetuating the need for such a contract, Negri has invoked a vision of radical democracy guided by "constituent power."

Critiques of sovereignty have also been directed at its philosophical underpinnings. French philosopher Jean-Luc Nancy (1991) has criticized the way the concept has shaped our very conception of the individual. Drawing on the work of Martin Heidegger, Nancy enjoins us to recognize how our lives are fundamentally contingent upon that which is outside of us. According to Nancy, every time we draw a sphere of autonomy around the individual and pretend that it is not inherently in-relation, we perpetuate the myth of sovereignty. Fully scalable, this dynamic is exacerbated when we draw a perimeter around "community" and deny its relation to the outside. For Nancy, any absolute that pretends to be absolutely alone is always exposed to an outside through which it is relationally co-constituted.

A social and political thinker and defender of indigenous knowledge, Marie Battiste, found that while the Canadian government was intent on establishing territorial lines to demarcate jurisdictions, indigenous leaders noted that communities depended on natural systems that necessarily exceeded such borders (Battiste and Henderson 2000). As a result, Battiste noted an inherent failure of communication between these two ways of seeing the world—one based on Western conceptions of sovereignty as autonomous, territorially defined jurisdictions, and the other based on a more relational approach that implicitly challenges the foundational assumptions of sovereignty.

Similarly, though he has acknowledged that some indigenous communities have made gains by advancing sovereign claims,

Taiaiake Alfred (2002) has argued that such claims cannot repair the ills wrought by centuries of anti-indigenous racism. This is so not least because such claims have been co-opted by the state, manipulated by the courts, capitalized upon by profit-hungry resource extraction companies, and left many communities more dependent upon the colonial occupier (Alfred 2002, 468–70). For Alfred, what has been lost through claims to sovereignty is indigenous autonomy. In contrast, a rejection of sovereignty both at the level of the individual and at the level of formal political authority would allow indigenous cultures and relationships to flourish. Somewhat distinct from Alfred's critique, Andrea Smith (2010) found that indigenous women articulated definitions of sovereignty that emphasized mutual responsibilities and a project of community realization. For Smith, indigenous nationhood is not just about land rights. Instead, it is about a mutual relationship with the land and the commitments that such a relationship entails. In this view, moving beyond state-centric models of governance based on recognition and representation becomes central to decolonization.

Radicals today need to think carefully about how their claims to "rights" and "autonomy" might perpetuate the sovereign legacies ingrained in our conceptions of liberty, freedom, the individual, and community. This requires more than spurning state sovereignty. Instead, it demands perpetual vigilance against any and all conceptions that allow the myth of sovereignty to persist.

SEE ALSO: Authority; Colonialism; Community; Democracy; Hegemony; Nation; Occupation; Representation; Responsibility; Victory

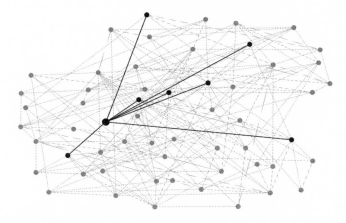

SPACE

Kanishka Goonewardena

THE MEDIATION OF POLITICS BY SPACE IS AS OLD AS
politics and space, even if it appears that the word
"space" attained keyword status in radical discourse
only recently. In *A Dictionary of Marxist Thought*
(Bottomore 1991), Henri Lefebvre and David Harvey
are conspicuously absent, and "space," the concept with
which these renowned thinkers are often associated,
is omitted. The term is also missing from Raymond
Williams's *Keywords* (1983). As such, these books may
seem as if they belonged to an old thought-world predating the age of globalization and postmodernism, in
which "space" rolls off many tongues with noticeable
ease and frequency.

The current popularity of "space" owes something to the sheer diversity of meanings it has acquired. Consider the notion of "safe space" advocated by LGBTQ, feminist, anti-racist, and other activists. The purpose of this formulation is to safeguard the marginalized bodies, relationships, homes, workplaces, habitats, discourses, and imaginaries from dominant social forces (Harris 2015). Even in this particular usage, however, "space" assumes many meanings: physical space (the body, bedroom, classroom, street, square, neighborhood, etc.), social space (domestic space, private space, work space, public space, etc.), political-juridical space (citizenship, human rights, civil rights, etc.), and discursive space (what can and cannot safely be said, even thought). Likewise, the feminist conceptual distinction between "public" and "private" stretches across various spatial scales from the body to the nation and beyond.

Despite these variations, some uses of "space" highlight the term's political lineages better than others, The events of the Arab Spring (e.g., Tahrir Square, Gezi Park) and the Occupy Movement (originating in Zuccotti Park), for example, revealed that "space" is both an essential mediation of politics and an unmediated object of political struggle. Even as commentators dwelled primarily on communication technology (e.g., email, Facebook, Twitter) and organizational innovation (e.g., democratic horizontalism), those movements themselves clearly revealed their attachment—both phenomenological and political—to space. According to *New York Times* architecture critic Michael Kimmelman (2011): "We tend to underestimate the political power of physical places. Then Tahrir Square comes along. Now it's Zuccotti Park, until four weeks ago an utterly obscure city-block-size downtown plaza with a few trees and concrete benches. . . . A few hundred people with ponchos and sleeping bags have put it on the map."

Watching "the Zuccotti Park demonstrators hold one of their 'general assemblies'" made Kimmelman think of "Aristotle, of all people," who "believed that the human voice was directly linked to the civic order." To underscore this point, he quoted Occupy activist Jay Gausson reflecting upon the significance of the "mic check," invented after megaphones were banned from Zuccotti

Park: "We're so distracted these days, people have forgotten how to focus. But the 'mic check' demands not just that we listen to other people's opinions but that we really hear what they're saying because we have to repeat their words exactly." Gausson called Zuccotti Park the "ground zero" of a new "architecture of consciousness" (Kimmelman 2011).

Echoing similar sentiments, urban theorist and activist Mike Davis (2011) noted that "activist self-organization—the crystallization of political will from free discussion—still thrives best in actual urban fora." In contrast, "most of our internet conversations are preaching to the choir." In his view, the movement's occupations actualized the promising formal features of urban space celebrated by Lefebvre (2003), especially centrality and difference. These were the qualities that turned those squares not only into "lightening rods. . . . for the scorned, alienated ranks of progressive Democrats," but also into "the common ground. . . . for imperilled, middle-aged school teachers to compare notes with young, pauperized college grads" (Davis 2011). Witnessing the same spaces, the US historian and journalist Jon Wiener (2011) exclaimed: "hardhats and hippies—together at last."

The space of Occupy was not only physical, but also symbolic. After more than two decades of neoliberal hegemony, one associates Zuccotti Park above all with capitalism's inherent inequity, the 99% and the 1%. But perhaps the "spatial moment" of greatest symbolic significance in the Western radical tradition is the Communards' toppling of the Vendôme Column on May 19, 1871. Anti-Communard poet Catulle Mendès voiced the spontaneous distress of his class at the impending fate of this Parisian monument glorifying Napoleonic imperialism:

> Don't think that demolishing the Vendôme Column
> is just toppling over a bronze column with an em-
> peror's statue on top; it's unearthing your fathers to
> slap the fleshless cheeks of their skeletons and to say
> to them: You were wrong to be brave, to be proud, to
> be grand! You were wrong to conquer cities, to win

> battles. You were wrong to make the world marvel at the vision of a dazzling France. (quoted in Ross 2015, 5)

A few days later, Communard Louis Barron recalled it otherwise:

> I saw the Vendôme Column fall. . . . Immediately a huge cloud of dust rose up, while a quantity of tiny fragments rolled and scattered about, white on one side, gray on the other. . . . This colossal symbol of the Grand Army—how it was fragile, empty, miserable. It seemed to have been eaten out from the middle by a multitude of rats, like France itself. . . . and we were surprised not to see any [rats] run out. . . . The music played fanfares, some old greybeard declaimed a speech on the vanity of conquests, the villainy of conquerors, and the fraternity of the people, and we danced in a circle around the debris, and then we went off, very content with the little party. (quoted in Ross 2015, 5–8)

In her research on the Paris Commune, Kristin Ross demonstrates how the demolition of the Vendôme Column etched the Communards' "anti-hierarchical" and "horizontal" political imaginary into popular consciousness. This ideology rejected divisions "between genres, between aesthetic and political discourses, between artistic and artisanal work, between high art and *reportage*" while extending radical-democratic "principles of association and cooperation into the workings of everyday life" (2015, 5). For Ross, the Commune was a "primarily spatial event" that manifested itself in the wake of the "European transformation of space into colonial space, and in the establishment of an international division of labour":

> To mention just a few of the spatial problems posed by the Commune, consider, for example, the

relationship of Paris to the provinces, the Commune as an immense "rent strike," the post-Haussmann social division of the city and the question of who, among the citizens, has a "right to the city"—the phrase is Lefebvre's—or the military and tactical use of city space during the street fighting. (2015, 4)

Following Ross, we may recall Lefebvre's demand that the Paris Commune be considered an *urban* revolution—or, in the words of the Situationists, *"the only implementation of revolutionary urbanism* to date" (Debord, Kotányi, and Vaneigem 1962). In their view, where the term "urban" refers to the processes of urbanization and the production of space, decisive social change ought to be understood not only with respect to time, but also with respect to social space and everyday life, precisely the material to be transformed in any revolution worthy of the name. Methodologically, both Lefebvre and the Situationists reject the conception of space as a mere container or reflection of social relations. Instead, they insist on the dialectical relationship between space and society and the fundamental role played by the production of space in social and political life. In *The Production of Space*, Lefebvre asks: "Is it conceivable that the exercise of hegemony might leave space untouched?" And replies: "No" (1991, 11). But he was by no means the first to comprehend the co-constitution of spatial and social relations from a revolutionary perspective. Indeed, the Communards and their allies—such as the great anarchist geographers Élisée Reclus and Peter Kropotkin—were amply aware of the spatiality of politics, especially in their pioneering vision of "anarchist communism" as a global federation of self-governing communes: a "Universal Republic" (Ross 2015).

Famously alleged to have said "I am a Marxist today so that I can be an anarchist tomorrow," Lefebvre is rightly credited for pioneering a spatial perspective within twentieth-century critical theory.[1] In this regard, the most common Lefebvre citation refers

---

1. By geographer Edward Soja, based on a conversation with Lefebvre in Los Angeles in the early 1980s.

to his triadic conception of "conceived space," "perceived space," and "lived" space (Lefebvre 1991). Nevertheless, Lefebvre's most significant "spatial" contribution to critical theory lies in his novel conception of social *totality*, which involves three *levels* of social reality—a "global" or "universal" level consisting of the logics of capital and state, an "everyday" or "lived" level consisting of the contestations between the aspirations and the routines of everyday life, and a "mediating level" consisting of the dynamics of "urbanization" and the "production of space" (Lefebvre 2003). Such is the holistic framework within which we can see, for example, how his theorization of the role of the state as the territorial organization of hierarchical social relations leads to a concept of *"autogestion"* ("self-management") as well as a (re)definition of (neo)colonialism: "Wherever there is a dominated space generated and mastered by a dominant space—where there is periphery and centre—there is colonization" (Lefebvre 1978, 174). The same conceptual constellation clarifies why he called for *"the right to the city"* in opposition to the "abstract," "homogeneous" and "hierarchical" space produced by capital and state in the "bureaucratic society of controlled consumption" (Lefebvre 1971). For Lefebvre's concept of totality links such seemingly disparate strategies—spatial and political—by showing that they are in fact complementary demands for a quite different world in which the production of space becomes a non-alienating, radical-democratic praxis.[2]

Lefebvre's thoughts regarding *autogestion* and "the right to the city" can be traced through the contemporary movement notion of "commoning," which advocates the use of space for communal purposes at odds with capital and state. This orientation is evident in a wide array of activist groups subscribing to a diversity of political ideologies and organizational strategies. These include "Reclaim the Streets" groups setting up Temporary Autonomous Zones, the Shack Dwellers Movement in South Africa pursuing more permanent claims to urban space, the neighbourhood associations advocating for better living conditions in the *favelas* and *barrios*

---

2. For a brief introduction to the wide range of Lefebvre's thought, see Goonewardena 2011, 44–64).

of Central and Latin America, and the slum dwellers of India confronting hegemonic possessors of political and economic power, all claiming their own space in the city. Likewise, the landless people's movement in Brazil (*Sem Terra*), the peasant and rural mobilizations in India, indigenous activists in Bolivia and Canada, and the Zapatistas in Chiapas have all advocated the self-government of their traditional territories in the face of the plunder of their habitats and ways of life by what Marx called "so-called primitive accumulation."

An instructive urban movement from the US, the Right to the City Alliance (RTTC) coalesced a variety of dispersed activist groups organizing around several issues—upon the catalytic awareness that they shared a common interest in appropriating city space (social, political, symbolic). On their website, RTTC describes itself as "a national alliance of racial, economic and environmental justice organizations" that "is building a national movement for racial justice, urban justice, human rights, and democracy" (Right to the City 2016). Significantly, and "in the realm of ideas," the group lists "Lefebvre's 1968 book *Le Droit à la ville* (Right to the City)" as "a key resource and touchstone." To be sure, Lefebvre has inspired many activist groups, including radical architects and planners in Brazil who translated *Le Droit* into Portuguese in 1969. In fact, exemplary practitioners and theoreticians of architecture and urbanism such as Anatole Kopp, Lucien Kroll, Hassan Fathy and Peter Marcuse are among the best exponents of "the right to the city" tradition. The title of Brazilian communist and architect Oscar Niemeyer's (2013) autobiography captures the essence of their intentions: "We Must Change The World."

Although *A Dictionary of Marxist Thought* occludes "space," it is impossible after reading Lefebvre and his kindred spirits to ignore the many spatial concepts of Marxism: uneven development, imperialism, colonialism, "so-called original accumulation," and so on (1857; 1871; 1867b). Likewise, although Williams's *Keywords* contains no entry on "space," space *is* the keyword underlying his most impressive work. According to Williams, his "central case in *The Country and the City* was that these two apparently opposite and separate projections—country and city—were in fact indissolubly linked, within the general and crisis-ridden development of a capitalist economy which had itself produced this division in its modern forms" (1989, 227). More recently, US Marxist critic Fredric Jameson has alerted us to nature and land amidst the growing "preponderance of space over time in late capitalism," arguing that "in our time all politics is about real estate." If indeed "postmodern politics is essentially a matter of land grabs, on a local as well as global scale"—as Jameson (2015) and many activists now realize—then space is surely an ineluctable and timely keyword for radicals.

SEE ALSO: Accessible; Commons; Community; Experience; Occupation; Politics; Utopia

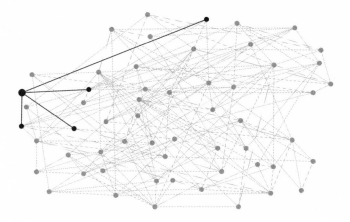

SUSTAINABLE

Patrick Bond

IN 2015, FACEBOOK BOSS MARK ZUCKERBERG FAMOUSLY declared his practical, financial opposition to net neutrality: "It's not sustainable to offer the whole Internet for free," he opined (Newman 2015). Without a commercial incentive, many facets of life end up falling short of "sustainability" in the classical sense of a financial rate of return greater than zero. Originally from the Latin "*sustinere*" ("to hold" or, in other evolutions, "long-lasting"), it is through the word's recent etymological trajectory that the banal terminology of economic profitability was temporarily displaced by environmental signposting. In radical scenes, "sustainable" is also used to describe processes—particularly in organizing contexts—that do not lead to "burnout," a major cause of movement disengagement. This usage, however, tends to invoke a metaphoric homology with both the ecological and the economic usage. It is therefore necessary to consider how such usages came to be.

The idea of "sustainability" as an ecological concept gained popularity in 1972 with the first Earth Summit in Stockholm and in *The Limits to Growth* (Club of Rome 1972), culminating in a 1987 United Nations Commission and the 1992 Rio Earth Summit. Co-opted by corporations during the 1990s, "sustainability" was downgraded in favor of neoliberal ideologues' advocacy of export-led growth and the commodification of nature. Nevertheless, the concept emerged once again at the 2002 UN Earth Summit in Johannesburg, which fused the UN's strategy with privatizers, carbon traders, and mega-corporations supporting its "Global Compact." Then, finding "Green Economy" rhetoric, biodiversity offsetting, and market-centric climate change policy to be fertile soil at the 2012 Rio Summit, "sustainability" once again flowered, leading to fears of "neoliberalized nature" (Büscher et al. 2014). Despite extensive critique by the scholar-activist network The Rules (2015) and others, "sustainable development goals" have become a mantra of the UN and many other multilateral agencies.

The return of "sustainability" will inevitably be contested by radical critics and attacked by pollution-intensive capitalist forces. But it is the torture of "sustainability" through "ecological modernization" (e.g., the World Business Council on Sustainable Development, established by Swiss construction billionaire Stephan Schmidheiny) to which critics must pay closest attention. Like so many forms of greenwashing, the term is deployed in the course of commodifying, financializing and destroying nature. The financialization of nature is underway with carbon markets and other forms of emissions trading and virtual water sales, increasingly packaged in exotic investment instruments (Bond 2012). In ecological modernization's most advanced form, Deutsche Bank's Pavan Sukhdev initiated "The Economics of Ecosystems and Biodiversity" (TEEB) within the UN Environment Program to "make nature's values visible" and thus "help decision-makers recognize the wide range of benefits provided by ecosystems and biodiversity, demonstrate their values in economic terms and, where appropriate, capture those values in decision-making" (TEEB n.d.).

TEEB's search for optimal resource use emphasizes "low-hanging fruit" that can achieve the least costly form of market-facilitated environmental management. Likewise, the World Bank's (2012) *Inclusive Green Growth* mandated that "care must be taken to ensure that cities and roads, factories and farms are designed, managed, and regulated as efficiently as possible to wisely use natural resources while supporting the robust growth developing countries still need . . . [to move the economy] away from suboptimalities and increase efficiency— and hence contribute to short-term growth— while protecting the environment." Not mentioned by World Bank staff were capitalism's recent distortions in the food system, carbon markets, and real estate, most proximately caused by financial speculation in commodities, nature, and housing. Nor would the World Bank admit that overproduction tendencies in the world economy are amplified by the "increased efficiency" required for successful export-led growth, nor that irrationality characterizes a large share of international trade. Silences in neoliberal versions of sustainability discourse tell us just as much about the real agenda behind co-optation of this sort.

This is the weak, corporate-dominated version of the sustainability narrative, but there was once a stronger one. Gro Harlem Brundtland's World Commission on Environment and Development (1987) defined "sustainable development" as meeting "the needs of the present without compromising the ability of future generations to meet their own needs." Moving beyond simple intergenerational equity, Brundtland also allowed mention of two central concepts that reflected a more favorable balance of forces for the environmental left. First was "the concept of 'needs', in particular the essential needs of the world's poor, to which overriding priority should be given." Second was "the idea of limitations imposed by the state of technology and social organization on the environment's ability to meet present and future needs." These relatively radical red and green agendas were briefly married in 1987. As a result, the idea of "sustainability" should have been a strong site for contesting capitalism had activists more jealously guarded the term.

It was not to be. As John Drexhage and Deborah Murphy (2012) explained, "over the past 20 years ["sustainable development"] has often been compartmentalized as an environmental issue. Added to this, and potentially more limiting for the sustainable development agenda, is the reigning orientation of development as purely economic growth." It is worth dwelling on this artificial bifurcation because, within the discipline of economics, two lines of argument had emerged by the early 1990s. The first was the visionary work of Herman Daly, who edited the seminal *Toward a Steady State Economy* (1973) but then labored fruitlessly at the World Bank to inject environmental values into financial considerations. Daly (1996, 220) had offered a tougher definition of "sustainability" than Brundtland, calling for "development without growth beyond environmental carrying capacity, where development means qualitative improvement and growth means quantitative increase." At the World Bank, he found that this framing "just confirmed the orthodox economists' worst fears about the subversive nature of the idea, and reinforced their resolve to keep it vague."

Daly (1996, 88–93) proposed four sustainability policy recommendations for both the World Bank and for governments centered on preserving the ecological inheritance, which came to be known as "natural capital." These were to stop counting natural capital as income, to tax labor and income less and resource throughput more, to maximize the productivity of natural capital in the short run and invest in increasing its supply in the long run, and to move away from export-led growth and toward domestic production for internal markets. By 1995, Daly (1996, 220) had grown frustrated because, "although the World Bank was on record as officially favoring sustainable development, the near vacuity of the phrase made this a meaningless affirmation. . . . The party line was that sustainable development was like pornography: we'll know it when we see it, but it's too difficult to define."

Laying down the party line on the other side of the bifurcation, was World Bank chief economist Lawrence Summers (1991), who dramatically reworked the idea of sustainability: "I think the economic logic behind dumping a load of toxic waste in the lowest-wage country is impeccable and we should face up to that," he asserted. For Summers, sustainability at a global scale allowed evasion or evisceration of state regulations designed to "internalize the externalities" associated with pollution or ecological damage. Summers' version meant simply displacing these externalities to wherever the immediate environmental implications were least visible. After all, Summers (1991) continued, inhabitants of low-income countries typically died before the age at which they would begin suffering prostate cancer associated with toxic dumping. Using the "marginal productivity of labor" as his guiding measure, Summers implied that low-income Africans were not worth very much, nor were their aesthetic concerns with air pollution as substantive as were those of wealthy northerners. In this view, "sustainability" actually permitted dumping toxic waste on poor people instead of halting the production of toxins.

"Your reasoning is perfectly logical but totally insane," rebutted Brazilian environment secretary José Lutzenberger. "Your thoughts are a concrete example of the unbelievable alienation, reductionist thinking, social ruthlessness and the arrogant ignorance of many conventional 'economists' concerning the nature of the world we live in" (quoted in Summers, 1991). Lutzenberger was subsequently fired by a conservative Brazilian president (later impeached for corruption). In contrast, Summers rose to the positions of US Treasury Secretary under Bill Clinton, Wall Street investment advisor, and President of Harvard University (a position from which he was fired for sexism). He also became Barack Obama's economic czar, and in this role, arranged trillions of dollars' worth of bailouts following the hazardous deregulation of banking he had championed. Summers personifies unsustainability, and, thanks to displacement of the "dirty industries," pollution largely generated in the North (or caused by northern overconsumption) began to shift to new production sites including Mexican maquiladoras and newly

420 | KEYWORDS FOR RADICALS

industrializing countries like Hong Kong, Singapore, Taiwan, and South Korea.

In part because of rampant socio-environmental unsustainability in these sites, the world began hitting what the Club of Rome (1972) had long warned would be "planetary boundaries." Of these, the most serious immediate threat overshooting the carrying capacity for greenhouse gases that cause climate change and, in turn, ocean acidification. There are others: biodiversity loss, stratospheric ozone depletion, chemical pollution, freshwater adulteration and evaporation, and shortages of arable land. As Fred Magdoff and John Bellamy Foster (2011, 12) remark, "Staying within each of these boundaries is considered essential to maintaining the relatively benign climate and environmental conditions that have existed during the last 12,000 years (the Holocene epoch). The sustainable boundaries in three of these systems . . . have already been crossed, representing extreme rifts in the Earth system."

Addressing these systemic threats, powerful institutions and companies are increasingly proposing technological silver-bullet fixes to unsustainability. These include "clean energy," biofuels, carbon capture and storage, and other geo-engineering gimmicks like genetically modified trees, air sulfates to shut out the sun, iron filings in the sea to create algae blooms (to sequester CO2), large-scale solar reflection, and artificial microbes to convert plant biomass into fuels, chemicals, and other products. Many of these tech-fix strategies violate the precautionary principle, create land-grab pressure, have excessive capital costs, require increased energy, are unproven in technological terms, and are many years—if not decades— away from implementation.

Can capitalism repair the damage being done? Some, including Al Gore (2009), believe in a "green capitalism" strategy based on arguments by Paul Hawken, Amory Lovins, and L. Hunter Lovins (1999). However, as Ariel Salleh (2012) has pointed out, a serious consideration of externalized costs should include at least three kinds of surplus extractions not considered by the "green capitalist": 1) the social debt to inadequately paid workers, 2) an embodied debt to women and family caregivers, and 3) an ecological debt to nature.

In contrast to this weak form of "sustainability," the left has stressed distributional equity, non-materialist values, and a critique of the mode of production. These ideas found early expression in the environmental justice vision articulated by African American activists in North Carolina during in the 1980s (Bullard 2000), and in the "anti-extractivism" and "rights of nature" positions articulated by Ecuadorean and Bolivian activists as well through the Andean indigenous peoples' versions of "*buen vivir*." They also found expression in allied ideas, including "degrowth" ("*décroissance*") (Latouche 2004), post-GDP "well-being" national accounting (Fioramonti 2014), "the commons" (Linebaugh 2008), and eco-socialism (Kovel 2007). Strategies for transitioning to genuinely sustainable societies and economies are also hotly debated (Swilling and Anneke 2012; Scoones, Leach, and Newell 2015).

With such creative options flowering, determining genuine sustainability does ultimately depend on the nature of the critique of unsustainability. Perhaps the most popular systemic analysis comes from Annie Leonard's (2007) *Story of Stuff* film and book, which link the spectrum of extraction, production, distribution, consumption, and disposal. Naomi Klein's (2014) *This Changes Everything* puts the onus on capitalism for climate change. For their part, Joan Martinez-Alier and Jochen Spangenberg (2012) explain what is truly at stake: "Unsustainable development is not a *market failure* to be fixed but a *market system failure*: expecting results from the market that it cannot deliver, like long-term thinking, environmental consciousness and social responsibility."

SEE ALSO: Care; Labor; Materialism; Nature

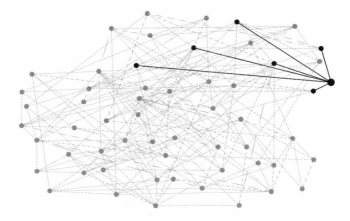

TRANS*/-

Dan Irving

During recent Trans* Pride events in cities like Vancouver, Toronto, Seattle, and New York, participants chanted slogans like "trans power" and "trans rights now!" Such slogans highlight contemporary meanings assigned to the term "trans*/-" and are indicative of the ambivalent political work this keyword performs. Derived from the Latin, the prefix *"trans-"* means "to move across." Reflecting the hegemony of Western and Anglophone gender activists in a global context, the term "trans" now refers to moving across the sex-gender binary from the sex or gender assigned at birth toward one asserted through acts of self-determination. Since the mid-1990s, trans identities have expanded beyond "transsexual" and "transgender" to include people identifying as "genderqueers," "genderfuckers," and "no gender."

As a mode of being and doing, "trans*" is the ontological and political term currently favored by trans scholars, nonprofit organizers, and grassroots activists to describe nonconforming gender identities. As a concept, "trans*" affirms the nonconforming and disruptive aspects of people's movement between, across, or beyond normative male/female and masculine/feminine categories. By virtue of such movement, trans people pose an implicit and sometimes explicit challenge to biologically determinist, essentialist, and naturalized conceptions of the sex/gender binary system. Drawing on computing language where an asterisk following a term broadens search results, "trans*" was popularized around 2010 through online debates concerning its utility (Tompkins 2014). This symbolic modifier also creates a porous border around trans networks to enable the future inclusion of other gender-nonconforming individuals, with the aim of resisting additional manifestations of gender oppression.

As with "queer" and "crip," there is a tension between the fluidity that "trans*" permits and the fixity of identity required to be intelligible within the human rights framework established by liberal democracy. Here trans people have been systemically erased via state administration (e.g., government-issued documents), legislation (e.g., lack of protection for gender identity), institutional policies (e.g., education and health care), and social services (Namaste 2000). Within this context, establishing rights becomes necessary because the socio-economic consequences of erasure (e.g., unemployment, homelessness, and sexual, physical, and emotional violence) threaten the lives of many trans people. As with previous struggles to secure rights on the grounds of sex, disability, indigeneity, and race, struggles to gain rights on the basis of gender identity have often relied on narrow categorical definitions; however, such a homogenous understanding detracts from the work that "trans*" does as a flexible signifier.

In an effort to combat the normalization of non-trans identities, many scholars and activists now juxtapose "trans*" as a gender identity to "cis-" individuals. The prefix "cis" means "on the side of" and encompasses the non-trans majority. Similar to white, middle-class, or heterosexual privilege, "cis-" denotes a structurally advantageous social location. In this case, cisgender and/or cissexual individuals benefit materially from fitting more comfortably within the sex/gender binary. Cis men and women are recognized at all levels of society as "authentic" or "normal" men and women. Consequently, they do not have the life experiences that make rights based on gender identity necessary. Feminist debates about trans women accessing women's shelters reveal how cis women are viewed as "legitimate" while trans women are rendered suspect. The *Nixon v. Vancouver Rape Relief* case illustrates how cis women are considered to be authentic while trans* women are excluded from the category woman. Kimberly Nixon was denied the opportunity to train as a volunteer phone counselor at Vancouver Rape Relief (VRR) once her transsexual history was uncovered. Nixon had experienced sexual trauma, received assistance from a rape crisis center, and desired to assist other women dealing with sexual assault. VRR denied her the opportunity to receive training for this position because her alleged "male socialization" meant that she could not be considered a peer to other women (Lakeman 2006). As trans activist, community worker, and scholar Jake Pyne demonstrates, cis privilege continues to inform the exclusion of trans* identified people from social services (2011).

Despite its widespread use, some trans* scholars and activists refuse to use the term "cis" on account of its potential divisiveness and because it creates another binary (Irving and Raj 2014). Others have chosen to highlight key issues trans people face while working to create solidarity between trans and cis people on account of their common subjection to restrictive gender norms (Serano 2014).

Within academia, scholars in the new field of Transgender Studies have used "trans-" (with a hyphen) as a theoretical framework for recognizing the specificity of trans subjectivities as they emerge through horizontal movements across sex and gender categories. Given that this interdisciplinary field often merges scholarship and activism, the hyphen denotes an intention to challenge the fixity of identity both theoretically and politically. "Trans-" motions toward understanding how gender-based governance interconnects with capitalism, nationalism, and colonialism.

In its present iterations, "trans*/-" denotes a way of being (*) and acting (-) that refuses to be contained by existing gender norms. According to pioneering Transgender Studies scholar and activist Sandy Stone, "trans*/-" works by spinning, rotating, and shifting terrains "guerilla" style (2014). In this view, the concept's elusiveness works to create possibilities for solidarity among oppressed peoples and across political movements. Groups like the Gender Justice League (Seattle) and the Sylvia Rivera Law Project (New York) as well as nonprofit organizations like Queers for Racial and Economic Justice (dissolved in 2014) engage in solidarity politics that link struggles against trans* oppression to queer, anticapitalist, and anti-racist social justice organizing.

The Free CeCe McDonald campaign exemplifies the conceptual work that "trans*/-" performs. Between 2012 and 2014, trans* activists demanded the release of McDonald, a Black trans woman serving a forty-one-month plea-bargained sentence for manslaughter. In 2011, McDonald stabbed and killed a man who had subjected her to racist, homophobic, and transphobic slurs before physically assaulting her. Trans*/- analysis uncovers the racist, sexist, and transphobic violence underlying an everyday reality in which particular bodies are declared monstrous, cast out from the social realm, and rendered disposable. McDonald's case also highlighted the means by which poor people who are part of racial, sexual, and gender minorities are increasingly criminalized and warehoused in prisons. Many activists contributing to campaigns to free CeCe McDonald worked to make these interconnections explicit. For example, the late transgender activist Leslie Feinberg said: *"CeCe McDonald survived a fascist hate crime; now she's sentenced as she struggles to survive an ongoing state hate crime. . . . As a white, working-class, Jewish, transgender lesbian revolutionary I will not be silent as this injustice continues!" (Adelman 2012).*

"Trans*/-" was preceded by terms such as "trans(s)exual" (with both one "s" and two), "transgenderist," and "transgender."

"Transsexuality" emerged primarily from clinical environs. In 1949, Dr. David O. Cauldwell introduced the term to refer to individuals who identified as opposite to their birth-assigned sex, exhibited cross-gender behaviors, and expressed desires for hormonal and surgical treatments. Cauldwell argued that transsexuality was a mental disorder and condemned medical professionals who operated on "gender dysphoric" individuals for engaging in medical mutilation (Cauldwell 1951; 1955). The lasting legacy of pathologization, which continues to find expression in particular medical and psychiatric communities, has impacted the trajectory of trans*/- politics.

In addition to the clinic, "transsexuality" also garnered meaning through popular culture. During the 1950s, Christine Jorgenson's "sex change" operation and subsequent career as an entertainer and educator expanded the reach of the term beyond medical and psychiatric milieus. During the 1960s, many grassroots "transsexual" groups continued to use the term—albeit with one "s"—to denote their rejection of medicalizing frameworks. In this way, "transsexuality" entered the public lexicon (although in a limited fashion) to represent a viable identity.

"Transexuality" was fraught with tensions, however. Despite their non-normative experiences and bodies, some transsexuals sought assimilation into mainstream white, heteronormative, and middle-class society. Nevertheless, even those who could disappear remained haunted by the derogatory slur "tranny." For their part, racialized and impoverished transexual women whose gender alterity was visible confronted this epithet and its consequences daily. "Tranny" came to denote transsexual individuals and was used primarily in reference to women of color doing sex work. Throughout, it served to govern trans people by vilifying some and spurring others to disassociate.

"Trans*" also emerges from the term "transgenderist," which was coined in the 1970s by Virginia Prince to refer to individuals who crossed the gender binary to live full-time as women (male-identified transgenderists were not mentioned) (Salah 2014). "Transgenderism" differentiated these women from transsexuals who sought surgery, drag queens who performed hyper-feminine gender pantomimes, and cross-dressers for whom wearing women's attire brought sexual satisfaction. Given that transsexuality and cross-dressing were considered pathological, the term "transgenderist" was associated with efforts to establish respectability (Salah 2014).

"Transgender" first appeared during the 1960s as part of an "organic, grassroots process that emerged from many sources, in many conversations, happening in many different locations" (Cristan Williams 2014, 223). Nevertheless, Holly Boswell's article "The Transgender Alternative" (1991) is credited with instigating its widespread use. Subsequently, Sandy Stone's article "The Empire Strikes Back: A Posttranssexual Manifesto" (2006), first published in 1992, did much to shape the intellectual and political agenda of the transgender movement (Stryker 2008). "Transgender" was intended (and sometimes functioned) as a unifying term for those resisting the pathologization, medicalization, and criminalization of transsexuals and transvestites (Stryker and Currah 2014). Joining together subgroups of gender nonconforming people with various identities and experiences, "transgender" performed a unifying function throughout the 1990s. In 1992, transgender lesbian Marxist Leslie Feinberg sought to unite gender oppression and socialist politics with hir pamphlet "Transgender Liberation: A Movement Whose Time Has Come."

For Susan Stryker and Paisley Currah—two leading scholars in Transgender Studies and senior editors of the journal *Transgender Studies Quarterly* (*TSQ*)—"transgender" denotes "inherently unfinishable combinational work" (2014, 1) with the potential to build social networks and develop intersectional political goals. However, gender nonconforming identities do not inevitably lead to political unity. Indeed, differences of class, gender, race, and ability produced significant fissures among those under the transgender umbrella. For instance, the struggle for transgender rights often reflected the concerns of white, middle-class individuals with considerable social and cultural capital. However, others sought to use "transgender" as a means of uncovering the "textual violence inscribed within the [gendered] body" (Stryker and Currah 2014, 3). Such tensions pointed both to the possibilities of "transgender" for transforming structural power relations and to the fact that umbrella terms can become governing devices that discipline individuals by fixing narrow identity-based criteria. For those who have embraced it, "trans*/-" represents a return to the radical potential of "transgender" without the imputed identity constraints.

Trans*/- resistance involves navigating between transgression and transformation. Trans histories of erasure, pathologization, and criminalization made it necessary to affix specific meaning to "trans*" in order for trans* people to achieve recognition, rights, and access to institutional, social, and cultural spaces. Indeed, trans-specific inclusion within the workplace (for example) can help to improve the immediate life chances of gender-nonconforming people. Nevertheless, trans*/- organizers have refused to limit their activism to singular identity categories; instead, they have challenged the limits of formal equality and symbolic recognition (Spade 2011) by linking their struggles to other queer, decolonial, and anticapitalist mobilizations for substantial equality (Mandlis 2011).

"Trans*/-" is not a homogenous category, nor does it signify a unified political movement. Within its very construction, "trans*/-" bears the histories of different labels—both identifying and objectifying—and works to complicate the politics of gender oppression. While "trans*" signified movement across or beyond the sex/gender binary, "trans*/-" seeks to acknowledge how both material embodiment and experiences of gender variance are mediated by capitalism, colonialism, and nationalism. For example, Beatriz Preciado's work (2013) demonstrates the interconnection between biocapitalism and embodied gender. Trans scholar Aren Aizura (2011) addresses the colonial and national geopolitics of sexual reassignment as a form of medical tourism. Viviane Namaste, a feminist scholar and activist, interrogates how "transgender" identities and politics reinforce Anglo-chauvinism in Canadian contexts. Similarly, Australian based trans scholar Vek Lewis addresses the ways that tracing the etymology of "transgender" and "trans" obscures past and current manifestations of colonialism (Namaste 2011).

The material lives of trans* people reveal the ways that complex regimes of governance—race, gender, colonialism, class, ability—are sutured together. The dismissal of transgender issues as cultural, petty bourgeois, and frivolous demonstrates how radicals themselves enact political erasure. Serious engagement with "trans*/-" will enable non-trans-identified radicals to reflect on the ways their organizing creates insiders and outsiders. In a moment marked by crises, radical movements need to develop the capacity to mobilize various marginalized groups while contributing to the momentum achieved by others. In the end, while "transgender" demonstrates the limitations of homogenous meaning and inspires hope by demonstrating unforeseen possibilities, "trans*/-" signals the potential for future becomings.

SEE ALSO: Bodies; Crip; Gender; Misogyny; Queer; Rights

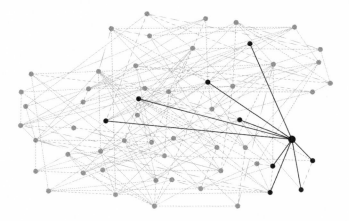

UTOPIA

David McNally

THE INTERNATIONAL LEFT-WING MOVEMENTS OF THE
1990s and early 2000s renewed activists' investment in
the concept of "utopia." From the Zapatistas' 1996 call
for an "international of hope" (1998, 13) to the 2001 con-
vening of the World Social Forum in Porto Alegre, Brazil
under the banner "Another World Is Possible," radicals
organizing against neoliberalism embraced a search for
radical alternatives. Confronted with the narrowing of
political horizons induced by the defeats of the neoliberal era—such as Margaret Thatcher's defeat of the British
coal miners' union in 1985 or the destruction of the tin
miners' union in Bolivia the same year—radicals have
since the 1990s frequently invoked utopia as a signature

category for imagining the new world that might be built on the ashes of the old.

Coined from the Greek "*ou*," meaning "not" and "*topos*" meaning "place," "utopia" literally means "no place." Its usage signifies the search for a place that does not yet exist but which ought to be created. Since the 1930s, "utopia" has been linked to the affirmation of hope in the face of barbarism and oppression, making the concept of "hope" utopia's key companion. In gesturing toward a better world yet to be made, the invocation of hope encapsulates what German Marxist philosopher Ernst Bloch described in 1918 as "the spirit of utopia." For Bloch, the principle of hope is the driving impulse of utopian politics. One glimpses this sensibility today in the Zapatista declaration "We will know how to resist to the end. We will know how to hope" (Womack 1999, 283) or in the banner carried at the May Day 2001 demonstration in London that implored participants to "overthrow capitalism—and replace it with something nicer!"

For their part, numerous critical theorists confirmed their allegiance to utopia by revisiting previous revolutionary engagements with the concept. Daniel Bensaid's 1995 *Marx l'intempestif* was the first of these efforts, followed by David Harvey's *Spaces of Hope* (2000) and the *Socialist Register 2000*, which bore the title "Necessary and Unnecessary Utopias" (Panitch and Leys 1999). The more recent collection of essays *Anarchism and Utopianism* (Davis and Kinna 2014) reflects the wide-ranging use of utopia as a central concept in contemporary anarchist thought. Often these utopian injunctions have come with qualifications. In particular, critics distance themselves from a variety of "bad utopias" marked by an elitist tendency to prescribe what a future society ought to look like. Nevertheless, utopia has come to be associated with a reinvigorated politics that boldly push the boundaries of the social imaginary. Drawing on science fiction, architecture, folklore, visual and plastic arts, insurgent histories, and all manner of cultural and political experimentation, this renewed left utopianism implores us to imagine revolutionary transformations without precedent in human social relations, in the interactions between humans and the natural environment, and in the values that animate all dimensions of social life.

Critical deployment of the concept of utopia is usually traced back to Thomas More's 1516 text, *Utopia* (More 1965). Inevitably More's work is deeply marked by its time and by the author's privileged social position. For instance, More operates with profoundly patriarchal assumptions and is untroubled by the moderate use of slavery (though not of a racialized variety). Nonetheless, many recognizably utopian themes animate his text—most notably the vision of an egalitarian society without money and private property. More was indebted to centuries of utopian folklore spanning many cultures, all of which featured similar images of infinite abundance and a life free of suffering and oppression. In the Ancient Greek comedy of Telecleides, for instance, we are offered an image of a society in which "the earth produced no terror and disease... Every torrent flowed with wine, barley-cakes strove with wheat-loves for men's lips... Fishes would come to the house and bake themselves."

With the rise of modern capitalism, utopia took on new significance. Exploitation, urban poverty, colonialism, the factory system, and the slave trade all induced efforts to imagine their undoing. Louis-Sébastien Mercier's 1771 novel *L'an 2440* is among the most inspiring of these in its depiction of a slave revolution that overturns all colonial relations. The heroic figures of an actual slave revolution in Haiti (1791–1804) later gave substance to such utopian visions, which inspired Black surrealist visions of the marvelous throughout the twentieth-century (Kelley 2002, 157–94).

The utopian socialist perspectives and experiments that developed in Europe and America during the nineteenth century all sought to grapple with the "social question" that emerged during the transition to industrial capitalism: why did mass poverty exist in a society experiencing explosive growth in machinery and new technologies, and how could such misery be eliminated? Some, like Henri de Saint-Simon in France and Robert Owen in Britain, celebrated modern machinery and industry for their potential to end poverty, while others were considerably more cautious in this regard. However, all called for principles of cooperation to displace those of competition. And while a number of these socialist critics looked to the state to plan society from above, others promoted the formation of cooperative communities. Indeed, Owen used some of his own fortune as a wealthy manufacturer to establish one such community, known as New Lanark, in Scotland. Similar principles and experiments were also at work in parts of the United States, where an Owenite community called Utopia was founded in Ohio in 1847.

In the *Communist Manifesto*, Marx and Engels famously criticized utopian socialism. Nevertheless, they were far more favorable toward the utopians than is often recalled. As much as they chastised the likes of Owen and Fourier for attempting to conjure up "recipes for the future," they also praised their writings as "full of the most valuable materials for the enlightenment of the working class" (1973, 96). What troubled Marx and Engels most was the utopians' tendency to ignore the central role of workers in their own self-emancipation.

Still, radical utopianism continued to find expression in literature. In 1888, the American socialist Edward Bellamy published his highly influential novel *Looking Backward*, in which a young Bostonian awakens in the year 2000 to a post-capitalist future. Two years later, the English Marxist William Morris brought out *News from Nowhere*, in which a new society emerges from a victorious working-class revolution. These texts, however, were exceptions to a general trend in many Marxist quarters, where a critical approach to utopian socialism hardened into a sterile dogma.

In opposition to utopianism, Marx and Engels argued for a "scientific" socialism, and the concept became the basis for Engels' 1880 text *Socialism: Utopian and Scientific*. By "scientific," they meant that socialist politics should be grounded in actual social-historical movements and struggles rather than in the theoretical speculations of individual critics. By the 1890s, however, notions of "science" had been stripped of their earlier philosophical meanings and were often conflated with mechanical models of cause and effect like those that had come to dominate the natural sciences. As a result, social democratic theorists like Karl Kautsky and Eduard Bernstein frequently insisted that the victory of socialism and the working class was an inevitable product of history's evolutionary laws. Consequently, they encouraged a gradualist and reformist approach that neglected the conscious action of actual human beings. Those who continued to talk of revolutionary will and action—like the Polish-German leftist Rosa Luxemburg—were thus subsequently dismissed as unscientific "utopians." While the initial excitement following the 1917 Russian revolution pointed in a different direction (as can be witnessed through a consideration of John Reed's classic *Ten Days that Shook the World*), the spirit of mechanical determinism began to infiltrate the communist parties as revolution receded and the Stalinist era began.

During the early twentieth century, the spirit of utopia largely resided within parts of the anarchist movement. While Peter Kropotkin's *Mutual Aid: A Factor of Evolution* (1902) is often seen as a key text, his earlier book *Fields, Factories and Workshops* (1898) better embodied the utopian impulse. In that work, Kropotkin advanced a vision of a social order in which people would be relieved of poverty and toil thanks to tools and machinery capable of drastically reducing the time devoted to labor. By the 1930s, Marxists were once again affirming the spirit of utopia.[1] With the defeat of revolutions in Hungary, Germany, Italy, and China (1918–27) followed by the rise of European fascism, a group of critical Marxist thinkers set out to rehabilitate utopianism for revolutionary politics. Essays by Ernst Bloch—particularly "The Fairy Tale Moves on Its Own in Time" (1930) and "Marxism and Poetry" (1935)— invoked utopian folklore and literature as imaginative resources necessary to renew Marxism in the face of European barbarism (Bloch 1988). Bloch's meditations in this area were later expanded into *The Principle of Hope* (1995), a monumental three-volume study in which his notion of *concrete utopia* would receive its fullest elaboration. One finds a more nuanced utopian impulse in the 1930s writings of another German Marxist, Walter Benjamin. For Benjamin, utopian possibilities took the form of fragments from

---

1. Significantly, *The Spirit of Utopia* was the title of an important 1923 volume authored by Ernst Bloch.

the past, which embodied the afterlives of revolutionary dreams and aspirations (Benjamin 1999). A key task for revolutionary politics, he urged, was to reactivate the utopian energies buried in these fragments by bringing them into contact with the struggles of the present. Some of these themes can be found in a less overtly political form in the subsequent writings of "Frankfurt School" theorists like Herbert Marcuse and Theodor Adorno. In particular, Marcuse's writings of the late 1960s and early 1970s stimulated visions of a new society characterized by "the convergence of technology and art and the convergence of work and play" (Marcuse 1970, 68).

Notwithstanding such efforts, left-utopianism barely survived the Second World War and the subsequent Cold War. With the emergence of a global New Left during the 1960s, however, a young generation of radical activists began to seek out a left-wing politics that was distinct from the bureaucratic approaches of communist and social-democratic parties. "Be realistic, demand the impossible," intoned the radical slogan found on walls throughout France during May and June of 1968. Such injunctions captured the utopian impulse that flourished during the mass worker and student uprising of those months. In the heady days of insurgent antiwar, Black Power, and women's liberation movements, utopian themes—embracing anti-racism, feminism, anarchism, and socialism—emerged once again in influential novels like Ursula K. Le Guin's *The Dispossessed* (1974) and Marge Piercy's *Woman on the Edge of Time* (1976). Amid these social upheavals, a utopian cultural politics began to develop, deploying science fiction to depict new forms of social life beyond gender, race, and class hierarchies. These efforts left invaluable legacies in art and cultural production. Nevertheless, in contrast to the 1970s, contemporary utopian art (and theory) tends generally to be disconnected from mass politics.

For left movements, utopia is politically and strategically ambiguous. On the one hand, images of utopia carry a critical charge capable of fueling our imaginative sense of other possible futures. On the other hand, a utopianism detached from real movements can too easily become a purely in-house operation in which artists and intellectuals imagine themselves (rather than the majority of oppressed people) to be the real harbingers of social change. It can become tempting for left-wing currents in the Global North, which often lack any real roots in working-class communities and organizations, to attempt to create spaces (from co-ops to communes) consisting of handfuls of people who imagine that they operate on a higher moral plane than the wider society. These efforts are typically characterized by the substitution of lifestyle choices for real mass organizing. At the same time, much of what passes for mass politics on the contemporary left is often found to be singularly lacking in the utopian impulse. Especially under conditions of neo-liberal assault and the daily grind of parliamentary politics, NGO work and trade union organizing tends to produce a cautious "routinism" hostile to insurgent mobilizations and utopian visions of radical change.

All of this reinforces Ernst Bloch's calls for *concrete utopia*—a revolutionary vision of a world turned upside-down that resists becoming disconnected from the real, living struggles of the present. We need, says Bloch, "to hope materialistically," by which he meant that radicals must envision means of overturning the present social order that remains rooted in and speaks to masses of real people (Bloch 1995, 1, 335). Without utopianism, we will never get there. But the utopianism we need must move to the pulse of the concrete.

SEE ALSO: Commons; Community; Demand; Future; Hope; Politics; Prefiguration; Revolution; Space

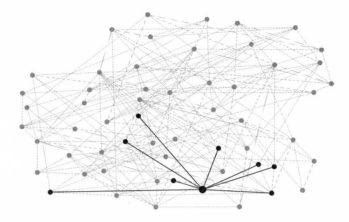

VANGUARD

Alan Shandro

THE WORD "VANGUARD" DERIVES FROM LATE MIDDLE English and originally denoted the foremost part of an advancing army or naval force. Etymologically, it is a shortening of the Old French "*avan(t) garde*" (meaning "before guard"). Current political usages date from the nineteenth and early twentieth centuries. It is sometimes used interchangeably with "avant-garde," though the two terms carry distinct (if overlapping) connotations.

The idea that communists might play the role of vanguard in the class struggle can be traced back to the *Communist Manifesto*, in which they are said to constitute, "practically, the most advanced and resolute section of the working-class parties of every country, that section which pushes forward all the others" while having over the mass of the workers, theoretically, "the advantage of clearly understanding the line of march, the conditions and the ultimate general results of the proletarian movement" (Marx and Engels 1976b, 497). Here "understanding the line of march" establishes a connection between theory and practice in the leadership of the working-class movement. Where "the line of march" is construed teleologically, the corresponding "understanding" has tended to be disparaged as an oracular vision, with the vanguard playing the role of prophet. In line with the *Manifesto*'s hardheaded rhetorical stance against the illusions of utopian socialism, however, the formulation is perhaps more reasonably read as an appreciation that placating the bourgeoisie could never advance the workers' struggles. It was thus incumbent upon those in the vanguard to establish principles of solidarity on a class foundation and dispel the illusion of supra-class solidarity. But if Marx's writing suggested a link between working-class movement practice and the development of theory (and if he thus established a matrix within which political agency could be situated and political leadership exercised), the link would become more rigid with the turn to orthodoxy within the Second International (1889–1914).

For example, Karl Kautsky associated the vanguard with the German Social Democratic Party (SPD), its Marxist theory, and its activists, while at the same time associating it with particular sections of the working class based on their position in the most advanced (productive, concentrated, socialized) forms of capitalist production. According to this position, since the logic of capitalist production transforms particular struggles into a universal one, the position of these most advanced strata bears—in organization, consciousness, and discipline—the universal interest of the whole working class. In contrast, the rear echelons of the movement struggle to disengage from the particularistic claims that diffuse their efforts. Nevertheless, the former were seen to embody the future of the latecomers. It is almost as though, as a result of their consciousness, members of the vanguard transcend their particular circumstances. However, the most advanced strata of the Social Democratic proletariat were not simply workers. They were, for instance, by and large skilled, urban, Protestant, German, male, and so on. For his part, Kautsky failed to address these concrete features. As a result, the "universality" of socialist consciousness donned the particular lenses of the advanced workers. When counterposed to the narrow particularism of the backward strata of the movement, such unity fueled tensions and resentments between workers and abetted bourgeois efforts to divide the movement by separating particular short-term interests from the general interest of the class. Ultimately, the SPD failed to address the latent contradictions within the working-class movement.

Though the metaphor of an advancing column *en march* infused Marxist self-understanding, it is notable that the word "vanguard" (*Avantgarde* in German) did not often figure in Marxist writings. Indeed, the leader-movement relation was more frequently conveyed through the term "representative." In 1898, SPD leader August Bebel counterposed SPD leadership as "the political representative of [a] proletariat" to the individualistic understanding of agency that anarchist "propaganda of the deed" shared with liberalism. Similarly, the word "vanguard" does not appear in the text of the *Communist Manifesto*. However, it does figure (albeit without reference to "consciousness") in the preface to the Russian edition of 1882. There, in the context of the assassination of Alexander II by members of the populist Narodnaya Volya, Marx and Engels note that the tsar no longer figured as the "chief of European reaction" since, holed up in his summer home at Gatschina, he had effectively become a prisoner of the revolution. In contrast, Marx and Engels found that "Russia forms the vanguard of revolutionary action in Europe." This relation is spelled out as follows: "If the Russian Revolution becomes the signal for a proletarian revolution in the West ... the present Russian common ownership of land may serve as the starting point for a communist development." In this usage, "vanguard" denotes the first clash of forces, which gives the signal for a wider revolutionary explosion. Such a role perhaps calls more for courage than for foresight.

The question of the vanguard would come to be posed with particular acuity in tsarist Russia. It is in this context that Lenin could assert in *What Is to Be Done?* that "*the role of vanguard* [Russian:

avangardnyy] *fighter can be fulfilled only by a party that is guided by the most advanced theory.*" In this formulation, the spontaneous working-class movement figured as both the mainspring of socialist agency and as a target of bourgeois ideology and strategy. Contending for hegemony required not only conscious resistance to bourgeois influence but also the capacity to rally potential allies (peasants, oppressed nationalities, etc.) around the workers' struggles. If the logic of the class struggle is refracted through the struggle for hegemony, then shifting circumstances demand that the vanguard readjust theory and adapt practice to account for the shifting terrain of battle. Indeed, for Lenin, the working class constitutes itself as a political force by rallying other forces around itself.

Such an analysis implies that vanguard political agency is multidimensional. Marx tried to understand the struggle for socialism through the construction of the "political form[s]" needed "to work out the economical emancipation of labor." He might have added that the "working out" would always need to be revised in view of altered needs, capacities, and circumstances. As understood by Lenin, the function of the vanguard might be characterized as generating "concrete analysis of the concrete situation" and orchestrating diverse fractions in the political process of "working out." With the advent of the First World War, and as a result of Lenin's analysis of imperialism (1952), the logic of the struggle for hegemony became generalized. And with the Bolsheviks establishing a socialist beachhead in Russia, Lenin's approach spread through working-class and progressive movements worldwide.

Lenin argued that the vanguard's effective intervention in the class struggle depended upon its organization into a political party distinct from the spontaneous working-class movement—hence, "vanguard party," as formulated in *The State and Revolution*: "By educating the workers' party, Marxism educates the vanguard of the proletariat, capable of assuming power and leading the whole people to socialism, of directing and organizing the new system, of being the teacher, the guide, the leader of all the working and exploited people in organizing their social life without the bourgeoisie and against the bourgeoisie" (Lenin 1964a, 409). The distinction between class and party and the apparent identification of the vanguard with the latter elicited criticism from Lenin's adversaries. Invoking a Marxist trope, these responses would come to shape how ideas about the vanguard would be received in much wider circles. The critique involved two claims: first, that the working class, unlike previous exploited classes, was capable of autonomous revolutionary activity. Second, not only does the working class come to understand its emancipation as entailing the end of capitalism and the construction of a socialist society, this end can be accomplished only through the independent activity of the working class itself. When this thesis is counterposed to the notion of "vanguard," the latter is seen as providing a rationale for the subordination of workers to the authority of revolutionary intellectuals. Trotsky famously outlined this position when he argued that, when followed to its logical conclusion, "the party organization substitutes itself for the party [which at the time he equated with the class], the Central Committee substitutes itself for the party organization, and finally a dictator substitutes himself for the Central Committee."

Framed in this way, the Leninist vanguard party appears to be central to the development and degeneration of the Bolshevik revolution and the Soviet Union. However, much of the rhetorical force of the critique depends upon an ambiguity that can be discerned once the question is raised as to whether proletarian self-emancipation is a generalization of individual self-consciousness or requires distinct concepts (e.g., "vanguard" and "masses") to come to grips with the collective character of the process. In the former case, self-emancipation is inconsistent with any attempt at influencing the direction of workers' movements. If, however, self-emancipation refers to a collective process, the notion of a vanguard refers fundamentally not to a particular organization or group of individuals, but to the performance of certain political functions in the movement of the class. In principle, any member of the masses could perform such functions.

In *Can the Bolsheviks Retain State Power?*, for example, Lenin praises the soviet as "an organizational form for the vanguard, i.e., for the most class-conscious, most energetic and most progressive section of the *oppressed* classes, the workers and peasants . . . by means of which the vanguard of the oppressed classes can elevate, train, educate and lead *the entire vast mass* of these classes" (Lenin 1964b, 103–4). Correlatively, the socialist consciousness that informs the vanguard is to be understood not as a set of propositions belonging to a certain group but rather as the capability of adjusting the socialist project to the changing circumstances of the class struggle— something that could only develop through the dynamic interaction of vanguard and masses, consciousness and spontaneity.

While "vanguard" and its variants are sometimes employed (usually, though not always, pejoratively) in the context of other social movements, these usages are largely derivative of Marxist debates. The recent neologism "vanguardism" (carrying the sense of sectarianism) reflected disillusion with the failure of would-be Maoist and Trotskyite "vanguards" formed during the social and political upheavals of the 1960s (see Camejo 1984). But where "sectarianism" invoked a distinction between self-absorbed sect and mass-oriented party, "vanguardism" insinuated that sect-like narcissism was implicit in the very notion of a vanguard project. Again, Gramsci is praised in Hardt and Negri's Occupy-era *Commonwealth* for supposedly understanding that "the vanguard of industrial workers can no longer serve as the subject of an active proletarian revolution" and for questioning "the desirability of the worker vanguard" (Hardt and Negri 2009, 366). In this view, revolutionary agency is no longer consistent with any type of representation, any vanguard acting on behalf of others. In its place, what's now required is the direct action of the multitude. The tension between representation and direct action informing the Negri-Hardt stance echoes both the anarchist positions critiqued by Bebel and the objections addressed to Lenin's conceptualization of the vanguard.

Since the mid-nineteenth century, the term "avant-garde" has been applied to cutting-edge artists or works of art that take a critical stance vis-à-vis the conformism of mainstream art and culture. Incorporated into the critique of consumer capitalism by Theodor Adorno and others, this connotation might suggest a fusion of artistic provocation and political commitment. As Adorno wrote in "Commitment," "Even 'vanguard' critics . . . accuse so-called abstract texts of a lack of provocation, of social aggressivity" (Adorno 1982, 301). To the extent that both the Leninist injunction to concrete analysis and the notion of self-emancipation might convey a sense of politics as artistic practice, they share an affinity with this sense of "avant-garde," especially in bohemian and artistic circles. Established in Greenwich Village in 1935 (the Popular Front era), the Village Vanguard became a venue for jazz, blues, and folk music as well as politically conscious poetry, comedy, and commentary. The venue also enabled Black, white, and Latino people to mix and mingle and evoked both the affinity and the tensions underlying the artistic and political senses of the term. During the 1960s, the Village Vanguard featured a Monday "Speak Out" on controversial political and social subjects of the day, though the tenor of political controversy had lost its radical edge in the wake of McCarthyism.

Where the distinction that informs the Leninist notion of "vanguard" contrasts the spontaneous movement of the workers to the conscious agency of those at the forefront of their class, the distinction at work in the artistic sense of "avant-garde" is between the critically thinking (and therefore anti-authoritarian) artist-intellectual and the passively conformist or even authoritarian masses. If the relation between spontaneous and conscious activity permits us to think of leadership as a process of weaving together disparate forces into a community of struggle and thereby inflecting the direction of the struggle, the avant-garde acts out its critically innovative character not really as leadership at all but as a kind of internal exile from the stifling conformism of capitalist society. When the former is read in terms of the latter's connotations, the notion of leadership simply vanishes in a puff of smoke and mirrors—hence the lyrical cynicism of David Rovics' satirical song "Vanguard": "I am the vanguard of the masses / And all of you should just follow me / And if you doubt my analysis / You must be in the petty bourgeoisie" (Rovics 2003).

SEE ALSO: Agency; Conspiracy; Demand; Leadership; Representation; Revolution; Victory; Violence

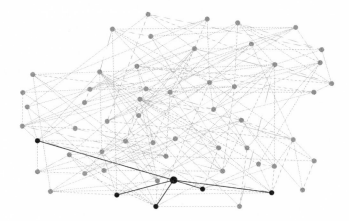

VICTORY

Heather Hax

THE *OXFORD ENGLISH DICTIONARY* DEFINES "VICTORY" AS "an act of defeating an enemy or opponent in a battle, game, or other competition." The etymological root of the word—"*vincere*"—means "to conquer." Through its common association with the word "win," "victory" also invokes the Old English "winnan," which means to "strive, contend." Meanwhile, the term's Germanic roots suggest that winning a victory requires that one "subdue and take possession of, acquire."

A recent *Waging Nonviolence* article asked how more social movements can "win victories like same sex marriage." According to Mark Engler and Paul Engler (2014b), the fight for same-sex marriage in America was victorious because activists organized tirelessly on multiple fronts, won the war of public opinion, and secured incremental gains that led to "victories [that] started coming in furious succession." In this view, shifting the tide of public opinion can lead to sweeping changes in public policy. As a result, declaring victory becomes a question of strategy. Occupy Wall Street claimed victory simply for having existed as long as it did (Meyerson 2011). Many contemporary social movements declare victory when they meet the goals of a campaign. A victory can also be proclaimed when a movement successfully draws attention to a social problem that had previously gone unnoticed. But while such developments should be celebrated, do they really constitute "victory" in the sense implied by the term's definition?

After the revolutions of 1848, Karl Marx and Friedrich Engels (1850) addressed the Communist League and spoke of victory. "It goes without saying," they said, "that in the bloody conflicts to come . . . it will be the workers, with their courage, resolution and self-sacrifice, who will be chiefly responsible for achieving victory." The challenge, they argued, was to keep the bourgeois democrats with whom the workers stood in coalition from usurping that victory in the final instance. In order to achieve this aim, the proletariat needed to temper "the victory euphoria and enthusiasm for the new situation which follow every successful street battle, with a cool and cold-blooded analysis of the situation and with undisguised mistrust of the new government." Concretely, this meant that, "from the very moment of victory the workers' suspicion must be directed no longer against the defeated reactionary party but against their former ally, against the party which intends to exploit the common victory for itself." In this view, accomplishing revolutionary victory involves shrewd, long-term, and flexible strategizing. This means that those who were once allies might at some later point become adversaries. In other words, incremental victories change the field and create a new array of antagonists in a dialectical procession of ever-evolving strategy—that is, until the game has been played through until its end.

In an exchange with Joseph Stalin, Young Communist League staff propagandist Ivan Philipovich observed that the "final victory of Socialism implies the solution of the external contradictions," which meant that the Soviet Union needed to be "fully guaranteed against intervention and, consequently, against the restoration of capitalism" (1938). Similarly, when reflecting on the dynamics of the Sino-Japanese war, Mao Zedong warned against the self-defeating tendencies that arose from premature declarations of victory. In particular, he condemned the temptation to declare victory on the basis of objectively improved social conditions that did not yet amount to complete revolutionary transformation. For Mao (1992), "final victory" required both "protracted war" and internal cooperation and organization among the people. When modifications of the system yielded important gains, it was necessary to confront both complacency and the defeatist belief that no further gains could be made. He also specifically warned against the defeatist assertion that "final victory" was impossible and that China's subjugation to Japanese armies was inevitable.[1]

Similarly, in a set of Party directives penned in 1965 during the early stages of the Guinea-Bissau War of Independence against Portuguese colonial rule, Amilcar Cabral (1974) urged his followers to "tell no lies" and "claim no easy victories." Significantly, his comments began by delimiting the field upon which victories could be won to the material realm. "Always bear in mind," he wrote, "that the people are not fighting for ideas, for the things in anyone's head. They are fighting for material benefits, to live better and in peace, to see their lives go forward, to guarantee the future of their children."

In these examples, "victory" means correctly identifying one's adversaries and eradicating them so as to ensure that they do not threaten the society one is struggling to create. Although "victory" is still announced when a discrete battle is won, it is understood that such battles are ultimately in the service of a larger, revolutionary war. However, even though victories were declared in several communist revolutions during the twentieth century, eliminating

---

1.   Indeed, the Chinese revolutionary forces were able to defeat the Japanese imperialists. Nevertheless, the Chinese system could best be described as "state-capitalist" rather than as socialist or communist.

external threats and achieving total social transformation—the "final victory"—remained elusive.

By the mid-twentieth century and with the rise of new social movements, "victories" came to be conceived very differently. New social movements arose in response to a labor movement that had failed to include (and at times actively excluded) women and people of color from their efforts (Leary 2005). Additionally, organized labor had forged an increasingly cozy relationship with management and shifted its focus away from fundamentally challenging the economic order. In response, new social movements created a model of organizing that began from the varied experiences of oppressed people and located deeply embedded hierarchies in the fabric of everyday life. Some aimed to prefigure the world they wanted by adopting practices that challenged the entrenched hierarchical relations that seemed to make victory so elusive (Day 2005). In practice, however, many of these movements restricted themselves to single-issue campaigns demanding greater inclusion in mainstream institutions (Melucci 1996). Subsequently, much of this organizing was criticized for failing to fundamentally uproot systems of domination. From a revolutionary standpoint, their victories seemed partial and their politics complacent.

It is in this political landscape that "victory" has come overwhelmingly to mean winning a campaign or securing a concrete change of some sort. In her contribution to *Beautiful Trouble: A Toolbox for Revolution*, Janice Fine defines a campaign as "a series of tactics deployed over a specified period of time, each of which builds the strength of the organization and puts increasing pressure on the target until it gives in on your specific demands. . . . A campaign is not endless; it has a beginning, middle and end. It ends, ideally, in a specific victory" (2014, 52).

Often, these campaigns claim victory through legislative change or reform in mainstream social institutions. The most lauded victories of this kind in the late-twentieth and early twenty-first century have involved substantial human rights gains for marginalized groups—including, but not limited to, the Civil Rights, Women's Liberation, and LGBTIQ movements. The Environmental Justice movement has also laid claim to important victories over the past thirty years, including the establishment of stricter oversight and regulation on pollution and conservation by environmental regulation agencies. Many of these advances have been secured through the work of social movement organizations and the growth of a huge nonprofit and nongovernmental organization sector. Taken together, these victories have had a profound impact on people's lives. However, each has amounted to a limited "victory" rather than to "victory" per se.

It has been argued that however much reforms and direct services relieve the suffering caused by an injustice, they do little to change the system that caused the problem in the first place. In fact, such reforms may even *bolster* the very systems they are meant to change—making final "victory" ever more elusive. For example, in the Turbulence Collective's anthology *What Would It Mean to Win?*, Paul Sumburm warns,

> After years of drawing attention to the facts of climate change, suddenly the issue is everywhere, and everyone, it seems, is calling for action to reduce greenhouse gas emissions. In some senses this is a rare victory, a response both to the pressure of activists and the scientific consensus channeled powerfully by the United Nation's Intergovernmental Panel on Climate Change. But, of course, some see the potential to expand the sphere of capital's influence: most mainstream talk is of market-friendly technological solutions, "carbon trading" and oil companies dabbling in renewable energy. (2010, 27)

For the most part, the victories that newer social movements have secured have been far from revolutionary. Even in the wake of profound victories such as those won by the Civil Rights, Women's, LGBTIQ, and Environmental movements, underlying mechanisms of domination have remained intact. As a result (and echoing the position advanced earlier by Cabral), radicals have been reluctant to claim victories since doing so might draw attention away from revolutionary aspirations. According to *Getting Past Capitalism* author Cynthia Kaufman, "There is a cultural norm on the left of being afraid to declare victory, which is related to the binary of reform/revolution." Specifically, "whereas reformists are winning small gains, revolutionaries don't want people to be satisfied with those small victories because they worry this will lead to acceptance of the bigger picture of capitalist domination so they find a way to turn every victory into a defeat" (Jensen 2014). Movement-based author Rebecca Solnit (2012) echoed Kaufman's concern when, in a letter addressed to her "dismal allies on the US left," she lamented how she "constantly encounter[s] a response that presumes the job at hand is to figure out what's wrong, even when dealing with an actual victory, or a constructive development."

As Mueller and Sol (2007) note, "It is nice to have our victories once in a while." However, this can result in a related but inverse tendency in which radicals become self-congratulatory by declaring victory prematurely (Dixon 2014). This dynamic arises in part from the tendency to prioritize tactics over strategy. For example, as a result of the fetishization of tactics like blockades or consensus-based decision-making, their very use is taken to be a measure of victory.

In the wake of the victorious blockade disruption of the 1999 WTO meetings in Seattle, global justice activists sought to reproduce these blockades all over the globe. Writing about the anti-G8 protests in Heiligendamm, Germany in 2007, summit protesters noted that their blockades were "indeed a victory" (Mueller and Sol 2007). Yet this victory was measured in terms of two criteria: first, for their disruptive nature, and second, as "a 'reconstitutive moment' of the conflictive potential of global movements." Upon reflection, however, what seemed like a victory for the protesters turned out to be a victory for the G8 as well. Although the blockades were victorious, they failed to fundamentally delegitimize the G8. That is, the G8 was still able to establish itself as the victor— the force that could solve the problems of neoliberal globalization the protesters had highlighted (Mueller and Sol 2007).

In a more recent example, several social movement theorists and movement participants have noted that Occupy Wall Street's primary power was to prefigure participatory democracy on the ground instead of engaging with the powers that be to demand reform (Graeber 2011; Barber 2012). Tracing "the anarchist DNA of Occupy," Dana Williams argued that, in its prefigurative practices of consensus and the (temporary) occupation of space, "Occupy has already enjoyed many victories, convincing countless people of the potential for radical social change" (2012, 20). In light of this, it is wise to ask what the strategic implications of claiming victory can be.

According to social movement scholars like Devashree Gupta (2009), declaring victory can yield mixed results for movements. On the one hand, a victory (or series of victories) can help to drum up support. This can expand the capacity of the social movement, which in turn can help to build its power and effectiveness. According to James Jasper, "Movement groups often expand their goals if they are victorious, and trim them if they meet unexpected resistance" (2004, 8). Likewise, declaring victory can carry tremendous psychological value by energizing a movement and its participants or keeping them from burning out (Solnit 2012). On the other hand, declaring victory can lead to what Gupta has called the "satiety" effect (2009). If movements declare a series of victories, supporters may conclude that they've got matters under control. As a result, a strategically misguided declaration of victory may decrease the support a movement might otherwise receive.

Like a litmus test, the evolving use of "victory" seems indicative of social-movement aims and accomplishments. In this way, it restages the historic debate about the tension between revolution and reform. However, since the Revolution seems a long way off, contemporary declarations of "victory" are significant primarily on account of their strategic value for morale and for creating openings for further strategic intervention. In "The Shock of Victory," David Graeber asks radicals to appreciate when they are victorious—even if the victories are solely tactical—and to understand that their interventions are part of a long historical arc. "The question is how to break the cycle of exaltation and despair and come up with some strategic visions (the more the merrier) about how these victories build on each other, to create a cumulative movement towards a new society" (2007, 12). In this view, victories themselves can serve to resolve the tension between revolution and reform—providing that movement participants are willing and able to use them to stimulate a grander vision.

SEE ALSO: Ideology; Revolution; Sovereignty; Vanguard; War

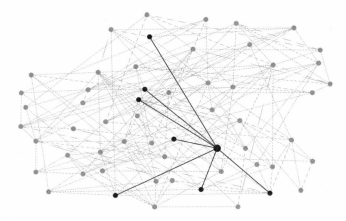

VIOLENCE

Peter Gelderloos

"Violence" may be one of the most contested, ambiguous terms in the radical lexicon today. Among its various deployments, one can find normative usages of both the favorable and proscriptive variety, failed attempts to build consensus on a literal usage, and even rejections of the term itself. Activists who advocate nonviolence or pacifism give the term a normative usage. Here violence is conceived as an unnecessary evil—either ethically impermissible or strategically counterproductive—that must be banished from social movements and replaced with some positive, transformative form of nonviolence.

The nonviolence guidelines published by Veterans for Peace (Occupy Winston Salem 2011) adequately sum up the behaviors to be prohibited under this normative conception. Aside from the obvious ban on physically attacking anyone, the guidelines include several significant points. "We will not vandalize or destroy property"; "We will not run or make threatening motions"; "We will not use or carry alcohol or illegal drugs"; "We will not insult, swear, or attack others." For proponents of nonviolence, property destruction has long been considered a form of violence. The subsequent inclusion by Veterans for Peace of running, drinking, and swearing helps to reveal the underlying logic.

In this usage, "violence" and "disorder" become synonymous, while "nonviolence" becomes orderliness. The final two guidelines in the Veterans for Peace list specifically address the problem of conflicting conceptions of acceptable behavior and the need to impose a unitary order: "As members of a nonviolent action, we will follow the directions of the designated coordinators" and, "if an individual has a serious disagreement with the organizers of the action, the individual will withdraw from the action" (Occupy Winston Salem 2011).

The order imposed by this framework privileges the normative and coercive functions of the state. The prohibition on running and "threatening motions" can reasonably be read as a law enforcement–friendly measure. Similarly, the ban on "weapons of any kind" is in practice only applied to protesters. Though many advocates of the normative rejection of "violence" may envision a world in which the police are disarmed or even absent, their evident priority in the short-term is disarming movement participants and avoiding hostilities with the police. In fact, in heterogeneous crowds where not everyone has pledged to uphold the guidelines (or played any role in drafting them), "organizers" have occasionally turned dissidents over to the police. Within the Occupy Movement, the physical assault of "violent" protesters by "nonviolent" ones became a familiar phenomenon, though it had already appeared in prior decades (Gelderloos 2013).

This normative conception was given further expression during the 2011 occupation of Plaça de Catalunya in Barcelona, when self-proclaimed organizers prohibited the conversion of a grassy section of the plaza into an urban garden. As a violation of the civic behavior ordinances, the guerrilla gardening was—in their own words—an act of violence (CrimethInc. 2011). Unknowingly they echoed the logic of the federal judge who handed down sentences to protesters in 2002 following an act of civil disobedience during the annual SOA Watch protests. From the judge's perspective, these protestors could not claim the mantle of nonviolence since they had carried out an illegal act.

Many radicals attempt to contain such extreme, legalistic, and state-privileging definitions of violence. Some argue that property destruction does not constitute violence. Others make the same case for self-defense. The ACME Collective, which participated in the black bloc that wreaked havoc during the 1999 Seattle WTO protests, wrote: "We contend that property destruction is not a violent activity unless it destroys lives or causes pain in the process. By this definition, private property—especially corporate private property—is itself infinitely more violent than any action taken against it" (ACME Collective 1999). Such rhetoric is still based on a normative, proscriptive conception of violence. However, it tries to limit the definition in order to legitimize a wider range of tactics.

A more developed outgrowth of such normative accounts can be found among critics of structural violence. These commentators equate violence with harm and, rather than focusing on protest tactics, draw attention to the invisibilized yet far greater harm perpetuated by dominant structures through "structural violence." In a typical example, the call-out for an activist conference in western Michigan in early 2015 mentioned the need to "investigate the often unseen and unnamed realities of structural violence that exist within economic policy, police departments, the military and the Prison Industrial Complex" (Change U 2015). Similarly, the anarchist poster that appeared in Barcelona following the riots that took place during the September 2010 general strike recounted how "the greatest violence was returning to normality." Though violence in this sense is still presented in a negative light, it ceases to be exceptional and is instead viewed as a constant reality in capitalist society.

Consequently, people are given more leeway in choosing how to fight back.

At the opposite end of the normative spectrum, one finds moralizing claims that valorize the violence of the oppressed. Such usages abound in the writings of groups like the Informal Anarchist Federation and Conspiracy Cells of Fire. A communiqué for an April 2012 attack on several banks in Poland (carried out in solidarity with Lambros Foundas, Conspiracy Cells of Fire, and prisoners in Chile and Indonesia) reads in part: "Violence is an integral part of our lives, concealed behind a mask of abstract social relations. Pushed to the ghettos of poverty, filling the prison cells, residing in the slums of the Third World. . . . We will come from darkness of the night and attack state and capitalist targets, every time more violently and with a stronger belief in the rightness of our actions" (Night Aurora 2012).

The clash between these two contradictory ethics became the subject of a witty 2009 anti-election poster that could be seen throughout Athens: "Sometimes, not doing anything is the greatest violence of all. Don't vote."

Finally there is the position that violence is such an ambiguous, moralistic, and media-driven concept that anyone interested in challenging dominant relations should never use the word in a categorical or analytical way (Gelderloos 2013). Indeed, the original uses of the term were both normative and subjective. The earliest uses of "violence" date back to the Old French of the thirteenth century and refer to vehemence or rash emotion. And though this "emotion" shared philological bonds with "riot" ("émeute"), "violence" was not yet a political category since it referred primarily to personal affect. In this original sense, one could kill peacefully or speak violently.

All that began to change when figures like Thoreau, Tolstoy, and Gandhi embraced nonviolence as a political position, thus forcing "violence" to take on categorical weight. According to Tolstoy, "To use violence is impossible; it would only cause reaction. To join the ranks of the Government is also impossible—one would only become its instrument. One course therefore remains—to fight the

Government by means of thought, speech, actions, life" (Tolstoy 1900). One might ask why these thinkers chose to use an ambiguous and morally weighted word when more precise, legalistic terms also existed. Still, the term "violence" was not as charged a hundred years ago as it is today. Radicals of previous generations were less inclined to debate what did or did not constitute violence. Both the ruling class and the underclasses spoke about class war with an implicitly violent language and evidently without the need to define their proposals as either "violent" or "nonviolent."

Nowadays, statements by the likes of Warren Buffet—who famously said that "there's class warfare, all right, but it's my class, the rich class, that's making war, and we're winning" (Stein 2006)—remain shocking and underreported. However, bourgeois newspapers at the end of the nineteenth century often explicitly advocated violence against strikers, protesters, and others. Radicals, for their part, advocated returning the favor. Although anarchists like Kropotkin and Malatesta painted a peaceful vision of anarchist struggle, it was one that nevertheless had to pass through violence since the ruling classes would never relinquish their power. In their usage, "violence" retained its negative, moralistic connotations; however, they accepted it as a necessary and justified evil. In contrast, anarchists like Luigi Galleani, Johann Most, and Jules Bonnot proactively advocated violence against the ruling class.

In *The End of Anarchism?*, Galleani (1925) advanced a negative, a neutral, and a positive usage of the term in rapid succession. These included the violence of "political and economic privilege," a "violent shock" to the senses, and violence as synonymous with a "rebellious act." The latter usage, however, stood as an exception, since Galleani (like most writers of his age) tended to use "violence" primarily to mean unjust force or to convey something shocking. Advocating the assassination of kings and the expropriation of banks, Galleani clearly admitted that such acts constituted "violence." However, he almost exclusively reserved the word for the actions of oppressors. Consider, for example, his insistence that the proletariat "repel violence by force of arms."

Similarly, in their short-lived daily newspaper *Izvestia*, the workers and sailors of the failed 1921 Kronstadt rebellion against Lenin and the New Economic Policy identified "violence" with "the dictatorship of the communist party with their Cheka and their state capitalism." However, they did not foreswear bloodshed. Referring to the "third revolution" inaugurated by the mutiny and prior to the descent of the Red Army, they wrote: "The first step has been taken . . . without a shot or a drop of blood, the spilling of which the workers have no need and which they will only spill in the case of legitimate defense" (Voline 1947).

For their part, Lenin and Trotsky used even more explicit language. In a warning to Kronstadt aired on Radio Moscow, they exclaimed: "If you persist, you will be riddled with bullets like partridges. . . . Don't you know that the soldiers of [White Army leader] General Wrangel, taken to Constantinople, died there in the thousands, like bugs, of hunger and sickness? The same fate awaits you if you don't come immediately to your senses." (Voline 1947). Though neither Lenin and Trotsky nor the workers and sailors of Kronstadt tended to qualify their own acts as "violent," they were far from shy when describing the methods they advocated. Violence, it seems, rested on whether or not the cause was righteous. Consequently, the use of the term reflected a degree of moralism. Nevertheless, violence was also understood to be a fact of life and an inevitable part of the revolution.

Through World War I, the rise of fascism, and the ultimate triumph of democracy, the bourgeoisie won the class war. Most of what had previously been referred to as "violence" became invisible and, with the defeat of an anticapitalist imaginary, structural violence became natural. Media conditioning and popular acceptance of structural violence paved the way for "violence" to become a category concerned solely with the abnormal. These conditioning processes also informed government strategies and police procedures. When the US Civil Rights Movement entered the media spectacle during the 1950s and 1960s, police quickly learned to avoid dramatic confrontations and opt instead for invisible forms of repression. According to some movement veterans, "whites began to understand the tactic, and nonviolence became less powerful" (SNCC Project Group). Ineffectiveness notwithstanding, the media narrative gave the movement's nonviolence credit for transformations that had not actually taken place.

By the 1980s, new social movements began referring back to the spectacular narrative. Rather than learning directly from previous movements and establishing an intergenerational continuity, they responded instead to the expansive definition of "violence" authored by the forces of law and disseminated by the media. This elite intervention did not only affect pacifists. The spectacular, vanguardist armed groups of the 1960s and 1970s, for instance, played their part by effectively performing the new idea of violence that the pacifists opposed. Here, "violence" became the mark of abnormal extremism. And though these groups followed in the tradition of "armed agitation," there were some important differences.

"Armed agitation" was a form of struggle developed by anarchists in France, Spain, and Argentina during the 1920s. As distinct from centralized military strategies, armed agitation was carried out in urban or rural settings by small affinity groups that did not view themselves as either a party or a vanguard. Instead, they sought to support class struggle by expropriating money, arming the population, carrying out sabotage, and creating mechanisms of collective self-defense. They maintained a horizontal, complementary relationship with other forms of struggle like strikes, social centers, and neighborhood assemblies.

In the 1960s, Marxist-Leninists became predominant in the movements where armed agitation was used. A mediatic few discarded the horizontal relationship with the class and declared themselves the vanguard. Their performance of violence-as-extremism won them the media attention necessary to claim a leading role within the ongoing social struggles and allowed the media to replace complex movements with a spectacular narrative featuring easily identifiable antagonists. Fifty years later, groups like the Red Army Faction still dominate official histories of those decades.

A legacy of such groups is that as soon as the word "violence" comes up, someone will invariably question the sanity of bombings or assassinations. The debate takes on neurotic tone, as activists ostensibly deliberating about strategy express anxieties about how they will be portrayed in the media. By sharing a mutual concern for "violence," the media traps dissidents in a virtual conversation that privileges elite values and perpetuates historical amnesia. In contrast, recovering the history of violence enables radicals to refuse bourgeois morality and mediatic spectacle so that we might re-create a culture of struggle with our own history, language, social relations, and all the tactics—both creative and destructive—that have defined our movements.

SEE ALSO: Class; Domination; Love; Politics; Revolution; Vanguard; War

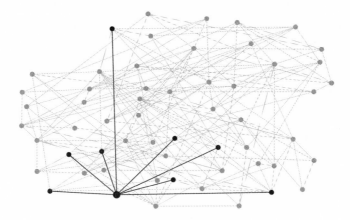

WAR

Neil Balan

DESCRIBING WAR AS "ACTUAL, INTENTIONAL, AND widespread armed conflict between political communities" (Orend 2008) fails to grasp how contemporary state militaries (let alone insurgents or activists) understand the term. While the *Oxford English Dictionary* defines "war" as a state of armed conflict between different countries or between different groups within a country or state, it also defines it as "a state of competition or hostility between different people or groups" and as "a sustained campaign against an undesirable situation." Beyond belligerent armed confrontation, the latter two definitions imply abstract, indiscrete, and nonlethal measures. In English, "war" derives from "*were*," which follows from the French "*guerre*," the Frankish "*werra*" ("riot or disturbance"), and the older Germanic Saxon words "*werran*" and "*verwirren*" ("to confuse and perplex"; "to bring into confusion"). This etymology suggests a general condition of things being out of sorts. Old English roots also link "war" to the word "*gewim*" ("struggle" or "strife"), from the Latin "*bellum*." The turn toward French and German variants through the course of the term's development reflected an effort to avoid ambiguity with the Latin "*bello*" ("beautiful")—though both "*bello*" and "*bellum*" are deployed in state-centric "just war" theory and customary war law (*jus ad bellum*, "right to war"; *jus in bello*, as "acceptable conduct or means of war").

War is acute, "kinetic," and lethal, but it is also ambient, slow, and difficult to discern; its hostility and violence are often justified as humane, proportionate, and restrained "lesser evils" (Weizman 2012). War may be conducted against indefinite nouns—drugs, terror, poverty, the environment—but wars waged against people, populations, and communities tend to remain undeclared. Contemporary military philosophy relies on semiotic camouflage to obscure martial violence. Indexed to intentionally vague modifiers like "contingency" and "stability," doctrine manuals on adaptive dispersed operations (Canadian Forces 2011) and on counterinsurgency (US Army and US Marine Corps 2014) unbind "war" from conventional battlefields while helping it to rhetorically disappear into a continuum of security and policing. Irregular war is normalized in military doctrine. Drones, data, and derivatives allow for new targeting practices that individualize war and make it a "manhunt" (Gregory 2014, 11; Chamayou 2011). Military intellectuals now admit that reciprocal war between states is actually an aberration. Indeed, the assumed sovereign state prerogative to monopolize war is more fiction than reality, as "atypical" engagements reveal themselves to be the norm (Gorka and Kilcullen 2011, 16–17).

The left, meanwhile, has its own theories of war. Marx envisioned that class struggle would end in a brutal "coming upheaval" that would pit "bodies against bodies" (Marx 2009). Maoist revolutionary war and people's war—campaigns waged first as *guerrilla* warfare before scaling up to become society-wide military struggle—follow from this tradition. Frantz Fanon took these insights to their logical conclusion when describing the "bare reality" of decolonization as a war waged against colonial power (Fanon 1963, 2). For his part, Gramsci introduced the distinction between the "war of position" and the "war of maneuver" (1971), thus broadening the means by which hegemony might be challenged. Gramsci understood these terms sequentially as part of a wider, two-stage process of insurrection. Given the complexities of capitalism and its naturalization as a system of power relations, a wider and longer-term cultural struggle (the war of position) was first required to prepare society for revolutionary transformation (the war of maneuver).

Later, Foucault traced the emergence of war as a rationality of government in modern liberal societies (Foucault 2003, 46–47). Modeled in part upon earlier forms of pastoral power (in which the clergy worked to shape the earthly conduct of their flock in the interest of saving their souls), this rationality also developed through biomedical conceptions of disease and contamination and through the boomerang effects of colonial occupations (which subsequently induced forms of "internal colonialism" within liberal states). The "peace" achieved in this way ultimately amounted to social war pursued by other means (Foucault 2003, 48; Clausewitz 1976, 87). In contrast, Gilles Deleuze and Felix Guattari's (1986) elaboration of the "war machine" aimed at calling the state's monopoly on war into question. As a dynamic of deterritorialization, the war machine is not about waging war per se; instead, it describes an assemblage of relations between people, their environments, and their forms of life that undoes the striations of state form. But while the deterritorializing dynamics of the war machine are common to all, its energies are also susceptible to capture. As a result, its intensity is perpetually under threat of being marshaled by state forces to organize, mobilize, and govern populations.

Resurgent indigenous movements like Idle No More and the Indigenous Nationhood Movement reveal that "war" remains an

466 | KEYWORDS FOR RADICALS

important means of describing settler colonialism, occupation, direct and indirect killing, and land expropriation (Waziyatawin 2010, 193; Ward 2014). Indigenous activists (and especially those working in the Haudenosaunee tradition) argue for waging war in holistic terms—though with disagreement concerning the types of social, civil, and military tactics necessary to its conduct (Alfred and Lowe 2005; Hill 2009). A revolutionary pan-Onkwehón:we, "indigenous 'north amerikan'" organization, Onkwehón:we Rising "explicitly mobilizes to undertake indigenous national liberation and struggle against colonization, genocide, and ecocide in Occupied Turtle Island." In their words, primitive accumulation and ecological destruction are manifestations of "the imperialist war machine." The group's glossary alludes to *rotiskenhrakete* ("a warrior tasked with carrying the burden of peace"), *Wasáse* ("war dance,"), warrior societies, and Mohawk and Cree terms of warfare. Throughout, the act of making war is implied but expressed in terms of decolonization, mobilization, struggle, and revolution. In many ways, the group's allusion to "war" suggests less about the offensive measures of indigenous movements than it does about the need to make state, capitalist, and legal procedures intelligible as measures of war incorporated into a normal continuum of social operations.

Such a framing makes clear that, today, war is always-already civil war. Nevertheless, contemporary discussions on the left concerning efficacy, outcomes, and the "diversity of tactics" tend to oppose more aggressive types of militancy (including armed struggle) with methods that are no less antagonistic but are considered to be less explicitly hostile. War, as civil war, remains a description of social reality rather than a practice through which to shape it. A noun rather than a verb, it is the state in which we find ourselves rather than the thing we do to get out of it. Despite the multiple expressions of war that constitute contemporary reality, radicals remain less likely to wage civil war than they are to name it while remaining its target.

Between 1999 and 2001, the anonymous French insurrectionist group Tiqqun released a series of tracts in which they foregrounded the state of civil war. Distilling the concept to its point of greatest abstraction, they associated it with "the free play between forms-of-life" in an era when sovereign state power was waning under the uneven flows of neoliberal globalization (Tiqqun 2010, 32–33). Like Foucault, they sought to "show how civil war continues even when it is said to be absent or provisionally brought under control" through means of an "*armed* peace" that makes it "impercept-ible" (60, 199). Proceeding along similar lines, Subcommandante Marcos of the Zapatistas described "the Fourth World War" as the new form of total war waged with military assets and neoliberal capital "at any moment, in any place, under any circumstances" (2001). Under such conditions, "everyone is a part, there are no neutrals, you are either an ally or you are an enemy." War thus becomes a corollary to security and police, blurring interior and exterior jurisdictions (Hardt and Negri 2004, 20). It is no longer an exceptional condition but a perpetual "active mechanism that constantly creates and reinforces the present global order" (21). The global "war on terror" (now re-anointed as overseas contingency operations) extends this logic: "This War on Terrorism requires the passive support of all those who have not yet been 'assessed' as terrorists. First they come for the most radical. Eventually they'll come for you" (Gelderloos 2009). Further, "even those of us in ap-parently open and peaceful countries are deeply involved in a war. It is a social and a political war. . . . It is a war between the includ-ed and the excluded" (Seaweed 2009, 1). Insofar as we internalize these conditions, civil war becomes a local and global collection of dividing practices producing and sustaining "new apartheids" (Žižek 2008, 423–24). Like post-Fordist "just in time" production, war is now flexible, instantaneous, and incipient. "No longer punc-tual, like a battle. It's on low boil all the time" (Massumi 2010).

At a time when imagining radical action is at a crossroads, civil war poses a conundrum. If we are all subject to its asymmetric pro-cedures, then what are we to make of the egregious corporeal vio-lence of "real" wars? Are we at risk of conflating "war" with force or coercion, or of reducing it to mere metaphor? If everything every-where is war, how do we recognize the experience of those whose lives are marked by grievous high-intensity violence? Austerity, ecological destruction, racialized policing, gentrification: these *are* different theaters of operation that constitute today's civil wars, yet we may avoid describing them as such. The way out of this trap is to acknowledge that this is a fundamental element of the civil war's psychological dimension, where "shock and awe" preempts experiments in fighting on a continuum, building solidarity across territorial enclosures, and developing tactical counter-conducts. Such counter-conducts include occupying a physical land base, whether through temporary measures like the Occupy Movement or through the more concerted efforts of indigenous communities. It may be about ongoing actions to challenge racial profiling, stop immigrant detention and deportation, and ensure access to essential services for undocumented people. It may also mean revoking "nonviolence," since bellicosity and hostility need not mean guns and bombs. Different types of violence must be contextualized and addressed on their own terms; they are all parts of civil war.

Though they are now significantly curtailed, the war powers we hold in common are by no means annulled. Moreover, if neoliberal globalization amounts to civil war, then we are already in the fight regardless of what our individual position or experience may be. Lifetime is wartime. Nevertheless, today's left remains reluctant to conceive of civil war in terms other than asymmetric armed revolt. Be this as it may, considering how civil war might look and feel (predicting how to engineer desired outcomes through direct and indirect actions) seems fundamental to any future victory. In short, the concept's contemporary generalization calls upon us to discover a new empowering practice of civil war that we can embrace as willing, indignant, irregular belligerents.

SEE ALSO: Domination; Friend; Leadership; Nation; Occupation; Revolution; Victory; Violence

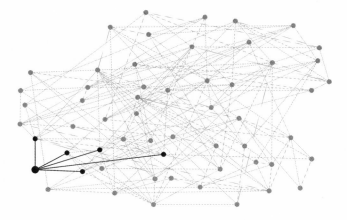

ZIONISM

Illan Pappé

ALTHOUGH USAGES OF "ZIONISM," "ZION," AND "Zionist" have varied historically, there are common etymological threads and mutual ideological influences underlying their various deployments. Today "Zionism" is primarily associated with the Jewish political movement that colonized Palestine. However, in Victorian Britain, among North American settlers, and from the Caribbean islands to South Africa, the adjective "Zionist" tended to be deployed by Christian cults and churches for whom the idea of a transcendental promised land became dogma. These usages originated in the Holy Scriptures. The New Testament adopted the Old Testament's reference to Jerusalem as "Zion," though it distinguished the "earthly" geographical manifestation from the "spiritual" one. Some congregations aspired to both, though most have been more attracted by Zionism's spiritual promise than its earthly manifestation.

"Zionism" became a dominant metaphor in the era of settler colonialism, during which it appealed to settlers and colonized people alike. To understand this pattern, it is necessary to consider how "Zion" and "Zionism" developed as intellectual reference points in nineteenth-century Europe. "Zion" had a powerful appeal for Victorian thinkers in Britain, as evidenced by the term's many appearances in the writings of both Matthew Arnold and his rivals (Dawson and Pfordresher 2013).[1] For these authors, "Zion" denoted both the Christian way of life as well as the lively intellectual scene in which they operated. For George Sainsbury (1916), "Zion" was the milieu to which cultural critics, writers, and poets belonged during the second half of the twentieth century: "I have in common with all the youth of Zion to acknowledge [Mathew Arnold's] vindication of our faith and freedom from the chain of Philistia."

In Arnold's usage, "Zion" was interchangeable with Hebraism—a commitment to obedience he contrasted to the pursuit of truth animating Hellenism (Dawson and Pfordresher 2013, 324–26). Hellenism (the intellectual pursuit of knowledge, self-discipline, and moral behavior emphasized during the Renaissance) was exemplified in the positions of the churches during Arnold's time. And, without a proper equilibrium between Zionism and Hellenism, there was a danger of a crisis. Consequently, Arnold viewed "Zion" as the traditional Semitic and Christian heritage that should not be forsaken, though Hellenism might be considered a more advanced cultural achievement. Accordingly, he thought that a good dose of Zion might free society from an overdose of Hellenism. For this reason, "Zion" became a powerful metaphor and orientation toward the new settler-colonial reality in North America.

According to Fuad Shaban (2005), the idea of Zion in America can be traced back to Christopher Columbus, whose westward

---

1. For late-twentieth-century theorists like Edward Said and Robert Young, Arnold was a dubious thinker who popularized supremacist ideas through catchphrases and metaphors (Dawson and Pfordresher 2013, 324).

voyages revived visions of the Crusaders. As it unfolded, it also came to be viewed as a "Quest for Zion." The idea would subsequently become ingrained in the Puritan and Mormon settler projects. The first Britons who came to New England referred to the territory as Zion, and their "saints" dubbed the settlement "the new Zion on the hill":

> Where righteous men govern,
> where Zion is rising.
> To spread forth her glory to every shore.
> 'Tis the rest of the Saints,
> and my home of adoption,
> Oh, England! I'll call thee my country no more

> (*"Diary of a Voyage from Liverpool to New Orleans on Board the Ship International,"* quoted in Buchanan 1961).

From here, "Zion" spread easily to other parts of the continent. The Puritans who traveled to Virginia reported that they had found the new Zion, which they described as a paradise, a utopia come true through settler colonialism. They saw themselves as God's descendants and chosen people and America as the Promised Land. Like their counterparts in New England, they too wished to build Zion on the Hill. The same phenomenon also prevailed during the Civil War, when the North became Babylon in opposition to the Zion of the South. John Winthrop (1838), a puritan lawyer, wrote that he would create a "Wilderness Zion" in the newfound land.

The motivation for this kind of colonization came from the Latter Day Saint Movement, arguably the most Zionist among the European settlers of North America. They also provided the most "earthly" interpretation of "Zion," which they took to denote a specific location where members needed to live in anticipation of the millennial moment. Like the ancient city of Enoch, this "Zion" promised to be taken to heaven and back, with a temple in its midst. Jewish political Zionism would later adopt the Latter Day Saint's idea of a Third Temple, though they eschewed the more bizarre parts of the vision. Despite this difference, the two movements nevertheless shared common ground, and Christian Zionism extends enthusiastic support to Israel today. This affinity became even stronger when the Latter Day Saint Movement included the "Gathering of Israel" into its divine scheme. The "Gathering" was the return of the Jews from their exiles to Palestine, an event seen as precipitating the second coming of the Messiah and the resurrection of the dead. In the 1830s, Mormon leaders—notably Brigham Young—encouraged British Mormons to immigrate to the Utah desert and make it bloom to secure Zion for the "chosen people."

> On board the "International"
> All joyful and lighthearted.
> Bound Zionward, four hundred Saints,
> From Liverpool we started.
> We're English, Irish, Scotch, and Welsh
> Assembled here together;
> Resolved to do the will of God,
> Whate'er the wind and weather.

(quoted in Buchanan 1961)

In 1837, these Europeans rescued Zion—not the imagined haven but the actual one in Utah—with machinery, tools, and materials for the establishment of new settlements. Many years later, the more cruel aspects of this "Zionization" would be denied as history was rewritten to accommodate today's "multicultural" approach.

Zionism's metaphoric journey from colonization to multiculturalism is best understood through the history of Zion National Park, in southwestern Utah. This park is well excavated and toured. Consequently, we know about who lived there and when. The earliest known Native American inhabitants date back twelve thousand years. In 1860, European settlers (Mormons) arrived, destroyed the Native peoples and their culture, and called the place Zion. According to the park's website, Native Americans and settlers lived peacefully in Zion and united against the hardships of life. "Only the will to survive saw Paiute, Anasazi, and European descendants through great difficulties," the website reads. "Perhaps today Zion is again a sanctuary, a place of life and hope" (National Park Service 2015).

Depictions of the United States as Zion propelled colonization and settlement in South Africa as well. Under the American influence, the concept of Zion became both a missionary tool and a shield against the white man's oppression. Indeed, "Zionism" became a wayward term as it passed between periods and locations. Its usage by seventeenth-century Puritans was different from the inflection given to it by the Mormons. Eventually it took a new shape with the Christian Catholic Apostolic Church of Johan Alexander Dowie of Zion, Illinois. Dowie dispatched Daniel Bryant to institute Zionist churches throughout South Africa. The concept of Zion, a land where all is well, resonated with traditional views as well as with the new ideas brought by white settlers—a mixture that helped to confront oppression and hardship while maintaining native roots within the oppressors' faith (Elphick 1997, 229–30).

Zionist Christianity in South Africa also reconnected the community with the tribal dress code of the local culture. Eventually a Zion was built in Charlestown, Natal, and in several other locations in South Africa. Different successful offshoots of African Zionism fused with Zulu ambitions for statehood and sovereignty. Not surprisingly, the preacher Shembe thus presented himself as the prophet sent by God to the Zulu nation.

A similar religious movement known as the Great Revival or Revival Zion emerged in 1860s Jamaica. The sudden explosion of emotional religious activity on the island was not limited to the established Christian churches. Led by members with no theological training and little education, new "churches" sprang up without orthodox Christian sanction. These churches became cults (especially in Kingston's poorer parts and in the rural countryside) in which Zion and the Bible fused into a polytheistic belief system and a rich world of gods and spirits.

Better known is the role of Zion in the music and lyrics of the Rastafari Movement, which appeared as a religion in the 1930s. Ras Tafari was a title of the emperor Haile Selassie of Ethiopia, crowned in 1930 and regarded as the prophet by this church; his country was viewed as Zion upon earth. Rastafarians believe strongly in a genealogy that dates back to the lost tribes of Israel and hold that every Zion has a Babylon—the emblem of materialism and oppression. From "Train to Zion" to "On the Rivers of Babylon," Bob Marley's songs reveal the inspiration derived from the concept of a New Jerusalem (allegedly anchored in a real geographical location but, in practice, existing in one's mind and away from life's daily tribulations).

This spirituality does not exist in Zionism as a Jewish political movement. Founded in the late-nineteenth century in Eastern and Central Europe, this movement is now Israel's hegemonic ideology. Its premise is that Judaism is a national movement. Expelled from their homeland two thousand years ago, Jews began to find redemption through Zionism in the late nineteenth century. Geographically, Zionism conceives the Jewish homeland as the whole of historical Palestine—Israel and the occupied territories of today. Historically, however, Zionism was not initially associated with Palestine, nor did it require its faithful to settle there. It was born of two impulses. The first was a search for a safe haven during a particularly perilous time in which anti-Jewish legislation, pogroms, and expulsions engulfed Central and Eastern Europe. In response, some moved from Eastern Europe to the western region of the continent, where they were encouraged by the rise of democratic, socialist, and liberal ideas and made an effort to assimilate. Looking for a new world where ideas of equality had a better chance of improving their lives, others traveled to the United States.

Because of romantic nationalism—the second impulse motivating the emergence of Zionism—the competing destination was Palestine. Unable to assimilate into new or old national identities in Europe, educated and politically active Jews sought to redefine Judaism as nationalism and demand the right to self-determination and a homeland. Although movement founder Theodor Herzl considered places such as Uganda as possible destinations, many other Jewish nationalists singled out Palestine as the only place to fulfill their aspirations. They considered Palestine to be their ancestral homeland, which had been taken by force by the Romans. Pragmatically, they accepted help from willing international powers and persuaded a fifth of the world's Jews that the colonization would redeem their lost homeland.

Until the end of the First World War, Palestine was under Ottoman rule. Colonization was thus undertaken incrementally, in disguise, and with enormous obstacles. Many who arrived before 1917 soon departed. (At that time, for strategic, pious Christian, and anti-Semitic reasons, the British occupied Palestine.) Those who remained became the core group from which the future Zionist leadership in Palestine—and later Israel—would emerge.

The implementation of the Zionist project resulted in incremental dispossession between 1918 and 1948. Ethnic cleansing of the native people of Palestine began in 1948 when Zionist forces expelled half the population and demolished half of the country's villages and towns. For Palestinians, Zionism therefore was (and remains) an ideology that negates their existence.

In theory, Zionism still denotes the desire to bring all the world's Jews to Israel, and the Law of Return grants citizenship to any Jew arriving in Israel. In practice, however, various religious trends (such as Reform Judaism) were not recognized as religiously abiding. Similarly, ultra-Orthodox Jews, who do not believe the Jews can return without God's will, are marginalized and alienated. Nonetheless, since the Second World War, most Jews regarded Zionism as an insurance policy—an ideology that would provide them escape in time of trouble. Only in recent years has a strong anti-Zionist impulse found expression in Jewish communities that realize that this policy demands unconditional support for Israel.

Initially the adjective "Zionist" denoted anyone with full right to be part of the project of Israel. Being a Zionist meant that one regarded Israel (which, after 1967, included the whole of historical Palestine) as the Jewish homeland and nation state. Zionism dictated that the symbols of the state be Jewish and its laws Halachic.

It equated citizenship with religious identity. However, one-fifth of Israel's citizens were Palestinians who could not be Zionists or accept the Zionist narrative. The people in the occupied West Bank and Gaza Strip were living in regions that some Zionists believed were Israel. The Zionist desire to deny them citizenship left their fate unresolved. As people around the world watched the brutal repression of Palestinian resistance movements, "Zionism" became equated with Israel's policies of destruction and annihilation.

As ideology, "Zionism" could not save Israel from the need to choose between democracy and ethnic supremacy. And though Western political elites cynically accepted Israel's claims to being a Jewish democracy, the general public did not. When it became clear that the majority of Israeli Jews preferred an ethnic state to a democratic one, Israel's legitimacy came into question (see El Fassed and Perry 2003). Zionism's international reappraisal was triggered by the challenging power of the Palestinian narrative. This narrative influenced Jewish Israeli dissidents to become "post-Zionist." With time, however, the older term "anti-Zionist" replaced "post-Zionist" as Jews realized that reconciliation required the redistribution of resources, land, and privileges (see Pappé 2014, 126–53).

In response, the Israeli academic, political, and military establishment reacted by becoming "neo-Zionists." Deserting attempts to reconcile democratic values with Jewish ethnicity, they declared their wish to maintain a racist ethnic state in historical Palestine (Pappé 2014). Despite this development, and despite the famous UN resolution of 1975, Western political elites still refuse to accept that Zionism is racism. Moreover, efforts to associate anti-Zionism with anti-Semitism have gained some traction. However, this trend is changing, and many Jews now view Zionism as an unacceptable political position and question its equation with Judaism.

SEE ALSO: Colonialism; History; Ideology; Nation; Occupation

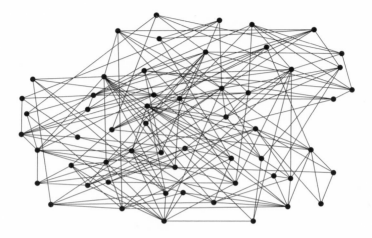

APPENDIX:
CONSTELLATIONS, COGNITIVE MAPS,
AND THE POLITICS OF
DATA VISUALIZATION

Derek Laventure

IN A GLOBAL CONTEXT DEFINED BY INCREASINGLY
complex webs of data, extracting and interpreting the information required to make sound political decisions can
be extremely difficult. In response, the growing field of
data visualization (Tufte 2001) has emerged to provide
a useful compromise between the subjective interpretation of data and a statistical-analysis approach aimed at
objective representation. Cognitively, the visual render-
ing of even moderate amounts of data can yield deeper
understandings of the subject matter while highlighting

the degree to which a data set is more than the sum of its parts. At its best, data visualization allows us to begin constructing what Frederic Jameson referred to as a "cognitive map," a "situational representation" of "the ensemble of society's structures as a whole" (1991, 51). Especially valuable in light of late capitalism's fragmentation of experience, such a map can help us to see relations that would otherwise go unnoticed and concretely determine "where we stand" in relation to the data points located throughout the spatialized array.

Like cartography (Jameson 1991), which had to pass through a subjective "itinerary" and objective "mimetic" phase before coming to terms with interpretive representational problems (e.g., how *do* you capture a swirling planetary orb on a little flat map?), data visualization is less about "the way it is" than about the manner in which the objective field might deliberately be navigated from a situated perspective. Despite proprietary constraints, the democratization of geographic information through tools like Google Maps (which combine scales while oscillating between itinerant and mimetic perspectives) hints at a corresponding cognitive development. The goal: thinking of ourselves as nodes within—and not merely as detritus upon—the swirling vortices of globalized capital.

Recognizing the value of creating a visual representation of the vocabulary explored in this volume, the editors of *Keywords for Radicals* asked me to help map the connections outlined in the "see also" lists contained at the end of each entry. Inspired by the work of neo-conceptual artist Mark Lombardi (1951–2000), whose hand-drawn "global networks" traced the connections binding together actors involved in financial scandals and other shady deals (Lombardi 2003), we aimed to devise our own cognitively rich strategy for representing the contested vocabulary of late-capitalist struggle. Following Raymond Williams (1983), we wanted to foreground how understanding this vocabulary required recognizing that the relative fixity of any given word was contingent upon its association with other words, which were in turn marked by their own conceptual relativity. For Williams, words played a key role both in producing and in giving expression to our reality.

Consequently, when a term's meaning fluctuated, it tended to signal a corresponding change in the world's social and material configuration. By perceiving these interconnections and locating ourselves among them, we can begin to consider how we might influence their development.

When I started researching how to produce a "semantic network" diagram to represent these keywords, I quickly discovered that researchers, developers, and hackers all over the world had been working collaboratively to produce a variety of opensource tools to aid with data visualization. These downloadable tools (along with their associated documentation) are free to use, to modify, and to repurpose. Since we had to produce a basic representation of the network, lay it out in a useful visual arrangement, and style it so that it could be published in print form, it became clear that no single tool would do everything we needed. After writing a couple of custom scripts to parse the simple textual representation of each keyword and its "see also" connections, I used the network visualization tools Gephi and Cytoscape to manipulate that representation into a serviceable graphical form. Finally, to get the styling right, I set up a semi-automated "command script" in Cytoscape to highlight each keyword and its immediate connections before exporting a scalable vector graphic of the results.[1]

Reflecting on this technical process, it became clear that the political importance of "free as in freedom" opensource tools was similar to that of the "cognitive mapping" process that had set us in motion. By developing collaborative, socially defined terms and tools, we become more capable of locating both our power and ourselves. With such tools, it becomes possible to begin producing meaning—and reality—in ways that connect rather than alienate. Like the constellation and the cognitive map, opensource software is a collective achievement. The field it enables us to visualize is one defined by struggle. However, with the right tools, it's a struggle we can win.

---

1. Those interested in learning more about the gory details can consult my technical blog post at http://tranzform.ca/keywords.

REFERENCES

Acklesberg, Martha. 2010. *Resisting Citizenship: Feminist Essays on Politics, Community and Democracy.* London: Routledge.

ACME Collective. 1999. "N30 Black Bloc Communiqué." Anarchist Library. http://theanarchistlibrary.org/library/acme-collective-n30-black-bloc-communique.

Adelman, Lori. 2012. "Lessons in Intersectionality: Gender Warrior Leslie Feinberg Arrested while Protesting CeCe McDonald's Incarceration." *Feministing.* http://feministing.com/2012/06/11/lessons-in-intersectionality-gender-warrior-leslie-feinberg-arrested-while-protesting-cece-mcdonalds-incarceration/.

Adorno, Theodore. 1982. "Commitment." In *The Essential Frankfurt School Reader*, edited by Andrew Arato and Eike Gebhardt, 300–18. New York: Continuum. First published 1962.

———. 1992. "How to Look at Television." In *Critical Theory: The Essential Readings*, edited by David Ingram and Julia Simon-Ingram, 68–76. New York: Paragon House.

AFL-CIO. 2012. "10 Ways to Rebuild the Middle Class." *AFL-CIO Now.* http://www.aflcio.org/Blog/Economy/10-Ways-to-Rebuild-the-Middle-Class.

"Against Conspiracy Theories: Why Our Activism Must Be Based in Reality." 2011. "The text of a talk given at Occupy Wellington, New Zealand, on October 27, 2011." Libcom. https://libcom.org/library/against-conspiracy-theories-why-our-activism-must-be-based-reality.

Agamben, Giorgio. 1993. *Infancy and History: The Destruction of Experience*. Translated by Liz Heron. London: Verso.

———. 1998. *Homo Sacer: Sovereign Power and Bare Life*. Stanford: Stanford University Press.

Against Equality. n.d. http://www.againstequality.org.

Agathangelou, Anna. forthcoming. "Global Raciality of Capitalism and 'Primitive' Accumulation: (Un)Making the Death Limit." In *Scandalous Economics*, edited by Aida Hozic and Jacquie True. Oxford: Oxford University Press.

Agathangelou, Anna, Daniel Bassichis and Tamara Spira. 2008. "Intimate Investments: Homonormativity, Global Lockdown, and Seductions of Empire." *Radical History Review*, (100): 120–44.

Ahmed, Sara. 2007. *Queer Phenomenology: Orientations, Objects, Others*. Durham: Duke University Press.

AIDS Action Now. n.d. http://www.aidsactionnow.org.

Aizura, Aren. 2011. "The Romance of the Amazing Scalpel: 'Race', Labour and Affect in Thai Gender Reassignment Clinics." In *Queer Bangkok*, edited by Peter A. Jackson, 143–62. Hong Kong: Hong Kong University Press.

Akpem, D. Denenge. 2011. "'Are You Ready to Alter Your Destiny?' Chicago and Afro-Futurism, Part 1 of 2." *Chicago Art Magazine*. July 2. http://chicagoartmagazine.com/2011/07/are-you-ready-to-alter-your-destiny-chicago-and-afro-futurism-part-1-of-2.

Alaimo, Stacy, and Susan Hekman, eds. 2009. *Material Feminisms*. Bloomington: Indiana University Press.

Alcoff, Linda. 1988. "Cultural Feminism versus Post-Structuralism: The Identity Crisis in Feminist Theory," *Signs* 13(3): 405–36.

———. 2015. *The Future of Whiteness*. Cambridge: Polity Press.

Alexander, Michelle. 2010. *The New Jim Crow*. New York: Free Press.

Alfred, Taiaiake. 2002. "Sovereignty." In *A Companion to American Indian History*, edited by Philip J. Deloria and Neal Salisbury, 460–74. Oxford: Blackwell.

Alfred, Taiaiake, and Jeff Corntassel. 2005. "Being Indigenous: Resurgences against Contemporary Colonialism." *Government and Opposition* 40(4): 597–614.

Alfred, Taiaiake, and Lana Lowe. 2005. "Warrior Societies in Contemporary

Indigenous Communities." *Upping the Anti* 2. http://uppingtheanti.org/journal/article/02-warrior-societies-in-contemporary-indigenous-communities.

Allan, Kathryn. 2011–14. "Keyword: Responsibility." *Keywords Project*. University of Pittsburgh. http://keywords.pitt.edu/keywords_defined/responsibility.html.

Allen, Ted and Noel Ignatiev. 1967. *White Blindspot*. https://www.marxists.org/history/erol/ncm-1/whiteblindspot.pdf.

Alleyne, Brian. 2002. "An Idea of Community and Its Discontents: Towards a More Reflexive Sense of Belonging in Multicultural Britain." *Ethnic and Racial Studies* 25(4): 607–27.

Althusser, Louis. 1971. *Lenin and Philosophy and Other Essays*. Translated by Ben Brewster. New York: Monthly Review Press.

———. 1977. *Lenin and Philosophy and Other Essays*. New York: New Left Books.

———. 1995. *Sur la reproduction*. Paris: Presse Universitaire de France.

Amnesty International. 2007. "Enduring Occupation: Palestinians under Siege in the West Bank." June 3. https://www.amnesty.org/en/documents/MDE15/033/2007/en.

Amsler, Sarah. 2015. *The Education of Radical Democracy*. London: Routledge.

Anaya, Rudolfo, and Francisco Lomeli. 1998. *Aztlán: Essays on the Chicano Homeland*. Albuquerque: El Norte Publications.

Andersen, Hans Christian. 1983. *The Emperor's New Clothes*. Boston: T. Y. Crowell Junior Books.

Andersen, Margaret, and Patricia Hill Collins. 2013. *Race, Class, and Gender: An Anthology*. 8th ed. Belmont, CA: Wadsworth Cengage Learning.

Anderson, Benedict. 1991. *Imagined Community*. London: Verso.

Anderson, Kip, and Keegan Kuhn. 2014. *Cowspiracy: The Sustainability Secret*. Santa Rosa, CA: Animals United Movement Films.

Anderson, Kristin J. 2015. *Modern Misogyny: Anti-Feminism in a Post-Feminist Era*. Oxford: Oxford University Press.

Anderson, Perry. 1976a. "The Antinomies of Antonio Gramsci." *New Left Review* (November/December): 5–78.

———. 1976b. *Considerations on Western Marxism*. London: Verso.

———. 1998. *The Origins of Postmodernity*. London: Verso.

Antaki, Mark. 2010. "Domination." In *Encyclopedia of Political Theory*, edited by Mark Bevir, 400–402. Thousand Oaks, CA: Sage.

Anzaldúa, Gloria, and Cherríe Moraga, eds. 1981. *This Bridge Called My Back: Writings by Radical Women of Color*. London: Persephone Press.

Appelbaum, Binyamin. 2012. "Regulator Rebuffs Obama on Plan to Ease Housing Debt." *New York Times,* July 31.

Arendt, Hannah. 1951. *The Origins of Totalitarianism.* New York: Harcourt, Brace.

———. 1963. *On Revolution.* New York: Viking Press.

Aronowitz, Stanley. 2002. Introduction to *Critical Theory: Selected Essays of Max Horkheimer.* New York: Continuum.

Artaraz, Kepa and Malania Calestani. 2014. "Suma Qamaña in Bolivia: Indigenous Understandings of Wellbeing and the Contribution to a Post-neoliberal Paradigm." *Latin American Perspectives* 30(20): 1–18.

Artrip, Nick. 2013. "No Fat, No Femme: The Politics of Grindr." *Feminist Wire,* November 8. http://www.thefeministwire.com/2013/11/no-fat-no-femme-the-politics-of-grindr.

Arvinth, Karthick. 2015. "Pope Francis Blasts 'New Colonialism' of Austerity in Fresh Attack on Capitalism." *International Business Times,* July 10. http://www.ibtimes.co.uk/pope-francis-blasts-new-colonialism-austerity-fresh-attack-capitalism-1510179.

Attawapiskat First Nation v. Canada. 2012. FC 948.

Austin, J. L. 1975. *How to Do Things with Words.* Cambridge, MA: Harvard University Press.

Averbeck, Robin. 2014. "Why I'm Not a Liberal." *Jacobin.* July 15. https://www.jacobinmag.com/2014/07/why-im-not-a-liberal.

Ayer, Alfred Jules. 1968. *The Humanist Outlook.* London: Rationalist Press Association.

Azzelini, Dario. 2015. *An Alternative Labour History: Worker Control and Workplace Democracy.* London: Zed Books.

Azzellini, Dario, and Marina Sitrin. 2014. *They Can't Represent Us! Reinventing Democracy from Greece to Occupy.* New York: Verso Books.

Bacon, Francis. 1964. "The Masculine Birth of Time." In *The Philosophy of Francis Bacon,* edited by Benjamin Farrington, 59–72. Chicago: University of Chicago Press. First published 1603.

———. 1991. *The New Atlantis and the Great Instauration.* London: Wiley-Blackwell. First published 1624.

———. 1994. *Novum Organum.* Chicago: Open Court. First published 1620.

Bady, Aaron and Mike Konczal. 2012. "From Master Plan to No Plan: The Slow Death of Public Higher Education." *Dissent,* Fall. http://www.dissentmagazine.org/article/from-master-plan-to-no

-plan-the-slow-death-of-public-higher-education.

Bakunin, Mikhail. 1869. *The Organization of the International*. www.marxists.org/reference/archive/bakunin/works/writings/ch02.htm.

———. 1871. "What Is Authority?" https://www.marxists.org/reference/archive/bakunin/works/various/authrty.htm.

———. 1990. *Statism and Anarchy*. Cambridge: Cambridge University Press.

Balibar, Etienne. 2010. "Marxism and War." *Radical Philosophy*. 160: 9–17.

Balibar, Etienne, and Immanual Wallerstein. 1991. *Race, Nation, Class: Ambiguous Identities*. London: Verso.

Banner, Stuart. 2007. *How the Indians Lost their Land: Law and Power of the Frontier*. Cambridge, MA: Harvard University Press.

Bannerji, Himani. 2000. *The Dark Side of the Nation: Essays on Multiculturalism, Nationalism and Gender*. Toronto: Canadian Scholars' Press.

———. 2014. "India and the Rise of Religious Nationalism: An Interview with Himani Bannerji" (Parts 1–3) *New Socialist Webzine*. http://www.newsocialist.org/763-india-and-the-rise-of-religious-nationalism-an-interview-with-himani-bannerji.

Barad, Karen. 2007. *Meeting the Universe Halfway: Quantum Physics and the Entanglement of Matter and Meaning*. Durham: Duke University Press.

Barber, Benjamin R. 1984. *Strong Democracy*. Berkeley: University of California Press.

———. 2012. "What Democracy Looks Like." *Contexts* 11(2): 14–16.

Barfield, Owen. 1967. *History in English Words*. Grand Rapids, MI: Eerdmans.

Barron, Anne. 2006. "Copyright." *Theory, Culture and Society* 23(2–3): 278–82.

Battiste, Marie, and James (Sa'k'ej) Youngblood Henderson. 2000. *Protecting Indigenous Knowledge and Heritage: A Global Challenge*. Saskatoon: Purich Press.

Bauman, Zygmunt. 2001. *Community: Seeking Safety in an Insecure World*. Cambridge, UK: Polity Press.

Bayertz, Kurt. 1999. "Four Uses of 'Solidarity.'" In *Solidarity*, edited by Kurt Bayertz, 3–28. Dordrecht: Kluwer.

Beasley-Murray, Jon. 2010. *Posthegemony: Political Theory and Latin America*. Minneapolis: University of Minnesota Press.

Bebel, August. 1898. "Assassinations and Socialism". Marxists Internet Archive. https://www.marxists.org/archive/bebel/1898/11/02.htm.

Belich, James. 2009. *Replenishing the Earth: The Settler Revolution and the Rise of the Anglo-World, 1783–1939*. Oxford: Oxford University Press.

Bell, Daniel. 1960. *The End of Ideology; On the Exhaustion of Political Ideas in the 1950s*. Glencoe, IL: Free Press.

Bell, Duncan. 2009. *The Idea of Greater Britain: Empire and the Future of World Order, 1860–1900*. Princeton, NJ: Princeton University Press.

Bellamy, Edward. 1986. *Looking Backward*. Harmondsworth: Penguin.

Benda, Julien. 2007. *The Treason of the Intellectuals*. New Brunswick, NJ: Transaction Publishers. First published 1928.

Bendix, Reinhard. 1964. *Nation Building and Citizenship*. New York: Wiley & Sons.

Benjamin, Walter. 1978. "Critique of Violence." *Reflections: Essays, Aphorisms, Autobiographical Writings*, edited by Peter Demetz, translated by Edmund Jephcott, 276–300. New York: Schocken Books.

———. 1999. *The Arcades Project*. Cambridge, MA: Harvard University Press.

Bennett, Jane. 2010. *Vibrant Matter: A Political Ecology of Things*. Durham: Duke University Press.

Bennett, Tony, Lawrence Grossberg, and Meaghan Morris, eds. 2005. *New Keywords*. Malden, MA: Blackwell.

Bensaïd, Daniel. 1995. *Marx L'impestif*. Paris: Fayard.

———. 2011. "Permanent Scandal." In *Democracy in What State*, edited by Giorgio Agamben et al., 16–43. New York: Columbia University Press.

Bentham, Jeremy. 1817. *A Table of the Springs of Action*. London: R. Hunter.

Berlatsky, Noah. 2013. "Good Day Care Was Once a Top Feminist Priority, and It Should Be Again." *Atlantic*. April 16. http://www.theatlantic.com/sexes/archive/2013/04/good-day-care-was-once-a-top-feminist-priority-and-it-should-be-again/275027.

Bernstein, Barton J., ed. 1968. *Toward a New Past: Dissenting Essays in American History*. New York: Vintage.

Bertram, B. 1995. "New Reflections on the 'Revolutionary' Politics of Ernesto Laclau and Chantal Mouffe." *Boundary 2* 22(3): 81–110.

Bey, Hakim. 1991. "The Temporary Autonomous Zone, Ontological Anarchy, Poetic Terrorism," T.A.Z. part 3. http://hermetic.com/bey/taz3.html.

———. 2004. *T.A.Z.: The Temporary Autonomous Zone, Ontological Anarchy, Poetic terrorism*. New York: Autonomedia.

Bhabha, Homi K. 1994. *The Location of Culture*. London: Routledge.

Bhaskar, Roy. 1975. *A Realist Theory of Science*. London: Verso.

———. 1979. *The Possibility of Naturalism: A Philosophical Critique of the Contemporary Human Sciences*. Atlantic Highlands, NJ: Humanities Press.

Bhattacharyya, Anindya. 2012. "Three Dimensions of Occupy." *Occupied Times*, March 24. http://theoccupiedtimes.org/?p=3033.

Black, Jeff. 2015. "ECB Adds 'Moral Hazard' to Emergency Liquidity Assistance Rules." *BloombergBusiness*. http://www.bloomberg.com/news/articles/2015-07-07/ecb-adds-moral-hazard-to-emergency-liquidity-assistance-rules.

Black Communist. 2014. "Liberalism in #BlackLivesMatter." *Black Communist*, December 22. http://theblackcommunist.tumblr.com/post/105934726166/liberalism-in-blacklivesmatter.

Blanchot, Maurice. 1988. *The Unavowable Community*. Barrytown: Station Hill Press.

Bloch, Ernst. 1971. *On Karl Marx*. New York: Herder and Herder.

———. 1988. *The Utopian Function of Art and Literature: Selected Essays*. Cambridge, MA: MIT Press.

———. 1995. *The Principle of Hope*. Cambridge, MA: MIT Press. First published 1959.

———. 1998. "Can Hope Be Disappointed?" In *Literary Essays*, 339–45. Stanford: Stanford University Press.

———. 2009. *Atheism in Christianity*. London: Verso. First published 1972.

Block, Daniel R., Noel Chavez, Erika Allen, and Dinah Ramirez. 2011. "Food Sovereignty, Urban Food Access, and Food Activism: Contemplating the Connections through Examples from Chicago." *Agriculture and Human Values*, 29(2): 203–15.

Blyth, Mark. 2015. "A Pain in the Athens: Why Greece Isn't to Blame for the Crisis." *Foreign Affairs*, July 7. https://www.foreignaffairs.com/articles/greece/2015-07-07/pain-athens.

Boccioni, Umberto, Carlo Carrà, Luigi Russolo, Giacomo Balla, and Gino Severini. 1910. "Manifesto of Futurist Painters." Niuean Pop Cultural Archive. http://www.unknown.nu/futurism/painters.html.

Boggs, Carl. 1977. "Marxism, Prefigurative Communism and the Problem of Workers' Control." *Radical America* 6 (Winter): 99–122.

———. 1979. "Marxism and the Role of Intellectuals." *New Political Science* 2(3): 7–23.

Boggs, Grace Lee. 2011. *The Next American Revolution: Sustainable Activism for the Twenty-First Century*. Berkeley: University of California Press.

Bolaria, B. Singh, and Peter S. Li. 1985. *Racial Oppression in Canada*. Toronto:

Garamond Press.

Bollier, David. 2003. *Silent Theft: The Private Plunder of Our Common Wealth.* New York: Routledge.

———. 2014. *Think Like a Commoner: A Short Introduction to the Life of the Commons.* Gabriola Island, BC: New Society Publishers.

Bollier, David, and Silke Helfrich. 2012. *The Wealth of the Commons: A World beyond Market and State.* Amherst, MA: Levelers Press.

Bond, Patrick. 2012. *Politics of Climate Justice: Paralysis Above, Movement Below.* Pietermaritzburg: University of KwaZulu-Natal Press.

Bondurant, Joan. 1971. *Conquest of Violence: The Gandhian Philosophy of Conflict.* Berkeley: University of California Press.

Bonilla-Silva, Eduardo. 2006. *Racism without Racists: Color-Blind Racism and the Persistence of Racial Inequality in the United States.* Oxford: Rowman and Littlefield.

Bookchin, Murray. 1995. *The Philosophy of Social Ecology.* Montreal: Black Rose Books.

Boon, Jeb. 2013. "Anonymous: Sorry FBI, you don't scare us." *Salon*, August 22. www.salon.com/2013/08/22/anonymous_sorry_fbi_you_dont_scare_us _partner/.

Bordo, Susan. 1993. *Unbearable Weight: Feminism, Western Culture and the Body.* Berkeley: University of California Press.

Boswell, Holly. 1991. "The Transgendered Alternative." *Chrysalis Quaterly* 1(2): 29–31.

Bottomore, Tom, ed. 1991. *A Dictionary of Marxist Thought.* Oxford: Blackwell.

Boyd, Andrew. 2012. "Prefigurative Intervention." In *Beautiful Trouble: A Toolbox for Revolution*, edited by Andrew Boyd and Dave Oswald Mitchell, 82–85. New York: OR Books.

Bradstock, Andrew. 2013. *Winstanley and the Diggers, 1649–1999.* London: Routledge.

Bravo, Luciano Ferrari. 1975. *Imperialismo e classe operaia multinazionale.* Milan: Feltrinelli.

Breines, Wini. 1980. "Community and Organization: The New Left and Michels' 'Iron Law.'" *Social Problems* 27(4): 419–29.

———. 1988. "Whose New Left?" *Journal of American History* 75(2): 528–45.

———. 1989. *Community and Organization in the New Left, 1962–1968: The Great Refusal.* New Brunswick, NJ: Rutgers University Press.

Brennan, Teresa. 2003. *Globalization and Its Terrors: Daily Life in the West.* New York: Routledge.

Brick, Howard, and Christopher Phelps. 2015. *Radicals in America: The U.S. Left Since the Second World War.* New York: Cambridge University Press.

"Bring Back the Feminists of W.I.T.C.H. (Women's International Terrorist Conspiracy from Hell)!" n.d. *Dangerous Minds.* http://dangerousminds.net/comments/bring_back_the_feminists_of_witch.

Brinkley, Alan. 1995. *The End of Reform: New Deal Liberalism in Recession and War.* New York: Vintage Books.

Brittain, Victoria. 2011. "Africa: A Continent Drenched in the Blood of Revolutionary Heroes." *The Guardian.* January 17. http://www.theguardian.com/global-development/poverty-matters/2011/jan/17/lumumba-50th-anniversary-african-leaders-assassinations.

Brooks Higginbotham, Evelyn. 1993. Righteous Discontent: The Women's Movement in the Black Baptist Church. Cambridge, MA: Harvard University Press.

Brown, Cynthia Stokes. 2002. *Refusing Racism: White Allies and the Struggle for Civil Rights.* New York: Teachers College Press.

Brown, Wendy. 2004. "'The Most We Can Hope for. . .': Human Rights and the Politics of Fatalism." *South Atlantic Quarterly* 103(2): 451–63.

Browning, Barbara. 1998. *Infectious Rhythm: Metaphors of Contagion and the Spread of African Culture.* New York: Routledge.

Brubaker, Rogers. 1996. *Nationalism Reframed: Nationhood and the National Question in New Europe.* Cambridge: Cambridge University Press.

Brushwood Rose, Chloe, and Anna Camilleri, eds. 2003. *Brazen Femme: Queering Femininity.* Vancouver: Arsenal Press.

Buchanan, Frederick S. 1961. "The Emigration of Scottish Mormons to Utah, 1847–1900." Masters thesis, University of Utah.

Buhle, Mari Jo. 1998. "Free Love." In *The Encyclopedia of the American Left*, edited by Paul Buhle, and Dan Georgakas, 242–44. New York: Oxford University Press.

Buhle, Paul, and Nicole Schulman. 2005. *Wobblies: A Graphic History of the Industrial Workers of the World.* London: Verso.

Bullard, Robert. 2000. *Dumping in Dixie: Race, Class and Environmental Quality.* Boulder, CO: Westview Press.

Burbach, Roger. 1994. "Roots of the Postmodern Rebellion in Chiapas." *New*

Left Review 205: 113–24.

———. 1996. "For a Zapatista Style Postmodernist Perspective." *Monthly Review* 47 (March): 4–41.

Burke, Edmund. 1775. "Speech on Conciliation with the Colonies." In *The Founders' Constitution*, vol. 1, edited by Philip B. Kurland and Ralph Lerner, 464–71. University of Chicago Press, 1987.

———. 2001. "Reflections on the Revolution in France." In *The Philosophy of Human Rights*, edited by Patrick Hayden, 88–94. St. Paul, MN: Paragon House.

Burkett, Elinor. 2015. "What Makes a Woman?" *New York Times*. June 8.

Burkett, Paul. 2014. *Marx and Nature*. Chicago: Haymarket Books.

Büscher, Bram, Wolfram Dressler, and Robert Fletcher, eds. 2014. *Nature™ Inc. Environmental Conservation in the Neoliberal Age*. Tucson: University of Arizona Press.

"But Some of Us are Brave." 2005. www.feministpress.org/books/gloria-hull/some-us-are-brave.

Butler, Judith. 1990. *Gender Trouble: Feminism and the Subversion of Identity*. New York: Routledge.

———. 1993. *Bodies That Matter: On the Discursive Limits of Sex*. New York: Routledge.

———. 1997. *Excitable Speech: A Politics of the Performative*. New York: Routledge.

———. 1999. "A 'Bad Writer' Bites Back." March 20. *New York Times*.

———. 2003. *Giving an Account of Oneself*. New York: Fordham University Press.

Byrd, Jodi. 2011. *The Transit of Empire: Indigenous Critiques of Colonialism*. Minneapolis: University of Minnesota Press.

Cabral, Amilcar. 1974. "Tell No Lies, Claim No Easy Victories." Marxists Internet Archive. https://www.marxists.org/subject/africa/cabral/1965/tnlcnev.htm.

Caffentzis, George. 2012. "A Tale of Two Conferences: Globalization, the Crisis of Neoliberalism and the Question of the Commons." *Borderlands e-Journal: New Spaces in the Humanities* 11(2): 1–32.

Caffentzis, George, and Silvia Federici. 2013. "Commons against and beyond Capitalism." *Upping the Anti: A Journal of Theory and Action* 15: 83–97.

Calderón, J Love. 2012. *Occupying Privilege: Conversations on Love, Race and Liberation*. Love-N-Liberation Press.

Camejo, Peter. 1984. "Problems of Vanguardism." Marxists Internet Archive.

https://www.marxists.org/archive/camejo/1984/19841001.htm.

Canadian Forces. 2011. *Designing Canada's Army of Tomorrow: A Land Forces 2021 Publication.* Kingston: Directorate of Land Concepts and Designs.

Canadian Labour Congress. 2015. http://canadianlabour.ca.

Candeias, Mario. 2015. "Democratic Rebellion: Some Lessons from the Municipal and Regional Elections in Spain." *Bullet* (Socialist Project), no. 1135. July 1. http://www.socialistproject.ca/bullet/1135.php.

Carmichael, Stokley. 1966. "Student Nonviolent Coordinating Committee Position Paper: The Basis of Black Power." Sixties Project. http://www2.iath.virginia.edu/sixties/HTML_docs/Resources/Primary/Manifestos/SNCC_black_power.html.

Carolyn. 1993. "Politicizing Gender: Moving toward Revolutionary Gender Politics." Spunk Library. http://www.spunk.org/texts/pubs/lr/sp001714/gender.html.

Carrigan, Ana. 1995. "Chiapas: The First Post-Modern Revolution." *Fletcher Forum* 19(1): 71–98.

Carson, Rachel. 1962. *Silent Spring.* Boston: Houghton Mifflin.

Carter, Bob. 2014. "'They Can't Be the Buffer Any Longer': Front-Line Managers and Class Relations under White-Collar Lean Production." *Capital and Class* 38(2): 323–43.

Casanova, Pablo Gonzalez. 1965. "Internal Colonialism and National Development." *Studies in Comparative International Development* 1(4): 27–37.

Castel, Robert. 2007. *La discrimination négative. Citoyens ou indigènes?* Paris: Seuil.

Catalyst Project. 2015. "The Catalyst Project: Anti-Racism for Collective Liberation." Catalyst Project. http://collectiveliberation.org/in-the-time-of-ferguson.

Cauldwell, D. O. 1951. *Sex Transmutation—Can One's Sex Be Changed?* Girard, KS: Haldeman-Julius.

———. 1955. "Is 'Sex Change' Ethical?" *Sexology* 22: 108–12.

Celeste, Anguatia. "Safety Is an Illusion: Reflections on Accountability." 2011. http://anarchalibrary.blogspot.ca/2011/01/safety-is-illusion-reflections-on.html.

Centre for Independent Living in Toronto. 2015. "Attendant Services Overview." http://www.cilt.ca.

Chamayou, Grégoire. 2011. "The Manhunt Doctrine." *Radical Philosophy* 169: 2–6.

Change U. 2015. "Confronting Structural Violence: Our Fight Is against a White Supremacist, Militaristic, Capitalist, Cis-Heterosexist Patriarchy." Crand Valley State University, http://www.gvsu.edu/socialjustice/confronting-structural-violence-29.htm.

Chatterjee, Partha. 1993. *The Nation and Its Fragments: Colonial and Postcolonial Histories.* Princeton: Princeton University Press.

Chen, Ching-In, Jai Dulani, and Leah Lakshmi Piepzna-Samarasinha. 2011. *The Revolution Starts at Home: Confronting Intimate Violence within Activist Communities.* New York: South End Press.

Chen, Mel Y. 2012. *Animacies: Biopower, Racial Mattering, and Queer Affect.* Durham: Duke University Press.

Cherlin, Andrew. 2015. "The Missing Working Class." *Washington Post*, February 13.

Chomsky, Noam. 2013. "Noam Chomsky on Conspiracy Theories." October 2. http://www.youtube.com/watch?v=BDkbaPedIz4.

Chun, Lin. 2014. "The Language of Class in China." In *Socialist Register 2015: Transforming Classes*, edited by Leo Panitch and Greg Albo, 24–53. London: Merlin Press.

Churchill, Ward. 2003. "The Bloody Wake of Alcatraz: Repression of the American Indian Movement in the 1970s". In *Acts of Rebellion: The Ward Churchill Reader*, 151–70. London: Routledge.

Clare, Eli. 1999. *Exile and Pride: Disability, Queerness, and Liberation.* Cambridge, MA: South End Press.

Clark, Meredith. 2013. "For Allies, a Question of How to Use Privilege for Good." MSNBC, July 21. http://www.msnbc.com/melissa-harris-perry/allies-question-how-use-privileg.

Clark, Sam. 2007. *Living without Domination: The Possibility of an Anarchist Utopia.* Aldershot: Ashgate.

Class Action. 2015. "What Is Classism?" http://www.classism.org/about-class/what-is-classism.

Classen, Albrecht. 2011. "Friends and Friendship in Heroic Epics: With a Focus on *Beowulf, Chanson de Roland*, the *Nibelungenlied*, and *Njal's Saga*." *Neohelicon*, 38: 121–39.

Clausewitz, Carl von. 1976. *On War.* Edited by Michael Howard and Peter Paret. Princeton: Princeton University Press.

Cleaver, Harry. 1994. "The Chiapas Uprising and the Future of Class Struggle in

the New World Order." http://la.utexas.edu/users/hcleaver/kcchiapasuprising
.html.

———. 2000. *Reading Capital Politically*. Oakland: AK Press.

Club of Rome. 1972. *The Limits to Growth*. New York: Universe Books.

Coates, Ken. 2015. *#IdleNoMore and the Remaking of Canada*. Regina: University of Regina Press.

Coates, Ta-Nehisi. 2013. "What We Mean When We Say Race is a Social Construct." *The Atlantic*. www.theatlantic.com/national/archive/2013/05/what-we-mean-when-we-say-race-is-a-social-construct/275872.

Cohen, Anthony P. 1985. *The Symbolic Construction of Community*. London: Routledge.

Cohn, Candace. 2015. "Privilege and the Working Class." *SocialistWorker.org*. International Socialist Organization, April 15.

Cohn, Martin Regg. 2013. "Arguments against Unions Are Ideological, Not Empirical." *Toronto Star*. September 5.

Colectivo Situaciones. 2012. *19 & 20: Notes for a New Social Protagonism*. Translated by Nate Holdren and Sebastián Touza. New York: Minor Compositions.

Colford, Paul. 2013. "'Illegal Immigrant' No More." April 2. Associated Press. http://blog.ap.org/2013/04/02/illegal-immigrant-no-more.

Collins, Patricia Hill. 1990. "Black Feminist Thought in the Matrix of Domination." In *Black Feminist Thought: Knowledge, Consciousness, and the Politics of Empowerment*, 221–38. Boston: Unwin Hyman.

Colours of Resistance Network. n.d. "Definitions for the Revolution." http://www.coloursofresistance.org/definitions-for-the-revolution.

———. n.d. "Whose Ally? Thinking Critically about Anti-Oppression Ally Organizing, Part 1." http://www.coloursofresistance.org/370/whose-ally-thinking-critically-about-anti-oppression-alay-organizing-part-1.

Colombo, Pamela, and Tomás Bril Mascarenhas. 2003. "We're Nothing; We Want To Be Everything." In *We Are Everywhere: The Irresistible Rise of Global Anti-Capitalism*, edited by Notes from Nowhere, 458–63. New York: Verso.

Colson, Daniel. 2001. "Domination". In *Petit lexique philosophique de L'anarchisme de Proudhon à Deleuze*. Paris: Librairie Générale Française.

Combahee River Collective. 1977. "The Combahee River Collective Statement." *Circuitous.org*, http://circuitous.org/scraps/combahee.html.

Combe, Holly. 2012. "Song the day: Nina Simone/various- Strange Fruit."

22 August. http://www.thefword.org.uk/2012/08/song_nina_simone _strange_fruit/

Commoner, Barry. 1971. *The Closing Circle*. New York: Alfred P. Knopf.

Comrades from Cairo. 2011. "Solidarity Statement from Cairo." October 24. http://occupywallst.org/article/solidarity-statement-cairo.

Connolly, James. 1916. *Notes on the Front*. www.marxists.org/archive/connolly/1916/02/fronta.htm.

"A Conspiracy of Hope." *Wikipedia*. https://en.wikipedia.org/wiki/A _Conspiracy_of_Hope.

Conspire to Resist. https://conspiretoresist.wordpress.com.

Coole, Diana, and Samantha Frost, eds. 2010. *New Materialisms: Ontology, Agency and Politics*. Durham: Duke University Press.

Cooper, Brittney. 2014. "It's Not about You, White Liberals: Why Attacks on Radical People of Color Are So Misguided." *Salon*, April 8. http://www.salon.com/2014/04/08/its_not_about_you_white_liberals_why_attacks_on_radical_people_of_color_are_so_misguided.

Cooper, Melinda, and Catherine Waldby. 2014. *Clinical Labor: Tissue Donors and Research Subjects in the Global Bioeconomy*. Durham: Duke University Press.

Coordinating Committee Black Liberation Army. 1976/1977. "A Political Statement from the Black Underground." http://www.assatashakur.org/message.htm.

Corporate Watch. 2015. "Gaza: Life beneath the Drones." *Corporate Watch*. February 20. http://www.corporatewatch.org/news/2015/feb/20/gaza-life -beneath-drones.

Corsianos, Marilyn. 2007. "Mainstream Pornography and 'Women': Questioning Sexual Agency." *Critical Sociology* 33: 863–85.

Coulthard, Glen. 2014. *Red Skin, White Masks: Rejecting the Colonial Politics of Recognition*. Minneapolis: University of Minnesota Press.

Council of Canadians with Disabilities. 2015. "What's at Stake in Friday's Supreme Court Decision on Assisted Suicide." February 4. Council of Canadians with Disabilities. http://www.ccdonline.ca/en/humanrights/endoflife/media-release-4Feb2015.

Coward, Barry and Julian Swan, eds. 2004. *Conspiracies and Conspiracy Theory in Early Modern Europe*. Burlington, VT: Ashgate.

Cox, Laverne. 2014. "Laverne Cox Talks to *Time* about the Transgender Movement: The *Orange Is the New Black* Star on Politics, Happiness and

Why Genitalia Isn't Destiny." *Time*, May 29. http://time.com/132769/transgender-orange-is-the-new-black-laverne-cox-interview.

Cranford, Cynthia J. 2005. "From Precarious Workers to Unionized Employees and Back Again? The Challenges of Organizing Personal-Care Workers in Ontario." In *Self-Employed Workers Organize: Law, Policy and Unions*, edited by Cynthia J. Cranford, Judy Fudge, Eric Tucker and Leah F. Vosko, 96–135. Montreal: McGill-Queen's University Press.

Crary, Jonathan. 2001. *Suspensions of Perception: Attention, Spectacle, and Modern Culture*. Cambridge, MA: MIT Press.

CrimethInc. Ex-Workers' Collective. 2001. *Days of War, Nights of Love*. Atlanta: CrimethInc.

———. 2002. *Fighting for Our Lives: An Anarchist Primer*. Salem, OR: CrimethInc. Free Press.

———. 2006. "Prudence." *Rolling Thunder: An Anarchist Journal of Dangerous Living* 3: 5.

———. 2010. "Against Ideology?" CrimethInc. Ex-Workers' Collective Online Reading Library. http://www.crimethinc.com/texts/recentfeatures/ideology.php.

———. 2011. "Fire Extinguishers and Fire Starters: Anarchist Interventions in the #Spanish Revolution." CrimethInc. Ex-Workers' Collective Online Reading Library. http://www.crimethinc.com/texts/atoz/barc.php.

———. 2013a. "English and the Anarchists' Language." CrimethInc. Ex-Workers' Collective Online Reading Library. http://www.crimethinc.com/texts/recentfeatures/language.php.

———. 2013b. "For All We Care: Reconsidering Self-Care." CrimethInc. Ex-Workers' Collective Online Reading Library. http://www.crimethinc.com/texts/recentfeatures/selfcare.php.

———. 2013c. *Accounting for Ourselves: Breaking the Impasse Around Assault and Abuse in Anarchist Scenes*. http://www.crimethinc.com/blog/2013/04/17/accounting-for-ourselves.

———. n.d. "The Age of Conspiracy Charges." CrimethInc. Ex-Workers' Collective Online Reading Library. http://www.crimethinc.com/texts/recentfeatures/conspiracy.php.

———. n.d. "Definition of Terms." *Harbinger*. CrimethInc. Ex-Workers' Collective Online Reading Library. http://www.crimethinc.com/texts/harbinger/definition.php.

———. n.d. "No Masters." CrimethInc. Ex-Workers' Collective Online Reading Library. http://www.crimethinc.com/texts/atoz/nomasters.php.

———. n.d. "Undermining Oppression." CrimethInc. Ex-Workers' Collective Online Reading Library. http://www.crimethinc.com/texts/atoz/underminingoppression.php.

———. n.d. "What is Security Culture?" CrimethInc. Ex-Workers' Collective Online Reading Library. http://www.crimethinc.com/texts/atoz/security.php.

———. n.d. "Why We're Right and You're Wrong: Towards a Non-D(en)ominational Revolution," *Harbinger.* CrimethInc. Ex-Workers' Collective Online Reading Library. http://www.crimethinc.com/texts/harbinger/infighting.php.

Crimp, Douglas. 1990. *AIDS DemoGraphics.* Seattle: Bay Press.

"Cripteori." 2012. Special issue. *lambda nordica* 1–2.

Critchley, Simon. 2007. *Infinitely Demanding: Ethics of Commitment, Politics of Resistance.* London: Verso.

"Critique of Ally Politics." 2015. *Revolutionary Solidarity: A Critical Reader for Accomplices*, 5–18. https://archive.org/download/RevolutionarySolidarity ACriticalReaderForAccomplices/revsol-SCREEN.pdf.

Cunneen, Joyce. n.d. "Cultural Diversity" ELDER Project, Fairfield University School of Nursing.

Curry, Marshall. 2011. *If a Tree Falls: A Story of the Earth Liberation Front.* Marshall Curry Productions.

Dace, Karen, ed. *Unlikely Allies in the Academy: Women of Color and White Women in Conversation.* New York: Routledge: 2012.

Dalla Costa, Mariarosa. 1975. "Women and the Subversion of the Community." In *The Power of Women and the Subversion of the Community*, edited by Mariarosa Dalla Costa and Selma James. Bristol, UK: Falling Wall Press.

———. 2008. "Food Sovereignty, Peasants and Women." *Commoner.* http://www.commoner.org.uk/wp-content/uploads/2008/06/dallacosta_food-sovereignty-farmers.pdf.

Daly, Herman, ed. 1973. *Toward a Steady State Economy.* San Francisco: W. H. Freeman.

———. 1996. *Beyond Growth: The Economics of Sustainable Development.* Boston: Beacon Press.

Daly, Mary. 1978. *Gyn/ecology: The Metaethics of Radical Feminism.* Boston:

Beacon Press.

Darder, Antonia, and Rodolfo Torres. 2004. *After Race: Racism after Multiculturalism*. New York: NYU Press.

Davidson, Carl. 2011. *Revolutionary Youth and the New Working Class*. Pittsburgh: Changemaker Publications.

Davis, Angela. 1993. "Surrogate Mother and Outcast Mothers: Racism and Reproductive Politics in the Nineties." In *American Feminist Thought at Century's End: A Reader*, edited by Linda S Kauffman, 355–66. Cambridge, UK: Basil Blackwell.

———. 1998. "From the Prison of Slavery to the Slavery of Prison: Frederick Douglass and the Convict Lease System." In *The Angela Y. Davis Reader*, edited by Joy James. Malden, MA: Blackwell.

Davis, Laurence, and Ruth Kinna. 2014. *Anarchism and Utopianism*. Manchester, UK: Manchester University Press.

Davis, Mike. 2011. "No More Bubblegum." *Los Angeles Review of Books*, October 21.

Dawson, Carl, and John Pfordresher, eds. 2013. *Matthew Arnold: The Critical Heritage*, vol. 1, *Prose Writings*. London: Routledge.

Dawson, J. A., ed. 1950. "Anton Pannekoek: Workers' Councils 1941–42 (–44, –47)." Marxists Internet Archive. https://www.marxists.org/archive/pannekoe/1947/workers-councils.htm.

Day, Richard. 2005. *Gramsci Is Dead: Anarchist Currents in the Newest Social Movements*. London: Pluto Press.

De Angelis, Massimo. 2006. *The Beginning of History: Value Struggles and Global Capital*. London: Pluto Press.

———. 2009. "The Tragedy of the Capitalist Commons." *Turbulence* 5: 32.

———. 2012. "Crises, Capital and Co-optation: Does Capital Need a Commons Fix?" In *The Wealth of the Commons*, edited by David Bollier and Silke Helfrich, 184–91. Amherst, MA: Levelers Press.

Dean, Jodi. 2012. *The Communist Horizon*. New York: Verso.

Debs, Eugene. 1895. "*Labor Omnia Vincit*." Written in jail in Woodstock, Illinois, August 5. Marxists Internet Archive. https://www.marxists.org/archive/debs/works/1895/laboromnia.htm.

Debord, Guy, Attila Kotányi, and Raoul Vaneigem. 1962. *Theses on the Paris Commune*. http://www.bopsecrets.org/SI/Pariscommune.htm.

Delacoste, Frédérique, and Priscilla Alexander, eds. 1987. *Sex Work: Writings by*

Women in the Sex Industry. Berkeley: Cleis Press.

Delanty, Gerard, and Krishan Kumar, eds. 2006. *The Sage Handbook of Nations and Nationalism.* London: Sage Publications.

Deleuze, Gilles, and Felix Guattari. 1986. *Nomadology: The War Machine.* Los Angeles: Semiotexte.

———. 1987. *A Thousand Plateaus: Capitalism and Schizophrenia.* Minneapolis: University of Minnesota Press.

Delgado, Richard. 2003. "Liking Arms: Recent Books on Interracial Coalitions as an Avenue of Social Reform." *Cornell Law Review* 88(3): 855.

della Porta, D. 2009a. *Democracy in Social Movements.* London: Palgrave.

———. 2009b. *Another Europe.* London: Routledge.

———. 2015. *Social Movements in Times of Austerity.* Oxford: Polity Press.

Delphy, Christine. 1993. "Rethinking Sex and Gender." *Women's Studies International Forum* 16(1): 1–9.

Demanuele, Gaye. 2013. "Why Birth Is a Feminist Issue." *The Organiser: The Australian Voice of Revolutionary Feminism.* December. http://www.socialism .com/drupal-6.8/organiser-articles/why-birth-feminist-issue.

Democracy Now. 2010. "Percy Schmeiser vs. Monsanto: The Story of a Canadian Farmer's Fight to Defend the Rights of Farmers and the Future of Seeds." September 19. http://www.democracynow.org/2010/9/17/ percy_schmeiser_vs_monsanto_the_story.

———. 2015a. "Noam Chomsky on Black Lives Matter: Why Won't U.S. Own Up to History of Slavery & Racism?" March 3. http://www.democracynow .org/2015/3/3/noam_chomsky_on_black_lives_matter.

———. 2015b. "Watch: Full Video of Hillary Clinton's Meeting with Black Lives Matter Activists." http://www.democracynow.org/blog/2015/8/19/ watch_full_video_of_hillary_clintons.

Denoon, Donald. 1983. *Settler Capitalism.* Oxford, UK: Clarendon Press.

Derrida, Jacques. 1992. "The Force of Law: The 'Mystical Foundation of Authority.'" In *Deconstruction and the Possibility of Justice*, edited by Drucilla Cornell, Michel Rosenfeld and David Gray Carlson, 3–67: Routledge.

———. 1994. *Specters of Marx: The State of Debt, the Work of Mourning, and the New International.* Translated by Peggy Kamuf. New York: Routledge.

Desil, Junie, Kirat Kaur and Gary Kinsman. 2005 "Anti-Oppression Politics in Anti-Capitalist Movements." *Upping the Anti* 1. http://uppingtheanti.org/ journal/article/01-anti-oppression-politics-in-anti-capitalist-movements/.

Devall, Bill, and George Sessions. 1985. *Deep Ecology*. Layton, UT: Gibbs Smith.

Devji, Faisal. 2014. *Muslim Zion: Pakistan as a Political Idea*. Cambridge, MA: Harvard University Press.

Dillon, Michael, and Julian Reid. 2009. *Killing to Make Life Live: The Liberal Way of War*. London: Routledge.

Dinerstein, Ana Cecilia. 2015. *The Politics of Autonomy in Latin America: The Art of Organizing Hope*. New York: Palgrave Macmillan.

Dinerstein, Ana Cecilia and Séverine Deneulin. 2012. "Hope Movements: Naming Mobilization in a Post-Development World." *Development & Change* 43(2): 585–602.

Dion, Jack. 2012. "Pour le Monde, Mélenchon = Le Pen = populistes!" *Marianne*. February 12. http://www.marianne.net/Pour-le-Monde-Melenchon-Le-Pen-populistes-_a215291.html.

Dixon, Chris. 2014. *Another Politics: Talking across Today's Transformative Movements*. Oakland: University of California Press.

Dobson, Andrew. 1995. *Green Political Thought*. New York: Routledge.

Dohrn-Van Rossum, Gerhard. 1996. *History of the Hour: Clocks and Modern Temporal Orders*. Chicago: University of Chicago Press.

Dominelli, L. 1998. "Anti-oppressive practice in context." In *Social Work: Themes, Issues and Critical Debates*, edited by R. Adams, L. Dominelli, and M. Payne. London: Macmillan.

Douglass, Frederick. 1845. *Narrative of the Life of Frederick Douglass, an American Slave*. Chapel Hill: Academic Affairs Library, University of North Carolina, 1999.

———. 1852. "Frederick Douglass: The Hypocrisy of American Slavery." History Place. http://www.historyplace.com/speeches/douglass.htm.

———. 1857. *If There Is No Struggle, There Is No Progress*. BlackPast.org. http://www.blackpast.org/1857-frederick-douglass-if-there-no-struggle-there-no-progress.

Downer, Carol. 1980. "Battle against Population Controllers Unite [*sic*] Radical Feminists and People of Color." Originally published in "Women's Health Movement Paper, July 1980." *Femwords*. http://femwords.blogspot.ca/2010/10/battle-against-population-controllers.html.

Drexhage, John, and Deborah Murphy. 2012. "Sustainable Development: From Brundtland to Rio 2012." Background paper prepared for consideration by the High Level Panel on Global Sustainability, United Nations, New York.

Drone Wars UK. 2014. *Israel and the Drone Wars: Examining Israel's Production, Use and Proliferation of UAV's.* Drone Wars UK. https://dronewarsuk.files. wordpress.com/2014/01/israel-and-the-drone-wars.pdf.

Du Bois, W. E. B. 1903a. *The Souls of Black Folk.* New York: Bantam Classic.

———. 1903b. "The Talented Tenth." http://teachingamericanhistory.org/ library/document/the-talented-tenth.

———. 1992. *Black Reconstruction in America, 1860–1880.* New York: The Free Press.

———. 2007. *Dusk of Dawn: An Essay Toward an Autobiography of a Race Concept.* Oxford: Oxford University Press.

———. 2013. *Black Reconstruction in America: Toward a History of the Part Which Black Folk Played in the Attempt to Reconstruct Democracy in America, 1860– 1880.* New Brunswick, NJ: Transaction.

Duffield, Mark. 2007. *Development, Security, and Unending War: Governing the World of Peoples.* Cambridge: Polity Books.

Duggan, Lisa. 1995. "Making It Perfectly Queer." In *Sex Wars: Sexual Dissent and Political Culture*, edited by Lisa Duggan and Nan D. Hunter, 155–72. New York: Routledge.

———. 2003. *Twilight of Equality: Neoliberalism, Cultural Politics and the Attack on Democracy.* Boston: Beacon Press.

Dunbar-Ortiz, Roxanne. 2014. *An Indigenous People's History of the United States.* Boston: Beacon Press.

Dunne, Stephen. 2007. "What Is Corporate Social Responsibility Now." *Theory and Politics in Organization* 7(2): 372–380.

———. 2008. "Corporate Social Responsibility and the Value of Corporate Moral Pragmatism." *Culture and Organization* 14(2): 135–49.

Durkheim, Emile. 1982. *The Rules of Sociological Method.* Translated by W.D. Halls. New York: The Free Press.

———. 1995. *The Elementary Forms of the Religious Life.* Translated by Karen E. Fields. New York: The Free Press.

Dworkin, Andrea. 1974. *Woman Hating.* New York: Dutton.

———. 1978. *Right Wing Women.* New York: Perigee Books.

———. 1996. "Dworkin on Dworkin." "An interview that appeared in *Radically Speaking*." *RANCOM!* rancom.wordpress.com/2011/12/30/andrea -dworkin-interview.

Dykes for an Amerikan Revolution. 1976. "Lesbian Feminist Declaration '76."

Lesbian Tide. September 1.

Eckersley, Robyn. 1992. *Environmentalism and Political Theory.* Albany: State University of New York Press.

Ecologist. 1993. *Whose Common Future?* London: Earthscan.

Ehrenreich, Barbara, and John Ehrenreich. 2013. *Death of a Yuppie Dream: The Rise and Fall of the Professional Managerial Class.* New York: Rosa Luxemburg Stiftung.

Elam, Diane. 1994. *Feminism and Deconstruction.* New York: Routledge.

El Fassed, Arjan, and Nigel Perry. 2003. "Israel Discovers the Democracy Is Not an Israel Value." May 22. *Electronic Intifada.* https://electronicintifada.net/content/israel-discovers-democracy-not-israeli-value/4593.

Elphick, Richard. 1997. *Christianity in South Africa: A Political, Social and Cultural History.* Berkley: University of California Press.

Emmanuel, Arghiri. 1972. "White-Settler Colonialism and the Myth of Investment Imperialism." *New Left Review,* May/June, 35–57.

Emirbayer, Mustafa, and Ann Mische. 1998. "What Is Agency?" *American Journal of Sociology* 103 (4): 962–1023.

Endnotes. 2010. "Crisis in the Class Relation." *Endnotes,* no. 2 ("Misery and the Value Form"). http://endnotes.org.uk/en/endnotes-crisis-in-the-class-relation.

———. 2013. "The Holding Pattern." *Endnotes,* no. 3 ("Gender, Race, Class and Other Misfortunes"). September. http://endnotes.org.uk/en/endnotes-the-holding-pattern

Engels, Friedrich. 1882. "Letter to Karl Kautsky." Marxists Internet Archive. https://www.marxists.org/archive/kautsky/1907/colonial/appendix.htm.

———. 1845. "Condition of the Working Class in England." Marxists Internet Archive. https://www.marxists.org/archive/marx/works/1845/condition-working-class/ch13.htm

———. 1934. *Dialectics of Nature.* Moscow: Progress Publishers.

———. 1968. "Engels to Franz Mehring, London, July 14, 1893." Marxists Internet Archive. https://www.marxists.org/archive/marx/works/1893/letters/93_07_14.htm.

Engler, Mark, and Paul Engler. 2014a. "Should We Fight the System or Be the Change?" *Dissent.* June 10. http://www.dissentmagazine.org/blog/should-we-fight-the-system-or-be-the-change.

———. 2014b. "When the Pillars Fall—How Social Movements Can Win More Victories Like Same-Sex Marriage." *Waging*

Nonviolence. July 9. http://wagingnonviolence.org/feature/pillars-fall -social-movements-can-win-victories-like-sex-marriage.

Epstein, Barbara. 1991. *Political Protest and Cultural Revolution: Nonviolent Direct Action in the 1970s and 1980s.* Berkeley: University of California Press.

Esteva, Gustavo. 2012. "Hope From the Margins." In *The Wealth of the Commons: A World Beyond Market and State*, edited by David Bollier and Silke Helfrich. Amherst, MA: Levelers Press.

Esteva, Gustavo, and Madhu Prakash. 1998. *Grassroots Postmodernism: Remaking the Soil of Cultures.* New York: Zed Books.

Evans, Brad. 2011. "The Liberal War Thesis: Introducing the Ten Key Principles of Twenty-First-Century Biopolitical Warfare." *South Atlantic Quarterly* 110(3): 747–56.

Evans-Pritchard, Ambrose. 2015. "Greek Deal Poisons Europe as Backlash Mounts against 'Neo-colonial Servitude.'" *Telegraph*, July 13.

Euronews. 2015. "Tsipras Champions Hope for Ordinary Greeks." January 19. http:// www.euronews.com/2015/01/19/tsipras-champions-hope-for-ordinary -greeks.

"Exclusive: When Hillary Clinton Met Black Lives Matter." 2015. *Rachel Maddow Show*, August 17, MSNBC. http://www.msnbc.com/rachel-maddow-show/ watch/when-hillary-clinton-met-black-lives-matter-507155523571.

Fanon, Frantz. 1963. *Wretched of the Earth.* London: Grove Press.

———. 1967. *The Wretched of the Earth.* New York: Grove Press.

———. 1986. *Black Skin, White Masks.* London: Pluto Press.

Faraj, Gaidi. 2007. "Unearthing the Underground: A Study of Radical Activism in the Black Panther Party and the Black Liberation Army." PhD diss., African American Studies, University of California, Berkeley.

Farber, Samuel. 2014. "Reflections on 'Prefigurative Politics.'" *International Socialist Review* 92. http://isreview.org/issue/92/reflections-prefigurative-politics.

Fausto-Sterling, Anne. 2000. *Sexing the Body.* New York: Basic Books.

Featherstone, David. 2012. *Solidarity: Hidden Histories and Geographies of Internationalism.* London: Zed Books.

Federici, Silvia. 2004. *Caliban and the Witch: Women, the Body, and Primitive Accumulation.* New York: Autonomedia.

———. 2011. "On Affective Labor." In *Cognitive Capitalism, Education and Digital Labor*, edited by Michael A. Peters and Ergin Bulut, 57–74. New York: Peter Lang.

———. 2012. *Revolution at Point Zero: Housework, Reproduction, and Feminist Struggle.* Oakland: PM Press.

———. 2015. *Wages for Housework and the Women's Liberation Movement 1973–1976: History, Theory and Documents.* Brooklyn: Autonomedia.

Feel Tank Chicago. 2015. "Pathogeographies." http://pathogeographies.net.

Feinberg, Leslie. 2006. "Transgender Liberation: A Movement Whose Time Has Come." In *Transgender Studies Reader*, edited by Susan Stryker and Stephen Whittle, 205–20. New York: Routledge. First published 1992.

———. 2012. "Transgender Liberation: A Movement Whose Time Has Come." In *Feminist Theory Reader: Local and Global Perspectives*, edited by Carole McCann and Seung-Kyung Kim, 148–61. New York: Routledge.

Fenton, Anthony, and Jon Elmer. 2013. "Building an Expeditionary Force for Democracy Promotion." *Empire's Ally: Canada and the War in Afghanistan*, edited by Jerome Klassen and Greg Albo, 306–38. Toronto: University of Toronto Press.

Fields, Karen, and Barbara Fields. 2014. *Racecraft: The Soul of Inequality in American Life.* London: Verso.

"Fierce Accountability Training Program." Fierce Inc. http://www.fierceinc.com/programs/accountability.

Fine, Janice. 2014. "Choose Tactics That Support Your Strategy." In *Beautiful Trouble: A Toolbox for Revolution*, edited by Andrew Boyd and Dave Oswald Mitchell, 52–54. Toronto: Between the Lines.

Fine, Michael D. 2007. *A Caring Society? Care and Dilemmas of Human Service in the 21st Century.* New York: Palgrave Macmillan.

Fioramonti, Lorenzo. 2014. *How Numbers Rule the World.* London: Zed Books.

Fitzsimmons, Emma. 2014. "A Scourge Is Spreading. M.T.A.'s Cure? Dude, Close your Legs." *New York Times.* December 20.

Fletcher, Bill, and Fernando Gapasin. 2008. *Solidarity Divided: The Crisis in Organized Labor and a New Path toward Social Justice.* Berkeley: University of California Press.

Fletcher, Ian. 2001. "Forum: Reflections on Radical History." *Radical History Review* 79: 75–121.

Floyd, Kevin. 2015. "Gendered Labor and Abstract Life." "Plenary Talk, HM 2015." http://www.pdf-archive.com/2015/08/03/kevin-floyd/preview/page/1.

Foley, Tadhg. 2011. "'An Unknown and Feeble Body': How Settler Colonialism Was Theorized in the Nineteenth Century". In *Studies in Settler Colonialism,* edited by Fiona Bateman and Lionel Pilkington, 10–27. Houndmills, UK: Palgrave Macmillan.

Forbes, Jack. 1993. *Africans and Native Americans: The Language of Race and the Evolution of Red-Black Peoples*. Chicago: University of Illinois Press.

Foucault, Michel. 1972. *The Archaeology of Knowledge and the Discourse on Language*. Translated by A. M. Sheridan. New York: Pantheon.

———. 1975. "Docile Bodies"; "The Means of Correct Training." In *Discipline and Punish: The Birth of the Prison*. Translated by Alan Sheridan, 135–38, 141–45. New York: Random House.

———. 1978. *The History of Sexuality*, vol. 1, *An Introduction*. New York: Pantheon.

———. 2003. *Society Must Be Defended: Lectures at the Collège de France 1975–76*. Edited by Michel Senellart, translated by Graham Burchell. New York: Picador.

———. 2009. *Security, Territory, Population: Lectures at the Collège de France, 1977–78*. Edited by Michel Senellart, translated by Graham Burchell. New York: Picador.

Foucault, Michel, and Duccio Trombadori. 1991. *Remarks on Marx: Conversations with Duccio Trombardori*. Los Angeles: Semiotext(e).

Fraser, Nancy. 2010. "Who Counts Dilemmas of Justice in a Postwestphalian World." *Antipode* 41(1): 281–97.

———. 2013. "Against Anarchism." *Public Seminar*. April 9. http://www.publicseminar.org/2013/10/against-anarchism/#.Vdefy0V41UU.

Frederick, William C. 1994. "From CSR1 to CSR2." *Business & Society* 33(2): 150–64.

Free Geek Vancouver. 2013. "What is Anti-oppression?" wiki.freegeekvancouver.org/article/What_is_Anti-Oppression%3F.

Freeman, Jo. 2002. "The Tyranny of Structurelessness." In *Quiet Rumours: An Anarcha-Feminist Reader*, edited by Dark Star, 54–62. Edinburgh: AK Press UK.

Freire, Paulo. 1970. *Pedagogy of the Oppressed*. New York: Herder and Herder.

———. 2000. *Pedagogy of the Oppressed*. London: Continuum. First published 1970.

———. 2004. *Pedagogy of Hope*. London: Continuum.

———. 2005. *Pedagogy of the Oppressed*. New York: Continuum.

Friedman, Jocelyn, and Jessica Valenti. 2008. *Yes Means Yes! Visions of Female*

Sexual Power and a World without Rape. Seattle: Seal Press, 2008.

Fritsch, Kelly. 2013. "Neoliberal Circulation of Good Affects: Happiness, Accessibility, and the Capacitation of Disability." *Health, Culture and Society* 5: 135–49.

Fritsch, Kelly, Clare O'Connor and AK Thompson. 2014. Introduction to *Keywords for Radicals.* http://keywordsforradicals.net/introduction.html.

Galeano, Eduardo. 1997. *Open Veins of Latin America: Five Centuries of the Pillage of a Continent.* New York: Monthly Review Press.

Galleani, Luigi. 1925. *The End of Anarchism?* Translated by Max Sartin and Robert D'Attilio. Sanday, Orkney: Cienfuegos Press.

Garriga, Elisabet, and Domènec Melé. 2004. "Corporate Social Responsibility Theories: Mapping the Territory." *Journal of Business Ethics* 53: 51–71.

Garvey, Amy Jacques, ed. 2012. *More Philosophy and Opinions of Marcus Garvey.* London: Frank Cass.

Garza, Alicia. 2014. "The Herstory of the #BlackLivesMatter Movement." *Feminist Wire,* October 7. http://www.thefeministwire.com/2014/10/blacklivesmatter-2.

Gates, Henry Louis Jr. 2013. "Who Really Invented the 'Talented Tenth'?" *The Root,* February 18. http://www.theroot.com/articles/history/2013/02/talented_tenth_theory_web_du_bois_did_not_really_invent_it.html.

Geary, Patrick J. 2003. *The Myth of Nations: The Medieval Origins of Europe.* Princeton: Princeton University Press.

Gelderloos, Peter. 2009. "Against the War on Terror." *ZNet.* May 20. http://zcomm.org/znetarticle/ against-the-war-on-terrorism-by-peter-gelderloos.

———. 2013. *The Failure of Nonviolence.* Seattle: Left Bank Books.

Gellner, Ernest. 1983. *Nations and Nationalisms.* Cambridge, UK: Blackwell.

Geoghegan, Vincent. 2008. "Pandora's Box: Reflections on a Myth." *Critical Horizons,* 9: 24–41.

Geras, Norman. 1987. "Post-Marxism?" *New Left Review,* 163: 40–83.

Gerbaudo, Paolo. 2013. "When Anarchism Goes Pop." *openDemocracy,* November 6. https://www.opendemocracy.net/paolo-gerbaudo/when-anarchism -goes-pop.

Ghobadian, Abby, Kevin Money, and Carola Hillenbrand. 2015. "Corporate Responsibility Research: Past Present Future." *Group & Organization Management* 40(3): 271–94.

Giddens, Anthony. 1984. *The Constitution of Society: Outline of the Theory of*

Structuration. Oxford, UK: Polity Press.

Gill, Rosalind. 2007. "Technobohemians or the New Cybertariat? New Media Work in Amsterdam, a Decade after the Web." Report prepared for the Institute of Network Cultures. http://www.networkcultures.org/_uploads/17.pdf.

Gilroy, Paul. 2002. *Against Race: Imagining Political Culture beyond the Color Line.* Cambridge, MA: Harvard University Press.

Girard, René. 1977. *Violence and the Sacred.* Baltimore: Johns Hopkins University Press.

Glenn, Evelyn Nakano. 2010. *Forced to Care: Coercion and Caregiving in America.* Cambridge, MA: Harvard University Press.

Global Exchange. 2006. *Anti-Oppression Reader.* www.energyactioncoalition.org/sites/wearepowershift.org/files/AO_Reader_2007.pdf

Goldberg, David, and Trevor Griffey. 2010. *Black Power at Work: Community Control, Affirmative Action, and the Construction Industry.* Ithaca, NY: Cornell University Press.

Goldman, Emma. 1914. "Intellectual Proletarians." Anarchist Library. http://theanarchistlibrary.org/library/emma-goldman-intellectual-proletarians.

———. 1932. *Living My Life*, vol. 1. London: Duckworth.

———. 1969. *Anarchism and Other Essays.* New York: Dover.

———. 1970. *Living My Life: Volume II.* New York: Dover.

Goldner, Loren. 1997. "Race and the Enlightenment: From Anti-Semitism to White Supremacy." *Race Traitor* #7. Dorchester, MA.

Goldstein, Dana. 2014. "The Tough Lessons of the 1968 Teacher Strikes." *Nation*, September 24. http://www.thenation.com/print/article/181757/tough-lessons-1968-teacher-strikes.

Gooding, Judson. 1970. "Blue-Collar Blues on the Assembly Line." *Fortune*, July: 112–113.

Goodman, Amy. 2011. "Occupy Wall Street Emerges as 'First Populist Movement' on the Left Since the 1930s." *Democracy Now.* October 10. http://www.democracynow.org/2011/10/10/occupy_wall_street_emerges_as_first.

Goonewardena, Kanishka. 2011. "Henri Lefebvre" in *The Wiley-Blackwell Companion to Major Social Theorists.* Eds. George Ritzer and Jeffrey Stepnisky. London: Wiley-Blackwell.

Gordon, Uri. 2008. *Anarchy Alive! Anti-Authoritarian Politics from Practice to Theory.* London: Pluto.

Gore, Al. 2009. *Our Choice.* New York: Rodale.

Gorka, Sebastian, and David Kilcullen. 2011. "An Actor-Centric Theory of War: Understanding the Difference Between COIN and Counterinsurgency." *Joint Force Quarterly* 60: 14–18.

Graeber, David. 2002. "New Anarchists." *New Left Review*, 13: 61–73.

———. 2004. *Fragments of an Anarchist Anthropology.* Chicago: Prickly Paradigm Press.

———. 2007. "The Shock of Victory." Anarchist Library. http://theanarchistlibrary.org/library/david-graeber-the-shock-of-victory.

———. 2009. *Direct Action: An Ethnography.* Oakland: AK Press.

———. 2011. "Occupy Wall Street's Anarchist Roots." *Aljazeera.* November 30. http://www.aljazeera.com/indepth/opinion/2011/11/201111 12872835904508.html.

———. 2012. *The Democracy Project: A History, a Crisis, a Movement.* London: Allen Lane.

———. 2013. *The Democracy Project: A History, a Crisis, a Movement.* New York: Spiegel & Grau.

Grafton, Anthony. 1997. *The Footnote: A Curious History.* Cambridge, MA: Harvard University Press.

Graham, Mark. 2016. "Settler Colonialism from the Neo-Assyrian to the Roman Empire." In *The Routledge Handbook of the History of Settler Colonialism*, edited by Edward Cavanagh and Lorenzo Veracini. London: Routledge, forthcoming.

Graham, Robert. 2005. *Anarchism: A Documentary History of Libertarian Ideas*, vol. 1. Montreal: Black Rose Books.

Graham, Stephen. 2012. "When Life Itself Is War: On the Urbanization of Military and Security Doctrine." *International Journal of Urban and Regional Research* 36: 136–55.

Gramsci, Antonio. 1971. *Selections from the Prison Notebooks of Antonio Gramsci.* New York: International Publishers.

Green, John Richard. 1881. *A Short History of the English People.* New York: Harper and Brothers.

Greenwald, Glenn. 2014. *No Place to Hide: Edward Snowden, the NSA and the US Surveillance State.* New York: Picador/Holt.

Gregory, Derek. 2014. "Drone Geographies." *Radical Philosophy* 183: 7–19.

Greif, Mark. 2015. "What's Wrong with Public Intellectuals?" *Chronicle*

of Higher Education. February 13. http://chronicle.com/article/Whats
-Wrong-With-Public/189921.

Griffiths, Jay. 1996. "Life in the Fast Lane on the M41: Jay Griffiths Parties without Reservation at the Invitation of Reclaim The Streets." July 17. *Guardian.*

Grotius, Hugo. 2001. "The Rights of War and Peace" In *The Philosophy of Human
Rights*, edited by Patrick Hayden, 48–54. St. Paul, MN: Paragon House.

Gubar, Susan. 1994. "Feminist Misogyny: Mary Wollstonecraft and the Paradox of 'It Takes One to Know One.'" *Feminist Studies* 20(3): 453–74.

Gudynas, Eduardo. 2011. "Buen Vivir: Today's Tomorrow." *Development*
54(4): 441–47.

Guevara, Ernesto Che. 1968. "Socialism and Man in Cuba, and Other Works."
Marxists Internet Archive. https://www.marxists.org/archive/guevara
/1965/03/man-socialism.htm.

———. 2006. *Guerrilla Warfare.* "Authorized Edition with Corrections Made
by Che Guevara." Melbourne: Ocean Press.

Gumbs, Alexis Pauline. 2010. "We Can Learn to Mother Ourselves: The Queer
Survival of Black Feminism, 1968–1996." PdD diss., Duke University.

Gupta, Devashree. 2009. "Small Victories and Partial Losses: How Incremental
Outcomes Affect Social Movement Organizations." *Mobilization: An International Journal* 14(3): 417–32.

Habermas, Jürgen. 1991. *The Structural Transformation of the Public Sphere: An
Inquiry into a Category of Bourgeois Society.* Cambridge: MIT Press.

Hackman, Rose. 2015. "'We Need Co-conspirators, Not Allies': How White
Americans Can Fight Racism." *Guardian.* June 26.

Hahn, Steven. 2009. *The Political Worlds of Slavery and Freedom.* Cambridge:
Harvard University Press.

Haiven, Max. 2014. *Crises of Imagination, Crises of Power: Capitalism, Creativity
and the Commons.* London: Zed Books.

Haiven, Max, and Alex Khasnbish. 2014. *The Radical Imagination: Social Movements in the Age of Austerity.* Blackpoint, Winnipeg: Fernwood Books.

Hale, Charles R., ed. 2008. *Engaging Contradictions: Theory, Politics, Method.*
Berkeley: University of California Press.

Hall, Anthony. 2003. *The American Empire and the Fourth World.* Montreal: Mc-
Gill-Queen's University Press.

Hall, Stuart. 1988. *The Hard Road to Renewal: Thatcherism and the Crisis of the
Left.* London: Verso.

———. 1996a. "On Postmodernism and Articulation: An Interview with Stuart Hall." In *Stuart Hall: Critical Dialogues in Cultural Studies*, edited by David Morley and Kuan-Hsing Chen, 131–50. London: Routledge.

———. 1996b. "The Problem of Ideology: Marxism without Guarantees." In *Stuart Hall: Critical Dialogues in Cultural Studies*, edited by David Morley and Kuan-Hsing Chen, 25–46. London: Routledge.

———. 1997. *Stuart Hall: Representation and the Media*. Directed by Sut Jhally. Media Education Foundation.

Halliday, Josh, and Charles Arthur. 2010. "Wikileaks: Who are the hackers behind Operation Payback?" *The Guardian*, December 8. http://www.theguardian.com/media/2010/dec/08/anonymous-4chan-wikileaks-mastercard-paypal

Hamilton, Neil. 2002. *American Social Leaders and Activists*. New York: Facts on File.

Hampton, Fred. 1969. "Power Anywhere Where There's People." http://www.historyisaweapon.com/defcon1/fhamptonspeech.html

Hande, Mary Jean, and Christine Kelly. 2015. "Organizing Survival and Resistance in Austere Times: Shifting Disability Activism and Care Politics in Ontario, Canada." *Disability & Society* 30(7): 961–75.

Haraway, Donna. 1991. *Simians, Cyborgs and Women: The Reinvention of Nature*. New York: Routledge.

Harden, Joel. 2013. *Quiet No More: New Political Activism in Canada and around the Globe*. Toronto: James Lorimer.

Hardin, Garrett. 1968. "The Tragedy of the Commons." *Science* 162: 1243–48.

Harding, Sandra. 1986. *The Science Question in Feminism*. Ithaca, NY: Cornell University Press.

Hardt, Michael. 2012. *The Procedures of Love*. Ostfildern, Germany: Hatje Cantz.

Hardt, Michael, and Antonio Negri. 2001. *Empire*. Cambridge, MA: Harvard University Press.

———. 2004. *Multitude: War and Democracy in the Age of Empire*. New York: Penguin Press.

———. 2009. *Commonwealth*. Cambridge, MA: Harvard University Press.

Harlow, Barbara. 1991. "The Intellectuals and the War: An Interview with Edward Said." *Middle East Report* 171: 15–20.

Harney, Stefano, and Fred Moten. 2013. *The Undercommons: Fugitive Planning and Black Study*. New York: Minor Compositions.

Harris, Michael. 2015. "What is 'Safe Space'?" *Fusion*. November 19. http:

//fusion.net/story/231089/safe-space-history/?utm_source=twitter& utm_medium=social&utm_campaign=FusionRSS.

Harrison, Hubert. 2001. *A Hubert Harrison Reader*. Middletown: Wesleyan University Press.

Hart, Gillian. 2013. "Gramsci, Geography and the Languages of Populism." In *Gramsci: Space, Nature, Politics*, edited by Mike Ekers, Gillian Hart, Stefan Kipfer, Alex Loftus, 301–20. Oxford, UK: Blackwell.

———. 2014. *Rethinking the South African Crisis: Nationalism, Populism, Hegemony*. Athens: University of Georgia Press.

Harring, Sidney. 1994. *Crow Dog's Law: American Indian Sovereignty, Tribal Law, and United States Law in the Twentieth Century*. Cambridge: Cambridge University Press.

Harrington, Michael. 1962. *The Other America: Poverty in the United States*. New York: Touchstone.

Harvey, David. 2000. *Spaces of Hope*. Berkeley: University of California Press.

———. 2003. "The Right to the City." *International Journal of Urban and Regional Research* 27(4): 939–41.

———. 2005. *A Brief History of Neoliberalism*. Oxford: Oxford University Press.

———. 2012. *Rebel Cities: From the Right to the City to the Urban Revolution*. London: Verso.

Hawken, Paul, Amory Lovins, and L. Hunter Lovins. 1999. *Natural Capitalism*. Boston: Little, Brown.

Hayden, Tom. 2011. Foreword to *Conspiracy to Riot in Furtherance of Terrorism: The Collective Autobiography of the RNC 8*, edited by Leslie James Pickering and Tom Hayden, 1–5. Binghamton, NY: Arissa Media Group.

Hebdige, Dick. 1993. "From Culture to Hegemony." In *The Cultural Studies Reader*, edited by Simon During, 357–67. London: Routledge. First published 1979.

Hechter, Michael. 1975. *Internal Colonialism: The Celtic Fringe in British National Development, 1536–1966*. London: Routledge & Kegan Paul.

Heckert, Jamie. 2012. *Gender*. Lexicon Pamphlet Series. Washington, DC: Institute for Anarchist Studies.

Hegel, G. W. F. 1802. "II History and Critique of the Constitution of the German Empire." *The German Constitution*. www.marxists.org/reference/archive/hegel/works/gc/ch02.htm.

———. 1970. *The Philosophy of Nature*. London: George Allen and Unwin. First published 1830.

Heideman, Paul. 2014. "Bulletproof Neoliberalism." June. *Jacobin*. https://www.jacobinmag.com/2014/06/bulletproof-neoliberalism.

Hennessy, Rosemary. 2013. *Fires on the Border: The Passionate Politics of Labor Organizing on the Mexican Frontera*. Minneapolis: University of Minnesota Press.

Hennessy, Rosemary, and Chrys Ingraham, eds. 1997. *Materialist Feminism: A Reader in Class, Difference, and Women's Lives*. New York: Routledge.

Heraclitus. 1987. *Fragments: A Text and Translation with a Commentary by T. M. Robinson*. Toronto: University of Toronto Press.

Hill, Gord. 2009. *500 Years of Indigenous Resistance*. Oakland: PM Press.

Hill, Mike, and Tom Cohen. 2009. "Black Swans and Pop-Up Militias: War and the 'Re-Rolling' of Imagination." *Global South* 3: 1–17.

Hixson, Walter L. 2013. *American Settler Colonialism: A History*. New York: Palgrave Macmillan.

Hobbes, Thomas. 1962 [1651]. *Leviathan, or the Matter, Forme, and Power of a Commonwealth Ecclesiastical and Civil*. Edited by Michael Oakeshott. New York: Macmillan.

———. 1992. "Leviathan." In *Classics of Modern and Political Theory*, edited by Michael L. Morgan, 651. Cambridge: Hackett.

———. 2008. *Leviathan*. Edited by J. C. A. Gaskin. Oxford: Oxford University Press.

Hobsbawm, Eric J. 1971. "From Social History to History of Society," *Daedalus* 100: 20–45.

———. 1995. *Age of Extremes: The Short Twentieth Century 1914–1991*. London: Abacus.

Hoelzl, Michael. 2004. "Recognizing the Sacrificial Victim: The Problem of Solidarity for Critical Social Theory." *Journal for Cultural and Religious Studies* 6: 45–64.

Holsaert, Faith, et al., eds. 2010. *Hands on the Freedom Plow: Personal Accounts by Women in SNCC*. Urbana: University of Illinois Press.

Holy Bible. 1982. New King James Version. Nashville: Thomas Nelson.

Honeywell, Carissa. 2007. "Utopianism and Anarchism." *Journal of Political Ideologies* 2(3): 239–54.

hooks, bell. 1982. "Race and Gender: The Issue of Accountability." *Ain't I a Woman? Black Women and Feminist*. Boston: South End Press.

————. 1992. *Black Looks: Race and Representation*. New York: South End Press.

————. 2000. *Feminist Theory: From Margin to Center*. Cambridge, MA: South End Press.

hooks, bell, and Amalia Mesa-Bains. 2006. *Homegrown: Engaged Cultural Criticism*. Cambridge, MA: South End Press.

Horton, Myles and Paolo Freire. 1990. *We Make the Road by Walking*. Philadelphia: Temple University Press.

House, Robert J. and Ram M. Aditya. 1997. "The Social Scientific Study of Leadership: Quo Vadis?" *Journal of Management*, 23. no. 3, 409–473.

Hurston, Zora Neale. 1979. "How it Feels to be Colored Me." In *I Love Myself when I Am Laughing ... and Then Again when I Am Looking Mean and Impressive: A Zora Neale Hurston Reader*, 152–5. New York: CUNY Press.

Huws, Ursula. 2003. *The Making of a Cybertariat: Virtual Work in a Real World*. New York: Monthly Review Press.

"Identity in Crisis." 2012. *Baeden 1: Journal of Queer Nihilism*, 3–18.

Iglesias, Pablo. 2015. "Podemos: notre stratégie." *Le Monde Diplomatique*. July 1, 7.

Iggers, Georg G., and J. Powell, eds. 1990. *Leopold von Ranke and the Shaping of the Historical Discipline*. Syracuse: Syracuse University Press.

Ignatieff, Michael. 2001. *Human Rights as Politics and Idolatry*. Princeton: Princeton University Press.

Incite! Women of Color Collective. 2009. *The Revolution Will Not Be Funded: Beyond the Non-Profit Industrial Complex*. Boston: South End Press.

Indigenous Action Media. 2014. "Accomplices Not Allies: Abolishing the Ally Industrial Complex: An Indigenous Perspective and Provocation." May 4. http://www.indigenousaction.org/accomplices-not-allies-abolishing-the-ally-industrial-complex.

Inoperative Committee. 2011. "Preoccupied: The Logic of Occupation." In *Dispatches from the Ruins: Documents and Analyses from University Struggles, Experiments in Self-Education*, 3–7. New York: 1000 Little Hammers.

Institute for Anarchist Studies. 2012. "Lexicon Pamphlet Series: About." Institute for Anarchist Studies. http://anarchiststudies.org/lexicon-pamphlet-series/lexicon-series-about.

Invisible Committee. 2009. *The Coming Insurrection*. Los Angeles: Semiotexte; Cambridge, MA: MIT Press.

————. 2015. *To Our Friends*. South Pasadena, CA: Semiotexte; Cambridge,

MA: MIT Press.

Irving, Dan, and Rupert Raj, eds. 2014. *Trans Activism in Canada: A Reader*. Toronto: Canadian Scholar's Press.

Isaac, Benjamin H. 2006. *The Invention of Racism in Classical Antiquity*. Princeton: Princeton University Press.

Iseman, Myre. 2010. *Race Suicide*. Charleston: Nabu Press.

Isla, Ana. 2009. "Who Pays for the Kyoto Protocol?" In *Eco-Sufficiency & Global Justice: Women Write Policial Ecology*, edited by Ariel Salleh, 199–217. London: Pluto Press.

"Is the Anarchist Man Our Comrade?" 2010. http://anarchalibrary.blogspot. ca/2010/10/is-anarchist-man-our-comrade-2010.html.

Italian Revolution Milano. 2011. "Dal presidio permanente al presidio diffuso." http://italianrevolutionmilano.jimdo.com.

Jacoby, Russell. 1987. *The Last Intellectuals: American Culture in the Age of Academe*. New York: Basic Books.

———. 1994. "The Myth of Multiculturalism." *New Left Review* 208: 121–26.

Jagose, Annamarie. 1996. *Queer Theory: An Introduction*. New York: New York University Press.

James, Cedric L. R. 2001. *The Black Jacobins: Toussaint L'Ouverture and the San Domingo Revolution*. New York: Penguin.

James, Joy. 2005. *Imprisoned Intellectuals: America's Political Prisoners Write on Life, Rebellion and Liberation*. Lanham, MD: Rowman & Littlefield. https://repositories.lib.utexas.edu/handle/2152/7098.

James, Selma. 2012. *Sex, Race, and Class: The Perspective of Winning*. Oakland: PM Press.

Jameson, Frederic. 1981. *The Political Unconscious: Narrative as a Socially Symbolic Act*. Ithaca, NY: Cornell University Press.

———. 1991. *Postmodernism, or, The Cultural Logic of Late Capitalism*. Durham: Duke University Press.

———. 2015. "The Aesthetics of Singularity." *New Left Review* 92, 101–132.

Jasper, James. 2004. "A Strategic Approach to Collective Action: Looking for Agency in Social Movement Choices." *Mobilization: An International Journal* 9(1): 1–16.

Jay, Martin. 1973. *The Dialectical Imagination: A History of the Frankfurt School and the Institute of Social Research, 1923–1950*. Berkeley: University of California Press.

———. 2004. *Songs of Experience: Modern American and European Variations on a Universal Theme.* Berkeley: University of California Press.

Jefferson, Thomas. 1816. "Letter to Isaac H. Tiffany." TeachingAmerican History.org, http://teachingamericanhistory.org/library/document/letter-to-isaac-h-tiffany.

Jensen, Derrick. n.d. "Beyond Hope." *Orion Magazine.* https://orionmagazine.org/article/beyond-hope.

Jensen, Robert. 2014. "Declaring Victory Wherever We Can: An Interview with Cynthia Kaufman on Getting Past Capitalism." *Truth-Out.* February 9. http://www.truth-out.org/opinion/item/21755-declaring-victory-wherever-we-can-an-interview-with-cynthia-kaufman-on-getting-past-capitalism.

Johnson, Cedric. *Revolutionaries to Race Leaders.* 2007. Minneapolis: University of Minnesota Press.

Johnson, Merri Lisa, and Robert McRuer, eds. 2014. "Cripistemologies." *Journal of Literary and Cultural Disability Studies* 8: 2–3.

Johnson Reagon, Bernice. 1983. "Coalition Politics: Turning the Century." Kitchen Table Press. *Home Girls: A Black Feminist Anthology.*

Jordan, June. 1998. *Affirmative Acts: Political Essays.* New York: Doubleday.

Joseph, Miranda. 2002. *Against the Romance of Community.* Minneapolis: University of Minnesota Press.

———. 2014. *Debt to Society: Accounting for Life under Capitalism.* Minneapolis: University of Minnesota Press.

Joseph, Peniel E. 2009. "The Black Power Movement: A State of the Field." *Journal of American History* 96: 751–76.

Joyce, Joyce A. 1987. "'Who the Cap Fit': Unconsciousness and Unconscionableness in the Criticism of Houston A. Baker, Jr., and Henry Louis Gates, Jr." *New Literary History* 18: 371–84.

Jumonville, Neil, and Kevin Mattson. 2007. *Liberalism for a New Century.* Berkeley: University of California Press.

Justseeds. n.d. "About." justseeds.org/about/who_we_are.html.

Kafer, Alison. 2013. *Feminist, Queer, Crip.* Bloomington: Indiana University Press.

Kantorowicz, Ernst. 1957. *The King's Two Bodies: A Study in Medieval Political Theology.* Princeton: Princeton University Press.

Kautsky, Karl. 1892. *The Class Struggle.* New York: W. W. Norton.

Kazin, Michael. 2011. *American Dreamers: How the Left Changed a Nation.* New

York: Vintage Books.

Kelley, Robin D. G. 2002. *Freedom Dreams: The Black Radical Imagination*. Boston: Beacon Press.

———. 2014. "Why We Won't Wait," *Counterpunch*. November 25. http://www.counterpunch.org/2014/11/25/75039.

Kennedy, David. 2005. *The Dark Sides of Virtue: Reassessing International Humanitarianism*. Princeton: Princeton University Press.

Kern, Stephen. 2003. *The Culture of Time & Space (1880–1918)*. Boston: Harvard University Press.

Keyt. 1993. "Aristotle and Anarchism." *Reason Papers* 18: 133–52.

Khasnabish, Alex. 2008. *Zapatismo beyond Borders: New Imaginations of Political Possibility*. Toronto: University of Toronto Press.

Khiari, Sadri. 2013. "Le Peuple et le Tiers-Peuple." In *Qu'est-ce qu'un Peuple*, edited by Alain Badiou et al., 115–36. Paris: La Fabrique.

Klein, Naomi. 2007. *The Shock Doctrine: The Rise of Disaster Capitalism*. Toronto: Knopf Canada.

———. 2014. *This Changes Everything*. New York: Simon and Schuster.

Kimmelman, Michael. 2011. "In Protest, the Power of Place." *New York Times*, October 15.

King, Martin Luther. 1964a. "Acceptance Speech." Nobelprize.org. http://www.nobelprize.org/nobel_prizes/peace/laureates/1964/king-acceptance.html.

———. 1964b. "Speech on Civil Rights, Segregation and Apartheid South Africa" December 7. *Democracy Now*. http://www.democracynow.org/2015/1/19/exclusive_newly_discovered_1964_mlk_speech.

King, Miriam. 2014. "Mother Earth Water Walk around Local Lakes Sending a Message." *Barrie Examiner*. June 27.

Kino-nda-niimi Collective. 2014. *The Winter We Danced: Voices from the Past, the Future, and the Idle No More Movement*. Winnipeg: Arbeiter Ring.

Kipfer, Stefan, and Gillian Hart. 2013. "Translating Gramsci in the Current Conjuncture." In *Gramsci: Nature, Space, Politics*, Mike Ekers, Gillian Hart, Stefan Kipfer and Alex Loftus eds., 323–44. London: Routledge.

Kirmayer, Laurence J. 1988. "Mind and Body as Metaphors: Hidden Values in Biomedicine." In *Biomedicine Examined*, edited by Margaret Lock and Deborah Gordon, 57–93. Dordrecht: Kluwer Academic.

Kitschelt, H. 1993. "Social Movements, Political Parties, and Democratic Theory" *Annals of the American Academy of Political and Social Science* 528: 13–29.

Kittay, Eva Feder. 1999. *Love's Labour: Essays on Women, Equality, and Dependency*. New York: Routledge.

Kivel, Paul. 1996. *Uprooting Racism: How White People Can Work for Racial Justice*. Gabriola Island, BC: New Society Publishers.

———. 2011. *Uprooting Racism: How White People Can Work for Racial Justice*. 3rd ed. Gabriola Island, BC: New Society Publishers.

Kolárová, Katerina. 2014. "The Inarticulate Post-Socialist Crip: On the Cruel Optimism of Neoliberal Transformations in the Czech Republic." *Journal of Literary and Cultural Disability Studies* 8: 257–74.

Kolisetty, Akhila. 2011. "Let Us Not Deny Them Agency." August 15. *Journeys toward Justice*. http://akhilak.com/blog/2011/08/15/let-us-not-deny -them-agency.

Kolko, Gabriel. 1963. *The Triumph of Conservatism: A Reinterpretation of American History, 1900–1916*. New York: Free Press.

Kovel, Joel. 2007. *The Enemy of Nature: The End of Capitalism or the End of the World*. London: Zed Books.

Koyama, Emi. 2003. "The Transfeminist Manifesto." In *Catching A Wave: Reclaiming Feminism for the Twenty-First Century*, edited by Rory Dicker and Alison Piepmeier, 244–59. Boston: Northeastern University Press.

Kraniauskas, John. 2014. "Rhetorics of Populism: Ernesto Laclau, 1935–2014." *Radical Philosophy* 186: 29–37.

Krauss, Rosalind. 1994. "In the Name of Picasso." *The Originality of the Avant-Garde and Other Modernist Myths*. Cambridge, MA: MIT Press.

Kristof, Nicholas. 2014. "Professors, We Need You!" *New York Times*, February 15.

Kropotkin, Peter. 1898. *Fields, Factories and Workshops*. New York: G. P. Putnam.

———. 1902. *Mutual Aid: A Factor of Evolution*. London: William Heinemann.

———. 1970. "Law and Authority." In *Kropotkin's Revolutionary Pamphlets*, edited by Roger N. Baldwin, 195–218. New York: Dover.

———. 2014. "Communism and Anarchy." In *Direct Struggle against Capital: A Peter Kropotkin Anthology*. Edited by Iain McKay, 631–42. Oakland: AK Press.

Kruks, Sonia. 2001. *Retrieving Experience: Subjectivity and Recognition in Feminist Politics*. Ithaca, NY: Cornell University Press.

Kulchyski, Peter Keith. 2013. *Aboriginal Rights Are Not Human Rights: In Defence of Indigenous Struggles*. Winnipeg: Arbeiter Ring.

Kulick, Don. 2000. "Gay and Lesbian Language" *Annual Review of Anthropology* 29: 24385.

Kuppers, Petra. 2011. *Disability Culture and Community Performance: Find a Strange and Twisted Shape*. New York: Palgrave.

Kurwa, Nishat. 2014. "'Black Lives Matter' Slogan Becomes a Bigger Movement." NPR. December 4. http://www.npr.org/2014/12/04/368408247/black -lives-matter-slogan-becomes-a-bigger-movement.

Kushner, David. 2014. "The Masked Avengers." *The New Yorker*, September 14.

Laclau, Ernesto. 1977. *Politics and Ideology in Marxist Theory: Capitalism, Fascism, Populism*. London: Verso.

———. 2005. *On Populist Reason*. London: Verso.

Laclau, Ernesto, and Chantal Mouffe. 1985. *Hegemony and Socialist Strategy*. London: Verso.

Lakeman, Lee. 2006. "Sustaining Our Resistance to Male Violence: Attacks on Women's Organizing and Vancouver Rape Relief and Women's Shelters." *Canadian Women's Studies* 25: 129–32.

Lambert, Renaud. 2015. "Podemos, le parti qui bouscule l'Espagne" *Le Monde Diplomatique*. January 1.

Lamm, Nomy. 2015. "This Is Disability Justice." *The Body Is Not an Apology*. http://thebodyisnotanapology.com/magazine/this-is-disability-justice.

Landstreicher, Wolfi, Shawn Wilbur, and Vincent Stone. 2014. *Disruptive Elements: The Extremes of French Anarchism*. San Francisco: Ardent Press.

Langman, L. 2013. "Occupy: A New, New Social Movement." *Current Sociology* 61(4): 510–24.

Lasch, Christopher. 1979. *The Culture of Narcissism*. New York: W. W. Norton.

Lash, Scott. 2007. "Power after Hegemony: Cultural Studies in Mutation?" *Theory, Culture, and Society* 24(3): 55–78.

Latouche, Serge. 2004. "Degrowth Economics." *Le Monde Diplomatique*. November 14.

Latour, Bruno. 2004. "How to Talk about the Body? The Normative Dimension of Science Studies." *Body and Society* 10(2–3): 215–29.

———. 2005. *Reassembling the Social: An Introduction to Actor-Network Theory*. Oxford: Oxford University Press.

Lattman, Peter. 2012. "Former Citigroup Manager Cleared in Mortgage Securities Case." *New York Times*, July 31.

Lavin, Chad. 2008. *The Politics of Responsibility*. Urbana: University of

Illinois Press.

Law, Victoria, and China Martens, eds. 2012. *Don't Leave Your Friends Behind: Concrete Ways to Support Families in Social Justice Movements and Communities*. Oakland: PM Press.

Le Guin, Ursula. 1974. *The Dispossessed*. New York: Harper and Row.

Leakey, Richard E., and Roger Lewin. 1995. *The Sixth Extinction*. New York: Doubleday.

Leary, Elly. 2005. "Crisis in the U.S. Labor Movement: The Roads Not Taken." *Monthly Review* 57(2): 28–37.

Lefebvre, Henri. 1971. *Everyday Life in the Modern World*. Trans. Sasha Rabonovitch. Harmondsworth: Allen Lane. First published 1968.

———. 1978. *De l'état*, tome IV. Paris: Union générale d'éditions.

———. 1988. *Le nationalisme contre les nations*. Paris: Méridiens Klincksieck.

———. 1991. *The Production of Space*. Trans. David Nicholson-Smith, afterword by David Harvey. Oxford: Blackwell. First published 1974.

———. 2003. *The Urban Revolution*. Trans. Robert Bononno, foreword by Neil Smith. Minneapolis: University of Minnesota Press. First published 1970.

Leiss, William. 1972. *The Domination of Nature*. Boston: Beacon Press.

Lemisch, Jesse. 1975. *On Active Service in War and Peace: Politics and Ideology in the American Historical Profession*. Toronto: New Hogtown Press.

Lenin, Vladimir Ilyich. 1919. "Letter to Gorky." Revelations from the Russian Archives (exhibition), Library of Congress. http://www.loc.gov/exhibits/archives/g2aleks.html.

———. 1920. "The Tasks of the Youth Leagues: Speech Delivered at the Third All-Russia Congress of the Russian Young Communist League." Marxists Internet Archive. https://www.marxists.org/archive/lenin/works/1920/oct/02.htm.

———. 1932. *The State and Revolution*. New York: International Publishers.

———. 1952. *Imperialism: The Highest Stage of Capitalism*. Moscow: Foreign Languages Publishing House.

———. 1961. "What Is to Be Done?" Marxists Internet Archive. https://www.marxists.org/archive/lenin/works/1901/witbd.

———. 1963. "Reformism in the Russian Social-Democratic Movement." In *Collected Works*, vol. 17, 229–40. Moscow: Foreign Languages Publishing House. First published 1911.

———. 1964a. "The State and Revolution: The Marxist Theory of the State and the Tasks of the Proletariat in the Revolution" In *Collected Works* vol. 25, 385–499. Moscow: Progress Publishers. First published 1917.

———. 1964b. "Can the Bolsheviks Retain State Power?" In *Collected Works* vol. 26, 87–136. Moscow: Progress Publishers. First published 1917.

———. 1977. "A Letter to the Northern League." In *Collected Works*, vol. 6, 161–71. Moscow: Progress Publishers.

Leonard, Annie. 2007. *Story of Stuff.* Berkeley: Free Range Studios.

Letts, Marcus. 2009. "Obama's Discourse of 'Hope': Making Rhetoric Work Politically." Working paper no. 4/09, SPAIS (School of Sociology, Politics and International Studies), University of Bristol, Bristol, UK.

Levine, Andrew. 2007. *Political Keywords: A Guide for Students, Activists and Everyone Else.* Wiley Press.

Levine, Cathy. 2002. "The Tyranny of Tyranny". In *Quiet Rumours: An Anarcha-Feminist Reader*, edited by Dark Star, 63–86. Edinburgh: AK Press UK.

Levine, Debra. 2009. "How to do Things With Dead Bodies." *E-Misferica* 61. http://hemisphericinstitute.org/hemi/en/e-misferica-61/levine.

———. 2012. *Demonstrating ACT UP: The Ethics, Politics, and Performance of Affinity.* PhD diss., New York University.

Levitas, Ruth. 1997. "Educated Hope: Ernst Bloch on Abstract and Concrete Utopia." In *Not Yet: Reconsidering Ernst Bloch*, edited by J. O. Daniel and T. Moylan, 65–79. London: Verso.

Liberti, Stefano. 2011. *Land Grabbing. Come il mercato delle terre crea il nuovo colonialismo.* Rome: Minimum Fax.

Liberty Mutual Insurance. 2015. "The Responsibility Project." Liberty Mutual Insurance. www.libertymutual.com/responsibility-project.

Linebaugh, Peter. 2008. *The Magna Carta Manifesto: Liberties and Commons for All.* Berkeley: University of California Press.

———. 2014a. *Midnight Notes Goes to School: Report from the Zapatista Escuelita.* Brooklyn: Autonomedia.

———. 2014b. *Stop Thief! Commons, Enclosures, Resistance.* Oakland: PM Press.

Lixinski, Lucas. 2011. "Selected Heritage: The Interplay of Art, Politics and Identity." *European Journal of International Law* 22: 81–100.

Locke, John. 1828. *An Essay concerning Human Understanding.* London: J. F. Dove.

———. 1995. *Treatise of Government and a Letter Concerning Toleration.* Edited by Charles L. Sherman. New York: Irvington Press.

Loewe, B. 2012. "An End to Self-Care." *Organizing Upgrade*. http://www
.organizingupgrade.com/index.php/blogs/b-loewe/item/729-end
-to-self-care.

Lombardi, Mark. 2003. *Mark Lombardi: Global Networks*. New York: Independent
Curators International.

Longo, Stefano, Rebecca Clausen, and Brett Clark. 2015. *The Tragedy of the
Commodity*. New York: Routledge.

Lorde, Audre. 1980. *The Cancer Journals*. San Francisco: Aunt Lute.

———. 1988. *A Burst of Light: Essays by Audre Lorde*. Ithaca, NY: Fire-
brand Books.

Lorenzano, Luis. 1998. "Zapatismo: Recomposition of Labour, Radical Democracy and Revolutionary Project." In *Zapatista! Reinventing Revolution
in Mexico*, edited by John Holloway, and Eloina Peláez, 126–58. London:
Pluto Press.

Losurdo, Domenico. 2011. *Liberalism: A Counter-History*. London: Verso.

Lowe, Lisa. 1998. *Immigrant Acts: On Asian American Cultural Politics*. Durham:
Duke University Press.

Löwy, Michael. 1988. *Marxism and Liberation Theology*. Note Books for Study
and Research. Amsterdam: IIRE.

———. 2014. "Dix Thèses Sur l'Extrême Droite en Europe." *Les Alternatifs*. June
2. http://www.alternatifs44.com/2014/06/ce-serait-une-erreur-de-croire
-que-le.html.

Lukács, Georg. 1971. *History and Class Consciousness: Studies in Marxist Dialectics*. Translated by Rodney Livingstone. Cambridge, MA: MIT Press.

Luxemburg, Rosa. 1968. *The Accumulation of Capital*. New York: Monthly Review Press.

Macauley, T. Babington. 1835. "Minute by the Hon'ble T. B. Macauley, date
the 2nd February, 1835." http://www.columbia.edu/itc/mealac/pritchett/
00generallinks/macaulay/txt_minute_education_1835.html.

MacKinnon, Catherine. 2001. "Rape, Genocide, and Women's Human Rights."
In *The Philosophy of Human Rights*, edited by Patrick Hayden. St. Paul: Paragon House.

Mackintosh, James. 2015. "Playing Morality with Greek Markets." *Financial
Times*. July 6.

Macpherson, Crawford Brough. 1962. *The Political Theory of Possessive Individualism*. Oxford: Oxford University Press.

Madondo, Obert. 2012. "What Chief Spence's Hunger Strike Says about Canada." *Huffington Post*, Canada ed. December 14. http://www.huffingtonpost.ca/obert -madondo/cheif-hunger-strike-democracy_b_2298786.html.

Magdoff, Fred, and John Bellamy Foster. 2011. *What Every Environmentalist Needs to Know about Capitalism: A Citizen's Guide to Capitalism and the Environment*. New York: Monthly Review Press.

Makin, Kirk. 2013. "How Canada's Sex-Assault Laws Violate Rape Victims." *Globe and Mail*, October 5.

Malacrida, Claudia. 2015. *A Special Hell: Institutional Life in Alberta's Eugenic Years*. Toronto: University of Toronto Press.

Malcom X. 1964. "Malcom X's Speech at the Founding Rally of the Organization of Afro-American Unity." BlackPast.org. http://www.blackpast. org/1964-malcolm-x-s-speech-founding-rally-organization-afro-american -unity.

———. 1999. *Autobiography of Malcolm X*. New York: Random House.

Mandlis, Lane. 2011. "'Formal Equality Can Actually Be Seen to Function as a Barrier to Substantive Equality': An Interview with Lane Mandlis." In *Sex Change, Social Change: Reflections on Identity, Institutions and Imperialism*, 2nd edition, edited by V. Namaste, 169–79. Toronto: Toronto Women's Press.

Mankiller, Wilma, and Michael Wallis. 1993. *Mankiller: A Chief and Her People*. New York: St. Martin's Press.

Mann, Susan Archer. 2012. *Doing Feminist Theory: From Modernity to Postmodernity*. New York: Oxford University Press.

Mannheim, Karl. 1954. *Ideology and Utopia: An Introduction to the Sociology of Knowledge*. New York: Harcourt, Brace & Co.

Mao Zedong. 1938. "On Protracted War." Marxists Internet Archive. https:// www.marxists.org/reference/archive/mao/selected-works/volume-2/ mswv2_09.htm.

———. 1992. "Problems of War and Strategy." In *Mao's Road to Power: Revolutionary Writings 1912–1949*, vol. 6, edited by R. Stuart Schram and Nancy Jane Hodes, 548–59. Armonk, NY: M. E. Sharpe.

Marazzi, Christian. 2008. *Capital and Language: From the New Economy to the War Economy*. Los Angeles: Semiotext(e).

Marcos, Subcomandante. 2001. "The Fourth World War." October 23. *La Jornada*.

———. 2004. *Ya Basta! Ten Years of the Zapatista Uprising*. Edited by Žiga

Vodovnik. Oakland: AK Press.

Marcuse, Herbert. 1964. *One-Dimensional Man: Studies in the Ideology of Advanced Industrial Society.* Boston: Beacon Press.

———. 1970. *Five Lectures.* Boston: Beacon Press.

Marinetti, Filippo. 1909. "Manifesto of Futurism." Italian Futurism. http://www.italianfuturism.org/manifestos/foundingmanifesto.

Marshall, T. H. 1992. "Citizenship and Social Class." In *Citizenship and Social Class*, edited by Marshall, T. H. and Tom Bottomore, 3–51. London: Pluto Press.

Martel, James. 2012. *Divine Violence: Walter Benjamin and the Eschatology of Sovereignty.* New York: Routledge.

Martin, Randy. 2002. *Financialization of Daily Life.* Philadelphia: Temple University Press.

Martinez-Alier, Joan, and Joachim Spangenberg. 2012. "Green Growth." *EJOLT.* http://www.ejolt.org/2015/09/green-growth.

Martínez, María Elena. 2011. *Genealogical Fictions: Limpieza de Sangre, Religion, and Gender in Colonial Mexico.* Palo Alto: Stanford University Press.

Marx, Karl. 1843. Marx's Letters to Arnold Ruge. Marxists Internet Archive. https://www.marxists.org/archive/marx/letters/ruge.

———. 1857. Introduction to *Grundrisse.* Marxists Internet Archive. https://www.marxists.org/archive/marx/works/1857/grundrisse/ch01.htm.

———.1857. *Grundrisse.* www.marxists.org/archive/marx/works/1857/grundrisse/.

———. 1863. "Theories of Surplus Value." Marxists Internet Archive. https://www.marxists.org/archive/marx/works/1863/theories-surplus-value/

———. 1867a. "The Labour-Process and the Process of Producing Surplus-Value." Marxists Internet Archive. https://www.marxists.org/archive/marx/works/1867-c1/ch07.htm.

———. 1867b. "The Secret of Primitive Accumulation." *Capital, Vol 1.* www.marxists.org/archive/marx/works/1867-c1/ch26.htm

———. 1871. "The Paris Commune." *The Civil War in France.* www.marxists.org/archive/marx/works/1871/civil-war-france/ch05.htm

———. 1963. *The Poverty of Philosophy.* New York: International Publishers.

———. 1964. *The Economic and Philosophic Manuscripts of 1844.* New York: International Publishers.

———. 1973. *Grundrisse.* London: Penguin.

———. 1974. "Concerning Feuerbach." In *Marx, Early Writings*, translated by Rodney Livingstone and Gregor Benton, 421–23. London: Penguin.

———. 1976. *Capital: A Critique of Political Economy*, vol. 1. London: Penguin.

———. 1978. "On the Jewish Question." In *The Marx-Engels Reader*, edited by Robert C. Tucker, 26–46. New York: Norton.

———. 1981. *Capital: A Critique of Political Economy*, vol. 3. London: Penguin.

———. 1982. *Critique of Hegel's 'Philosophy of Right'*, edited by Joseph O'Malley. Cambridge: Cambridge University Press.

———. 1993. *Capital: A Critique of Political Economy*, vol. 2. London: Penguin.

———. 2004. "Theses on Feuerbach." In *The German Ideology*. New York: International Publishers.

———. 2009. *The Poverty of Philosophy*. Marxists Internet Archive. https://www.marxists.org/archive/marx/works/1847/poverty-philosophy/index.htm. First published 1847.

———. 2010a. "The 18th Brumaire of Louis Bonaparte." Marxists Internet Archive. http://www.marxists.org/archive/marx/works/download/pdf/18th-Brumaire.pdf.

———. 2010b. *The Civil War in France*. Marxists Internet Archive. http://www.marxists.org/archive/marx/works/1871/civil-war-france/index.htm.

Marx, Karl, and Friedrich Engels. 1850. "Address of the Central Committee to the Communist League." Marxists Internet Archive. https://www.marxists.org/archive/marx/works/1847/communist-league/1850-ad1.htm.

———. 1973. "Manifesto of the Communist Party." In *The Revolutions of 1848*. Harmondsworth: Penguin Books.

———. 1976a. *Collected Works*, vol. 5. New York: International Publishers.

———. 1976b. "Manifesto of the Communist Party." In *Collected Works*, vol. 6, New York: International Publishers.

———. 1978. *The German Ideology*. New York: International Publishers.

———. 2012. *The Communist Manifesto: A Modern Edition*. London: Verso.

Mary Nardini Gang. 2011. "Toward the Queerest Insurrection." In *Queer Ultra Violence: Bash Back! Anthology*, edited by Fray Baroque and Tegan Eanelli, 256–68. San Francisco: Ardent Press.

Massad, Joseph A. 2007. *Desiring Arabs*. Chicago: University of Chicago Press.

Massumi, Brian. 2010. "Perception Attack: Brief on War Time." *Theory & Event* 13(3).

Matthews, Dylan. 2012. "Rick Santorum Says Stay in School, Work Hard, Wait to Have Kids, and You'll Avoid Poverty. It's Not That Simple." *Washington Post.* August 29.

May, Todd. 2012. *Friendship in an Age of Economics: Resisting the Forces of Neoliberalism.* Lanham, MD: Lexington Books.

Mayer, Margit. 2013. "Preface." In *Squatting in Europe: Radical Spaces, Urban Struggles*, edited by Squatting Europe Kollective. Wivenhoe, Englad: Minor Compositions.

Mbembe, J. A. 2003. "Necropolitics." *Public Culture* 15(1): 11–40.

Mbiti, John. 1990. *African Religions and Philosophy.* Johannesburg: Heinemann Educational Publishers.

McBean, Shanice. 2015. "I Was Born a Baby Not a Boy: Sex, Gender and Trans Liberation." *She Is Revolutionarily Suicidal.* https://sheisrevolutionarilysuicidal .wordpress.com/author/shaniceoctaviamcbean.

McCann, Carole, and Seung-Kyung Kim. 2013. "Introduction: Theorizing Feminist Times and Spaces." In *Feminist Theory Reader: Local and Global Perspectives*, edited by Carole McCann and Seung-Kyung Kim, 11–29. New York: Routledge.

McDermott, Mary. 2014. "Commons Sense: New Thinking about an Old Idea." *Community Development Journal* 49, suppl. 1, i1–i11.

McDonnell, Mary-Hunter, Brayden G. King, and Sarah A. Soule. 2015. "A Dynamic Process Model of Private Politics: Activist Targeting and Corporate Receptivity to Social Challenges." *American Sociological Review* 80(3): 654–78.

McIntosh, Peggy. 1988. *White Privilege: Unpacking the Invisible Knapsack.* www. deanza.edu/faculty/lewisjulie/White%20Priviledge%20Unpacking%20 the%20Invisible%20Knapsack.pdf

———. 1988. *White Privilege and Male Privilege: A Personal Account of Coming to See Correspondences Through Work in Women's Studies.* http://www.collegeart. org/pdf/diversity/white-privilege-and-male-privilege.pdf

McKay, George. 1996. *Senseless Acts of Beauty: Cultures of Resistance Since the Sixties.* London: Verso.

McKibben, Bill. 1989. *The End of Nature.* New York: Random House.

McNally, David. 1988. *Political Economy and the Rise of Capitalism: A Reinterpretation.* Berkeley: University of California Press.

———. 2001. *Bodies of Meaning: Studies on Language, Labor, and Liberation.* Albany: SUNY Press.

McPherson, James. 1999. "Was Blood Thicker than Water? Ethnic and Civic Nationalism in the American Civil War." *American Philosophical Society*. 143(1),102–108.

McRuer, Robert. 2006. *Crip Theory: Cultural Signs of Queerness and Disability*. New York: NYU Press.

Means, Russell, and Marvin Wolf. 1995. *Where White Men Fear to Tread: The Autobiography of Russell Means*. New York: St. Martin's.

Meiksins, Peter. 1986. "Beyond the Boundary Question." *New Left Review* I/157 (May-June): 101–20.

Melucci, Alberto. 1989. "The Democratization of Everyday Life." In *Nomads of the Present: Social Movements and Individual Needs in Contemporary Society*, edited by John Keane and Paul Mier, 165–79. Philadelphia: Temple University Press.

———. 1996. *Challenging Codes: Collective Action in the Information Age*. Cambridge: Cambridge University Press.

Memmi, Albert. 2003. *The Colonizer and the Colonized*. London: Earthscan.

Merchant, Carolyn. 1980. *The Death of Nature*. New York: Harper and Row.

———. 1995. "Reinventing Eden: Western Culture as a Recovery Narrative." In *Uncommon Ground: Toward Reinventing Nature*, edited by William Cronon, 132–59. New York: W. W. Norton.

———. 2012. *Radical Ecology: The Search for a Livable World*. New York: Routledge.

Messner, Michael A., Max A Greenberg, and Tal Peretz, 2015. *Some Men: Feminist Allies and the Movement to End Violence against Women*. Oxford: Oxford University Press.

Meyerson, JA. 2011. "Anatomy of a Victory: Occupy Wall Street Wins a Big One." *Truth-Out*. October 15. http://www.truth-out.org/news/item/3998:anatomy-of-a-victory-occupy-wall-street-wins-a-big-one.

Midnight, Dori. 2012. "More Healing, More of the Time." *Midnight Apothecary*. http://midnightapothecary.blogspot.ca/2012/10/more-healing-more-of-time.html.

Midnight Notes Collective. 1990. *The New Enclosures*. Jamaica Plain, MA: Midnight Notes Collective.

———. 2001. *Auroras of the Zapatistas. Local and Global Struggles in the Fourth World War*. Brooklyn: Autonomedia.

Milstein, Cindy, ed. 2015. *Taking Sides: Revolutionary Solidarity and the Poverty of Liberalism*. Oakland: AK Press.

Mies, Maria. 1986. Patriarchy and Accumulation on a World Scale: Women and the International Division of Labour. 2nd ed. London: Zed.

———. 1999. *The Subsistence Perspective: Beyond the Globalized Economy*. London: Zed Books.

Mies, Maria, and Vandana Shiva. 2014. *Ecofeminism*. London: Zed Books.

Milgram, Stanley. 1974. *Obedience to Authority*. New York: Tavistock.

Miller, John G. 1998. *Personal Accountability: Powerful and Practical Ideas for You and Your Organization*. Denver: Denver Press.

———. 2004. *The Question behind the Question: Practicing Personal Accountability in Business and in Life*. New York: G. P. Putnam's Sons.

Miller, Mike. 2014. "Prefigurative Politics and the Student Nonviolent Coordinating Committee." *Berkeley Journal of Sociology*. http://berkeleyjournal.org/2014/11/prefigurative-politics-and-the-student-nonviolent-coordinating-committee.

Milstein, Cindy. 2010. *Anarchism and Its Aspirations*. Oakland: AK Press/Institute for Anarchist Studies.

———. 2015. "Solidarity, as Weapon and Practice, against Killer Cops and White Supremacy." In *Revolutionary Solidarity: A Critical Reader for Accomplices*, zine edited by Anonymous, 51–62. https://archive.org/download/Revolutionary SolidarityACriticalReaderForAccomplices/revsol-SCREEN.pdf.

Mingus, Mia. 2010a. "Changing the Framework: Disability Justice." *RESIST Newsletter*, November/December. https://leavingevidence.wordpress.com/2011/02/12/changing-the-framework-disability-justice.

———. 2010b. "Interdependency (Excerpts from Several Talks)." *Leaving Evidence*. https://leavingevidence.wordpress.com/2010/01/22/interdependency-exerpts-from-several-talks.

———. 2011. "Access Intimacy: The Missing Link." *Leaving Evidence*. https://leavingevidence.wordpress.com/2011/05/05/access-intimacy-the-missing-link.

———. 2014. "Talking Transformative and Disability Justice with Mia Mingus." *Project As[I]Am*. http://project-as-i-am.com/talking-transformative-and-disability-justice-with-mia-mingus.

Mitchell, David, and Sharon Snyder. 1995. *Vital Signs: Crip Culture Talks Back*. Fanlight Productions.

"Modern Gangs Have Roots in Racial Turmoil of '60s." 1988. *Los Angeles Times*.

Mohanty, Chandra Talpade. 2003. *Feminism without Borders: Decolonizing*

Theory, Practicing Solidarity. Durham: Duke University Press.

Mongia, Radhika. 2007. "Historicizing State Sovereignty: Inequality and the Form of Equivalence." *Comparative Studies in Society and History* 49(2): 384–411.

Moore, Rosemary. 2013. "Seventeenth Century Context and Quaker Beginnings." In *The Oxford Handbook of Quaker Studies.* Oxford: Oxford University Press.

Moraga, Cherríe and Gloria E. Anzaldúa, eds. 1981. *This Bridge Called My Back: Writings by Radical Women of Color.* New York: Kitchen Table/Women of Color Press.

More, Thomas. 1965. *Utopia.* Harmondsworth, UK: Penguin Books.

Morgan, Robin. 1970. *Sisterhood Is Powerful: An Anthology of Writings from the Women's Liberation Movement.* New York: Random House.

Morin, Rich, and Seth Motel. 2012. "A Third of Americans Now Say They Are in the Lower Classes." Pew Research Center. September 10. http://www.pewsocialtrends.org/2012/09/10/a-third-of-americans-now-say-they-are-in-the-lower-classes.

Morris, William. 1993. *News from Nowhere and Other Writings.* Harmondsworth, UK: Penguin.

Moscoso, Melania. 2013. "'De aquí no se va nadie': del uso del discapacitado para el aleccionamiento moral." *Constelaciones: Revista de Teoría Crítica* 5: 170–83.

Moye, J. Todd. 2013. *Ella Baker: Community Organizer of the Civil Rights Movement.* Lanham, MD: Rowman and Littlefield.

Moylan, Tom. 1997. "Bloch against Bloch: The Theological Reception of *Das Prinzip Hoffnung* and the Liberation of the Utopia Function" In *Not Yet: Reconsidering Ernst Bloch*, edited by Jamie Owen Daniel, and Tom Moylan, 96–121. London: Verso.

Moynihan, Daniel Patrick. 1965. *The Negro Family: The Case for National Action.* Washington, DC: U.S. Department of Labor, Office of Policy Planning and Research.

Mueller, Tadzio, and Kriss Sol. 2007. "A Tale of Two Victories? Or, Why Winning Becomes Precarious in Times of Absent Antagonisms". *Transform.* June 28. http://transform.eipcp.net/correspondence/1183042751#redir#redir.

Mulberry, Matt. 2014. "Physical Space and 'Occupy' Tactics: A New Trend in Civil Resistance?" *Open Democracy.* November 19. https://www

.opendemocracy.net/civilresistance/matt-mulberry/physical-space -and-%E2%80%98occupy%E2%80%99-tactics-new-trend-in-civil-resistance.

Muñoz, José Esteban. 1999. *Disidentifications: Queers of Color and the Performance of Politics*. Minneapolis: University of Minnesota Press.

———. 2009. *Cruising Utopia: The Then and There of Queer Futurity*. New York: New York University Press.

Murphy, Alexander B. 2005. "The Role of Geography in Public Debate." *Progress in Human Geography* 29(2): 165–93.

Murphy, Piaras. 2002. "Solidarity Best Weapon for Unions—SIPTU." *Irish Times* October 11.

Murray, Daniel. 2014. "Prefiguration or Actualization? Radical Democracy and Counter-Institution in the Occupy Movement." *Berkeley Journal of Sociology*, November 3. http://berkeleyjournal.org/2014/11/prefiguration -or-actualization-radical-democracy-and-counter-institution-in-the -occupy-movement.

Nail, Thomas. 2013. "Zapatismo and the Origins of Occupy." *Journal for Cultural and Religious Theory*. 12(3): 20–35.

Nair, Yasmin. 2011. "Fuck Love." *No More Potlucks* 18. http://nomorepotlucks. org/site/fuck-love.

Namaste, Viviane K. 2000. *Invisible Lives: The Erasure of Transsexual and Transgender People*. Chicago: University of Chicago Press.

———. 2005. *Sex Change, Social Change*. Toronto: Women's Press.

———. 2011. "Critical Research and Activisms on Trans Issues in Latin America: An Interview with Vek Lewis." In *Sex Change, Social Change: Reflections on Identity, Institutions and Imperialism*, 2nd ed., 181–204. Toronto: Women's Press.

Nancy, Jean-Luc. 1991. "The Inoperative Community". In *The Inoperative Community*, translated by Simona Sawhney and edited by Peter Connor, 1–42. Minneapolis: University of Minnesota Press.

Nas. 1994. "Represent." In *Illmatic*. Columbia Records.

National Park Service. 2015. "[Zion National Park] History and Culture." http://www.nps.gov/zion/learn/historyculture/index.htm.

Navdanya. 2015. "Food Sovereignty." *Navdanya*. http://www.navdanya.org/ earth-democracy/food-sovereignty.

Negri, Antonio. 1999. *Insurgencies: Constituent Power and the Modern State*.

Minneapolis: University of Minnesota Press.

Neocleous, Mark. 2011. "The Police of Civilization: The War on Terror as Civilizing Offensive." *International Political Sociology* 5: 144–59.

———. 2010. "War as Peace, Peace as Pacification." *Radical Philosophy*. 159: 8–17.

Neill, Monty. 2001. "Rethinking Class Composition Analysis in Light of the Zapatistas." In *Auroras of the Zapatistas: Local and Global Struggles in the Fourth World War*, edited by the Midnight Notes Collective. Brooklyn: Autonomedia.

Newman, Lily Hay. 2015. "Mark Zuckerberg: 'It's Not Sustainable to Offer the Whole Internet for Free.'" *Slate*, May 4. http://www.slate.com/blogs/future_tense/2015/05/04/zuckerberg_announces_changes_to_internet_org_responding_to_net_neutrality.html.

Newport, Frank. 2015. "Fewer Americans Identify as Middle Class in Recent Years." Gallup, April 28. http://www.gallup.com/poll/182918/fewer-americans-identify-middle-class-recent-years.aspx.

Newton, Huey P. 1968. "Huey Newton Talks to the Movement about the Black Panther Party, Cultural Nationalism SNCC, Liberals and White Revolutionaries." *Movement*, August.

New York Times. "History Is Bunk, Says Henry Ford." 1921. *New York Times*, October 28.

Nez, H. 2012. "Délibérer au sein d'un mouvement social: ethnographie des assemblées des Indignés à Madrid." *Participations* 3: 79–101.

Niemeyer, Oscar. 2013. *Wir müssen die Welt verändern*. München: Verlag Antje Kunstmann Gmbh

Nietzsche, Frederick. 1908. *Human, All Too Human: A Book for Free Spirits*. Translated by Alexander Harvey. Chicago: C. H. Kerr. Available via Hathi Trust Digital Library. http://babel.hathitrust.org/.

Night Aurora. 2012. "Lublin, Poland: Direct Action in Solidarity with Political Prisoners across the World." *Contra Info*. http://en.contrainfo.espiv.net/2012/04/04/lublin-poland-solidarity-with-political-prisoners/comment-page-1.

Nkrumah, Kwame. 1965. *Neo-Colonialism: The Last Stage of Imperialism*. London: Thomas Nelson & Sons.

Northover, Kylie. 2014. "Melbourne Comedy Festival Causes Nervous Laughs." *Sydney Morning Herald*. March 15.

Notes from Nowhere, eds. 2003. *We Are Everywhere: The Irresistible Rise of Global*

Anticapitalism. New York: Verso.

O'Connor, Clare. 2011. "What Moves Us Now? The Contradictions of 'Community.'" In *Whose Streets? The Toronto G20 and the Challenges of Summit Protest*, edited by T. Malleson and D. Wachsmuth, 187–200. Toronto: Between the Lines.

O'Hara, Mary. 2006. "No Fears, No Frills." *Guardian*, June 21.

Oakeshott, Michael. 2006. *Lectures on the History of Political Thought.* Charlottesville, VA: Imprint Academic.

Oakley, Ann. 1985. *Sex, Gender and Society.* New ed. Burlington, VT: Ashgate. First published 1972.

Obama, Barack. 2009. "Remarks by the President to a Joint Session of Congress on Health Care." September 9. https://www.whitehouse.gov/the-press -office/remarks-president-a-joint-session-congress-health-care.

———. 2011. "Transcript: George Stephanopoulos' ABC News/Yahoo! News Exclusive Interview with President Obama." http://abcnews.go.com/Politics/transcript-george-stephanopoulos-abc-news-yahoo-news-exclusive/ story?id=14659193.

———. 2012. "Victory Speech". *Guardian.* November 7.

Occupy Patriarchy. 2011. Flyer. October 27. http://occupypatriarchy. feministpeacenetwork.org/wp-content/uploads/2011/10/occupy-patriarchy-flyer.jpg.

Occupy Winston Salem. 2011. "Non-violence Guidelines and Principles." October 8. http://occupywinstonsalem.org/2011/10/08/non-violence-guidelines -and-principles/#.VelOoZN8tkU.

Omi, Michael, and Howard Winant. 1994. *Racial Formation in the United States: From the 1960s to the 1990s.* New York: Routledge.

Oldenberg, Ray. 1999. *The Great Good Place.* Boston: Da Capo Press.

Onkwehón:we Rising. n.d. "What We Understand, What We Want." *Onkwehón:we Rising.* https://web.archive.org/web/20141216223937/http:// onkwehonwerising.wordpress.com/resources-for-knowledge/ onkwehonwe-rising-basic-points-of-unity.

Oppenheim, James. 1911. "Bread and Roses." *American Magazine.*

Orend, Brian. 2008. "War." In *The Stanford Encyclopedia of Philosophy*, edited by Edward N. Zalta. http://plato.stanford.edu/archives/fall2008/entries/war.

Orwell, George. 1950. *Nineteen Eighty-Four.* Signet Classic.

Osterhammel, Jürgen. 1997. *Colonialism: A Theoretical Overview.* Princeton, NJ:

Markus Wiener.

Osterweil, Willie. 2011. "A (Very, Very) Brief History of Occupation Tactics." *Shareable*. December 21. http://www.shareable.net/blog/a-very-very-brief-history-of-occupation-tactics.

Ostrom, Elinor. 1990. *Governing the Commons: The Evolution of Institutions for Collective Action*. New York: Cambridge University Press.

#OWS POC Working Group. 2011. *Call Out to People of Color from the POC Working Group*. October 4. http://pococcupywallstreet.tumblr.com/post/11049895469/call-out-to-people-of-color-from-the-ows-poc.

Oxfam. 2007. "Investing for Life: Meeting Poor People's Needs for Access to Medicines through Responsible Business Practices." Oxfam Briefing Paper, November 2007. https://www.oxfam.org/sites/www.oxfam.org/files/bp109-investing-for-life-0711.pdf.

Palmer, Bryan. 1990. *Descent into Discourse: The Reification of Language and the Writing of Social History*. Philadelphia: Temple University Press.

———. 2000. *Cultures of Darkness: Night Travels in the Histories of Transgression*. New York: Monthly Review Press.

———. 2013. "Reconsiderations of Class: Precariousness as Proletarianization." In *Socialist Register 2013: Transforming Classes*, edited by Leo Panitch and Greg Albo, 40–62. London: Merlin Press.

Pan, Jennifer. 2013. "She Came to Riot." *Jacobin*. http://jacobinmag.com/2013/09/she-came-to-riot.

Panitch, Leo, and Leys, Colin. 1999. *The Socialist Register 2000: Necessary and Unnecessary Utopias*. London: Merlin Press.

Pannekoek, Anton. 1927. *Social Democracy and Communism*. Marxists Internet Archive. https://www.marxists.org/archive/pannekoe/1927/sdc.htm.

Pappé, Ilan. 2014. *The Idea of Israel: History of Power and Knowledge*. London: Verso.

Parker, Ian, Hazel Self, Vic Willi, and Judith O'Leary. 2000. *Power Shift*. Toronto: Centre for Independent Living Toronto (CILT).

Pastor, Manuel. 2015. "How Immigrant Activists Changed L.A." *Dissent*, Winter. https://www.dissentmagazine.org/article/how-immigrant-activists-changed-los-angeles.

Pateman, Carole. 1970. *Participation and Democratic Theory*. Cambridge: Cambridge University Press.

Pavlich, George. 2001. "The Force of Community." In *Restorative Justice and*

Civil Society, edited by Heather Strang and John Braithwaite, 56–69. Cambridge, UK: Cambridge University Press.

Peerla, David. 2012. *No Means No: The Kitchenuhmaykoosib Inninuwug and the Fight for Indigenous Resource Sovereignty.* Cognitariat Publishing. http://www.miningwatch.ca/sites/www.miningwatch.ca/files/No%20 Means%20No.pdf.

Peterson, Bob. 2014/2015. "A Revitalized Teacher Union Movement: Reflections from the Field." *Rethinking Schools* 29(2).

Phelan, Peggy. 1993. *Unmarked: The Politics of Performance.* New York: Routlege.

Philipovich, Ivan, and Joseph Stalin. 1938. "On the Final Victory of Socialism in the U.S.S.R." Marxists Internet Archive. https://www.marxists.org/ reference/archive/stalin/works/1938/01/18.htm.

Piercy, Marge. 1976. *Woman on the Edge of Time.* New York: Random House.

Piterberg, Gabriel. 2008. The *Returns of Zionism.* London: Verso.

Piterberg, Gabriel, and Lorenzo Veracini. 2015. "Wakefield, Marx and the World Turned Inside Out." *Journal of Global History* 10(3): 457–78.

P.M. 2014. *"The Power of Neighborhood"and The Commons.* Brooklyn: Autonomedia.

Poloz, Stephen. 2014. "Stephen Poloz on Youth Unemployment." *Globe and Mail* November 4.

Poole, Deborah. 2010. "Interview with Mario Palacios." *NACLA Report on the Americas* 43(5): 30–33.

Pope Francis. 2015. "Discurso del Papa Francisco." *América Latina en Movimiento (ALAINET).* October 7. http://www.alainet.org/es/articulo/170996#sthash .JCHrW9Zf.dpuf.

Postill, John. 2011a. "Democracy in an Age of Viral Reality (2)." November 2. http:// johnpostill.com/2011/11/02/democracy-in-the-age-of-viral-reality-2.

———. 2011b. "Democracy in an Age of Viral Reality (4)." November 15. http:// johnpostill.com/2011/11/15/democracy-in-the-age-of-viral-reality-4.

Postone, Moishe. 2003. *Time, Labor, and Social Domination: A Reinterpretation of Marx's Critical Theory.* Cambridge: Cambridge University Press.

Precadio, Beatriz. 2013. *Testo Junkie: Sex, Drugs, and Biopolitics in the Pharmaco-pornographic Era.* Translated by Bruce Benderson. New York: Feminist Press.

Precarias a la deriva. 2005. "A Very Careful Strike: Four Hypotheses." *Caring Labor: An Archive.* https://caringlabor.wordpress.com/2010/08/14/ precarias-a-la-deriva-a-very-careful-strike-four-hypotheses.

Puar, Jasbir K. 2007. *Terrorist Assemblages: Homonationalism in Queer Times.* Durham: Duke University Press.

———. 2013. "Rethinking Homonationalism." *International Journal of Middle East Studies* 45(2): 336–39.

Put a Rainbow On It. n.d. http://www.putarainbowonit.com.

Pyne, Jake. 2014. "The Governance of Gender Non-conforming Children: A Dangerous Enclosure." *Annual Review of Critical Psychology* 11: 76–96.

———. 2011. "Unsuitable Bodies: Trans People and Cisnormativity in Shelter Services." *Canadian Social Work Review/Revue canadienne de service social* 28: 129–37.

Queer Nation New York. 2013. "Queer Nation New York History." http://queernationny.org/history.

Rabinow, Paul, and Nicolas Rose. 2003. "Thoughts on the Concept of Biopower Today." http://www.lse.ac.uk/sociology/pdf/RabinowandRose-Biopower-Today03.pdf.

Radical Women's Kitchen. 2010. "i. communique." https://occupyca.wordpress.com/2010/08/22/i-communiqué.

Rancière, Jacques. 1999. *Disagreement: Politics and Philosophy.* Translated by Julie Rose. Minneapolis: University of Minnesota Press.

———. 2001. "Ten Theses on Politics," *Theory & Event* 5(3).

———. 2011. "The Thinking of Dissensus: Politics and Aesthetics." In *Reading Rancière: Critical Dissensus*, edited by Paul Bowman and Richard Stamp, 1–17. New York: Continuum.

———. 2013. "L'introuvable populisme." In *Qu'est-ce qu'un peuple* edited by Alain Badiou, et al., 137–45. Paris: La Fabrique.

Randall, Vicky. 1996. "Feminism and Child Daycare." *Journal of Social Policy* 25(4): 485–505.

Rankine, Claudia. 2014. *Citizen: An American Lyric.* Minneapolis: Graywolf Press.

Ransby, Barbara. 2005. *Ella Baker and the Black Freedom Movement.* Chapel Hill: University of North Carolina Press.

———. 2015. "Ella Taught Me: Shattering the Myth of the Leaderless Movement." *Colorlines*, June 12. http://www.colorlines.com/articles/ella-taught-me-shattering-myth-leaderless-movement.

Ratner, Carl. 2015. "Neoliberal Co-optation of Leading Co-op Organizations, and a Socialist Counter-Politics of Cooperation." *Monthly Review* 66(9).

http://monthlyreview.org/2015/02/01/neoliberal-co-optation-of-leading
-co-op-organizations-and-a-socialist-counter-politics-of-cooperation.

"Reclaim the Streets!" 1997. *Do or Die* 6: 1–10.

Reed, John. 2007. *Ten Days That Shook the World*. Harmondsworth: Penguin.

Rehmann, Jan. 2013. "Occupy Wall Street and the Question of Hegemony: A Gramscian Analysis." *Socialism and Democracy* 72(1): 1–18.

Reisman, David. 2011. *The Economics of Alfred Marshall*. New York: Routledge.

Rex v. Russell et al. 1919. 29 Man R. 511 (C.A.). Marxists Internet Archive.

Rhodan, Maya. 2015. "Transcript: Read Full Text of President Barack Obama's Speech in Selma." *Time*. March 7. http://time.com/3736357/barack-obama-selma-speech-transcript.

Rich, Adrienne. 1979. "Disloyal to Civilization: Feminism, Racism, Gynephobia." In *On Lies, Secrets, and Silence: Selected Prose, 1966–1978*, 276–310. New York: W. W. Norton.

Ridgway, Shannon. 2013. "19 Examples of Ability Privilege." *Everyday Feminism*. March 5. http://everydayfeminism.com/2013/03/19-examples-of-ability-privilege.

Rieff, David. 2002. *A Bed for the Night: Humanitarianism in Crisis*. New York: Simon & Schuster.

Rifkin, Jeremy. 1989. *Time Wars: The Primary Conflict in Human History*. New York: Touchstone.

Right to the City. 2015. "Mission & History." http://righttothecity.org/about/mission-history/.

R. L. 2014. "Indistinguishable Fire: Ferguson and Beyond." *Mute*. November 17. http://www.metamute.org/editorial/articles/inextinguishable-fire-ferguson-and-beyond.

Roberts, Ed. 2015. "Highlights from Speeches by Ed Roberts." Collected by Jon Oda. World Institute on Disability. http://www.wid.org/about-wid/highlights-from-speeches-by-ed-roberts.

Robin, Corey. 2014. "When Intellectuals Go to War." *Jacobin*, May 27. https://www.jacobinmag.com/2014/05/when-intellectuals-go-to-war.

Robinson, Cedric. 2000. *Black Marxism: The Making of the Black Radical Tradition*. Chapel Hill: University of North Carolina Press.

Rodgers, Daniel. 1998. *Atlantic Crossings: Social Politics in a Progressive Age*. Cambridge, MA: Harvard University Press.

Rodriguez, Dylan. 2005. *Forced Passages: Imprisoned Radical Intellectuals and the*

U.S. Prison Regime. Minneapolis: University of Minnesota Press.

Rogue, J. 2012. "De-essentializing Anarchist Feminism: Lessons from the Transfeminist Movement." In *Queering Anarchism: Addressing and Undressing Power and Desire*, edited by C. B. Daring et al., 25–32. Oakland: AK Press.

Rorty, Richard. 1989. *Contingency, Irony, and Solidarity.* Cambridge: Cambridge University Press.

Rosanvallon, P. 2006. *La contre-démocratie. La politique a l'age de la defiance.* Paris: Seuil.

Rose, Willie Lee Nichols, ed. 1976. *A Documentary History of Slavery in North America.* New York: Oxford University Press.

Ross, Kristin. 1988. *The Emergence of Social Space: Rimbaud and the Paris Commune.* Minnesota: University of Minnesota Press.

———. 2015. *Communal Luxury: The Political Imaginary of the Paris Commune.* London: Verso.

Rotunda, Ronald D. 1968. "The 'Liberal' Label: Roosevelt's Capture of a Symbol." In *Public Policy*, edited by John D. Montgomery and Albert O. Hirschman, 377. Cambridge, MA: Harvard University Press.

Rousseau, Jean-Jacques. 1988. The Social Contract and Discourses. Translated by J. D. H. Cole. London: J.M. Dent and Sons.

———. 2002. *The Social Contract and the First and Second Discourses.* Edited by Susan Dunn. New Haven: Yale University Press.

Rousselle, Duane, and Süreyyya Evren. 2011. *Post-Anarchism: A Reader.* London: Pluto Press.

Rovics, David. 2003. "Vanguard." In *Behind the Barricades.* AK Press/Daemon Records. http://lyrics.wikia.com/David_Rovics:Vanguard.

Rowbotham, Sheila. 1973. *Hidden from History: 300 Years of Women's Oppression and the Fight Against It.* London: Pluto.

Roy, Jessica. 2015. "What Happens When a Woman Walks Like a Man?" *New York Magazine.* January 8. http://nymag.com/thecut/2015/01/manslamming-manspreading-microaggressions.html.

Rubin, Gayle. 1975. "The Traffic in Women: Notes on the 'Political Economy of Sex." In *Toward an Anthropology of Women*, edited by Rayna Reiter, 157–210. New York: Monthly Review Press.

———. 2005. "The Traffic of Women: Notes in the Political Economy of Sex." In *Feminist Theory: A Reader,* edited by Wendy Kolmar and Frances

Bartkowski 273–88. Boston: McGraw-Hill.

The Rules. 2015. "SDGs." http://therules.org/tag/sdgs.

Russell, Joshua Kahn, and Arun Gupta. "Tactic: Occupation." In *Beautiful Trouble: A Toolbox for Revolution*. http://beautifultrouble.org/tactic/occupation.

Rutherdale, Myra, Erin Dolmage, and Carolyn Podruchny. 2014. "Bodies of Water, Not Bodies of Women: Canadian Media Images of the Idle No More Movement." *Active History*. http://activehistory.ca/papers/bodies-of-water-not-bodies-of-women-canadian-media-images-of-the-idle-no-more-movement.

Sagan, Aleksandra. 2015. "Caitlyn Jenner's Transition Doesn't Represent Most Transgender Experiences." *CBC World*. June 3. http://www.cbc.ca/news/world/caitlyn-jenner-s-transition-doesn-t-represent-most-transgender-experiences-1.3096911.

Said, Edward. 1978. *Orientalism*. London: Vintage.

———. 1994. *Representations of the Intellectual*. New York: Vintage Books.

Sainsbury, George. 1916. "Critical Introduction on Matthew Arnold." In *English Prose, Selections with Critical Introductions by Various Writers and General Information to Each Period*, edited by Henry Craik, 699–704. New York: Macmillan.

Saint Augustine. 1961. *Confessions*. London: Penguin Books.

———. 1962. *The Political Writings of St. Augustine*. Edited by Henry Paolucci. Washington, D.C.: Regnery Publishing.

Saint-Simon, Henri. 1972. *The Doctrine of Saint-Simon*. Translated by George G. Iggers. New York: Schocken.

Sakai, J. 2014. *Settlers: The Mythology of the White Proletariat from Mayflower to Modern*. Montreal: Kersplebedeb. First published 1983.

Salah, Trish. 2014. "Gender Struggles: Reflections on Trans Liberation, Trade Unionism, and the Limits of Solidarity." In *Trans Activism in Canada: A Reader*, edited by Dan Irving and Rupert Raj, 149–69. Toronto: Canadian Scholars' Press.

Salamanca, Omar Jabary, Mezna Qato, Kareem Rabie, and Sobhi Samour. 2012. "Past Is Present: Settler Colonialism in Palestine." *Settler Colonial Studies* 2: 1–8.

Salleh, Ariel. 2009. *Eco-sufficiency and Global Justice: Women Write Political Ecology*. New York: Pluto Press.

———. 2012. "Women, Food Sovereignty and Green Jobs in China."

Friends of the Earth Australia. http://www.foe.org.au/women-food
-sovereignty-and-green-jobs-china.

Sanbonmatsu, John. 2004. *The Postmodern Prince: Critical Theory, Left Strategy, and the Making of a New Political Subject*. New York: Monthly Review Press.

Sanchez, John, and Mary E. Stuckey. 2000. "Rhetoric of American Indian Activism in the 1960s and 1970s." *Communication Quarterly* 48(2): 120–36.

Sandahl, Carrie. 2003. "Queering the Crip or Cripping the Queer? Intersections of Queer and Crip Identities in Solo Autobiographical Performance." *GLQ: A Journal of Lesbian and Gay Identities* 9(1–2): 25–56.

Sanger, Margaret. 1920. *Women and the New Race*. New York: Brentano's.

Sangster, Joan and Meg Luxton. 2013. "Feminism, Co-optation, and the Problems of Amnesia." *Socialist Register* 49: 288–309.

Sartre, Jean Paul. 2001. *Colonialism and Neocolonialism*. London: Routledge.

SB-967: Student Safety: Sexual Assault. [California] Senate Bill No. 967. September 28, 2014. http://leginfo.legislature.ca.gov/faces/billNavClient.xhtml?bill_id=201320140SB967.

Schmitt, Carl. 1996. *The Concept of the Political*. Chicago: University of Chicago Press.

———. 2005. *Political Theology: Four Chapters on the Concept of Sovereignty*. Translated by George Schwab. Chicago: University of Chicago Press.

Schneider, Nathan. 2013. *Thank You, Anarchy: Notes from the Occupy Apocalypse*. University of California Press.

Scoones, Ian, Melissa Leach, and Peter Newell. 2015. *The Politics of Green Transformation*. London: Routledge.

Scott, Joan. 1986. "Gender: A Useful Category of Historical Analysis." *American Historical Review* 91(5): 1053–75.

———. 1992. "Experience." In *Feminists Theorize the Political*, edited by Joan W. Scott and Judith Butler, 22–40. London: Routledge.

Seaweed. 2009. *Of Martial Traditions and the Art of Rebellion*. Santa Cruz: Quiver Press.

Seguin, Bécquer. 2014. "Populism and Other Epithets." *Dissent*. September 11. http://www.dissentmagazine.org/blog/populism-epithet-podemos-spain-pundits.

The Self Care Project. 2015. http://theselfcareproject.org.

Sellars, Kirsten. 2002. *The Rise and Rise of Human Rights*. Gloucester: Sutton.

Seltzer, Sarah. 2015. "Beyond Mansplaining: A New Lexicon of Misogyist Trolling

Behaviors." *Flavorwire.com*. March 24. http://flavorwire.com/511063/beyond-mansplaining-a-new-lexicon-of-misogynist-trolling-behaviors.

Serano, Julia. 2007. *Whipping Girl: A Transsexual Woman on Sexism and the Scapegoating of Femininity*. New York: Seal Press.

———. 2012. "Trans-Misogyny Primer." *Whipping Girl*. April 3. http://juliaserano.blogspot.co.nz/2012/04/trans-misogyny-primer.html.

———. 2014. "Cissexism and Cis Privilege Revisited." *Whipping Girl*. October 1. http://juliaserano.blogspot.ca/2014/10/cissexism-and-cis-privilege-revisited.html.

Sethness, Javier. 2014. "Noam Chomsky: Ecology, Ethics, Anarchism." *Truthout*, April 3. http://truth-out.org/news/item/22819-noam-chomsky-ecology-ethics-anarchism.

Sexton, Jared. 2010. "People of Color Blindness: Notes on the Afterlife of Slavery." *Social Text* 28(2 103): 31–56.

Shaban, Fuad. 2005. *For Zion's Sake: The Judeo-Christian Tradition in American Culture*. London: Pluto Press.

Shakespeare, William. 1963. *Macbeth*. New York: Dover.

———. 1992. *Romeo and Juliet*. Hertfordshire: Wordsworth.

Shakur, Assata. 1987. *Assata: An Autobiography*. London: Zed Books.

Sharp, Gene. 2012. *Dictionary of Power and Struggle: Language of Civil Resistance in Conflicts*. New York: Oxford University Press.

Sharpe, James. 2005. *Remember, Remember: A Cultural History of Guy Fawkes Day*. Cambridge, MA: Harvard University Press.

Shiva, Vandana. 1989. *Staying Alive: Women, Ecology and Development*. London: Zed Books.

———. 2005. *Earth Democracy*. Boston: South End Press.

———. 2012. "The Seed Emergency: The Threat to Food and Democracy". *Al Jazeera*. February 6. http://www.aljazeera.com/indepth/opinion/2012/02/201224152439941847.html.

Shotwell, Gregg. 2014. "A Practical Solution to an Urgent Need." *Monthly Review* 65(11): 36–48.

Silliman, Jael, Marlene Gerber Fried, Loretta Ross, and Elena R. Gutiérrez. 2004. *Undivided Rights. Women of Color Organize For Reproductive Justice*. Cambridge, MA: South End Press.

Simone, Nina. 1964. "Mississippi Goddamn." In *Nina Simone in Concert*. Philips Records.

Singh, Nikhil Pal. 2004. *Black is a Country: Race and the Unfinished Struggle for Democracy*. Cambridge, MA: Harvard University Press.

Sistering. 2007. *Anti-Oppression and Diversity Policy*. www.orgwise.ca/sites/ osi.ocasi.org.stage/files/resources/SISTERING%20Anti-Oppression%20 Policy.pdf

Sitrin, Marina. 2006. *Horizontalism*. Oakland: AK Press.

Smith, Adam. 1993. *The Wealth of Nations*. Oxford: Oxford University Press.

Smith, Andrea. 2010. "Queer Theory and Native Studies: The Heteronormativity of Settler Colonialism." *GLQ: A Journal of Lesbian and Gay Studies* 16(1–2): 41–68.

Smith, Andrea, with Sharmeen Khan, David Hugill, and Tyler McCreary. 2010. "Building Unlikely Alliances: An Interview with Andrea Smith." *Upping the Anti* 10. http://uppingtheanti.org/journal/ article/10-building-unlikely-alliances-an-interview-with-andrea-smith.

Smith, Anna Marie. 2002. "The Sexual Regulation Dimension of Contemporary Welfare Law: A Fifty State Overview." *Michigan Journal of Gender & Law* 8: 121–247.

Smith, Dorothy, E. 1990. *The Conceptual Practices of Power: A Feminist Sociology of Knowledge*. Toronto: University of Toronto Press.

Smith, Linda Tuhiwai. 1999. *Decolonizing Methodologies: Research and Indigenous Peoples*. London: Zed Books.

Smith, Mark J. 1998. *Ecologism*. Minneapolis: University of Minneapolis Press.

Smith, Neil. 2011. "Revolutionary Ambition in an Age of Austerity: An Interview with Neil Smith." *Upping the Anti* 13. http://uppingtheanti.org/ journal/article/13-neil-smith.

Smith, Nicholas. 2008. "Analyzing Hope." *Critical Horizons* 9(1): 5–23.

SNCC Project Group. "SNCC 1960–1966." http://www.ibiblio.org/sncc /nonviolence.html.

Snyder, Sharon L., and David T. Mitchell. 2006. *Cultural Locations of Disability*. Chicago: University of Chicago Press.

SOA Watch. n.d. "Principles and Practice of Anti-Oppression." http://soaw.org/ index.php?option=com_content&view=article&id=398.

Solnit, Rebecca. 2007. *Storming the Gates of Paradise: Landscapes for Politics*. Berkeley: University of California Press.

———. 2012. "A Letter to my Dismal Allies on the U.S. Left." *Guardian*. October 15.

Solty, Ingar. 2013. "The Crisis Interregnum: From the New Right-wing Populism to the Occupy Movement." *Studies in Political Economy* 91: 85–112.

Sonnie, Amy, and James Tracy. 2011. *Hillbilly Nationalists, Urban Race Rebels, and Black Power: Community Organizing in Radical Times*. New York: Melville House.

Spade, Dean. 2011. *Normal Life: Administrative Violence, Critical Trans Politics, and the Limits of Law*. Brooklyn: South End Press.

Speier, Hans. 1939. *The Salaried Worker in German Society*. New York: Columbia University.

Spence, Lester, and Mike McGuire. 2012. "Occupy and the 99%." *We Are Many: Reflections on Movement Strategy from Occupation to Liberation*. Oakland: AK Press.

Spinoza, Baruch. 2000. *Ethics*. Edited and translated by G. H. R. Parkinson. Oxford: Oxford University Press.

Springer, Kimberly. 2005. *Living for the Revolution: Black Feminist Organizations, 1968–1980*. Durham: Duke University Press.

Spronk, Susan, and Jeffrey Webber, eds. 2014. *Crisis and Contradiction: Marxist Perspectives on Latin America in the Global Political Economy*. Leiden: Brill.

Spivak, Gayatri Chakravorty. 1985. "The Rani of Sirmur: An Essay in Reading the Archives." *History and Theory* 24(3): 247–72.

———. 1994. *A Critique of Postcolonial Reason: Toward a History of the Vanishing Present*. Cambridge, MA: Harvard University Press.

Standing, Guy. 2011. *The Rise of the Precariat: The New Dangerous Class*. London: Bloomsbury Academic.

Stanley, Eric A. et al. eds. 2015. *Captive Genders: Trans Embodiment and the Prison Industrial Complex*, 2nd edition.

Stanton, Elizabeth Cady. 1995. "Declaration of Sentiments and Resolutions." In *Issues in Feminism: An Introduction to Women's Studies*, edited by Sheila Ruth, 541–43 . London: Mayfield.

Starhawk. 2011. *The Empowerment Manual: A Guide for Collaborative Groups*. Gabriola Island, BC: New Society Publishers.

Stavrakakis, Yannis. 2014. "Hegemony or Post-Hegemony? Discourse, Representation and the Revenge(s) of the Real" In *Radical Democracy and Collective Movements Today*, edited by Alexandros Kioupkiolis and Giorgios Katsambekis, 111–33. Farnham: Ashgate.

Stein, Ben. 2006. "In Class Warfare, Guess Which Class is Winning." *New York*

Times, November 26.

Stoler, Ann Laura. 1995. *The Education of Desire: Foucault's History of Sexuality and the Colonial Order of Things.* Duke: Duke University Press.

Stone, Sandy. 2006. "The Empire Strikes Back: A Posttranssexual Manifesto." In *Transgender Studies Reader*, edited by Susan Stryker and Stephen Whittle, 221–36. New York: Routledge. First published 1992.

———. 2014. "Guerilla." *Transgender Studies Quarterly* 1(1): 92–96.

Sterpka-King, Mary. 2010. "Preparing on the Instantaneous Battlespace: A Cultural Examination of Network-centric Warfare." *Topia: Canadian Journal of Cultural Studies* 23/24: 304–29.

STFU, White Liberals! http://stfuwhiteliberals.tumblr.com.

Stiegmann, Martha. 2012. "Confessions of a Reluctant Food Activist." In *Organize! Building from the Local for Global Justice*, edited by Aziz Choudry, Jill Hanley, and Eric Shragge, 266–77. Oakland: PM Press.

Striffler, Steve, and Mark Moberg, eds. 2003. *Banana Wars: Power, Production and History in the Americas.* Durham: Duke University Press.

Stryker, Susan. 2008. *Transgender History.* Berkeley: Seal Press.

Stryker, Susan, and Paisley Currah. 2014. "Introduction." *Transgender Studies Quarterly* 1: 1–18.

Sudbury, Julia. 1998. *Other Kinds of Dreams': Black Women's Organizations and the Politics of Transformation.* London: Routledge.

Sullivan, Patricia. 2006. "Voice of Feminism's 'Second Wave.'" *Washington Post.* February 5.

Sumburm, Paul. 2010. "A New Weather Front". In *What Would It Mean to Win?*, edited by Turbulence Collective, 27–32. Oakland: PM Press.

Summers, Lawrence. 1991. "The Memo." http://www.whirledbank.org.ourwords /summers.html.

Sun Tzu. *The Art of War.* Translated by Lionel Giles. http://classics.mit.edu/Tzu/ artwar.html.

Swilling, Mark, and Eve Annecke. 2012. *Just Transitions: Explorations of Sustainability in an Unfair World.* Cape Town: University of Cape Town Press.

Syriza. 2015. "About Syriza." http://www.syriza.gr/page/who-we-are.html.

Takaki, Ronald. 1989. *Strangers from a Different Shore: A History of Asian Americans.* Boston: Little, Brown and Company.

Taneja, Anup. 2005. *Gandhi, Women and the National Movement, 1920–1947.* Delhi: Har-Anand Publications.

Tarter, Jim. 2002. "Some Live More Downstream than Others: Cancer, Gender, and Environmental Justice." In *The Environmental Justice Reader: Politics, Poetics & Pedagogy*, edited by Joni Adamson, M. Mei Evans, and Rachel Stein, 213–28. Tucson: University of Arizona Press.

Tatum, Beverly. 1994. "Teaching White Students about Racism: The Search for White Allies and the Restoration of Hope." *Teachers College Record* 95: 463–76.

Teaching Tolerance. n.d. "On Racism and White Privilege." http://www.tolerance .org/article/racism-and-white-privilege.

TEEB [The Economics of Ecosystems and Biodiversity]. n.d. http://www.teebweb .org/about.

Terki-Mignot, Auriane. 2015. "Greece, Europe and the Troika: Colonialism in Action?" *Cambridge Globalist*. March 5. http://cambridgeglobalist. org/2015/03/05/greece-europe-troika-colonialism-in-action.

Test Their Logik. 2011. "Conspiracy Rap." *YouTube*, https://www.youtube.com/ watch?v=Kd_wJ5FOUR4.

Tester, Keith. 1991. *Animals and Society*. New York: Routledge.

Theorie Communiste. 2011. "The Present Moment." *Libcom.org*. https://libcom. org/library/present-moment-theorie-communiste.

Thomas, Carol. 2007. "Care and Dependency: A Disciplinary Clash." In *Sociologies of Disability and Illness: Contested Ideas in Disability Studies and Medical Sociology*, 85–119. New York: Palgrave Macmillan.

Thompson, AK. 2010. *Black Bloc, White Riot: Anti-Globalization and the Genealogy of Dissent*. Oakland: AK Press

———. 2014. "Waging War on Valentine's Day." *Truthout*. February 14. http:// truth-out.org/opinion/item/21795-waging-war-on-valentines-day.

Thompson, E. P. 1957. "Socialism and the Intellectuals." *Universities and Left Review* 1, no. 1: 31–36.

———. 1963. *The Making of the English Working Class*. London: Pelican Books.

———. 1966. *The Making of the English Working Class*. New York: Vintage.

———. 1978. *The Poverty of Theory and Other Essays*. London: Merlin.

Thompson, Shirley. 2003. "From a Toxic Economy to Sustainability: Women Activists Taking Care of Environmental Health in Nova Scotia." *Canadian Woman Studies* 21(1): 108–14.

Tiqqun. 2010. *Introduction to Civil War*. Los Angeles: Semiotexte.

Titchkosky, Tanya. 2011. *The Question of Access: Disability, Space, Meaning.*

Toronto: University of Toronto Press.

Todorov, Tzvetan. 1984. *Mikhail Bakhtin: The Dialogical Principle*. Translated by Wlad Godzich. Minneapolis: University of Minnesota Press.

Toffler, Alvin. 1970. *Future Shock*. New York: Random House.

Tolstoy, Leo. 1900. "On Anarchy." Anarchist Library. http://theanarchistlibrary.org/library/leo-tolstoy-on-anarchy.

———. n.d. *A Letter to a Hindu: The Subjection of India—Its Cause and Cure*. http://www.gutenberg.org/files/7176/7176-h/7176-h.htm.

Tometi, Opal, Alicia Garza, and Patrisse Cullors-Brignac. 2015. "Celebrating MLK Day: Reclaiming Our Movement Legacy." *Huffington Post*, January 18. http://www.huffingtonpost.com/opal-tometi/reclaiming-our-movement-l_b_6498400.html.

Tomkins, Adam. 2005. *Our Republican Constitution*. Oxford: Oxford University Press.

Tompkins, Avery. 2014. "Asterisk." *TSQ: Transgender Studies Quarterly* 1(1–2): 26–27.

Trotsky, Leon. 1910. "The Intelligentsia and Socialism." Marxists Internet Archive. https://www.marxists.org/archive/trotsky/1910/xx/intell.htm.

———. 1932. *The History of the Russian Revolution*. New York: Simon and Schuster.

———. 1938. *The Transitional Programme*. Marxists Internet Archive. https://www.marxists.org/archive/trotsky/1938/tp.

Trott, Ben. 2007. "Walking in the Right Direction?" *Turbulence* 1. http://turbulence.org.uk/turbulence-1/walking-in-the-right-direction.

Tsilhqot'in First Nation v. British Columbia, 2014 SCC.

Tufte, Edward R. 2001. *The Visual Display of Quantitative Information*, 2nd Edition. Cheshire, CT: Graphics Press

United Nations Livestock, Environment and Development Initiative. 2006. *Livestock's Long Shadow: Environmental Issues and Opinions*. ftp://ftp.fao.org/docrep/fao/010/a0701e/a0701e00.pdf.

United Press International. 1987. "Helms Calls for Aids Quarantine on Positive Tests." *Chicago Tribune*, June 16.

US Army and US Marine Corps. 2014. *Insurgencies and Countering Insurgencies*. FM 3-24/MCWP 3-33.5. Washington: Headquarters of the US Army/Marine Corps Combat Development Command.

US Citizenship and Immigration Service. 2015. "Citizenship Rights and Responsibilities." http://www.uscis.gov/citizenship/learners/citizenship-rights-and -responsibilities.

V for Vendetta. 2005. Directed by James McTeigue. Burbank, CA: Warner Brothers.

Vagrancy Act. 1714. 12 Ann. c. 23.

Vaneigem, Raoul. 2001. *The Revolution of Everyday Life*. Translated by Donald Nicholson-Smith. London: Rebel Press.

Van Meter, Kevin. 2012. "To Care is to Struggle." *Perspectives on Anarchist Theory* 14(1): 43–59.

Vasconcelos, Jose. 1979. *La Raza Cósmica*. Los Angeles: California State University Press.

Veracini, Lorenzo. 2010. *Settler Colonialism: A Theoretical Overview*. Houndmills, UK: Palgrave Macmillan.

———. 2013. "'Settler Colonialism': Career of a Concept." *Journal of Imperial and Commonwealth History* 41(2): 313–33.

———. 2015. *The Settler Colonial Present*. Houndmills, UK: Palgrave Macmillan.

Vico, Giambattista. 1968. *The New Science of Giambattista Vico*. Translated by Thomas Goddard Bergin, and Max Harold Fisch. Ithaca, NY: Cornell University Press. First published 1744.

Village Vanguard. 2015. "Village Vanguard [History]." Village Vanguard. http://www.villagevanguard.com/#!history/c1yi7.

Virno, Paulo. 2004. *A Grammar of the Multitude: For an Analysis of Contemporary Forms of Life*. New York: Semiotext(e).

Vobejda, Barbara. 1996. "Clinton Signs Welfare Bill amid Division." *Washington Post*, August 23.

Vogel, Lise. 1987. *Marxism and the Oppression of Women: Towards a Unitary Theory*. London: Historical Materialism.

Voline. 1947. *The Unknown Revolution: 1917–1921*. http://www.ditext.com/voline /unknown.html.

Voltaire, Francois-Marie Arouet de. 1962. *The Age of Louis XIV*. New York: Dutton Adult.

Vora, Kalindi. 2012. "The Limits of Labor: Accounting for Affect and the Biological in Transnational Surrogacy and Service Work." *South Atlantic Quarterly* 111(4): 681–98.

Wakefield, Edward Gibbon. 1968. "A Letter from Sydney The Principal Town of Australasia." In *The Collected Works of Edward Gibbon Wakefield*, edited by

M. F. Lloyd-Prichard. Glasgow: Collins.

Waldron, Jeremy. 1991. "Homelessness and the Issue of Freedom." *UCLA Law Review* 39: 2.

Walia, Harsha. 2012. "Decolonizing Together: Moving Beyond a Politics of Solidarity Toward a Practice of Decolonization." *Briarpatch Magazine*, January 1. http://briarpatchmagazine.com/ articles/view/decolonizing-together.

———. 2014. "Israel, Canada and Struggles for Decolonization." *Rabble.ca*, July 11. http://rabble.ca/columnists/2014/07/israel-canada-and -struggles-decolonization.

Walker, Julie. 2015. "#BlackLivesMatter Founders: Please Stop Co-opting Our Hashtag." *The Root.* March 17. http://www.theroot.com/articles/culture /2015/03/_blacklivesmatter_founders_please_stop_co_opting_our_ hashtag.html.

Walker, Martin. 1992. "L.A. Gangs Give Peace a Chance." *Guardian*, May 30.

Wang, Dan. 2011. "Second Report on the Wisconsin Movement." *Propositions Press*, February 23. http://prop-press.typepad.com/blog/2011/02/second-report -on-the-wisconsin-movement.html.

Wang, Esther. 2011. "The Responsibility of Radicals." *Left Turn*. July 30. http:// www.leftturn.org/responsibility-radicals.

Ward, Brian. 2014. "First Nations Fight against the Frackers." *Bullet* (Socialist Project) 924, January 6. http://www.socialistproject.ca/bullet/924.php.

Warren, Dorian. 2015. "Is the Public Intellectual a Thing of the Past?" *Nerding Out with Dorian Warren*. MSNBC, April 23. http:// www.msnbc.com/nerding-out/watch/is-the-public-intellectual -a-thing-of-past--432970819813.

Washington, James, ed. 1986. *A Testament of Hope: The Essential Writings and Speeches of Martin Luther King, Jr.* San Francisco: Harper and Row.

Waziyatawin. 2010. "Colonialism on the Ground." In *Unsettling Ourselves: Reflections and Resources for Deconstructing Colonial Mentality*, edited by Unsettling Minnesota, 191–99. Minneapolis: Unsettling Minnesota Collective.

Weber, Max. 1977. *Critique of Stammler*. New York: Free Press.

———. 1978. *Economy and Society: An Outline of Interpretive Sociology*, edited by Guenther Roth and Claus Wittich. Berkeley: University of California Press.

———. 2003. *The Protestant Ethic and the Spirit of Capitalism*. Translated by Talcott Parsons. Mineola, New York: Dover Publications.

Wedes, Justin. 2014. "On Founders and Keepers of Occupy Wallstreet." http://

www.occupy.com/article/founders-and-keepers-occupy-wall-street.

Weeks, Kathi. 2011. *The Problem with Work: Feminism, Marxism, Antiwork Politics, and Postwork Imaginaries.* Durham: Duke University Press.

Weil, Simone. 1955. *Oppression and Liberty.* Paris: Gallimard.

Weir, James, and Hekmatullah Azamy. 2014. "The Taliban's Transformation from Ideology to Franchise." October 17. http://foreignpolicy.com/2014/10/17/the-talibans-transformation-from-ideology-to-franchise/

Weizman, Eyal. 2012. *The Least of All Possible Evils: Humanitarian Violence from Arendt to Gaza.* London: Verso.

Wells, H. G. 1928. *The Open Conspiracy: Blueprints for a World Revolution.* London: Gollancz.

West, Cornell. 1994. *Race Matters.* New York: Vintage Books.

———. 1999. *The Cornell West Reader.* New York: Basic Civitas Books.

———. 2014. "Love and Justice." Alternative Radio, October 9. http://www.alternativeradio.org/products/wesc006#.

Whitman, Walt. 1855. "I Sing the Body Electric." Poetry Foundation. http://www.poetryfoundation.org/poem/174740.

White, Brent T. 2009. *Underwater and Not Walking Away: Shame, Fear and the Social Management of the Housing Crisis.* Arizona Legal Studies Discussion Paper No. 09-35. Tucson: University of Arizona, James E. Rogers College of Law.

White, Micah. 2011. "#OCCUPYWALLSTREET." *Adbusters*, July 13. www.adbusters.org/blogs/adbusters-blog/occupywallstreet.html.

Whitehead, Alfred North. 1920. *The Concept of Nature.* Cambridge: Cambridge University Press.

Wiegman, Robin. 2012. *Object Lessons.* Durham: Duke University Press.

Wiener, Jon. 2011. "Hard Hats and Hippies, Together At Last: The Action at Occupy Wall Street." *The Nation*, October 14.

Wild Roots Feral Futures Collective. n.d. *Anti-Oppression Policy.* http://feralfutures.blogspot.ca/p/blog-page.html

The Wikileaks Files: The World According to Empire. 2015. New York: Verso Press.

Wilde, Lawrence. 2013. *Global Solidarity.* Edinburgh: Edinburgh University Press.

Wilderson, Frank, III. 2010. *Red, White and Black: Cinema and the Structure of U.S. Antagonisms.* Durham: Duke University Press.

Wildt, Andreas. 1999. "Solidarity: Its History and Contemporary Definition."

In *Solidarity*, edited by Kurt Bayertz, 209–22. Dordrecht: Kluwer.

Wilkinson, David. 2008. "Hegemonia: Hegemony, Classical and Modern." *Journal of World-Systems Research* 14(2): 119–41.

Wilkinson, John Frome. 1891. *The Friendly Society Movement: Its Origin, Rise, and Growth; Its Social, Moral, and Educational Influences; the Affiliated Orders*. London: Longmans, Green.

Williams, Brett. 1994. "Babies and Banks: The 'Reproductive Underclass' and the Raced, Gendered Masking of Debt." In *Race*, edited by Steven Gregory and Roger Sanjek, 348–65. New Brunswick, NJ: Rutgers University Press.

Williams, Cristan. 2014. "Transgender." *Transgender Studies Quarterly* 1(1): 232–34.

Williams, Dana. 2012. "The Anarchist DNA of Occupy." *Contexts* 11(2): 19–20.

Williams, Douglas. 2015. "A Short Follow-up to the Previous Post on Black Lives Matter." *South Lawn*. http://thesouthlawn.org/2015/08/18/a-short-follow-up-to-the-previous-post-on-black-lives-matter.

Williams, Juan. 2006. "Getting Past Katrina." *New York Times*, September 1.

Williams, Kristian. 2014. "The Politics of Denunciation." *Toward Freedom*. February 20. http://towardfreedom.com/29-archives/activism/3455-the-politics-of-denunciation.

———. n.d. "Anarchism and the English Language." CrimethInc. Ex-Workers' Collective Online Reading Library. http://www.crimethinc.com/texts/recentfeatures/language.php.

Williams, Raymond. 1976. *Keywords: A Vocabulary of Culture and Society*. New York: Oxford University Press.

———. 1977. *Marxism and Literature*. Oxford: Oxford University Press.

———. 1980. "Means of Communication as Means of Production." In *Problems in Materialism and Culture: Selected Essays*, 50–66. New York: Verso.

———. 1983. *Keywords: A Vocabulary of Culture and Society*. Revised ed. New York: Oxford University Press.

———. 1989. *Resources of Hope*. London: Verso.

Williams, Sasha, and Ian Law. 2012. "Legitimizing Racism: An Exploration of the Challenges Posed by the Use of Indigeneity Discourses by the Far Right." *Sociological Research Online*. http://www.socresonline.org.uk/17/2/2.html.

Williamson, Bess. 2015. "Access." In *Keywords in Disability Studies*, edited by Rachel Adams, Benjamin Reiss, and David Serlin, 14–16. New York:

NYU Press.

Willig Levy, Chava. 1988. Introduction to *A People's History of the Independent Living Movement*. Farsta, Sweden: Independent Living Institute. http://www.independentliving.org/docs5/ILhistory.html.

Wilson, A. and P. Beresford. 2000. "'Anti-oppressive practice': emancipation or appropriation?" *British Journal of Social Work* 30(5): 553–573.

Wilson, E. O. 1978. *On Human Nature*. Cambridge, MA: Harvard University Press.

Wilson, Wes. 1984. "The Political Use of Conspiracy." *University of Toronto Faculty of Law Review* 42: 60–78.

Winthrop, John. 1838. "A Model of Christian Charity" *Collections of the Massachusetts Historical Society* Third Series 7: 31–48.

Withers, AJ. 2015. "Self-Determination, Disability and Anti-Colonialism or Self-Determination as Disablism and Colonialism." In *If I Can't Dance, Is It Still My Revolution?* January 25. http://stillmyrevolution.org/2015/01/25/self-determination-disability-and-anti-racism-or-self-determination-as-disablism-and-racism.

Witoszek, Nina. 2007. "Friendship and Revolution in Poland: The Eros and Ethos of the Committee for Workers' Defense (KOR)." *Critical Review of International Social and Political Philosophy* 10(2): 215–31.

Wittig, Monique. 1992. *The Straight Mind and Other Essays*. Boston: Beacon Press.
———. 2012. "One Is Not Born a Woman." In *Feminist Theory Reader: Local and Global Perspectives*, edited by Carole McCann and Seung-Kyung Kim, 246–52. New York: Routledge. First published 1981.

Wolfe, Patrick. 1999. *Settler Colonialism and the Transformation of Anthropology: The Politics and Poetics of an Ethnographic Event*. London: Cassell.

Wolff, Richard D. 2010. "Capitalism and the Useful Nation State" March 10. http://rdwolff.com/content/capitalism-and-useful-nation-state.

Womack, John. 1999. *Rebellion in Chiapas: An Historical Reader*. New York: New Press.

Womack, Ytasha. 2013. *Afrofuturism: The World of Black Sci-Fi and Fantasy Culture*. Chicago: Lawrence Hill Books.

Woo, Andrea. 2015. "On Eve of Bill C-51 Protests, Premier Sounds Note of Caution over Lost Freedoms" March 13. *Globe and Mail*.

Wood, Ellen Meiksins. 1995. "The Demos versus 'We, the People': From Ancient to Modern Conceptions of Citizenship." In *Democracy against Capitalism*,

204–37. New York: Cambridge University Press.

———. 1999. *The Retreat from Class: A New 'True' Socialism*. London: Verso.

Woodhull, Victoria C. 1871. "And the Truth Shall Make You Free: A Speech on the Principles of Social Freedom." November 20. Gifts of Speech: Women's Speeches from Around the World. http://gos.sbc.edu/w/woodhull.html.

World Bank. 1992. *World Development Report 1992*. Environment and Development. Washington, DC: World Bank.

———. 2012. *Inclusive Green Growth*. Washington: World Bank.

World Commission on Environment and Development Sustainability. 1987. *Our Common Future*. Oxford: Oxford University Press.

Wright, Melissa. 2003. "The Politics of Relocation: Gender, Nationality and Value in a Mexican Maquiladora." In *Ethnography at the Border*, edited by Pablo Vila, 1601–17. Minneapolis: Minneapolis University Press.

Wright, Michelle M. 2015. *Physics of Blackness: Beyond the Middle Passage Epistemology*. Minneapolis: University of Minnesota Press

Wynne, Kathleen. 2013. "Ontario's Apology to Former Residents of Regional Centres for People with Developmental Disabilities." *Ontario Ministry of Community and Social Services*. http://www.mcss.gov.on.ca/en/mcss/programs/developmental/Premier_Apology.aspx.

Yandle, Bruce. 1993. "Sir Edward Coke and the Struggle for a New Constitutional Order." *Constitutional Political Economy*, 4(2): 263–85.

Yates, Luke. 2015. "Rethinking Prefiguration: Alternatives, Micropolitics and Goals in Social Movements." *Social Movement Studies* 14(1): 1–21.

Young, Iris Marion. 1986. "The Ideal of Community and the Politics of Difference." *Social Theory and Practice* 12(1): 1–26.

———. 2005. *On Female Body Experiences: "Throwing like a Girl" and Other Essays*. Oxford: Oxford University Press.

Young, Michael P. 2006. *Bearing Witness against Sin: The Evangelical Birth of the American Social Movement*. Chicago: University of Chicago Press.

Young, Robert. 2006. "Putting Materialism Back into Race Theory: Toward a Transformative Theory of Race." *Red Critique*. Winter/Spring. http://www.redcritique.org/WinterSpring2006/puttingmaterialismbackintoracetheory.htm.

Yúdice, George. 2005. "Community." In *New Keywords: A Revised Vocabulary of Culture and Society*, edited by T. Bennett, L. Grossberg, and M. Morris, 51–3. Oxford: Blackwell.

Zapatistas. 1998. *Zapatista Encuentro: Documents from the 1996 Encounter for Humanity and against Neoliberalism*. Toronto: Seven Stories Press.

Zinn, Howard. 1980. *A People's History of the United States*. New York: Harper and Row.

Žižek, Slavoj. 2008. *In Defense of Lost Causes*. London: Verso.

———. 2014. "Only a Radicalised Left Can Save Europe." *New Statesman*, June 25. http://www.newstatesman.com/politics/2014/06/slavoj-i-ek-only -radicalised-left-can-save-europe.

Zweig, Michael. 2012. *The Working Class Majority: America's Best Kept Secret*. 2nd edition. Ithaca, NY: ILR Press.

COMMONLY CITED DICTIONARIES

An American Dictionary of the English Language (Noah Webster) 1828. http:// webstersdictionary1828.com.

Concise Oxford Dictionary, 10th ed. 1999.

Dictionnaire de L'Académie française, various editions, http://artfl.atilf.fr /dictionnaires/onelook.htm.

New College Latin and English Dictionary (John Traupman), 1979.

Oxford English Dictionary.

Online Etymology Dictionary, http://www.etymonline.com.

Roget's 21st Century Thesaurus, 3rd ed., http://www.thesaurus.com.

Webster's New International Dictionary of the English Language, 1913.

ABOUT THE CONTRIBUTORS

Anna Agathangelou is an associate professor in political science and a faculty member of the Institute for Science and Technology Studies at York University. She is also the co-director of the Global Change Institute in Nicosia, Cyprus, and has published in *American Political Science Review, International Studies Quarterly,* and *Millennium: Journal of International Studies.* She is currently working on a research project on reconstruction post-nuclear disaster and art.

Robin Marie Averbeck holds a PhD in American history from UC Davis, and her work and research focuses on postwar liberalism, race, and the politics of poverty. She has written essays for publications such as *Jacobin* and *Democracy* and currently blogs on a regular basis for the Society for US Intellectual History. Robin Marie is also an activist who looks for opportunities to merge her scholarly interests with the contemporary fight against racism, homophobia, transphobia, sexism, and class inequality.

Neil Balan has been a dad, a co-parent, a comrade and ally, a lover, an itinerant builder, a faculty member, a food sovereignty organizer, a sessional instructor, a harm-reduction frontline worker, and a long-time worker in the silviculture sector. He is partially aligned with the churning neoliberal production that is the public university. Having just completed a doctoral dissertation on war, violence, and biopolitics, he is ready for something else.

Himani Bannerji is a professor in the Department of Sociology at York University, Toronto, Canada. Her research and writing life extends between Canada and India. Her interests encompass anti-racist feminism, Marxism, critical cultural theories, and historical sociology. Publications include *Demography and Democracy: Essays on Nationalism, Gender and Ideology* (2011), *Of Property and Propriety: The Role of Gender and Class in Imperialism and Nationalism* (edited and co-authored with S. Mojab and J. Whitehead, 2001),

Inventing Subjects: Studies in Hegemony, Patriarchy and Colonialism (2001), *The Dark Side of the Nation: Essays on Multiculturalism, Nationalism and Racism* (2000), and *Thinking Through: Essays on Feminism, Marxism and Anti-Racism* (1995).

Patrick Bond is a professor of political economy at the University of the Witwatersrand. His recent books include *BRICS: An anti-capitalist critique* (co-edited with Ana Garcia, 2015), *Elite Transition: From Apartheid to Neoliberalism in South Africa* (3rd edition, 2014), *South Africa - The present as history* (with John Saul, 2014) and *Politics of Climate Justice* (2012). From 2004–16 he was based at the University of KwaZulu-Natal where he directed the Centre for Civil Society.

Johanna Brenner is professor emeritus of Women's Studies/ Sociology at Portland State University and author of *Women and the Politics of Class.*

George Caffentzis was a cofounder of the Midnight Notes Collective and a coordinator of the Committee for Academic Freedom in Africa. His is now working with the anti-debt organization, Strike Debt. He has taught in many US universities and at the University of Calabar (Nigeria). He is now emeritus professor of Philosophy at the University of Southern Maine. He has written many essays on social and political themes. His books include *Clipped Coins, Abused Words and Civil Government: John Locke's Philosophy of Money, Exciting the Industry of Mankind: George Berkeley's Philosophy of Money, In Letters of Blood and Fire: Work, Machines, and the Crisis of Capitalism,* and *No Blood for Oil!* (forthcoming). His coedited books include *Midnight Oil: Work Energy War 1973–1992), Auroras of the Zapatistas: Local and Global Struggles in the Fourth World War,* and *Thousand Flowers: Social Struggles against Structural Adjustment in African Universities.*

Heather Davis is a postdoctoral fellow at the Institute for the Arts and Humanities at Pennsylvania State University, where she researches the ethology of plastic and its links to petrocapitalism. She is the editor of *Art in the Anthropocene: Encounters Among Aesthetics, Politics, Environment and Epistemology* (Open Humanities Press, 2015) and *Desire/Change: Contemporary Feminist Art in Canada* (MAWA/McGill-Queen's Press, forthcoming).

Richard Day is an autonomy-oriented practitioner and theorist who lives on three acres north of Kingston, Ontario, where he, his sons, and partner build, garden, and get ready to move off the grid. Richard has been associated with a number of radical projects over the years, from community education to food and housing co-ops, indigenous solidarity, urban social centers, and rural intentional communities. He is currently involved in creating an intentional community that will exist somewhere in British Columbia (as this land is known in settler worlds). He is the author of *Multiculturalism and the History of Canadian Diversity* (2000), *Gramsci Is Dead* (2005), and *Utopian Pedagogies* (with Greig de-Peuter and Mark Coté 2007), and is currently working on a documentary about early-twenty-first-century protest movements, *After the Barricades: Insurrection and Institutionalization in Latin America*. He is founding editor of *Affinities: A Journal of Radical Theory, Culture, and Action*.

Donatella della Porta is professor of sociology in the Department of Political and Social Sciences at the European University Institute, where she directs the Centre on Social Movement Studies (Cosmos). She is also professor of political science at the Istituto Italiano di Scienze Umane (on leave). She is co-editor of the *European Political Science Review*. In 2011, she was the recipient of the Mattei Dogan Prize for distinguished achievements in the field of political sociology. Her main fields of research are social movements, the policing of public order, participatory democracy, and political corruption.

Ana Cecilia Dinerstein is associate professor in the Department of Social and Policy Sciences at the University of Bath, UK. She has published extensively on Argentine and Latin American politics, autonomy, subjectivity, labor, alternative economies, rural, urban and Indigenous movements, emancipatory struggles, and the politics of policy in *Social Movement Studies*, *Development & Change*, *Community Development Journal*, *Capital & Class*, *South Atlantic Quarterly*, *Historical Materialism*, *Realidad Económica*, *Herramienta*. Her books include *The Labour Debate* (co-edited with M. Neary, 2002), *La Ruta de los Piqueteros. Luchas y Legados* (2010), and *The Politics of Autonomy in Latin America: The Art of Organising Hope* (2014).

Stacy Douglas is Assistant Professor of Law and Legal Studies at Carleton University in Ottawa, Canada. Former co-director of the Centre for Law, Gender, and Sexuality at Kent Law School, as well as editorial board member of *Feminist Legal Studies* and feminists@law, she has published academic and political commentary in *Law and Critique*; *Law, Culture & the Humanities*; *Theory & Event*; *Radical Philosophy*; *Australian Feminist Law Journal*; *Canadian Dimension*; and *Truthout*; and she recently co-edited a special issue of the *Canadian Journal of Law and Society* on law and decolonization. She is winner of the 2014 Julien Mezey dissertation prize from the Association for Law, Culture, and the Humanities.

Silvia Federici is a longtime feminist activist, teacher, and writer. She was a co-founder of the International Feminist Collective, the New York Wages for Housework Committee, the Radical Philosophy Association Anti-Death Penalty Project, and the Committee for Academic Freedom in Africa. She has taught at the University of Port Harcourt (Nigeria) and is Emerita Professor of Political Philosophy and International Studies at Hofstra University. She has authored many essays and books on feminist theory and history. Her books include *Revolution at Point Zero: Housework, Reproduction and Feminist Struggle*, *Caliban and the Witch: Women, the Body and Primitive Accumulation*, *Enduring Western Civilization: The Construction of the Concept of Western Civilization and Its Others* (editor), *A Thousand Flowers: Social*

Struggles against Structural Adjustment in African Universities (co-editor), and *African Visions* (co-editor).

John Bellamy Foster is a professor of sociology at the University of Oregon and editor of *Monthly Review* (New York). His writings focus on the political economy of capitalism and economic crisis, ecology and ecological crisis, and Marxist theory. He is the author of *The Theory of Monopoly Capitalism* (1986, 2014), *The Vulnerable Planet* (1994), *Marx's Ecology* (2000), *Ecology against Capitalism* (2002), *Naked Imperialism* (2006), *The Ecological Revolution* (2009), The Great Financial Crisis (with Fred Magdoff, 2009), *The Ecological Rift* (with Brett Clark and Richard York, 2010), *What Every Environmentalist Needs to Know About Capitalism* (with Fred Magdoff, 2011), and *The Endless Crisis* (with Robert W. McChesney, 2012)—all published by Monthly Review Press; and of *Marx and the Earth* (with Paul Burkett, Brill, forthcoming).

Kelly Fritsch is a Banting Postdoctoral Fellow in Women and Gender Studies at the University of Toronto. She is associate editor of the *Review of Disability Studies: An International Journal*, and her work appears in *Feral Feminisms; Feminist Review; Foucault Studies; Disability & Society; Journal of Cultural and Literary Disability Studies; Health, Culture, and Society; The Canadian Journal of Disability Studies; Disability Studies Quarterly*; and *Critical Disability Discourse*. Between 2008 and 2012, Fritsch served on the editorial committee of *Upping the Anti: A Journal of Theory and Action*.

Peter Gelderloos is an anarchist and writer from Virginia. His published works include *How Nonviolence Protects the State, Anarchy Works, Consensus, The Failure of Nonviolence*, and *The Justice Trap*.

Sam Gindin was Research Director of the Canadian Auto Workers from 1974 to 2000 and over the next decade facilitated a course at York University on social justice and political activism (free to activists). He is currently retired but continues to be active around labor issues.

Kanishka Goonewardena was trained as an architect in Sri Lanka and now teaches urban design and critical theory in Toronto. He is co-editor (with Stefan Kipfer, Richard Milgrom, and Christian Schmid) of *Space, Difference, Everyday Life: Reading Henri Lefebvre* (2008) and is currently Associate Professor in the Department of Geography and Planning, University of Toronto.

Deborah Gould is an Associate Professor of Sociology at the University of California, Santa Cruz, and participated in ACT UP/ Chicago during the late 1980s and early 1990s. She co-founded the Chicago-based social justice activist group Queer to the Left, and she also co-founded Feel Tank Chicago, an arts/activist research collaborative. Her first book, *Moving Politics: Emotion and ACT UP's Fight against AIDS* (University of Chicago Press, 2009), won the Distinguished Contribution to Scholarship Award from the American Sociological Association's Political Sociology Section (2010) and the Ruth Benedict Book Prize from the American Anthropological Association (2010). Her work also appears in *Contemporary European History*, *Sociological Quarterly*, *Contexts*, and *Quarterly Journal of Speech*, and in *Methods of Exploring Emotions* (Routledge), *Politics and Emotions: The Obama Phenomenon* (VS Verlag), *Political Emotions: Affect and the Public Sphere* (Routledge), and *Gay Shame* (University of Chicago Press).

Heather Hax is a PhD candidate in Sociology at York University in Toronto. Her work focuses on cooperative workplaces and large-scale anticapitalist social transformation. Currently residing in Baltimore, Heather teaches Sociology at Towson University. She is currently a collective member of 2640 Space, a collectively run events space for radical politics and grassroots culture. She also teaches and practices Ashtanga yoga at an ungodly hour each morning.

Rosemary Hennessy is L. H. Favrot Professor of Humanities and Professor of English at Rice University in Houston. Before moving to Houston she was a member of the English department at the University of Albany, SUNY. Among her publications are

Fires on the Border: The Passionate Politics of Labor Organizing on the Mexican Frontera (2013); *Profit and Pleasure: Sexual Identities in Late Capitalism* (2000); *Materialist Feminism and the Politics of Discourse* (1993); *NAFTA from Below: Maquiladora Workers, Campesinos, and Indigenous Communities Speak Out on the Impact of Free Trade in Mexico* (co-edited with Martha A. Ojeda, 2006); and *Materialist Feminism: A Reader in Class, Difference, and Women's Lives* (co-edited with Chrys Ingraham, 1997). She has published numerous articles and book chapters and has essays in *The Sage Handbook of Feminist Theory*, *The Blackwell Companion to Critical and Cultural Theory*, and other critical guidebooks.

Mandy Hiscocks is an anarchist who tries but usually fails to strike a balance between activism and organizing, paid work, and friends and community. She has been active since the '90s in student, anti-poverty, animal liberation, prison abolition, anti-globalization, and environmental justice movements. She now focuses most of her energy on decolonization and land defense. In 2010 she was involved in organizing against the G20 Summit in Toronto, as part of the Toronto Community Mobilization Network and the Southern Ontario Anarchist Resistance. This effort was the target of police undercover work in the community, which led to her being charged with conspiracy and counseling as part of the "Main Conspiracy Group." The result was a group plea deal that saw her and five others do jail time while charges against the other eleven were dropped. From jail she wrote the blog *Bored but Not Broken*. Mandy lives in Guelph, Ontario, where she is a staff member at the Ontario Public Interest Reseach Group (OPIRG). When asked to speak publicly, she talks about the importance of embracing a diversity of tactics and centering Indigenous struggle and resistance in our movements, as well as the need for people with privilege to be willing to risk far more than most of us currently do.

Dan Irving is Associate Professor of Sexuality Studies and Human Rights at Carleton University. His research is located within

Transgender Studies, Masculinity Studies, and Critical Political Economy. His current research focuses on un(der)employment among trans* populations. His project, "Love the Way You Lie: Eminem, Male-Identified Youth and the Crisis of Masculinity," launched in the fall of 2015. He is the co-editor of *Trans Activism in Canada: A Reader* (2014), and his work has been published in *Radical History Review*, *Sexualities*, and the *Australian Feminist Review*.

Joy James is Presidential Professor of the Humanities and a professor in political science at Williams College. She is the author of *Shadowboxing: Representations of Black Feminist Politics*; *Transcending the Talented Tenth: Black Leaders and American Intellectuals*; and *Resisting State Violence: Radicalism, Gender and Race in U.S. Culture*. Her edited books include *Warfare in the American Homeland*; *The New Abolitionists: (Neo) Slave Narratives and Contemporary Prison Writings*; *Imprisoned Intellectuals*; *States of Confinement*; *The Black Feminist Reader* (co-edited with T. Denean Sharpley-Whiting); and *The Angela Y. Davis Reader*. James is completing a book on the prosecution of twentieth-century interracial rape cases, tentatively titled *Memory, Shame, and Rage*. She has contributed articles and book chapters to journals and anthologies addressing feminist and critical race theory, democracy, and social justice, and is curator of the Harriet Tubman Literary Circle (HTLC) digital repository, which is part of the University of Texas human rights archives.

Miranda Joseph is Professor and Director of Graduate Studies in Gender and Women's Studies at the University of Arizona. She teaches feminist, Marxist, poststructuralist, and queer theory, cultural studies methods, and LGBT Studies. Her research explores the relationship between economic processes and social formations. She is the author of *Debt to Society: Accounting for Life under Capitalism* (University of Minnesota Press, 2014) and *Against the Romance of Community* (University of Minnesota Press, 2002).

Sumayya Kassamali is currently a doctoral student in Anthropology at Columbia University in New York. She organized for some years with No One Is Illegal–Vancouver and Toronto, and she has long been involved in antiwar and Palestine solidarity organizing. She is currently living in Beirut, Lebanon, studying Arabic, and getting some space away from North America.

Kate Kaul is a doctoral candidate in Social and Political Thought at York University, Toronto, writing on disability theory, inter-disciplinarity, subjectivity, and experience. She is interested in a broad range of critical theory, including questions of form and content in pedagogy and accessible design. She teaches Writing and Disability Studies.

Christine Kelly is a Banting Postdoctoral Fellow in the Institute of Feminist and Gender Studies at the University of Ottawa. Informed by feminist and disability scholarship, Christine's research explores attendant services, care, personal support workers, youth, and Canadian disability movements. Christine's book *Disability Politics and Care: The Challenge of Direct Funding* (University of British Columbia Press, 2016) explores what it might mean to incorporate a rejection of care, as represented by disability activists, into the core of our theorizing, policies, and practices of support.

Ruth Kinna works in the Department of Politics, History and IR at Loughborough University, UK. She is the author of *A Beginner's Guide to Anarchism* (2005), editor of the journal *Anarchist Studies* and *The Bloomsbury Companion to Anarchism* (2014) and co-editor of *Anarchism and Utopianism*, with Laurence Davis (2009) and *Libertarian Socialism: Politics in Black and Red* (2013) with Alex Prichard, Saku Pinta and David Berry.

Markus Kip is a PhD candidate in Sociology at York University, Toronto. His doctoral work investigates practices of union solidarity with undocumented migrant workers in Germany. He is member of a union support center for undocumented migrant workers at the services sector union, ver.di, in Berlin. Prior to his studies, he gained experience as community organizer in San Salvador, El Salvador, and as a day laborer in North America, constituting an important source of inspiration for his research and activism. Publications include the co-edited book *Lumpencity: Discourses of Marginality | Marginalizing Discourses* (2011) and the co-edited anthology *Urban Commons: Moving beyond State and Market* (2015).

Stefan Kipfer teaches urbanization, urban politics, and planning in the Faculty of Environmental Studies, York University, Toronto. Informed by urban social theory, especially Henri Lefebvre, Frantz Fanon, and Antonio Gramsci, his research is focused on comparative politics, restructuring, and colonization in metropolitan regions.

Natalie Kouri-Towe is a Toronto-based academic and activist working on the politics of solidarity, questions of attachment, and queer activism in transnational social movements. She completed her PhD at the University of Toronto in 2015. Her dissertation, "Solidarity at Risk," examines the impacts of neoliberalism and homonationalism on contemporary practices of solidarity activism in the Queer Palestine Solidarity Movement. She has published in both academic and non-academic venues on topics relating to queer politics, including *Atlantis: Critical Studies in Gender, Culture & Social Justice, Briarpatch, FUSE Magazine, No More Potlucks*, and *Upping the Anti: A Journal of Theory and Action*.

Tammy Kovich is a Hamilton-based organizer and theory nerd. Currently working on a PhD in Gender, Feminist, and Women's Studies at York University, her research concerns questions pertaining to resistance, revolution, and gender. She enjoys coffee, the color black, and riot porn, and is involved in various anarchist projects.

Sarah Lamble teaches at Birkbeck College, University of London, researches issues of gender, sexuality, and criminal justice and co-edits Routledge's Social Justice book series. Sarah is a founding member of the Bent Bars Project, a letter-writing program for queer, trans, and gender-nonconforming prisoners in Britain.

Derek Laventure is an opensource advocate, web hacker, and political activist committed to working with technology to serve the needs of progressive communities and social mission organizations. A graduate of the Cognitive Science program at the University of Toronto, Derek has been working in the Toronto progressive technology community for over 10 years. Before that, he appropriated skills and experience in corporate technology support and development. Derek is keenly interested in technology that enhances and supports the liberation of human potential from alienation. He also enjoys hand work like knitting and sewing, earth work like gardening and camping, and is privileged to study and teach tai chi in Toronto.

Jaleh Mansoor received her PhD from Columbia University in 2007. She taught at SUNY Purchase, Barnard College, Columbia University, and Ohio University before joining the University of British Columbia where her areas of teaching and research include modernism, theories and histories of the revolutionary avant-garde, Marxism, and Marxist feminism. Mansoor's forthcoming book, *Marshall Plan Modernism*, addressed problems concerning aesthetic abstraction, real abstraction, and violence in the second half of the twentieth century, and the way that history continues to structure the matrix of our contemporary insurrectionary present.

Sara Matthews is Associate Professor in the Department of Global Studies at Wilfrid Laurier University. Her interdisciplinary work brings aesthetics and cultural theory to the study of violence and the dynamics of social conflict. Her current research considers how contemporary Canadian war artists are responding to Canada's military involvement in Afghanistan. She is also interested in how aesthetic practices can inform methods for cultural analysis, especially in the context of public engagements with visual representations of war and social conflict. Her new project, "The Cultural Life of Drones," explores social responses to technologies of military surveillance and mechanized killing such as drone warfare. In addition to her academic work, Sara curates aesthetic projects that archive visual encounters with legacies of war and social trauma. Her critical writing has appeared in *PUBLIC*, *FUSE Magazine*, and exhibition catalogs for the Art Gallery of Bishop's University and Toronto-based YYZ.

David McNally teaches political science at York University in Toronto and actively supports numerous social justice movements in that city. He is the author of six books: *Political Economy and the Rise of Capitalism* (1988); *Against the Market: Political Economy Market Socialism and the Marxist Critique* (1993); *Bodies of Meaning: Studies on Language, Labor and Liberation* (2001); *Another World Is Possible: Globalization and Anti-Capitalism* (2002; 2006); *Global Slump: The Economics and Politics of Crisis and Resistance* (2010); and *Monsters of the Market: Zombies, Vampires and Global Capitalism* (2011). He is also on the advisory editorial board for *Historical Materialism: A Journal of Critical Marxist Research* and is a member of the Toronto Historical Materialism Group, which organizes a biennial conference at York University.

Robert McRuer focuses on queer and crip cultural studies and critical theory. He is completing a book titled *Crip Times: Disability, Globalization, and Resistance*, considering locations of disability within contemporary political economies and the roles that disabled movements and representations play in countering hegemonic forms of globalization. He is the author of *Crip Theory: Cultural Signs of Queerness and Disability* and co-editor, with Anna Mollow, of *Sex and Disability*. Most recently, with Merri Lisa Johnson, he co-edited two special issues of the *Journal of Literary and Cultural Disability Studies* on "Cripistemologies."

Thomas Nail is an Associate Professor of Philosophy at the University of Denver. He has worked with Cascadia Forest Defense, No One Is Illegal, and Occupy Denver and is currently a member on the advisory board for *Upping the Anti: A Journal of Theory* *and Action.* He is the author of *Returning to Revolution: Deleuze, Guattari and Zapatismo* (Edinburgh University Press, 2012), *The Figure of the Migrant* (Stanford University Press, 2015), and *Theory of the Border* (under review, Oxford University Press). His work has appeared in *Angelaki, Theory & Event, Philosophy Today, Parrhesia, Deleuze Studies, Foucault Studies,* and elsewhere.

Clare O'Connor is a doctoral student in Communication at the University of Southern California. She is former Coordinator of the Public Interest Research Group at the University of Toronto and co-founder of Toronto-based activist training program Tools for Change. Her publications include the chapter "What Moves Us Now? The Contradictions of 'Community'" in *Whose Streets? The Toronto G20 and the Challenges of Summit Protest* (Between the Lines, 2011) and contributions to *Briarpatch Magazine.* Between 2008 and 2012 she served on the editorial committee of *Upping the Anti: A Journal of Theory and Action.*

Bryan Palmer is the author of thirteen books, editor of five collections of essays/oral biographies/pamphlets, and served as editor of the journal *Labour/Le Travail* from 1997–2014. Palmer's publications have been nominated for or won a number of academic prizes, including both the Canadian/American Historical Association's A. B. Corey Prize and the Canadian Historical Association's Wallace K. Ferguson Prize. Palmer's *James P. Cannon and the Origins of the American Revolutionary Left, 1890–1928* (2007, University of Illinois Press) was judged the best book published by a historian in Canada in a field other than Canadian history. His most recent books include the edited collection (with Joan Sangster) *Labouring Canada: Class, Gender, and Race in Canadian Working-Class History* (2008), *Canada's 1960s: The Ironies of Identity in a Rebellious Era* (2009), and *Revolutionary Teamsters: The Minneapolis Truckers' Strikes of 1934* (2013).

Ilan Pappé is a Professor of History and Director of the European Centre for Palestine Studies at the University of Exeter.

Rasheedah Phillips is a Philadelphia public interest attorney, mother, speculative fiction writer, creator of "The AfroFuturist Affair," and a founding member of Metropolarity Speculative Fiction Collective. She independently published her first speculative fiction collection, *Recurrence Plot (and Other Time Travel Tales)* and an anthology of experimental essays from Black visionary writers called *Black Quantum Futurism: Theory and Practice*, vol. 1. Phillips is a 2015 artist-in-residence with West Philadelphia Neighborhood Time Exchange.

Justin Podur has worked in the Canada Colombia Solidarity Campaign (2001–2003), and the International Solidarity Movement (2002). He has been a volunteer editor for *ZNet* since 1999 and is a founding member of the Pueblos en Camino collective. He is the author of *Haiti's New Dictatorship* (Pluto Press 2012) and has contributed chapters to *Empire's Ally: Canada and the War in Afghanistan* (University of Toronto Press, 2013) and *Real Utopia* (AK Press, 2008). He is an Associate Professor at York University's Faculty of Environmental Studies.

Nina Power is a Senior Lecturer in Philosophy at Roehampton University. She is author of *One-Dimensional Woman* (Zero Books), is the co-editor of Alain Badiou's *On Beckett* (Clinamen), and the author of several articles on European philosophy, pedagogy, art, and politics.

Maia Ramnath is a teacher, writer, activist, and dancer/aerialist/choreographer who teaches history at Penn State. She is the author of *The Haj to Utopia: How the Ghadar Movement Charted Global Radicalism and Attempted to Overthrow the British Empire* and *Decolonizing Anarchism: An Antiauthoritarian History of South Asian Liberation Struggle*. She is currently a member of the Institute for Anarchist Studies board and Historians Against War Palestine-Israel Working Group.

Conor Tomás Reed is an archivist, activist, student, and teacher at the City University of New York, a collective member of *Lost & Found: The CUNY Poetics Document Initiative*, and a co-founding participant of Free University-NYC. Conor researches twentieth- and twenty-first-century literatures of Africana social movements and urban freedom schools. Forthcoming and recent writing include "Diving into SEEK: Adrienne Rich and Social Movements at the City College of New York, 1968–1974," in an anthology on Adrienne Rich and Jayne Cortez (2016); "You Can't Evict a Movement," in *Viewpoint Magazine* (2015); "Remembering the Watts Rebellion," in *Mask Magazine* (2015); "Black Arts Boomerang," in *The New Inquiry* (2015); and "Organizing against Empire: Struggles over the Militarization of CUNY," in *Berkeley Journal of Sociology* (2014).

Rebecca Schein is Assistant Professor in the Human Rights program at Carleton University's Institute of Interdisciplinary Studies in Ottawa, Ontario.

Christian Scholl is a Brussels-based writer, researcher, and activist. His research interests revolve around globalization, social movements, and questions of transnational organizing and social control. He is co-author of *Shutting Down the Streets: Political Violence and Social Control in the Global Era* (New York University Press, 2011) and author of *Two Sides of a Barricade: (Dis)order and Summit Protest in Europe* (SUNY Press, 2013).

Mab Segrest is an American feminist, writer, and activist. She is best known for her 1994 autobiographical work *Memoir of a Race Traitor*. She joined the faculty of Connecticut College in the fall of 2002 and retired from teaching in 2014.

Alan Shandro is the author of *Lenin and the Logic of Hegemony: Political Practice and Theory in the Class Struggle* (Leiden: Brill, 2014) as well as a number of articles in Marxist theory. He is on the editorial board of *Science & Society* and teaches political and social theory at Laurentian University in Sudbury, Ontario.

Eliza Steinbock is assistant professor and a postdoctoral researcher in the Department of Film and Literary Studies at Leiden University. Eliza writes on contemporary philosophies of the body, visual culture, and transfeminist issues. Eliza is an American who completed a master's in cultural studies at the University of Leeds (with distinction, 2004) and a doctorate in cultural analysis at the University of Amsterdam, entitled "Shimmering Images: On Transgender Embodiment and Cinematic Aesthetics" (2011). Hir current funded research project, "Vital Art: Transgender Portraiture as Visual Activism," examines the worlds created in the visual arts to harbor at-risk trans subjects and to critique their discrimination. Recent publications include essays in the *Journal of Homosexuality*, *Photography and Culture*, and *TSQ: Transgender Studies Quarterly*.

Sunera Thobani is Associate Professor at the Institute for Gender, Race, Sexuality and Social Justice at the University of British Columbia. Her research focuses on critical race, postcolonial, and feminist theory, globalization, citizenship, migration, Muslim women, the "war on terror," and media. Her book *Exalted Subjects: Studies in the Making of Race and Nation in Canada* was published by the University of Toronto Press (2007), and she has also co-edited *Asian Women: Interconnections* (Canadian Scholars' Press, 2005) and *States of Race: Critical Race Feminist Theory for the 21st Century* (Between the Lines, 2010).

AK Thompson got kicked out of high school for publishing an underground newspaper called *The Agitator* and has been an activist, writer, and social theorist ever since. Currently teaching social theory at Fordham University, his publications include *Black Bloc, White Riot: Anti-Globalization and the Genealogy of Dissent* (2010) and *Sociology for Changing the World: Social Movements/Social Research* (2006). Between 2005 and 2012, he served on the editorial committee of *Upping The Anti: A Journal of Theory and Action*.

Seth Tobocman is a comic book artist whose work often deals with political issues from a radical point of view. He founded the magazine *World War 3 Illustrated* with Peter Kuper in 1979 and has been part of the editorial collective ever since. His work has appeared in the *New York Times*, *Village Voice*, *Heavy Metal*, and many other publications. He is author of a number of graphic books including *You Don't Have to Fuck People Over to Survive*, *War in the Neighborhood*, *Portraits of Israelis and Palestinians*, *Disaster and Resistance*, and *Understanding the Crash*. Tobocman's art has been shown at the Museum of Modern Art, the New Museum of Contemporary Art, the Museum of the City of Ravenna, Exit Art, and ABC No Rio.

Lorenzo Veracini is Associate Professor of History at the Swinburne University of Technology in Melbourne, Australia. His research focuses on the comparative history of colonial systems and settler colonialism. He has authored *Israel and Settler Society* (2006) and *Settler Colonialism: A Theoretical Overview* (2010). His *The Settler Colonial Present* is now in press with Palgrave. Lorenzo is managing editor of *Settler Colonial Studies*.

Simon Wallace is training to be a criminal lawyer. Based in Toronto, he is a member of the Law Union of Ontario and active in its prisoner justice group. He was an editor of *Upping the Anti* from 2010 to 2013.

Douglas Williams is a doctoral student in political science at Wayne State University in Detroit. His research revolves around labor policy and the effects that working-class social movements have had on policy outcomes. He writes on these topics and more on his blog *The South Lawn*.

Support **AK Press!**

AK Press is one of the world's largest and most productive anarchist publishing houses. We're entirely worker-run

& democratically managed. We operate without a corporate structure—no boss, no managers, no bullshit. We publish close to twenty books every year, and distribute thousands of other titles published by other like-minded independent presses from around the globe.

The Friends of AK program is a way that you can directly contribute to the continued existence of AK Press, and ensure that we're able to keep publishing great books just like this one! Friends pay $25 a month directly into our publishing account ($30 for Canada, $35 for international), and receive a copy of every book AK Press publishes for the duration of their membership! Friends also receive a discount on anything they order from our website or buy at a table: 50% on AK titles, and 20% on everything else. We've also added a new Friends of AK ebook program: $15 a month gets you an electronic copy of every book we publish for the duration of your membership. Combine it with a print subscription, too!

There's great stuff in the works—so sign up now to become a Friend of AK Press, and let the presses roll!

Won't you be our friend? Email friendsofak@akpress.org for more info, or visit the Friends of AK Press website: www.akpress.org/programs/friendsofak